IMPRESSION
Management

IMPRESSION
Management

THE SELF-CONCEPT,
SOCIAL IDENTITY, AND
INTERPERSONAL RELATIONS

BARRY R. SCHLENKER

University of Florida

Brooks/Cole Publishing Company
Monterey, California
A DIVISION OF WADSWORTH, INC.

To David, who arrived,
and Brandy, who departed,
and Patty, who, thankfully, was here all along.

Consulting Editor: *Lawrence S. Wrightsman*

Printed in the United States of America

10 9 8 7 6 5 4 3 2 1

Library of Congress Cataloging in Publication Data

Schlenker, Barry R
 Impression management.

 Bibliography: p.
 Includes indexes.
  1. Interpersonal relations. 2. Self-perception.
3. Social acceptance. I. Title.
HM132.S352   302   80-15047
ISBN 0-8185-0398-X

Acquisition Editor: *Claire Verduin*
Manuscript Editor: *John Joyner*
Production Editor: *Patricia E. Cain*
Interior Design: *Ruth Scott*
Cover Design: *Stanley Rice*
Typesetting: *Boyer & Brass, Inc., San Diego, California*

PREFACE

Impression management, or image control, is a central aspect of interpersonal relations. Consciously or unconsciously, people attempt to control images in real or imagined social interactions. By doing so, they define the nature of the interaction, the identities they and others possess, and the meanings of their interpersonal actions. What people believe they "are" and the outcomes they receive from social life are both predicated in large part on impression management.

The importance of studying impression management has been appreciated by many social psychologists. However, a number of obstacles have impeded work. First, the area has been somewhat fragmented and compartmentalized. Symbolic interactionists—social psychologists who happen to be housed primarily in sociology departments—and experimental social psychologists—housed primarily in psychology departments—have each made major contributions. But surprisingly little cross-fertilization has occurred, each group remaining cool, uninterested, and often ignorant of the work of the other. One goal of the present book is to provide an integrative approach to the area.

Second, a number of misconceptions exist about impression management. The term has numerous negative connotations that make it seem more appropriate for students of public relations than for students of social psychology. It brings to mind automatons programmed to smile appropriately and do everything in their power to please or even con an audience. Impression management can involve such behavior, but it also involves much more. In its full sense, impression management is integral to the study of the self, identity, and interpersonal relations. One goal of this book is to demonstrate the relevance of the topic to this wide array of phenomena.

Third, the impression-management approach frequently has been criticized for failing to develop specific, testable hypotheses. It is true that no definitive theory of impression management has yet been achieved. Yet the elements of such a theory are beginning to take form. The approach is becoming increasingly refined and is hardly lacking in precise hypotheses fit for the experimental crucible. No claims are made that this book presents a finalized theory, but it is hoped that it provides an impetus for theory development and enough hypotheses to generate even more work in the area.

Finally, there has been no book from which students could gain a general exposure to ideas and research in the area. The present book is intended to serve this purpose. It does not attempt to be encyclopedic in its coverage; several volumes would be required for that. Nor does it attempt to provide a detailed, critical examination of the methodology and research done in the area. Although such an examination would undoubtedly please some advanced readers, it would detract from the usefulness of the book for those who want only to gain a general appreciation of the area. Instead, my aim is to provide a single, reasonably concise volume that serves as an introduction to the study of impression management.

In places, the book seems to take a "how-to-do-it" turn, as when it discusses how to use nonverbal signals to increase interpersonal attraction. In general I tried to avoid that style, but I succumbed every now and then for at least three reasons. First, the data that exist in some areas are decidedly one-sided. In general there has been much less research on people's actions than on their reactions. There is research that shows how observers respond to a particular behavior used by an actor (for example, how observers respond when an actor uses one nonverbal action rather than another), but less research on the conditions that determine when an actor will use such behaviors. Thus, we often know what "works" on audiences but don't necessarily know that actors will use these efficacious strategies under appropriate conditions. It is reasonable, though, to believe that people learn what works during the course of their social lives and use these strategies when called for; indeed, a variety of anecdotal data (often found in explicit "how-to-do-it" books) suggests that people are sensitive to such audience reactions and take advantage of them. In presenting such material it is difficult to avoid statements such as "People who are attempting to increase their attractiveness to an audience should. . . ." Second, the question of how audiences react to particular strategies is interesting in its own right, and I didn't feel like excluding such material merely because research on the opposite side of the coin has not yet been done. Finally, it is often easier to write in a "how-to-do-it" manner than to stay committed to a more neutral style. I tried to fight the urge, but I plead guilty to slipping on occasion.

There are numerous people to whom I owe thanks for assisting in one way or another during the book's preparation. An array of ideas and constructive criticism were provided, both in informal discussion and in reviews of the manuscript, by colleagues and present and former students. In particular, I wish to thank E. E. Jones of Princeton University, James T. Tedeschi of SUNY at Albany, and Mark Snyder of the University of Minnesota, who reviewed the manuscript, and also Bruce Darby, Don Forsyth, Mark Leary, Nancy McCown, Rowland Miller, Marc Riess, Larry Severy, Marvin Shaw, and Starr Silver. Larry Wrightsman supplied an invaluable amount of encouragement and knowledge. Claire Verduin gets my vote for editor of the year. I also wish to thank the National Institute of Mental Health (Research Scientist Development Program, Grant No. 1 K02 MH 00183-01) and the National Science Foundation (Grant No. BNS 77-08182) for their support of my research on impression management and social identity. My parents provided a huge indirect contribution; they brought me up to appreciate the things I do and were always there when I needed them. Finally, my wife, Pat, had to put up with it all; as she knows, I am not the grandest companion while working on a project. But, somehow, we got through it all together.

Barry R. Schlenker

CONTENTS

PART THREE   THE LINES   167

PART ONE

SETTING THE STAGE

O N E

INTRODUCTION

Bob groggily appreciates the sound of rock music in the background. He slowly turns in bed and opens his eyes to see his new digital alarm clock/radio recording the time as 7:30 A.M. How contemporary and stylish the clock/radio is. (Bob had known it was for him the minute he saw it; he, too, has style.) He likes the song, even though it is only Number 16 on the current charts. Oh, well, if other people come to appreciate the song's subtle riffs and fine lyrical nuances as he does, it will soon be Number 1. But, then, most people buy certain records only because their friends do, not because they really understand music. Maybe it won't make Number 1, even though it should. (Bob has discerning tastes in an undiscerning world.) Now awake, he gingerly swings his feet over the side of the bed, whistles along with the music, and pops up ready to encounter another day. How lucky he is to be dynamic so early in the day; his roommate has to pull himself from bed in the morning, but not Bob. He knows he has a certain zest. Sliding the lever on the radio to another station, he tunes in the morning news. His roommate has often commented on Bob's desire to keep up with what's happening in the world. (Isn't that the duty of a serious contemporary college student?)

Looking in the bathroom mirror, Bob gives his head a little shake and sports one of his impish grins. (What a cavalier image.) As he picks up his toothpaste, he chuckles to himself about how some people buy that brand because of its advertised sex appeal. Those advertisements are so silly that they'd make him refuse to buy it; he wonders how others can be so gullible. He buys it because of its great taste.

As he looks into his closet to pick out the day's outfit, he thinks about the girl—no, woman (he's too mature to refer to them as girls)—in his first-period humanities class. Since it's the start of the second week of the semester, he should really talk to her today, or he might miss his opportunity for the rest of the term. What could he say? Several conversation openers come to mind, but they're all so trite. You can't begin a relationship by appearing too common; at least he can't. "Nice weather"—that went out years ago. Maybe she'll be wearing a T shirt with something odd printed on it—she did that the first day of class— that could start a conversation. She had smiled at him last week and seemed to orient toward his side of the room; she must like him. If only he'd said something then, but the time just wasn't right; besides, he couldn't really think of anything to say. But he'd be ready today. His yellow shirt with the orange and red flowers would be just the kind of thing to make him stand out. (Prominence and taste, a perfect combination.)

As he briskly strides toward class, he nonchalantly gazes at the sky, apparently pondering the mysteries of the universe. (Idealism but direction, a fine balance.) He seems unaware of those around him, who go about their mundane business on the campus. He takes his usual seat in the front center of the classroom; that's where the action is, since instructors spend more time looking at and talking to people there. Luckily, the woman Bob wants to meet is only a seat away. He picks up his notebook, places it on the desk arm, looks toward the front of the room, leans back in his seat, and puts his hand under his chin. (Relaxed, contemplative, but ready for action in his own confident way.)

Scores on the first week's quiz will be handed back in a moment. That would merit a comment to the attractive woman, especially since he knows he did well on it. Turning slowly to his right, almost oblivious to the presence of the other students (one shouldn't appear too anxious), he asks her how she likes the course so far. (Was his voice really that low in pitch? Well, masculine voices generally are bass and sexy.) She says she is enjoying the course, is a fine arts major, and really likes the instructor. Bob agrees that he too enjoys the course immensely (he is the kind of person who fully appreciates the humanities) but notes that the instructor, although quite knowledgeable, has a tendency to ramble off on a tangent. (Bob is obviously cultured and has similar opinions to hers, yet is discerning—one shouldn't agree about everything, or one would seem too conforming.) Bob asks what she thought about last week's quiz. He believes it was quite hard but fair. (A good score on a hard quiz means more than a good score on an easy one, so long as the test is fair.) How does he think he did, she asks. Oh, he probably did all right. (No need to brag; humility is a virtue, especially when one has something to be humble about. Besides, he knows she'll be able to see his "A" grade—he'll be able to place his paper in a conspicuous spot on the desk.)

Maybe she'd like to go with him to a football game next weekend. Better find out first if she likes football. Did she see the game this past weekend when the college team lost? Certainly was a big letdown for them to blow the game after we had won the weekend before. (Did that sound funny? *We* won, but *they* lost?) Bob suddenly notices that his foot is jiggling. He places the offending foot securely on the floor; after all, he can't appear nervous. So she says she does like football. Great—a woman who shares his appreciation of culture, yet can let her hair down and enjoy sports. He tells her how unusual he believes that is. (No need to tell her how beautiful she is; she's probably heard that so many times that it would have no impact. Much better to compliment her on her ideas and tastes. Besides, she may be "liberated" or think that he is someone who doesn't realize that beauty is only skin deep. She is beautiful, though.) After a few more minutes of conversation, she agrees to a date.

After class, Bob slowly closes his notebook. (Obviously deep in thought about that day's lecture.) Deftly, he places the notebook under his chemistry text. (Maybe she'll notice his scientific interests as well.) As he gets up, he clumsily catches his foot on the chair leg and mutters something about the newly waxed floor. It would trip up even an Olympic gymnast. Other challenges of the day await.

No matter how different people feel they are from Bob in terms of their interaction style or personality characteristics, certain things stand out in his morning experiences with which everyone can associate. People are social animals. Our lives are interwoven with the lives of those around us. When in the presence of others, the impressions we make dramatically affect our interpersonal relations, and this is true whether those others are strangers, friends, or family. Even when not in the immediate presence of others, their existence affects our actions in countless ways. Some of these are obvious. People rehearse upcoming interactions, plan what they will do and say, try to anticipate what others will do, and decide how to respond. An example is pondering what to do on a date later in the evening. People even take actions that they believe will help the future interaction along, as Bob did in selecting a shirt he thought would make a favorable impression on the attractive classmate. Other effects may be more subtle, such as when other people are used as standards for self-evaluations. Bob employed social comparisons regarding musical tastes and reasons for buying toothpastes, allowing him to feel good about his personal qualities. People's thought processes are guided by social meanings, and people's values, attitudes, and beliefs are influenced by others more than they usually care to admit.

Nearly every action can carry some social meaning that has implications for what a person is like and how he or she should be treated. The clothes people wear, the ways they decorate their rooms, the statements they make about themselves, others, and the world, the ways they walk and sit—all communicate and express things about them. There is hardly any action that couldn't give others some clue useful in categorizing and evaluating a person. Is the person pleasant or unpleasant? Competent or incompetent? Liberal or conservative? Enjoyable to be with or boring? Honest or deceptive? Moral or immoral? Independent or conforming? Naturally, people make the same kinds of inferences about themselves from their own actions. What do my actions express about me? Is it consistent or inconsistent with my image of the kind of person I am or want to be? Everyone is an amateur psychologist of sorts, examining and evaluating behaviors to reach conclusions about what he or she is really like. Simply put, actions carry social meanings that affect the impressions others form of the actor, the way they treat the actor, and the way the actor views himself or herself.

To live effectively as human beings, our actions can't be simply random; actions must follow some pattern or plan that establishes who we are, how we see ourselves and desire others to see us, and how we see the world and wish the world to treat us. Bob's behaviors are purposeful. He has a particular set of self-images—cavalier, dynamic, idealistic, discerning, intelligent, cultured, and sexy—and behaves in ways that he believes will express and maintain these qualities. Other images are not part of this desired picture, and he tries to dissociate himself from them. When Bob clumsily slipped while getting up after class, he immediately tried to account for the wayward behavior in a way he thought could negate the appearance of being a clod. When he noticed his foot wiggling, perhaps connoting nervousness or self-consciousness, he was quick to halt the offending behavior. His self-concept and the social identity he wishes to establish provide him with guidelines for actions.

A person's self-concept, though, isn't the only guideline that affects actions. Societal and situational forces, some salient and others scarcely noticed, exert powerful influences. Society provides norms for behavior that prescribe how people should act in particular situations. The guidelines for interacting with one's boss, for example, are quite different from those for interacting with one's family. These social rules direct interactions along particular courses, sometimes without the participant's full awareness of what is occurring. In a different vein, transient situational factors can steer actions in one or another direction. Bob, for example, was rather modest in answering his classmate's question about his test performance, knowing that she would be able to see that he had done extremely well. If the situation had been such that she could not have seen how well he had done, he probably would have been more of a braggart in his answer. Comparably, if his classmate had been a premed major rather than a fine arts major, he probably would have said different things to her, stressing different self-descriptions and opinions.

As the little slice from Bob's life illustrates, impressions, impression management, and interpersonal relations are integrally related. *Impression management is the conscious or unconscious attempt to control images that are projected in real or imagined social interactions.* When these images are self-relevant, the behavior is termed *self-presentation.* We attempt to influence how other people—real or imagined—perceive our personality traits, abilities, intentions, behaviors, attitudes, values, physical characteristics, social characteristics, family, friends, job, and possessions. In so doing, we often influence how we see ourselves. Impression management plays a key role in how we develop and maintain particular identities in social life. Identities define who we are; they shape and are shaped by our self-concepts, behaviors, other people, and situations.

Broadly, the study of impression management involves the study of self-concept, social identity, the relationship between the person and society, and the ways in which people influence themselves and others. Impression management is a central part of the very nature of social interaction; it is inconceivable to discuss interpersonal relations without employing the concept.

The idea of impression management or self-presentation is often met with a jaundiced eye, since it evokes images of a Machiavellian character concerned with outcomes and not principles. Some people might argue that a person who "uses" impression management is a crude caricature of a human being, a phony who is more concerned with appearance than substance and is too self-centered to enter into truly meaningful relationships. The more cynically minded might argue that the ultimate reality is one of appearance as substance, that a person who uses impression management is only recognizing the true depths of vanity, is honest enough to admit that facades exist and turn them to personal advantage. These opposite viewpoints express moral biases and are couched in value-laden terms. The "humanist" views impression management as false and deceptive, out of touch with one's "real" self. The "cynic" similarly views impression management as deceitful but concludes that deceit is more virtuous because of its naturalness and that there is no such thing as a real self when it is stripped of the external trappings. Neither of these views needs to be accepted.

All people control, more or less, through habit or conscious design, the ways they appear to themselves and others. Impression management often consists of well-ingrained, habitlike responses that are triggered in particular situations and need not involve intentional subterfuge. Bob, for instance, did not have to think through all of the implications of how a wiggling foot connotes nervousness and what appearing nervous would mean to the impression he was trying to create. He simply stopped the nervous wiggle as soon as it came to his attention. Similarly, he didn't have to weigh, strategically and consciously, the advantages and disadvantages of talking about the course in one way rather than another. Given what his classmate said, the appropriate verbal response flowed from his lips. Further, the impressions people attempt to create can be true or false and consistent or inconsistent with their self-concept. It is just as important to a priest to establish and maintain a consistent identity as a man of God and moral scruples as it is to some politicians to control their images to garner votes. The impressions people create are under internal as well as external control and can manifest socially desirable or undesirable motives. They can come about because of high moral standards or perfidious intentions. There is nothing intrinsic to the concept of impression management that dictates that it must involve dissimulation. In fact, over time, the "authentic" presentation of self—that is, showing ourselves as we believe we really are—is likely to be met by the greatest internal satisfaction and external approval. Thus to talk about social identity and impression management is simply to talk about life—what we are, what we do, and how we carve niches for ourselves in our worlds.

Unfortunately, the term *impression management* has connotations of intentionally attempting to be something one is not. The term *self-presentation* shares some of these negative connotations. I hope that the preceding discussion will alleviate some of this concern, since my use of the term is not limited to such intentional deceptions. The remainder of the book will also show why the terms should not be so limited. I was sorely tempted to get around this problem by using more neutral terms instead. For instance, we could substitute the term *self-projection* for *self-presentation*. Self-projection does not imply intention, nor does it imply subterfuge. However, since the research literature generously uses the terms *impression management* and *self-presentation*, I'll resist the switch.

How does the self-concept develop? How is it related to social identity? When don't we want to be seen as we feel we "really are"? Why do we adopt one rather than another set of self-images? How do these self-images affect actions? How do actions in turn affect self-images? When we behave in a fashion that is inconsistent with one of our self-images, under what conditions will we change the image to match the behavior? How do people use verbal actions (self-descriptions or attitude statements, for example) and nonverbal ones (body language, for example) for self-presentational purposes? How is impression management used for personal advantage as a form of social power, as in the business world or politics? How do situational factors and social forces affect the ways people present themselves to others? Why do some people seem to present themselves in socially undesirable ways, such as appearing hostile (the high school bully) or incompetent (the mental patient)? To what extent are self-serving perceptions used to protect and enhance one's identity? For example, how prevalent is Bob's tendency to associate himself with positive outcomes (the football team's win) and dissociate himself from negative outcomes (the team's loss)? How do people protect their identities when they lose face? When do people feel that their actions are truthful and self-revealing versus deceitful and manipulative?

These are just a few of the questions we'll be addressing. Before diving headfirst into the specifics of how people use impression management, it's wise to step back and inspect the terrain. There is no reason to leap into a tree before gaining an appreciation of the forest. So we'll first explore a little of interpersonal relations and the nature of human behavior.

TWO

Man alone desires to be both in one, a social solitary.
Jacob Bronowski

INTERPERSONAL BEHAVIOR: IMPRESSION MANAGEMENT AND THE STAGE OF LIFE

People have been characterized (or caricatured) in a multitude of ways. Some scientists view people as irrational animals controlled by biological drives and primitive emotions. Others view people as "sophisticated rats" who simply react to the rewards and punishments dispensed by the environment. To others, people are rational decision makers attempting to understand and control the environment, much like scientists in their quest for knowledge. Still others view people as social entities, the by-products of the society in which they were reared. The list could continue indefinitely. Each scientist and writer has a favorite view of what people are like. Each characterization might contain a germ of truth, but none tells the whole story. Each approaches people and interpersonal relations from a slightly different angle and leads to a slightly different conclusion.

In this chapter, we'll examine some key ideas that have influenced contemporary work relevant to impression management. These ideas can be woven together to form a general perspective on human behavior. By looking at this pattern, we can begin to understand the nature of impression management and its place in interpersonal relations. The pattern of ideas is somewhat like an imperfectly woven blanket—it has gaps and dangling threads. This is the nature of social science at the moment; it, too, is far from perfect. Yet it is progressing steadily, offering much in the way of understanding as it constantly seeks to improve our knowledge of people. Since a blanket with holes is better than none at all, though, we'll proceed.

PRAGMATISM: THE FUNCTIONS OF ACTION

The term *impression management* often evokes images of strategy and tactics, of people jockeying for position in the social world, trying to control how they appear in order to accomplish particular objectives. It sounds very pragmatic, and indeed it is.

Usefulness

Pragmatism is a school of American philosophy promulgated principally by three individuals: Charles Sanders Peirce (1839–1914), whom some regard as the greatest American philosopher to ever live, William James (1842–1910), the brilliant philosopher and psychologist who established the first psychology course taught in America, and John Dewey (1859–1952), the philosopher-educator whose work had an impact on psychology, sociology, and education. A basic theme of pragmatic philosophy is that ideas and actions must be evaluated in terms of their *usefulness*. For example, in deciding whether a particular idea is true or false, pragmatists ask about its consequences. Is the idea useful in understanding, explaining, or predicting something about the world? Do these implications aid us in functioning effectively in the world? For an idea to be true, it should be useful; that is, it should increase our understanding, our ability to predict, and the effectiveness of our functioning.

The View of Human Behavior. This theme is carried over into the pragmatists' view of human behavior. They believe that ideas and actions have uses, or functions, that are aimed at producing particular consequences. If we want to understand why a particular action occurred, we must analyze the functions it served for the individual; we must understand what he or she was attempting to achieve.

The functions of social actions are not apparent, though, if one views behavior as composed of elementary, unconnected, and nonmeaningful responses. To understand actions, we must understand their social character, their significance to the individual's functioning in social life (Dewey, 1922). Imagine a baseball player as he strides to the plate, glares menacingly at the pitcher, goes into a crouched position while cocking the bat off his shoulder, and takes a few practice swings to set up an intimidating aura. Some scientists might attempt to explain these actions by considering the specific stimuli and past reinforcements that could have triggered each of the minute movements and responses that constituted this sequence. The actions themselves, though, lose all social meaning when approached in such a molecular fashion. Pragmatists prefer to analyze behaviors in terms of coherent, integrated, and meaningful units rather than as sequences of discrete, unrelated responses.[1] In this case, the ballplayer might be trying to convince the pitcher, the cheering fans, and himself that he means business and is going to get a hit. If the pitcher is intimidated, the chances for a hit are increased; if the pitcher isn't, at least it's obvious to all concerned that the batter tried his best. Continuing the pragmatic tradition, we'll analyze actions in terms of socially meaningful, integrated units that imply a particular theme.

To function effectively in the world, people have to make sense out of it. They form beliefs that allow them to understand, explain, and predict events. Beliefs are functional; they "guide our desires and shape our actions" (Peirce, 1966a, pp. 7–8). Beliefs carry behavioral implications; they can steer people in directions that fulfill goals. A person with clear political beliefs "knows" how to vote in an upcoming election; a person with clear beliefs about his or her life goals "knows" what college courses to take. Our beliefs about other people can guide how we behave. Imagine a job interview with a new employer. You know you

[1]It is worth noting that the selection of a unit of analysis (molar or molecular) is somewhat arbitrary and depends on the goals of the theorist. A social psychologist is interested in molar actions that are unified by a common meaning, like the ballplayer's behaviors. An experimental psychologist might be more interested in an analysis of how a specific stimulus influences a particular response. A physiological psychologist might be more interested in a molecular analysis of neuronal events. A biochemist might be more interested in an even more molecular analysis of the chemical events occurring within and between particular cells. Choosing one of these units of analysis over another depends on what we want to explain, and says nothing about how "scientific" the explanation is. Complex sequences of meaningful actions can be treated just as scientifically as complex sequences of cellular events (see Schlenker, 1974, 1976, 1977).

want to make a favorable impression to get the job, but what is the best way of proceeding? Does the employer seem to value "company people" who will agree with the boss and not rock the boat? Or does the employer value independence that might facilitate getting the job done in the best possible way? Each of these beliefs carries quite different implications for what might be said to the employer during the interview, and it has been found that people do behave quite differently in such situations depending on which belief they hold. When they believe that the superior values productivity, they behave in an independent manner, but, when they believe that the superior values solidarity and "going along," they behave in a conforming manner (Jones, Gergen, Gumpert, & Thibaut, 1965).

Similarly, our beliefs about ourselves guide our actions. For instance, people who believe that they possess a particular attribute, such as independence, are more likely to act in ways that seem to express the attribute than are people who do not have the same self-belief (Carson, 1969). Our beliefs about the attributes we think we have and the tasks we think we can accomplish given those attributes steer us in one direction rather than another.

On the other hand, a state of doubt does not provide paths useful in obtaining goals. Peirce viewed doubt as an uncomfortable, irritable state from which relief is sought. Doubts serve only to cause us to acquire information useful in forming beliefs and courses of action.[2] Thus, a job applicant might attempt to get a feel for what the superior wants in an employee by talking to other workers at the company or by forming a belief based on how the superior looks and talks. Much of social life is spent acquiring information that can be used to guide action.

It would not be functional for people to have to concentrate on each and every implication of the myriad beliefs they hold; consequently, beliefs generate habits that don't demand constant attention. "The whole function of thought is to produce habits of action," habit being defined as "the establishment in our nature of a rule of action" (Peirce, 1966b, p. 13). A habit allows actions to flow without one's having to devote considerable conscious attention to the minute behaviors that constitute that habit (Kimble & Perlmuter, 1970). A skilled pianist finds it disruptive to concentrate on each finger movement that was once so arduously studied; a judge can't attend to the trial evidence if he

[2]The concept of unequivocal behavior orientation (Jones & Gerard, 1967) is a more formal statement and extension of the relationship among belief, doubt, and action described by Peirce. An unequivocal behavior orientation is an orientation that "permits effective and nonconflicted action" (Jones & Gerard, 1967, p. 719). We can't vote for both the Republican and Democratic presidential candidates; we can't be both submissive and assertive during the course of a short interview with a prospective employer. When such mutually exclusive paths exist, a belief is needed as a signpost. Once one path is taken, we further justify the belief by making the chosen path appear even better and the rejected one appear even worse than it may have initially seemed to us.

or she constantly ruminates about the appropriate rules of decorum that establish status and maintain authority. At one time, such actions may have been attended to quite carefully by the individual. But, because they served the individual well in the past, these ingrained responses are automatically triggered off by the appropriate cues in the situation. People become embedded in habit patterns that direct their actions, leading them on courses they once charted carefully but now have put out of mind.

In a classic passage, William James amplified the nature of habit.

> Habit is thus the enormous flywheel of society, its most precious conservative agent. It alone is what keeps us all within the bounds of ordinance, and saves the children of fortune from the envious uprisings of the poor. It alone prevents the hardest and most repulsive walks of life from being deserted by those brought up to tread in them. It keeps the fisherman and the deck-hand at sea through the winter; it holds the miner in his darkness, and nails the countryman to his log-cabin and his lonely farm through all the months of snow. . . . It dooms us all to fight out the battle of life upon the lines of our early choice, and to make the best of a pursuit that disagrees, because there is no other for which we are fitted, and it is too late to begin again. . . . Already at the age of twenty-five you see the professional mannerism settling down on the young commercial traveller, or the young counsellor-at-law. You see the little lines of cleavage running through the character, the tricks of thought, the prejudices, the ways of the 'shop,'. . . from which the man can by-and-by no more escape than his coat-sleeve can suddenly fall into a new set of folds. On the whole, it is best he should not escape. It is well for the world that in most of us, by the age of thirty, the character has set like plaster, and will never soften again [1890/1952, p. 79].

It is interesting to note in James' eloquent passage the examples of habits provided for our evaluation. All involve the enactment of identities in society. People become enmeshed in particular roles that direct their actions without continued conscious monitoring. These habits are more subtle than some other habitlike responses such as riding a bike, since they are patterns of social behavior that escape our deliberations at the moment they occur.

In sum, the pragmatists believed that understanding the world and effectively functioning in it go hand in hand. To understand human behavior, we have to examine the functions that thought and action serve. And to do this, we must appreciate that thoughts and actions have meanings, meanings that can be controlled by people to accomplish objectives. Actions are meaningful social units, and those that have been consciously enacted and practiced can become habit patterns that set people free to attend to others things and accomplish new goals. These pragmatic ideas will be encountered again as we continue to explore the nature of interpersonal relations.

HEDONISM: A BEHAVIOR CALCULUS

To many scientists, the primary function of action is to achieve happiness. Given the choice of a pleasurable or painful experience, it is not hard to predict which one people will choose. One of the oldest ideas about what motivates behavior is the principle of hedonism: people seek pleasure and avoid pain. This principle was articulated by ancient Greek philosophers and has endured in various forms to the present; more sophisticated statements of it serve as cornerstones of numerous contemporary psychological theories.

Aristippus of Cyrene, who lived during the age of Socrates, is often credited as the originator of hedonism. He felt that pleasure of the moment is "the only thing worthy of striving for and that . . . virtue [is] identical with the ability to enjoy" (Cofer & Appley, 1964, p. 28). Self-control, though, must guide the pursuit of pleasure, or the experience will not be of the highest type. Epicurus (342/1–270/1 B.C.), whose name has often been wrongly associated with luxurious self-indulgence (Epicurianism), also preached that the goal of life is to obtain pleasure. He distinguished, however, between active pleasures, undertaken to relieve pain or tension like hunger, and passive pleasures, which achieve a comfortable state of equilibrium. An example of the latter is eating regular and small amounts to avoid feeling either hungry or full. Epicurus believed that passive pleasures produce the greatest happiness and are superior to active pleasures. Thus, he advocated prudence, disdained self-indulgence, was thankful for a small piece of bread or cheese, discouraged sexual intercourse—he felt it was one of the most "active" of pleasures—and believed friendship was the safest of social pleasures (Russell, 1945).

The emphasis on the pleasures of this life offended Christian doctrines, so the principle of hedonism remained dormant until resurrected by social philosophers in the 18th and 19th centuries. Jeremy Bentham (1748–1832), well known to students of government and economics, maintained that pleasure and pain are our "sovereign masters." He spoke of the principle of utility—the ability of an action to produce happiness. Translating this principle into social and economic policies, the utilitarians believed that the object of governments is to produce "the greatest good for the greatest number" of people. Utilitarians such as John Stuart Mill (1806–1873) endorsed the belief that "to desire to do anything except in proportion as the idea of it is pleasant is a physical impossibility" (Allport, 1968, p. 11).

A more colorful statement of hedonism is presented by the popular author Robert Ringer (1977) in his best seller *Looking Out for Number One*. Ringer flatly asserts that "*all* people act in their own self-interest *all* the time" (p. 33).[3] Ringer describes a hypothetical Weight-and-Balance Happiness Scale with which we are all endowed and which we use in calculating what our self-interest is: "Your Weight-and-Balance Happiness Scale automatically weighs every known alternative available to you at a given moment and chooses the one it *believes* will bring you the most happiness" (p. 4). Of course, sometimes miscalculations occur and what one thinks should produce happiness turns out not to. But, to Ringer, it is inconceivable that people do something unless they believe that the action maximizes their potential happiness or minimizes their potential unhappiness.

The idea that people look out only for their self-interests and maximize their own happiness seems to reek of cynicism. However, seeking rewarding outcomes and avoiding punishing ones does not necessarily imply obtaining vast quantities of material goods, being callous toward the needs of other people, exploiting others, or behaving immorally. People's values differ. Although one person might desire material goods and hoard possessions, another might abhor them and be happy in a small cabin in the forest. People can also gain satisfaction by living up to their moral standards, however lofty or base these might be. Behaving exploitatively or immorally could produce unhappiness or happiness, depending on one's values and standards. Moreover, people are empathic; the joys, sorrows, happiness, and pains of others can trigger similar emotional reactions in themselves. Seeing joy in a child opening a present can be more valuable than any material good. Finally, maximizing our long-run best interests often necessitates establishing a particular kind of reputation (say, for honesty, helpfulness, understanding) and doing the types of things that live up to it. Thus, people's values, standards, empathic abilities, long-term goals, and similar considerations must be included when discussing self-interest.

Psychologists have long endorsed the principle of hedonism, although in somewhat more sophisticated forms than the above. Since the concepts of happiness and unhappiness are ambiguous, psychologists translated them into concepts that are more suited for quantification, measurement, and prediction. This produced the terms *reinforcement, rewards, and punishments*. Reinforcements are events that increase the probability of occurrence of a particular response; rewards are outcomes that are positively evaluated; and punishments are outcomes that are negatively evaluated. Psychologists also added a new dimension to the hedonic principle. Unlike Aristippus, who focused on hedonism of the present ("act to produce pleasure now"), or Ringer and the utilitarians, who focused on hedonism of the future ("act to produce

---

[3]From *Looking Out for Number One*, by Robert J. Ringer, Copyright © 1977 by Robert J. Ringer. (New York: Harper & Row Publishers, Inc., 1977). This and all other quotations from this source are reprinted by permission.

long-run pleasure"), psychologists originally emphasized hedonism of the past ("act now in ways that previously produced rewards and avoided punishments"). The law of effect (Thorndike, 1927), a principle discussed in virtually all introductory psychology texts, is that actions that produce satisfaction (rewards) become "stamped in" and repeated in similar situations, while actions that produce discomfort (punishments) become "stamped out" and avoided in similar situations. B. F. Skinner, the widely known contemporary psychologist, believes that behaviors are determined by an organism's reinforcement history; that is, we repeat those actions that produced reinforcements in similar situations in the past.

By way of illustration, picture our initial protagonist Bob on his first date with the attractive classmate. After the football game, they find themselves sitting across from each other in a candlelit Italian restaurant. The noisy crowd at the game permitted little conversation, so they are only now really getting acquainted. Bob mentions something about his home town in New York, but his California-reared date has little to contribute to this theme (no reinforcement for that topic). Bob next mentions how the restaurant reminds him of a scene from an old Humphrey Bogart movie. Her head perks up; she shows her approval by recounting another scene from the same movie (reinforcement!). He amplifies the theme, and soon both are engrossed in a mutually reinforcing conversation about old movies. This could be described as an instance of operant conditioning: the presentation of a reinforcement following a response increases the probability of occurrence of a similar future response.

When the waitress arrives, the fragrance of her perfume wafts in Bob's direction. The perfume is identical to that worn by Bob's former fiancée, who broke up with him after an emotional romance. He feels a pain deep inside and falls silent, his effervescent mood stilled by sadness. This could be described as an instance of classical conditioning: a previously neutral stimulus (the perfume), by being associated with a stimulus (the fiancée) that evokes a response (an emotional reaction), comes to elicit the response on its own.

Many psychologists once believed that the processes of classical and operant conditioning could explain all human learning and behavior. For example, Bob's selection of a particular shirt to wear on a date might have been explained as depending exclusively on how much reinforcement he had previously received for wearing it in comparable situations. Bob's self-descriptions might have been thought to be exclusively under the control of environmental factors such as discriminative stimuli and past reinforcement. Relatively few contemporary psychologists make such assertions (see Bandura, 1974, 1978; Carson, 1969; Hilgard & Bower, 1975; Mischel, 1973).

Simple conditioning processes do explain some behaviors, but they do not adequately explain the richness and complexity of most human and nonhuman actions. The concept of simple conditioning does not consider how cognitive processes affect behavior. Cognitive variables (mental states such as ideas, beliefs, expectations, attitudes, and goals) and cognitive processes (mental activities such as information processing, reasoning processes, and planning) are ignored. The meaning of interpersonal actions is given little attention. Psychologists have moved away from such radical forms of behaviorism toward a fuller understanding of the role of cognitive activities in affecting action (see Bandura, 1977a, 1978; Bolles, 1972; Carroll & Payne, 1976; Carson, 1969; Longstreth, 1971; Miller, Galanter, & Pribram, 1960; Mitchell & Biglan, 1971; Neisser, 1967, 1976; Rosenthal & Zimmerman, 1978; Schank & Abelson, 1977; Sperry, 1977; Wyer, 1974). We'll explore more fully some of these cognitive processes in the later section on social cognition.

The reacceptance of cognitive processes in the hedonic calculus brings us to something akin to Ringer's Weight-and-Balance Happiness Scale. People gather information about the environment, store it in memory, integrate it to arrive at a perspective they can use to organize experiences, and use it to help them in interacting with the environment. They form expectations of the consequences of their own and other people's actions, and they act on the basis of these expectations to obtain a favorable reward/cost ratio. A general hedonic proposition about behavior that is widely accepted by social psychologists is that *people act to maximize their expected rewards and minimize their expected punishments.* To do so, people develop goals for the future and plans for achieving them. Goals are desired end states we want to achieve. Plans are strategies for achieving these goals. More technically, a plan is defined as a hierarchically ordered sequence of operations (thoughts or behaviors) that has a particular goal (Miller et al., 1960). They are analogous to computer programs in that they exist for some purpose, guide the operations of that entity, and contain feedback loops that are responsive to changing circumstances. Plans do not have to be consciously formulated (Carson, 1969; Miller et al., 1960).

Returning to Bob and his date, we can explain their behaviors in terms of their attitudes, beliefs, goals, and plans. Bob, as we know, had evaluated her positively. One of his goals was to make her like him, and he felt that increasing his attractiveness would cause her to have, if she did not already, a favorable attitude. One of his beliefs is that, if people talk about mutually interesting topics, they will both feel comfortable and their mutual attraction will increase. He formulates a plan based on this belief and searches for a viable topic. When she fails to respond to his talk about his home town, he realizes that his goal can't be achieved by pursuing that topic, so he switches topics. When she shows pleasure with a discussion of old movies, he realizes he has found a topic that is mutually satisfying, and he proceeds to the second step of his plan—continuing the discussion. Her nod of approval served as information that was meaningful in terms of his plans.

In sum, when considering why people behave as they do, we will adopt the basic hedonic postulate that people act to maximize their expected rewards and minimize their expected punishments. To do so, people must gather information about the world, integrate it, interpret it, and use it, forming plans to accomplish their goals. The function of action, then, is to produce "happiness"—that is—achieve a desirable reward/cost ratio. Yet, as we shall now examine, everyday life is so interdependent that, to achieve happiness, people must take into consideration the impressions they create on others.

INTERDEPENDENCE, EXCHANGE, AND POWER

People sometimes dream about what it would be like to obtain all the outcomes they desire—love, friendship, money, success, property, reputation, contentment, or whatever (rank these any way you wish). Without debating the question of whether such a windfall would produce true happiness or just plain boredom, it is enough to note that people never get everything they want. They constantly strive to obtain desirable outcomes, and, once they obtain one goal, they set their sights on others.

Interdependence

Some of the most important and valuable outcomes people can receive in life are dependent, at least to some degree, on the actions of others. How many desirable outcomes can you think of that aren't? Love and friendship obviously are. To get a reputation, others must appreciate one's skills or attributes. To get money or the things it can buy, people must provide a skill, service, or other good that people are willing to pay for. Personal contentment and self-satisfaction are based on having achieved other goals; it is hard to be content when one has no friends, no job, no money, and a tarnished reputation. Even success is defined in terms of standards developed by others, although people may modify the standards to fit their own goals.

If other people don't act in the ways we wish, the outcomes evaporate or change. Interdependence of outcomes characterizes human life: the outcomes we receive are derived from the interplay of our own behaviors and those of others. As Robert Ringer (1977) put it, "What a paradox: to maximize my possibilities for a joyous life, I needed people. . . . One requires people in his life because one has needs, and it simply isn't possible for an individual to fill all his own needs" (p. 223).

Exchange: Tit for Tat and Value for Value

When people interact, their actions have consequences for both themselves and others. People are intermeshed in a social matrix in which their outcomes are linked. Consequently,

> Simple reasoning tells you that you must regard the interests of others (though not all others) in order to obtain your objectives. Fellow human beings represent potential values to you in business or personal relationships, and the rational individual understands that to harvest those values he must be willing to fill certain needs of others. In this way, the most rationally selfish individual is also the most "giving" person, since he best understands the soundness of value-for-value relationships [Ringer, 1977, pp. 34–35].

Thus, interdependence breeds exchange. Although Ringer's admonitions might sound cynical, they are rooted in basic social-psychological theory. Exchange theory (Blau, 1964; Homans, 1974; Thibaut & Kelley, 1959) provides a general perspective on social behavior that derives from psychological principles of reinforcement and from economic principles of the exchange of commodities. Just as businesspeople exchange goods, services, and money, in interpersonal relations people exchange commodities that have value. Some commodities are materialistic, such as gifts on holidays, birthdays, or even "no special occasion." Other commodities are less tangible but are nonetheless quite valuable. For example, we often exchange sentiments. Sentiments are behavioral indications of how one person regards or feels about another (Homans, 1974). For example, we show our friends that we like them and enjoy their company; we show our superiors deference and provide them with status; we show our teachers respect and indicate we admire their competence. Of course, we can also do the opposites, indicating our dislike, disrespect, or feelings that someone is incompetent. These outcomes are all worth something to the participants. They involve both rewards and costs. Hence, any interaction can be said to yield each of the participants a certain profit, which is the amount of reward minus the cost. According to the exchange approach, people want to maximize their profits from interactions. If the profits from a relationship are high and are better than what might be obtained in alternative relationships, the persons will be quite satisfied, and the relationship should prosper. If profits are low relative to what can be obtained in alternative relationships, the person will leave it for an alternative. If profits from the relationship are low, but no better alternative exists, the person will be dissatisfied but stuck, being dependent on that relationship for even the meager profits it provides. The exchange approach can be applied to any conceivable interaction, including the development and maintenance of love relationships (Blau, 1964).

The principles of exchange seem to be universal. *Reciprocity norms,* which prescribe that people should return benefit for benefit and harm for harm, have been found in every society studied (Gouldner, 1960).

Power and Influence

The nature of interdependence is such that we can't be certain of the outcomes we will receive from interactions: they depend in part on the actions of others. Therefore, in order to maximize our reward/cost ratios, it is necessary to exert social influence to guide others' actions in the directions we desire. Influence is the production of a change in the environment that otherwise would not have occurred. Social influence is the production of such a change in people (their attitudes and actions, for example). Social power is the ability to influence people.[4]

When one first thinks of power and influence, the images that come to mind usually involve unscrupulous characters who use power exploitatively. Power clearly can be used at the expense of others, as when a seller misleads a buyer or a dictator extracts taxes from his people to pay for his own comforts. Yet it can also be used to produce mutual benefit, as when a salesman advertises and sells a commodity for a fair price to a consumer who needs it or a government uses tax money to support services desired by the people.

All interactions involve influence, even when people don't recognize it. You want to eat dinner at a Chinese restaurant and your spouse or date wants to eat at a Mexican one. You want to study for a test; your roommate wants to party boisterously in the next room. You want your child to eat proper foods; the child expresses drastically different preferences. To resolve such minor conflicts, social influence occurs. Even when conflicts are less apparent, influence is at the forefront. You want your date to like you, or you want your boss to give you a raise, so you take appropriate actions to influence their attitudes and behaviors. Power and influence exist because of interdependence; the phenomena are real whether we want to use these terms or substitute euphemisms.

The Importance of Power. Philosophers and psychologists have defined power in general terms involving the ability to influence the environment, including people, but most theorists have focused on social (interpersonal) power. Unifying the themes of hedonism and power, the British social philosopher Thomas Hobbes (1588–1679) asserted that power was necessary to obtain pleasure. "The power of man, to take it

---

[4]Power and influence have been defined in numerous ways by numerous authors, but the definitions above are similar to the others and are sufficient for our purposes. For further discussions, see Cartwright (1959), Kipnis (1976), Pollard and Mitchell (1972), Schopler (1965), Tedeschi (1972), Tedeschi, Schlenker, and Bonoma (1973).

universally, is his present means to obtain some future good" (Hobbes, 1651/1952, p. 71). He believed people were unable to obtain a sense of personal worth, dignity, and honor without power, making it a central motive for human behavior. "I put for a general inclination of all mankind a perpetual and restless desire for power after power, that ceaseth only in death" (1651/1952, p. 76).

The German philosopher Friedrich Nietzsche (1864–1900) believed that all human actions reflect direct or disguised strivings for power; he posited a fundamental "will to power" from which everything else derives. He believed the will to power is superordinate even to a will to live: since people are sometimes willing to risk their lives, the will to live must be governed by the will to power. To Nietzsche, "All things . . . seek aggrandizement, seek to augment their power over other things. The strong use direct means, the weak indirect; and at length . . . all actions and codes of moral law can be explained as expressions of this one, basic drive" (Hollingdale, 1961, p. 26). He also believed that humans are quite similar to other animals save for one thing—a very few special humans could exhibit *self-overcoming*, rising above the constraints and controls of their environment and other people to become "supermen," the ultimate manifestation of the will to power. His idea of self-overcoming is similar to some 20th century notions of self-actualization (Maslow, 1968; C. R. Rogers, 1961).

Bertrand Russell (1872–1969), the great British philosopher and mathematician, believed that social scientists could not understand human behavior without understanding the nature of power. He stated that the "love of power is the chief motive producing the changes which social science has to study" (1938, p. 15). Further, "The fundamental concept in social science is power, in the same sense in which Energy is the fundamental concept in physics" (1938, p. 12).

The Bases of Power. What attributes allow a person to influence the attitudes and actions of others? Certainly, some people are very effective in getting their way in interactions, while others can claim modest success at best. One of the first attempts to list the bases of power was made by Hobbes. He included (1) servants and friends (one could form coalitions against others using united strengths), (2) riches joined with liberality (one can "buy" friends and servants so long as they feel they will be fully rewarded), (3) a reputation of power (others are not likely to test you), (4) popularity, (5) a quality that makes one loved or feared (it gets one the assistance and service of others), (6) success (it forms a reputation of wisdom or good fortune), (7) the esteem of those who have power, (8) eloquence (for persuasive purposes), (9) nobility (status), and (10) the "arts of public use" (skills that others need). Things have apparently not changed much since 1651. After delineating these attributes, Hobbes concluded that "the value or worth of a man is, as of all other things, his price; that is to say, so much as would be given for the use of his power, and therefore is not absolute, but a thing dependent on the need and judgment of another" (1651/1952, p. 73). It is a quite modern statement that recognizes the nature of interdependence and social exchange and how power is used to accomplish goals.

Numerous other analyses of power have been made by social psychologists. French and Raven (1959) concluded that five factors were fundamental: (1) reward power (possessing the ability to reward others), (2) coercive power (possessing the ability to punish others), (3) expert power (having another believe that you possess knowledge useful to him or her), (4) referent power (having another identify with you because of certain attractive qualities), and (5) legitimate power (possessing the "right" to get others to comply because they believe they "should," as when police exert authority over citizens). Social psychologists agree that being able to do one or both of the following is essential to power: (1) reward or punish the target personally or (2) affect the perceptions, beliefs, attitudes, and goals of the target, causing the target to believe that a particular course of action will produce his or her most favorable reward/cost ratio.

Impression management is a form of social influence. People affect their own outcomes by attempting to influence the impressions that others form of them. Through words and deeds, we leave impressions on others that shape how they approach and treat us. Controlling these impressions is a means of controlling others' actions, which, in turn, affect our own outcomes for better or worse.

SOCIAL COGNITION: CONSTRUCTING REALITIES

People use information to formulate beliefs, goals, and plans that permit successful transactions with others and the environment. A prominent area of psychology and sociology is the study of how such information is acquired, organized, and given meaning.

Constructive Alternativism

George Kelly (1955), a personality theorist, developed the analogy of people as scientists: people try to predict, control, and understand the things that transpire around them. They proceed the way scientists do, although perhaps less systematically. People gather facts, observations of objects and events, about the world and then fit these facts together to form beliefs, or hypotheses, about what is occurring. These beliefs are then tested against new observations to see whether the beliefs are supported or refuted. If supported, the belief increases in strength; if refuted, it may be abandoned, modified, or held with less confidence.

Facts and beliefs don't exist in isolation; they are given meaning only through a person's existing *constructs* about the world. A construct is a pattern or template created by the person that serves as a way of looking at the world. It is a cognitive category or generalization that can encompass numerous facts. For example, one may code oneself and others on such constructs as friendly versus unfriendly, strong versus weak, happy versus sad, and active versus passive. People use constructs as summary interpretations of what transpires around them—indeed, they must use them, since the world would seem too complex without them. Each of us uses a slightly different set of constructs when gathering and evaluating information, and constructs appropriate for one situation might not be for another. Since people can construe the world in different ways, Kelly spoke of *constructive alternativism,* the ability to shift constructs and gain new perspectives.

Bob, for example, may be trying to evaluate how attracted or unattracted his date feels. Right after entering the restaurant, she is quiet and leans slightly backward—away from him—in the booth. Momentarily Bob hypothesizes that she finds him unattractive. But perhaps she is simply shy or just tired after the noisy football game. Bob now has different hypotheses, based on different constructs, and certainly wants to test them.

After remembering some of the revealing clothes she wore to class and her cheering at the football game, Bob rejects the shyness hypothesis. After talking for a few moments about his home town and getting no reaction, he becomes slightly uneasy. Maybe she really doesn't like him. After he switches to a discussion of movies, she perks up. Now she's leaning toward him and talking freely. He reaches for her hand, and she doesn't move away—in fact, she returns his touch. She does like him; she must have been relaxing momentarily after the long afternoon and been uninterested in the first topic. As we see here, people's behaviors are guided by the constructs they employ to describe situations. In this case, Bob's behaviors probably would have been quite different had he concluded that his date was uninterested in him rather than tired.

Constructs give meanings to particular facts, and, by switching constructs, the same set of facts can be given a different appearance. Was Robin Hood a thief or a hero? It depends on the perceiver's perspective—a rich 12th century Englishman might apply the former construct, while a poor one might quickly employ the latter. Robin himself, had he actually existed, would have undoubtedly preferred the latter. By judiciously applying the constructs that "describe" facts, one can control the meanings the facts convey. By controlling meanings, one controls one's outcomes from social interactions. Impression management includes controlling meanings in this way.

Attributions

Fritz Heider (1958), a social psychologist, developed a theoretical position that bears many resemblances to Kelly's theory of personal constructs. Heider recognized that people develop organized views of their environments. People behave much like amateur psychologists, developing theories about human behavior: why people act in certain ways, what personality traits are related to certain behaviors, and so on. This is "naive psychology," so called because it is not always systematically thought out or even consciously appreciated. It is the psychology of the person on the street: "If we can understand the terms in which Everyman constructs social causation, we can understand what animates his actions and decisions" (E. E. Jones, in press, p. 45).

A central theme of the approach is that people want to understand events, and to do that they make attributions about what may have caused an event. *Attribution* is making a "connection or relation between some event and a source" (Heider, 1976, p. 16). The question of causation is particularly important when social events are involved. If a rock falls near you, you look around to discover why, but you don't, let us hope, attribute malicious motives to it or try to figure out why it hurled itself in your direction. People, on the other hand, do intend certain things, and their intentions have implications for our future interactions with them. All behaviors carry implications for what the actor is like as a person and what he or she is likely to do.

When making attributions about people's behavior, we break down the possible causes into two general classes: *personal dispositions* of the actor such as intentions and traits and *environmental forces* or pressures such as coercions in the situation and luck. Suppose a young executive arrives promptly at work every day in a conservative suit and acts very formally toward coworkers. Are these actions reflective of a conservative, formal, perhaps cold disposition? Or do they reflect the rules of that particular company or of a boss who demands promptness, conservatism, and formality from employees? Perhaps they are produced by some combination of the executive's dispositions and the work situation. If we make the attribution primarily to the person's dispositions, we have formed expectations of what the young executive is likely to do across a variety of situations, and we are likely to respond accordingly. If we make the attribution primarily to the situation, we don't feel we have learned what the person is "really like."

People are held most accountable for their actions when the actions are seen as uncoerced by external pressures or extenuating circumstances. A person who flies into a rage and injures another is seen as less accountable for the behavior if the other was taunting and holding a knife than if the other was calmly and quietly debating a point. The attributions people make about others affect how they view them, when they hold them accountable, and therefore how they treat them.

Attribution theorists (see Harvey, Ickes, & Kidd, 1976, 1978; Jones & Davis, 1965; Kelley, 1967; Shaver, 1975) have generated a great deal of information about how people make attributions about themselves, others, and the world. It is beyond our purpose to explore the details of these theories. But it is important to recognize that people act as naive scientists, creating their own theories about the world and making attributions about events. These attributions are the bases for their beliefs and ultimately their actions.

Not surprisingly, people attempt to control the attributions others make about them in order to maximize their own reward/cost ratios. If we can figure out how others are perceiving a situation, we can use this information to personal advantage in attempting to reinforce or change their attributions. The young executive might want to be seen as spontaneous and warm and therefore attempt to attribute his actions in the office more to the situation than to personal disposition. The person who harmed another might want a jury to see the action as self-defense, not indefensible cruelty. Thus, we not only make attributions about what causes other people to behave as they do but also attempt to ascertain and influence the attributions they make about us.

Symbolic Interaction: Symbols and People

Symbolic interactionism is a school of microsociology that traces its roots to the pragmatists. Its founders include John Dewey, George Herbert Mead, Charles Horton Cooley, and William I. Thomas.[5] As the name

---

[5]Since the 1950s, the two foremost proponents of symbolic interactionism have been Herbert Blumer, originally at the University of Chicago, and the late Manford H. Kuhn, at the University of Iowa. Although both continued in the grand traditions of the earlier theorists, they employed slightly different approaches. Their views came to be termed the "Chicago school" and the "Iowa school" of symbolic interactionism. Blumer employs an intuitive approach in trying to understand the nature of modern society, stresses the unpredictable and creative elements of social conduct, and advocates the use of introspective, personal methods of data gathering, such as observational techniques, case studies, and interviews. Kuhn, in contrast, sought principles of social conduct that had universal applicability, stressed the predictable elements of behavior, and advocated the use of operational measures of internal constructs in empirical research, such as defining the "self" as the answers a person gives to a question like "Who am I?" Despite these differences, the schools have in common the themes of symbolic interactionism (see Meltzer & Petras, 1972).

implies, symbolic interactionism stresses symbolic meaning and how symbols relate to social interaction. It is less of a theory than a grand perspective whose many implications lead down paths that otherwise might have remained unexplored.

The fundamental premise that unites symbolic interactionists is that the individual and society are "inseparable and interdependent units. Individuals, living together in society, [are] viewed as reflective and interactive beings possessing selves" (Meltzer & Petras, 1972, p. 43). The idea that the individual and society are interdependent is deceptively simple, reminiscent of John Donne's often-paraphrased line "No man is an island unto himself." Why? We've seen how people are interrelated in terms of outcomes. Beyond this, though, people are interrelated in their shared and symbolic perceptions of the world.

Symbolic interactionists focus on the importance of symbols in understanding the relationship between people and society. *Symbols* are mental representations of objects and events with agreed-upon social meanings. They are not tied directly to the external world, since they involve interpretations and can be manipulated by the mind. For example, we can have a mental image of our car that duplicates, in reasonably faithful detail, the physical characteristics of the actual car. As a symbol, though, the car means much more. If it is a Cadillac, it could symbolize that its owner has "arrived" financially. If a Porsche, it could be a symbol of a fast, free-wheeling, sporty life-style. If a Volkswagen, it could be a symbol of a practical, conservation-minded lifestyle. Actions also have symbolic meaning. Recall the way Bob sat in class, his body relaxed, his head facing the front of the room, his hand under his chin. These actions were symbolic of his self-characterization as a relaxed, confident, contemplative sort of person. He could express his self-definition through symbolic actions.

Through interactions with others, people learn how to view themselves and the world. Since symbols are shared by the people in a particular group, children must be taught the "appropriate" symbols for particular objects and actions. In order to interact effectively with others, people must learn to place themselves in the positions of others and try to see things from their perspectives. How do my actions look to them? What does the behavior reveal about me? Is that the impression I want to convey? What did she mean by that comment or action? What are his goals in this interaction? Learning society's codes of conduct, learning the meanings that society gives to actions, being able to take the perspective of others—these produce a socialized entity, a member of society fit to interact with others. In fact, our "selves" develop through social interaction; the self-concept emerges from the interrelatedness of the person and society (see Chapter 3). Through socialization, each person becomes a "society in miniature" (Meltzer, 1972, p. 11).[6]

As a society in miniature, each person can interact with himself or herself just as he or she can interact with other people. The process of thinking is often interactive. We "talk to ourselves," alternating the roles of speaker and audience. This is private dialogue, not monologue. Recall the way Bob bounced from bed in the morning and began thinking about music. "Good song, full of complex guitar riffs." "Yes, but I wonder why it's only Number 16 on the current charts?" "Well, you know how other people are, buying records because of social pressure and not because of any real understanding of music." "Oh, I know. It's a shame others can't be more independent." In this process of personal interaction, Bob engaged an agreeable alter ego who provided one of the most reassuring partners imaginable; where else could he find another person who shared so much in common?

Symbolic interaction breaks our literal bondage to the world; we are not chained to ongoing events and forced to perceive them as they "really are." Instead, we can organize and evaluate them from our own frames of reference. By way of illustration, some years ago a brutal football game took place between Princeton and Dartmouth. It was the last game of the season and a big one for both teams, particularly since Princeton was undefeated. During the game the star Princeton back, Dick Kazmaier (who achieved celebrity status by appearing on the cover of *Time* magazine), suffered a broken nose and was forced from the game. Shortly after, a Dartmouth player left the game with a broken leg. In the aftermath, the Princeton student paper accused Dartmouth of purposefully injuring their star; the Dartmouth paper said the injury

---

[6]It is as easy to exaggerate the influence of society as to ignore it. The individual and society are not one. People are not stamped out of common molds by their ancestors, remaining mere pawns of the customs, courtesies, laws, norms, and rules existing at the time and place of their births. Social movements, often beginning with a roughly honed idea in the mind of a single individual, can drastically modify societies. For every example of blind conformity to social pressures—the atrocities committed by Nazi underlings on the commands of their superiors, the My Lai massacre in which American soldiers said that they were "following orders" by executing Vietnamese peasants, or the "overzealous" enthusiasm of Nixon's aides in committing burglaries to help their cause—counterexamples can be given—the early Christians martyred without recanting their beliefs or Aleksandr Solzhenitsyn's refusing to bow to the official doctrines of Soviet society, leading to his imprisonment and eventual expulsion. People do not passively ingest whatever information the world offers. People actively digest the world by selecting what they wish to encounter and modifying what they take in to suit their purposes (R. Brown, 1965; Erdelyi, 1974). The individual is not subservient to society, nor are society and the individual equivalent. Individuals and society are interdependent. In the words of John Dewey (1922, p. 59): "To talk about the priority of 'society' to the individual is to indulge in nonsensical metaphysics. But to say that some pre-existent association of human beings is prior to every particular human being who is born into the world is to mention a commonplace."

was an accident, but accused Princeton of trying to gain revenge by illegal, dirty tactics.

A study was made in which films of the game were shown to students at both schools. Princeton students "saw" the game as rough and dirty because of the tactics of the Dartmouth players, and they "counted" twice as many rule infractions on the part of Dartmouth than Princeton. Dartmouth students though "saw" their own team make only half the infractions as did the Princeton students.

Hastorf and Cantril (1954, p. 133) concluded that "the data here indicate that there is no such 'thing' as a 'game' existing 'out there' in its own right which people merely 'observe.' The 'game' 'exists' for a person and is experienced by him only in so far as certain happenings have significance in terms of his purpose. Out of all the occurrences going on in the environment, a person selects those that have some significance for him from his own egocentric position in the total matrix."

Such potential ambiguity in how people see the world implies that situations must be defined by participants in interactions; otherwise, they will not be able to effectively communicate with and act toward one another. William I. Thomas (1923) first discussed how people use symbols to create a definition of a situation that can guide subsequent actions. The idea of defining situations has received ever-increasing attention by sociologists (see Berger & Luckman, 1967; McHugh, 1968; T. Scheff, 1968; Stebbins, 1967; Waller, 1932). Simply stated, objects, events, words, and actions lack meaning until placed in a situational context. Such a context must be constructed by people. Defining the situation is a "process by which the individual explores and feels out through behavior and thought the behavior possibilities of the situation" (Waller, 1932).

Suppose Bob and his classmate agree to a "study date." The range of possible behaviors on such a date is enormous, from serious, concentrated studying to amorous activities. Near the beginning of the date, the young woman defines the situation for Bob by explaining that she simply must do well on the next day's exam and has a great deal of work to do to accomplish that goal. Since he doesn't protest, Bob's role in the interaction has been set: he will study. After about an hour of studious behavior, Bob attempts to change the definition. He yawns, stretches, comments that it might be worthwhile to take a short break, and gets up to get two glasses of wine. Quickly, his date reaffirms the original definition of the situation by noting that she better not drink—she has too much work to do. By way of compromise, though, she adds that they'll have plenty of time to enjoy themselves tomorrow, after the exam. Bob returns empty-handed but with high hopes for the next day.

As seen here, a definition of the situation can be negotiated by the participants to arrive at mutually acceptable conclusions. When participants refuse to negotiate, conflict results. Such might have been the case had Bob tried to impose his definition on his date despite her refusal to accept it. Once the situation is defined, behaviors appropriate to it become obvious to the participants.

In sum, symbolic interactionists view people as symbol users and interpreters integrally related to others in their society. We are both the products of our social worlds and their creators. Through symbolic activity fantasies become realities. The aspects of life that we think of as intrinsically and distinctly human—art, culture, morality, poetry, philosophy—all derive from symbolic activity. Symbolic activities have been called the "central core" of human experience (Brittan, 1973).[7] Social meaning, one of the pragmatists' major concerns, is epitomized by the attachment of symbols to objects, events, actions, and people.

Scripts: Arranging the World in Meaningful Units

People's cognitive worlds are rich and dynamic. We gather information, form constructs, make attributions about causality, form mental pictures of people and events, and add social meanings to those pictures. Robert Abelson (1976) developed a theory of social cognition that integrates these elements. *Script theory*, as the approach is called, is based on the concept of a cognitive script, "a coherent sequence of events expected by the individual, involving him either as a participant or as an observer" (p. 33).

The "basic ingredient" of a script is a *vignette*, "an encoding of an event of short duration, in general including both an image (often visual) of the perceived event and a conceptual representation of the event" (p. 34). It resembles the picture-plus-caption format of a panel in a cartoon strip. A vignette depicts the people involved, the situation in which they are embedded, and a meaning for the scene. Abelson proposes that vignettes are the "raw constituents of remembered episodes in the individual's experience" (p. 34); they are the basic units we store in memory. When we remember an event, we don't recall every detail about it: we don't recall each of the sensations it generated; we don't

---

[7]Ernst Becker (1962) proposed that different response modes exist; that is, different processes govern behavior. *Simple reactivity* is based on instinctively programmed reactions of a very rudimentary stimulus-response nature: the organism's responses are innately tied to particular environmental stimuli. *Conditional reactivity* is comprised of classical and operant conditioning: the organism is freed from the inflexible innate responses that characterize the first mode and can learn new responses to changing environmental circumstances, but the organism is still a passive respondent to the environment. *Relational activity* is comprised of the cognitive learning of associations between objects and events: the organism uses mental activity to represent the world and guide actions, but these mental activities are still bound to concrete objects and events. *Symbolic activity* involves the use of symbols not tied directly to the world in order to understand the world and guide action. Organisms lower down the phylogenetic scale might possess only the first one or two modes, whereas humans possess primarily the last three.

think of it as a composite of millions of different elements. We remember it as an integrated, meaningful unit—a vignette. Without the structure of the vignette, each of the components loses meaning because it lacks a context (Abelson, 1976; Jenkins, 1974).

Scripts are comprised of sequences of vignettes, as a series of cartoon panels form a comic strip. Together, the vignettes tell a story, and so are stored in memory together in the form of scripts. Scripts are learned and modified through the course of our lifetimes. Different people have different learning histories and therefore might approach the same event with different scripts in mind. Yet, through socialization, there is remarkable commonality among the scripts employed by members of any particular group in society.

Vignettes can be established through three processes: episodic, categorical, and hypothetical. The episodic process involves storing a single experience. We see something; it makes an impression and is stored as such without complex interpretation. "I dropped my books" is an episodic vignette. This is the way we might store facts. At a more abstract level, experiences can be stored under categories. Dropping one's books could be stored as the categorical vignette "I am clumsy." Applying a construct seems to involve this type of vignette; the construct "clumsy" is applied to oneself and is triggered by the particular instance of it. Thus, a categorical vignette amounts to subsuming an experience under a construct. At the most abstract level, hypothetical processing involves dealing with lists of features that can be reasoned about. It is more semantic than the preceding types, since it involves coding dimensions and rules that might be important in the experience. For example, dropping the books could be stored as "I am a clumsy person, but only if I'm not a good athlete generally (in which case this incident would be an atypical accident) or didn't have sweaty hands (if my hands were slippery, dropping the books would not necessarily indicate I am clumsy) or wasn't overly tired (if I was tired, then a momentary slip is excusable and does not indicate habitual clumsiness)." Hypothetical vignettes are the bases of complex and abstract reasoning and of inference sequences; working through syllogistic logic and other such tasks seems to rely on this mode of processing. Cognitive scripts can be comprised of episodic, categorical, or hypothetical vignettes, or of a combination of them.

How might scripts affect behavior? According to Abelson (1976, p. 42), "Cognitively mediated social behavior depends on the occurrence of two processes: (a) the selection of a particular script to represent the given situation and (b) the taking of a participant role within that script." Scripts allow us to define situations; through them, possible sequences of events and their meanings are revealed. The participants can then act in a reasoned fashion. Without a script, a situation is a chaos of events, without reason or pattern. One's behavior in such an unfathomable situation might also follow a random, chaotic pattern. The statement "I can't make sense of it" translates to "I have no cognitive script for it." With a cognitive script, action possibilities emerge. People can proceed to make plans that they expect will yield a favorable reward/cost ratio.

Abelson readily admits that the cognitive-script approach is still vague, at least by scientific standards. It is relatively new and has yet to be systematically clarified and explored. Yet, considerable thought and research have converged on the concept, although work has frequently been done without knowledge that comparable work was in progress (cf. Abelson, 1976; Goffman, 1974; Harré, 1974, 1977; Harré & Secord, 1973; Jenkins, 1974; Minsky, 1975; Tulving, 1972).[8] The growing consensus is that it does not seem possible to explain human behavior without such a concept.

Script theory has the potential for integrating much of the work on cognitive processes that we've reviewed. It has a place for constructive alternativism (categorical vignettes represent the application of constructs to a particular situation), attribution theory (attributions are contained within the scripts and add cause-effect structure to them), symbolic interactionism (vignettes can have a social meaning, and, when the vignettes are stored as a script, they tell a meaningful story), and defining the situation (the script provides both the context and particulars that give meaning to a situation).

Script theory also provides a link between actions that are objects of conscious attention and those that are not. Information can be processed and stored in memory after much deliberation or after practically no conscious attention at all (Langer, 1978). Much of the time we seem to process information with little or no thought; we don't ruminate about precisely why we are forming a particular impression; we just do it. Many of our stereotypes are acquired nonconsciously as we merely accept what people have told us. Blondes have more fun, welfare reci-

---

[8]The *ethogenic approach* to social behavior (Harré, 1974, 1977; Harré & Secord, 1973) draws heavily on a concept much like a cognitive script. The approach challenges the way social psychologists have traditionally explained and explored social behavior and tries to weave together the work of some philosophers and microsociologists to offer a new perspective. It treats people as agents, not passive puppets of environmental stimuli, and views people as "rule-following" animals. We are assumed to learn rules ("scripts") for social behaviors that we follow when we enter relevant situations. According to this approach, the task of social psychology is to discover the rules that people use to guide their behaviors. If we know the rules, we know the behaviors, since they are directly linked. Although the approach offers many insights, it has faults that prevent it from being a complete perspective on human behavior (see Schlenker, 1977; Shaw, 1974). For example, people don't always follow social rules; they revise them and use them to achieve their goals. The concept of cognitive script is not directly embedded in this particular perspective on social behavior and can be easily integrated into the existing approaches that we've discussed. Thus, cognitive scripts determine how we interpret and what we expect from social situations, but people take these scripts and use them to maintain favorable reward/cost ratios from social relations.

pients are lazy, fat people are jolly—many generalizations are stored
in memory without critical assessment of whether or under what
conditions they may be true or false. Such information and its implications are stored in scripts. Thus, the acquisition of scripts, in
their entirety or in part, can be at a conscious or nonconscious level
(Langer, 1978).

Irrespective of how a particular script is acquired, moreover, it
later guides our actions when evoked by a cue in the situation. For
example, a person who is introduced to a shapely blonde might automatically engage a script that covers such interactions. He has certain
stereotyped expectations of what shapely blondes are like (dumb, fun
loving) and bases his subsequent behavior on these presumed attributes. This script is cued by the sight of the blonde and has obvious
implications for the interaction. Existing scripts, then, can be not only
acquired but also evoked, at either a conscious or nonconscious level
(Langer, 1978). Relevant cues in the situation engage an existing script
that might be appropriate, and this script can be either inside or outside
one's focus of attention.

Scripts engaged without conscious attention seem to be the cognitive backbone of the type of habit pattern that the pragmatists discussed. William James' descriptions of the deckhand at sea, the
counselor-at-law, and his other characters illustrate how existing
scripts become evoked automatically by relevant cues and how they
guide behavior. The complex, meaningful habit patterns of interest to
social psychologists are guided by scripts that are not the object of
attention at the particular moment they occur.

When a script is evoked without conscious attention, blind adherence to it is likely to follow, provided that nothing focuses the individual's attention on script-relevant matters. Many behaviors related to
impression management are based on scripts that are cued by the situation. The appropriate smile when the boss tells a tired joke, the self-
compliment when we describe our performance on the tennis court, the
subtle put-down of the person seeking the same job we are seeking—
these and other impression management behaviors often seem to be
based on scripts that we have learned in the past and then to be
triggered by relevant cues in a situation.

When scripts are engaged in with conscious attention, on the other
hand, people examine them critically and engage in hypothetical processing of information. They may ask "What's going on here?" "Is this
the correct interpretation?" "What other interpretations could there
be?" "How should I behave?" "Is this the best way for me to act given
all the particulars of the situation?" By consciously considering such
questions, people can arrive at the best script for the situation. By best I
mean the one they believe will maximize their expected rewards and
minimize their expected costs. Thus, conscious attention permits more

careful consideration of action possibilities and the deliberate meshing of actions and desired outcomes. The conscious, tactical use of impression management is typified by this type of response.

Scripts provide the structure we use to interact effectively with the environment. They are the cognitive maps that tell us where we are going and what we are doing. Keep in mind, though, that our own scripts often require trying to change those that others hold. We want others' vignettes and scripts about us to be desirable, so we attempt to help them along with the scripts they store in memory. A student who gets an "A" grade on a test would prefer a friend to remember "She is intelligent," not "She has an easy teacher." On the basis of the "A" alone, either of these interpretations is plausible. If the student is skillful in describing her grade to her friend, though, the friend should draw the desired conclusion. The student might mention that few other people did well, that she studied hard, that she has been getting good grades all semester, or that her teacher was tough. In a hundred little ways, the friend can be influenced to conclude what the student wants her to. Through impression management, we attempt to control the scripts people use when they think about us.

THE DRAMATURGICAL APPROACH: SELF-PRESENTATION AND IMPRESSION MANAGEMENT

There are numerous similarities between our daily lives and theater. We possess scripts that allow us to know what to expect in situations. We perform roles that symbolize how we wish to appear to others. We select words, gestures, and props to illustrate our character just as an author does in fleshing out the characters in a play. There is a front stage where we're "on" to our associates. A good performance can bring applause, praise, pay raises, esteem, and affection. A poor performance might close the show, bringing criticism, rejection, loss of job, disrespect, and dislike; we might even leave the stage through suicide. There is a backstage where we can relax and loosen up, out of sight of the audience. Alone at home, for example, we can engage in all the little eccentricities that we'd never dream of exhibiting in public.

The Life-as-Theater Model in Literature. The analogy between life and theater has been drawn by countless writers. Plato spoke of the "great stage of human life." In his *Laws*, he "developed the stage imagery in the moral fable of the human puppets, whose strings . . . are manipulated by the gods" (Burns, 1973, p. 8). Hobbes (1651/1952, p. 96) stated that "a person is the same as an actor is, both on the stage and in common conversation." The word *person* has its roots in the Latin word *persona*, which meant a mask used by a character in a play. The Globe Theatre in London, centerpiece for the Elizabethan performances of Shakespeare's (1564–1616) plays, had atop its entrance the phrase *Totus Mundus Agit Histrionem*—"All the World Is a Theatre." In his play *As You Like It*, Shakespeare's character Jaques amplified that theme:

> All the world's a stage,
> And all the men and women merely players.
> They have their exits and their entrances;
> And one man in his time plays many parts . . . .

Shakespeare's great contemporary Miguel de Cervantes (1547–1616), the Spanish dramatist who wrote *The History of Don Quixote de la Mancha*, presented a revealing exchange between the chivalrous dreamer, Don Quixote, and his faithful but pragmatic squire, Sancho Panza. After describing some elements of a play, Don Quixote continues: "the same thing happens in the comedy and intercourse of this world, where some play the part of emperors, others that of pontiffs—in short, all the characters that a drama may have—but when it is all over, that is to say, when life is done, death takes from each the garb that differentiates him, and all are at last equal in the grave." Reflecting on the analogy of life and theater, Sancho admitted "It is a fine comparison . . . though not so new but that I have heard it many times before."

Nicholas Evreinoff (1879–1953), a Russian dramatist, introduced the concept of *theatrocracy*: actions are governed by rules of the theater. In his book *The Theatre in Life* (1927), he wrote "Examine any . . . branch of human activity and you will see that kings, statesmen, politicians, warriors, bankers, business men, priests, doctors, all pay daily tributes to theatricality, all comply with the principles ruling on the stage." Perhaps professional performers grasp the similarities between life and theater more quickly than most people. Sammy Davis, Jr., once remarked "As soon as I go out of the front door of my house in the morning, I'm on Daddy, I'm on" (quoted in Burns, 1973, p. 37).

Implications for Social Science. The full impact of the life/theater analogy on social science did not occur until Erving Goffman explored its ramifications in several insightful and gracefully written books. Goffman is a sociologist who pursued graduate studies at the University of Chicago, falling under the influence of the symbolic interactionists. While accepting many of the basic premises of symbolic interactionism, he gave the study of social life a twist by accentuating the theatrical elements of even the most inconspicuous social gestures.

Goffman began his book *The Presentation of Self in Everyday Life* (1959) by describing what he believes are the basic differences between life and theater. The stage is make-believe, while life is real; and, while there are three parties in a play—actors, other characters, and audience—in real life there are only actor and audience. A person can even play both parts himself or herself, as occurs when we "talk to ourselves." That these are the only differences Goffman feels noteworthy may reflect strong belief in the power of the model.

Performances. When people participate in social interactions, real or imagined, they engage in *performances.* Goffman (1959, p. 15) defines a performance as "All the activity of a given participant on a given occasion which serves to influence in any way any of the other participants."[9] Virtually all social activity is thereby characterized as performance, including our fantasy interactions.

Why should so much fall under the rubric of performance? Following the line of thought of the symbolic interactionists, we can say that, whenever we are in the real or imagined presence of others, behaviors carry social meanings and have a promissory character. It is the very nature of interaction that when in the presence of others "the individual will have to act so that he intentionally or unintentionally expresses himself, and the other will in turn have to be impressed in some way by him" (Goffman, 1959, p. 2). Of course, one can be impressed unfavorably or favorably. The impressions define the way we appear in social life, and the reactions of others are governed by them. We become characterized as possessing specific desirable and undesirable attributes, and these in turn affect the ways we are treated and our outcomes from social interaction. Machiavelli (1469–1527), whose name has often been associated with the arts of impression management, remarked that "when men are spoken of, they are marked for qualities which bring them either praise or censure" (1513/1966, p. 56). The sociologist Nelson Foote (1951, p. 17) noted that "every man must categorize his fellows in order to interact with them. We never approach another person purely as a human being or purely as an individual." Our outcomes are integrally tied to our identities, which are shaped by our social activities. Consequently, "When an individual appears in the presence of others, there will usually be some reason for him to mobilize his activity so that it will convey an impression to others which it is in his interests to convey" (Goffman, 1959, p. 4). Our activities become performances that can be more or less revealing, more or less truthful, more or less deliberate—but performances nonetheless.

Face. Recall that the origin of the word *person* is the Latin word for *mask.* Goffman (1967, p. 2) draws a parallel in defining the term *face:* "The positive social value a person effectively claims for himself by the

[9]Excerpted from *The Presentation of Self in Everyday Life,* by Erving Goffman. Copyright © 1959 by Erving Goffman. This and all other quotations from this source are reprinted by permission of Doubleday & Company, Inc. Published in the British Commonwealth and reprinted by permission of Penguin Books Ltd.

line others assume he has taken during a particular contact. Face is an image of self delineated in terms of approved social attributes." One constructs and projects different faces for different audiences. We have one face for our parents, another for our children, another for our spouse, one for friends, another for enemies, one for our employer, another for our employees, and so on. These are not necessarily contradictory, but they do show the sides of us that are most relevant to the specific encounter. One may feel generally dominant and aggressive but still show deference to a parent or employer. One may feel generally detached or submissive but show aggression toward an adversary. Such changes in face represent not gross inconsistencies in personality, but simply different aspects of our identities called forth by the situation.

Each face provides advantages. Certain faces make demands on others that they are expected to fulfill. A judge is entitled to the prestige, status, and deference suitable to a member of that group. A child is entitled to be provided for by the parents. "Society is organized on the principle that any individual who possesses certain characteristics has a moral right to expect that others will value and treat him in an appropriate way" (Goffman, 1959, p. 13).

Each face, though, has accompanying obligations; the person ought to be what he or she claims to be, else a violation of the social contract occurs. A "con man" who impersonates a policeman is quickly censured and imprisoned for impertinently displaying a face he had no right to assume. No one wants to be duped into providing rewarding outcomes to a charlatan who is not entitled to them.

Once a particular face is established in an interaction, the actor is committed to presenting a comparable face to the same audience in the future, one unmarred by out-of-image blemishes. To switch mutually exclusive faces rapidly is to present an image of inconsistency. It marks the individual as not to be trusted to behave predictably in social interactions, a person who has no "real" face. A person who tells an audience that he is a plumber one moment and a symphony conductor the next risks confinement in a mental institution, unless he can find some socially acceptable explanation for these statements. A person who without apparent provocation behaves courteously one moment and rudely the next risks censure as an unreliable social participant. People would be shocked and offended if a judge, at the climactic moment of a trial, suddenly poured forth a shower of profanity. They would hardly raise an eyebrow if a member of a gang of street-corner hoods uttered the same words, but they would be surprised if the gang began talking "legalese."

Identities can be damaged in many ways. Imagine a socialite at a party of sophisticates. Her walk reflects years of training; her speech exudes qualities that come only from diction lessons. She has studied the rules of etiquette with the dedication of a scientist. Suddenly she tips her plate slightly too far, spills her hors d'oeuvres, bends to pick them up, and splits her dress, exposing her backside to the crowd. She straightens up in embarrassment, only to knock over the plate and glass of the gentleman standing next to her and loosen her wig, which falls to her feet. The symbols of her identity have lost their value. This rather extreme example shows the discomfort created for an actor when out-of-face behaviors occur. Even a less dramatic faux pas can disrupt the interaction, cause one to lose credibility, and create embarrassment for actor and audience both. For these reasons, face maintenance is an important aspect of social interaction. When out-of-face behaviors occur, people usually try to explain them away in socially acceptable ways.

Actions that catch people out of face have impact not only for the actor but also for the interaction and the social structure. Borrowing an example from Goffman (1959), let us consider a doctor who, during an operation, allows the patient to fall off the operating table. Forgetting for the moment the outcomes to the unfortunate patient (not that we are callous, only interested in making another point), consider the doctor, nurses, and other staff involved. First, at a personal level, the doctor has committed a severe breach of performance. An unforgivable event has occurred that catches him totally out of face. Embarrassment, anxiety, and guilt paralyze him as he contemplates what this means to his career, his reputation, and his financial future. Second, at an interaction level, the participants are momentarily stunned. The normal course of the interaction has been disrupted. As a nurse, what do you say to the doctor? Are there any immediately apparent courses of action that can recover the atmosphere that existed prior to the incident? The interaction itself disintegrates because of the behavior of one of its participants. At the third level, societal, the breach has consequences for the reputations of all those who claim similar faces—doctors will be trusted less than before. The profession has been tarnished by the ineptitude of one of its members. Thus, face maintenance has far-reaching consequences. It affects the performer who falls from face, it affects all participants associated with the disrupted interaction, and it affects the social structure by revealing something about a group of similar-faced individuals.

Front Performances, then, define a person's social identity, define and set the tone for the interaction, and allow people to know what to expect from one another during social commerce. The person (or actor, as Goffman terms the individual giving the performance) must maintain a particular *front* that expresses how he or she wishes and expects to be treated. Front is "that part of the individual's performance which regularly functions in a general and fixed fashion to define the situation for those who observe the performance. Front, then, is the expressive equipment of a standard kind intentionally or unwittingly employed by the individual during his performance" (Goffman, 1959, p. 22). A front is composed of *appearance, manner,* and *setting.* A person's appearance consists of "those stimuli which function at the time to tell us of the performer's social status" (Goffman, 1959, p. 24). A person's manner is "those stimuli which function at the time to warn us of the interaction role the performer will expect to play in the oncoming situation" (p. 24)—for example, friendly versus hostile, formal versus informal. The setting is the physical environment in which the performance occurs and includes such things as furniture, room decorations, room arrangement, and locale.

These components of the front should be consistent, else doubts will be raised about the propriety of the performance. For example, a queen's appearance should connote high status, as might be conveyed through elegant dress; her manner should connote authority rather than meekness and submission; and the settings of her performances should exude regality and pomp. If she wandered through side streets dressed like a beggar, cowering when people come near, serious questions would arise about her queenly ability. Goffman (1959, p. 120) recounts an anecdote about Queen Victoria's requirement that "anyone seeing her approach when she was driving in her pony-cart on the palace grounds should turn his head or walk in another direction; therefore great statesmen sometimes were required to sacrifice their own dignity and jump behind the shrubbery when the queen unexpectedly approached." Although perhaps sacrificing the fronts of others, she maintained her own against the possibility that others would get the "wrong impression."

People in business invest great amounts of time, effort, and money establishing fronts. Office colors can be judiciously chosen to convey a particular atmosphere: a businessman might paint his office blue, believing the color to be associated with status, dominance, and authority, with touches of white to convey a feeling of space and freedom and red—the color of blood—to instill fear (Korda, 1976, p. 91). Office furniture and decorations are selected to convey numerous impressions. Sales plaques on walls connote success; ornate furnishings show that the owner has "arrived." Furniture arrangement can set the mood for meetings held in a room, as when the occupant, in a luxurious high-backed chair, peers from behind an expensive desk down on the visitor forced to sit in a low chair on the other side. Immediate feelings of subservience are induced in the visitor. Clothes and shoes are selected with care, and brands that are currently "in" adorn the body (Korda, 1976). Every aspect of the setting is carefully controlled to establish an image that reinforces the desired manner and appearance and establishes a united and, it is hoped, impressive front.

Teams are used in the performances given to certain audiences. A *team* is "any set of individuals who cooperate in staging a single routine" (Goffman, 1959, p. 79). In business, for example, secretaries are informed how to treat particular clients so that a front can be maintained by the company team. A visitor might be told to wait because the boss is busy even if the boss is only killing time to build up the visitor's anxiety and assert power as the one who controls the time of the meeting. The secretary then must make sure that the visitor does not catch a glimpse of the boss as he or she puts golf balls into the wastebasket. Such backstage, or back region, behavior would destroy the image created in the front region.

Dramatized and Idealized Performances. Performances are often dramatized or idealized. A *dramatized performance* makes it clear to the audience exactly what is going on; it leaves no doubts about how the actor views the situation. A student may dramatize his performance in class by appearing so attentive and enthralled by the lecture that he actually loses track of what the lecturer is saying. An *idealized performance* is one that fulfills, and perhaps exceeds, the stereotypes held by the audience. A priest might present himself as being even more devout, more humble, more moral than he really believes himself to be. A college professor might convey the impression that she despises television as an unintellectual pastime fit only for the uneducated, although she actually rushes home after class to enjoy the evening's video offerings. Dramatized and idealized performances are illustrative of Bertold Brecht's comment "It is not the play but the performance that is the real purpose of all one's efforts" (quoted in Burns, 1973, p. 32).

Are dramatized and idealized performances true or false, honest or dishonest? Sometimes it is easy to make such judgments, as in the case of a student who tells people he studies 30 hours a week but actually spends only an hour or two at best. At other times, only a fuzzy boundary separates appearance from substance. What of the student who is unsure of the time spent studying, thinks it may be about 25 hours, but says 30 hours to impress a date? What of the person who recognizes a few personal faults but in conversation focuses only on personal strengths? "Sometimes when we ask whether a fostered impression is true or false we really mean to ask whether or not the performer is authorized to give the performance in question" (Goffman, 1959, p. 59).

The boundary between accurate self-presentation and self-misrepresentation further blurs when we realize that people are often taken in by their own performances, coming to believe that they really are the idealized or dramatized identities they project. An insecure employee suddenly elevated to a supervisory position begins to act self-confidently, in order to gain the respect of workers, and soon becomes self-confident. An army draftee acts in a very military manner only to escape from punishment or win the favors of superiors but soon becomes gung ho. Thus, performances that were once inaccurate self-reflections can become accurate as the self-concept changes. Even grossly deceitful actions can produce attitude change as the person comes to believe the lie (Collins & Hoyt, 1972; Festinger, 1957; Schlenker & Schlenker, 1975). In another vein, a wallflower who is actually shy may have her actions misinterpreted by admiring suitors who see her as demure, mysterious, and tantalizing. The suitors' attentions and compliments can transform the wallflower into the belle of the ball. Thus, self-concepts, identities, and actions can be changed through social reinforcements (S. C. Jones, 1973).

Reaction to the Dramaturgical Approach. Goffman's dramaturgical approach has been criticized on several counts, each of which contains some truth. But these criticisms are less of the perspective itself than of the points Goffman chooses to emphasize. First, Goffman has been accused of leaving too much of the person out of the interaction—for example, he does not view the self-concept as playing a major role in affecting behaviors (Gergen, 1968). Goffman (1959, p. 252) indeed states that "a correctly staged and performed scene leads the audience to impute a self to a performed character, but this imputation—this self—is a *product* of a scene that comes off, it is not a *cause* of it." Although the self-concept is partially defined through interactions, once it is formed, it also can shape interactions. A person's self-beliefs affect his or her goals and plans in interaction (see Chapters 3 and 4).

Second, in conjunction with the first point, it is argued that Goffman places too much stress on the role of social rules in determining behaviors (Brittan, 1973). Goffman (1959, 1967) focuses on "interaction rituals"—social rules that tell us how we should behave. In a wedding, the parts of all the performers are clearly prescribed in advance, and people go through the motions of the ritual. Goffman believes that rituals, although not all so rigid as those of a wedding, pervade all social interactions. The extremity of Goffman's position is expressed in the following: "Universal human nature is not a very human thing. By acquiring it, the person becomes a kind of construct, built up not from inner psychic propensities but from moral rules that are *impressed upon* him from without" (1967, p. 45, italics added). The individual is not digesting but simply ingesting. A script is handed down by society, and we are left at the mercy of it.

It is neither necessary nor correct to say that our behavior is exclusively determined by personal dispositions or the environment. Either extreme represents what is termed *unidirectional determinism*—the notion that one set of factors (personal or environmental) determines behavior independently of the other. Social behavior does not involve just individual factors such as personal traits, cognitions, and emotions, nor just environmental influences like interaction rituals and reinforcement contingencies. It involves both. There are some occasions like weddings when we can indeed predict behavior just by knowing the appropriate interaction rituals. On other occasions we can predict behavior just by knowing an individual's personal characteristics, as when an ambiguous situation is encountered and different people interpret it in their own idiosyncratic ways. But on the vast majority of occasions it is necessary to know both. This approach—stressing the mutual interaction between the person and the environment—is termed *reciprocal determinism* (Bandura, 1978). A person's cognitions, behaviors, and the environment continually interact with and affect one another. For example, the environment, our cognitive scripts, and our goals interact to determine our behaviors. These behaviors change the environment, which might change our goals, scripts, and subsequent behaviors. This process of continual reciprocal interaction between the person and the environment best seems to describe how we are both products and creators of our social worlds.

Finally, Goffman has often been criticized for paying too much attention to the conscious and deliberate use of impression-management tactics. Although many of his examples do seem to involve such deliberate performances, he acknowledges that impression management is not solely conscious in nature. Performances may become habits or be very useful for impression management purposes while remaining outside the actor's conscious awareness. In some respects, then, many impression-management strategies are reminiscent of William James' discussions of habits. We learn behavior patterns that support our identities and use them, often without conscious attention, to establish our place in the social world.

The criticisms of Goffman have merit, but none alters the fundamental utility of the dramaturgical approach. There is nothing about the approach that demands that we view people as ingestors, leave them at the mercy of the social script, deny them self-control, or view them as malicious purveyors of falsehoods. In these aspects, we will depart from Goffman and substitute more sensible assumptions. In doing so, though, we will continue to view people as actors who consciously or unconsciously engage in performances that shape their identities and destinies.

THE MELTING POT: SUMMARY

Interpersonal relations, identity, and impression management can be approached from numerous angles, as exemplified by the major schools of social-psychological thought. The positions taken by psychologists and sociologists are not mutually exclusive, but complementary. They cast slightly different lights on the nature of people and interpersonal relations. Without each, our understanding would be significantly dimmed. People are not just reinforcement-seeking machines or information processors, scientists or power seekers, pragmatists or symbol interpreters, script writers or actors on the stage of life. They are all of these. Each view explains something of human existence.

Together, these positions provide a perspective we will use in exploring interpersonal relations and impression management. People have private mental lives whose content is filled with social meanings. In order to function effectively, we acquire information, make attributions about events, and organize the information into theories, behaving much like scientists. Much of the information is symbolic, conveying social and personal meanings that have implications for how we see ourselves, others, and the situation. Most everyday experiences seem to be stored in memory in the form of cognitive scripts, which are analogous to cartoon strips in depicting a series of related vignettes, or figures plus captions. When entering a situation, we draw on these cognitive scripts to provide us with expectations of meaningful potential sequences of events. Cognitive scripts affect how we interpret, and hence respond to, situations. Employing one rather than another cognitive script establishes different expectations and interpretations of events. People define situations by attempting to make clear to one another the scripts that they want to be relevant.

Based on information, we formulate goals and plans for achieving them. Plans are formed in accord with the hedonic assumption that we act to maximize desirable outcomes and minimize undesirable ones. Most outcomes, though, are based on interdependence—what people achieve depends both on their own actions and those of others. People are thus constantly engaged in social influence, trying to affect the attitudes and behaviors of others in ways that facilitate reaching their own goals. Since actions can express something about us and influence others, people consciously or unconsciously control their actions to convey specific impressions. Like actors, we present particular identities to others that are shaped by our self-concepts and goals and by the pressures of the situation. As patterns of behavior stabilize over time, habits take over and allow us to act without conscious attention to the subtleties of some behaviors. Each action, of course, can produce new information, lead to new outcomes, and cause goals to be changed.

All too often, psychology-oriented social psychologists have accused their sociology counterparts of being too concerned with general, all-encompassing theories that cannot be tested and that lead to no clear predictions of specific actions in specific situations. The sociologist is pictured as a fuzzy-headed ivory-tower theorist not properly respectful of the power of empiricism and prediction. Just as often, sociology-oriented social psychologists have accused their psychology counterparts of being too enamored of data, so focused on computer printouts that they fail to see the forest because they are examining the very bark of a particular tree. The picture is that of a compulsive individual, magnifying glass in hand, so busy scrutinizing a stimulus-response contingency that he or she is unable to see that a thinking, feeling, empathic, social person is getting in the way of an elegant but sterile mathematical relationship. Both pictures, of course, are really caricatures, but they nonetheless exist. Our aim is to walk the line between these extremes without falling to either side. There is little doubt that we will occasionally slip, sometimes tumbling into fuzziness, other times lapsing into pickiness. But, as Francis Bacon said, "In this theater of man's life it is reserved only for God and the angels to be lookers on."

PART TWO

THE ACTOR

Impression management is an integral part of social life. Through self-presentations, people attempt to construct and maintain particular images of themselves that they project to real and imagined audiences. Building on the basic framework provided by Part I, we can now be more specific about the hows and whys of self-presentation.

Part II focuses on the actor, exploring the self and social identity. In Chapter 3 we'll examine the nature of the self-concept and social identity. What are they? How are they formed and shaped? How are they related to self-presentation? What major individual differences exist in self-presentation styles? In Chapter 4 we'll see how people construct identities by controlling the images with which they are associated. What are the advantages and disadvantages of claiming particular images? Why do people select one rather than another set of self-images? Are people egotistical, seeking only to glorify the self? How do people go about claiming particular images in order to associate themselves with desirable characteristics and dissociate themselves from undesirable ones? Finally, in Chapter 5, we'll explore how people protect and defend their identities when confronted by events that seem to challenge their claims. How do people account for embarrassing or undesirable events? When do people come to believe the excuses and justifications they offer to audiences?

THREE

> *I study myself more than any other subject; it is my metaphysic, and my physic.*
>
> Michel de Montaigne

> *There are three Things extreamly hard, Steel, a Diamond, and to know one's self.*
>
> Benjamin Franklin

THE SELF AND SOCIAL IDENTITY: GENESIS AND DEVELOPMENT

People ponder themselves. One can turn consciousness inward and revel or despair in the thoughts that are revealed. Everyone can list personal assets and liabilities, accomplishments and failures, hopes and future perils. Images are evoked of one's appearance, health, possessions, tastes, goals, reputation, habits, bonds to others—all one's attributes and relations with the world. There is a sense of continuity in all this. Each person has a beginning and an end, and one's adventures in between seem generated by some personal and unified force or whole—the self.

The concept of self is important to any theory of impression management. The images people have of themselves shape and are shaped by social interactions. If we know what people think about themselves, how they evaluate their attributes, and what they believe they can accomplish given their attributes and the situation, we can make predictions about how they are likely to present themselves to audiences. Knowing how they present themselves to others, we can sometimes make inferences about what they privately think of themselves.

The self has been the subject of much study, discussion, and theorizing. Several basic questions have stirred controversy among psychologists (see Epstein, 1973; Gergen, 1971; Gordon & Gergen, 1968; Pepitone, 1968; Wells & Marwell, 1976; Wylie, 1961, 1968, 1974, 1979). Is the self a process that guides behaviors and categorizes self-related information, or is it a structure that contains the contents of categorizations? Is it both? Do people have one self, a unitary and coherent whole that is the core of their being, or do people have many selves, each directed at a different audience? Is the self consistent over time, so that one will be the same person tomorrow as yesterday, or a momentary, fluctuating phenomenon with peaks and valleys? Is the self a fact, a substantial, physical entity located perhaps in the brain, or is it a concept that has no "real" existence? Is the concept of self necessary to understanding, explaining, and predicting behavior, or can everything that the self involves be explained without it? Indeed, is the concept of self a useful scientific construct, or is it merely a throwback to metaphysical and spiritual ideas such as the soul?

Part of the problem has been the many ways the self has been defined. Some theorists have used the term *self* to encompass the thoughts, feelings, and actions of individuals; individual differences have been presumed to arise because everyone has a unique self. In this very general usage, though, the term *self* becomes synonymous with the term *person*, and the study of the self becomes synonymous with human psychology. One set of terms is simply substituted for another, and we seem to gain no more understanding than we had when we started. We need a conceptualization that is tied to existing theories in psychology and sociology, has scientific meaning, and allows explanation and prediction.

THE SELF-CONCEPT: ORIENTATION

William James was the first psychologist to attempt to dissect systematically the nature of the self. His writings serve as the starting point for most contemporary analyses. James began by trying to make sense of what people are referring to when they talk of the self. *"In its widest possible sense . . . a man's Self is the sum total of all that he CAN call his,* not only his body and his psychic powers, but his clothes and his house, his wife and his children, his ancestors and friends, his reputation and works, his lands and horses, and yacht and bank account. All these things give him the same emotions. If they wax and prosper, he feels triumphant; if they dwindle and die away, he feels cast down—not necessarily in the same degree for each thing, but in much the same way for all" (James, 1890/1952, p. 188).

The self, of course, cannot literally be one's bank account, lands, or other external material objects, nor can it be one's ancestors, friends, or any other person. Such literal interpretations would render the concept of self meaningless. James seems rather to be referring to the fact that people perceive associations between some central core they consider the self and myriad other things, from their physical appearance and behavior to their possessions, family, and friends. Family units and friends are seen as associated, since the accomplishments or shame of one may be felt by all. One's appearance reflects on oneself, since it is the first personal sign that others come to know, recognize, and evaluate. Our possessions reflect on us, since they reveal our values, preferences, and perhaps our earning ability. The association perceived between the person and all these things seems to make them relevant to the self. When such associations exist, they reveal something about the person. The person is categorized (for example, handsome or ugly) and evaluated (handsome is "better") both by himself or herself and by others.

James believed that the constituents of the self were divided into two classes: the pure ego and the empirical self. The *pure ego* is the self-as-knower, the *I*, and the *empirical self* is the self-as-known, the *Me*. (George Herbert Mead made a very similar distinction.) The *I* was considered to be the "judging thought," which is "passive and subjective" (James, 1890/1952, p. 239). It does not judge and evaluate itself, nor is it even cognizant of itself. It acts and reacts to the circumstances that it finds—sensing, perceiving, thinking, learning, and behaving in ways that allow it to survive and perhaps prosper in its environment. The study of the *I* is the study of the experiencing being, of how we perceive, think, learn, remember, and so on. The *I* can never be experienced as the direct object of thought; it is inferred indirectly from the fact that one knows and does things. Essentially, it is the process that characterizes the thinking person. The inferences one makes about the *I* provide a sense of continuity to thoughts and actions, since these seem to arise from a central, internal locus.

The *Me*, the empirical self, is the person's self-perception as object or entity—the person as he or she enters into personal awareness. The *Me* does judge and evaluate itself. It evaluates itself from the standpoint of what it is as an object. It stands back from the *I* and gives its verdict about the *I*'s qualities. James further divided this empirical self into three components: the material self, the social self, and the spiritual self.

The *material self* consists of one's body, bodily adornments, family, friends, property, and possessions. They all can be cognitively associated with the person and, hence, be revealing.

The *social self* is the recognition a person receives from others. It is how the person believes other people view him or her. James posited an "innate propensity to get ourselves noticed, and noticed favorably, by our kind. No more fiendish punishment could be devised . . . than that one should be turned loose in society and remain absolutely unnoticed by all the members thereof" (p. 189). The perceived contents of what others notice become aspects of the social self. Although James believed that the self has a sense of continuity and wholeness, he also believed that a person can have numerous social selves. "Properly speaking, a man has as many social selves as there are individuals who recognize him and carry an image of him in their mind" (pp. 189–190). For each audience, a different social self can exist.

The *spiritual self* is "man's inner or subjective being, his psychic faculties or dispositions, taken concretely" (p. 191). The spiritual self should not be confused with the pure ego, which is the self-as-knower. The spiritual self exists not because people think but because they can think of themselves as thinkers. People know they think and act and can make judgments about their effectiveness. People categorize themselves as quick or slow, complex or simple, effective or ineffective in their thoughts and deeds. These categorizations and evaluations comprise the spiritual self—an empirical self with the person as thinker as its object.

James' material, social, and spiritual selves simply reflect a way of subdividing the content of how people conceptualize themselves. Not surprisingly, other writers also have attempted to list aspects of self-conceptualization and have often arrived at different subdivisions. We will refrain, at least for the moment, from discussions of how best to categorize the contents of self-conceptualizations. What is important for our purposes is that people can view themselves as objects; when they do, an abundance of information is revealed. People recognize that various things like attributes, possessions, and friends are associated with them and that they can be categorized and evaluated on the basis of these things, both by others and by themselves. (Naturally, the way a person is categorized and evaluated has implications for the outcomes he or she receives from real or imagined social interactions, but that is getting ahead of our story.)

The pure ego and the empirical self thus differ dramatically. The former is the person as an active entity. The latter is the person as self-conceptualized. When the pure ego is included in the definition of self, we are back to the point of having to deal with everything about the person at once—how he or she thinks, learns, remembers, behaves, and so on. But when the empirical self is employed as our construct, we can begin to examine people's ideas about themselves, how these ideas are formed and modified, and how they might affect social interactions. Therefore the empirical self, one's self-concept, will be our point of departure.

THE SELF-CONCEPT AS A SELF-THEORY

Chapter 2 discussed the theme that people are naive scientists who build theories to help them understand their environment and function effectively within it. These theories extend to the self. Seymour Epstein (1973, p. 407) defined the self-concept as "a theory the individual has unwittingly constructed about himself as an experiencing, functioning individual . . . part of a broader theory which he holds with respect to his entire range of significant experience." It contains a cache of personal facts of the types James discussed in describing one's bodily appearance, possessions, friends, and so forth. It contains self-constructs such as being friendly, intelligent, and independent. It contains hypotheses, or beliefs, that relate aspects of these facts and constructs to each other (for example, "I am independent and hence don't conform to the opinions of others"). One's aspirations can also enter the picture to produce a self-concept that represents a blend of one's actualities and potentialities (R. H. Turner, 1968).

Self-Constructs: Categorizing Ourselves

Self-constructs, also called *self-schemata*, are key aspects of the self-concept. Self-constructs are cognitive categories or generalizations about the self. People categorize themselves on construct dimensions such as conforming-independent, friendly-unfriendly, competent-incompetent, and dominant-submissive. Like other types of constructs, self-constructs are summary terms that subsume numerous facts. One can't keep track of each and every personal behavior or self-relevant fact, but one can deal with a limited number of constructs that seem to integrate these facts into meaningful categories. If, for example, you are asked to describe your mental abilities, you undoubtedly would be unable to recall all the behaviors that might be relevant. But it is quite easy to list self-descriptive constructs that encompass such facts: "moderately creative," "excellent memory," "strong on verbal fluency," "average on quantitative ability," and so on. People find it easy to explain their own actions within such frameworks.

Self-constructs are not uniquely or simply determined by facts. Imagine a person having a conversation with a co-worker who privately disagrees with the colleague's opinion but who publicly expresses some agreement with it. Is this person conforming, submissive, tactful, friendly, ingratiating, self-doubting, or something else? On the basis of the behavior alone it is impossible to tell. If you knew a variety of other facts about the person and situation, they could narrow the possibilities. For example, knowing that the person has high self-esteem might eliminate the construct "self-doubting." But even when many such facts are known, there are alternative constructs that could be applied to describe the same set of facts. There is never a situation where one set of facts can be explained by only one construct.

Instead of constructs' being dictated by facts, constructs help us to interpret facts. Facts are given meanings by the constructs. In the example, the act of publicly agreeing while privately disagreeing would be given meaning as soon as it were interpreted as, say, "ingratiation," and that meaning is quite different from the meaning associated with the construct "tactful." People have some latitude in the constructs they apply to interpret their behaviors, and they attempt to apply constructs that they find personally desirable in maximizing their outcomes from social interaction. Most people, for example, prefer the self-construct "tactful" over the self-construct "ingratiating" and will go to great lengths to convince themselves and others that the former rather than the latter "really" describes their behavior.

Self-constructs organize and guide the ways people process self-related information. Once a particular self-construct is well established—that is, formed, used continually, and supported by a lot of data—it becomes increasingly resistant to contradictory information. We tend to notice behaviors that support that construct and interpret behaviors in terms of that construct rather than another. A person who normally categorizes herself as tactful and independent is more likely to interpret the behavior in the example (publicly agreeing while privately disagreeing) as demonstrating tact and not conformity. Research indicates that established cognitive categories do become increasingly immune to overthrow by single instances (see Carson, 1969; Mischel, 1973; Neisser, 1967, 1976).

Once established, self-constructs serve as selective devices that "determine whether information is attended to, how it is structured, how much importance is attached to it, and what happens to it subsequently" (Markus, 1977, p. 64). Self-constructs give meanings to our worlds. To demonstrate the importance of self-constructs, Hazel Markus (1977) classified students into those who had well articulated self-constructs on an important dimension (independence versus dependence) and those who did not. Those with well articulated self-constructs were able to process construct-related information faster, made related judgments and decisions about themselves more easily, were better able to recall related behaviors, were more self-confident in predicting their own future relevant actions, and were more resistant to information that contradicted these self-constructs. Markus concluded that "only when a self-description derives from a well-articulated generalization about the self can it be expected to converge and form a consistent pattern with the individual's other judgments, decisions, and actions" (p. 65). Self-constructs thus affect actions by affecting how people attend to, interpret, and respond to situations (Markus, 1977; Rogers, Kuiper, & Kirker, 1977; Rogers, Rogers, & Kuiper, 1979; R. G. Turner, 1978). In this sense, people who know themselves or at least think they do—that is, have well-articulated self-constructs—can more easily process information and make decisions about what is best for them. They believe they know what they are and therefore what they should and can do in various situations.

Expectations: Deciding What to Do

Self-constructs affect our expectations of what we should do and can do in various situations. Suppose you viewed yourself as independent, and your roommate asked you to sign a petition supporting an issue you didn't really support. What should you do? The answer is clear: to be independent, you should resist your roommate's pressure and refuse to sign. If you didn't view yourself as independent, your answer might be quite different. Or suppose you view yourself as introverted, poor at social conversation, physically unappealing, and lacking in sex appeal. What do you think your chances are of getting the gregarious and attractive classmate you admire to go out on a date and return your affection? You would probably expect failure. If you held the opposite set of self-constructs, you would anticipate greater success. Thus, self-constructs can affect people's expectations about what they should do and how effective they will be in various situations.

Albert Bandura (1977b) discussed *self-efficacy expectations*, which are beliefs "that one can successfully execute the behavior required to produce" particular outcomes (p. 193). As Bandura indicates, self-efficacy expectations determine whether a person will begin to cope with a potentially unpleasant situation and will work to accomplish some goal, how much effort the person will expend to reach the goal, and how long the person will continue to work in the face of frustrations and aversions. People who believe they can effectively accomplish some goal will begin sooner, work harder, and continue longer than those who do not. Our expectations, which are influenced by our self-constructs, thus have great impact on our behaviors. If you expect that nothing you can do will get the attractive classmate to agree to a date, why even ask? You will just be rejected. If you expect that your agreeable and sophisticated manner will surely get him or her to say "yes," don't hesitate for a moment.

Functions of the Self-Concept

Epstein (1973, p. 407) argues that the self-concept has three major functions for a person. It should (a) "optimize the pleasure/pain balance of the individual over the course of a lifetime," (b) "organize the data of experience in a manner that can be coped with effectively," and (c) facilitate "the maintenance of self-esteem." The first two functions are familiar ones, involving hedonism and cognitive organization. People who "know themselves"—that is, can accurately gauge their own capabilities and potential accomplishments—can make decisions that increase their outcomes from life. The third function, self-esteem maximization, has been assumed by most personality theorists to be a basic human motive (see Hall & Lindzey, 1978). Self-esteem is usually defined as an overall self-evaluation or judgment of personal worth (Wells & Marwell, 1976). People desire to think well of themselves, their attributes, and their actions. Some of the ways people go about doing so will be explored in the next chapter.

The Scientific Status of the Self-Concept

When the self-concept is seen as a self-theory, scientific objections to its status lose their force. The self-concept "can no longer be dismissed as unscientific, or as a reincarnation of the soul, unless one is also willing to dismiss theory, in general, as unscientific" (Epstein, 1973, p. 415). Some people might argue that it is not necessary to talk of the self-concept. One could simply examine each of a person's self-relevant facts, constructs, and beliefs in isolation. Yet, as all scientists know, no fact, construct, or hypothesis (belief) exists in isolation. Facts are given meaning by constructs, constructs are given meaning through their place in a theory, and no hypothesis can be tested in total isolation from the rest of the elements of a theory (see Hempel, 1966; Nagel, 1961). People understand themselves and their place in the world through the integrated elements of their self-concepts and use the self-concept to facilitate functioning in social life.

THE DEVELOPMENT OF THE SELF-CONCEPT

Social identity—the way a person is known and regarded by others—and impression management are both social concepts: they exist in interpersonal relationships. The self-concept intuitively seems to be a very personal one. It exists "inside" the individual; it is present even when he or she is alone in a dark room. It would seem easy to place these two social concepts at opposite poles. The private self is often conferred a positive evaluation that one's public identity is never given. "To thine own self be true" we are advised. "Be yourself." "Don't play a role." As people behave consistently with their "true selves" they are seen as wise and content; to the degree that they behave for a public audience, they are seen as sycophantic, conformist, ingratiating, and shallow. It sometimes seems as if the self is real, having a substance that transcends our social interactions, while social identity is only an appearance. In extreme cases, this intuitive approach shows merit. People sometimes lie. They sometimes do things not because they want to but because of the impression it will leave on others. Yet in most cases the boundary between our private and public self is fuzzy. The truth is that the self-concept, social identity, and impression management are more closely associated than most people admit. They all have a similar genesis in the social-interaction process. As explained in Chapter 2, interdependence of the individual and society characterizes human life, and this is particularly true concerning the development of the self-concept.

Symbolic Interaction

Symbolic interactionists root the self-concept in the social-interaction process; this position is basically accepted by most psychologists and sociologists. One's relationships with others provide the sort of information that becomes incorporated into one's self-concept.

Charles Horton Cooley placed the genesis of the self in children's perceptions and feelings about how others treat them. A child quickly learns that a relationship exists between personal actions and others' reactions. This connection becomes manifest in the ability to influence—the possession of power in the world.

> The child appropriates the visible actions of his parent or nurse, over which he finds he has some control, in quite the same way as he appropriates one of his own members or a plaything, and he will try to do things with this new possession, just as he will with his hand or his rattle. A girl

six months old will attempt in the most evident and deliberate manner to attract attention to herself, to set going by her actions some of those movements of other persons that she has appropriated. She has tasted the joy of being a cause, of exerting social power, and wishes more of it. She will tug at her mother's skirts, wriggle, gurgle, stretch out her arms, etc., all the time waiting for the hoped-for effect [Cooley, 1902/1922, p. 196].[1]

Interdependence exists: one has power, exerts influence, and controls personal outcomes. This exquisite revelation is the first great social discovery we make. It follows from the nature of interdependence and power that, just as one's own actions are directed at others, others' actions are directed at oneself. Others are rewarding or punishing in relation to one's own attributes and behaviors.

What others do reflects something about oneself. This second great social discovery sets the stage for the development of the self-concept. One sees oneself reflected in others' actions; others become a looking glass for self-perception. As Cooley (1902/1922, p. 184) put it:

Each to each a looking-glass
Reflects the other that doth pass.

The "self-idea" that develops, as Cooley called it, had three major elements: "the imagination of our appearance to the other person; the imagination of his judgment of that appearance; and some sort of self-feeling, such as pride or mortification" (p. 184). Appearance includes both bodily appearance and the type of "character" being displayed. "We are ashamed to seem evasive in the presence of a straightforward man, cowardly in the presence of a brave one, gross in the eyes of a refined one, and so on" (p. 184). People are not only able to view themselves as they imagine they are viewed by others, but quickly learn to control that appearance either to be perceived in a particular way or to capitalize on others' "characters" to obtain desirable outcomes. "The young performer soon learns to be different things to different people. . . . If the mother or nurse is more tender than just, she will almost certainly be 'worked' by systematic weeping" (p. 197).

For Cooley, then, the self-concept emerges from the social-interaction process. As children, we learn the nature of interdependence and power. We influence others' actions, and their actions reflect, as a looking glass, ourselves. Since others' actions are tied to one's appearance, one's own actions can construct particular appearances that produce desired effects. The self-concept, interpersonal relations, and impression management are wedded.

George Herbert Mead (1934) also placed the self-concept in the

[1]From *Human Nature and the Social Order* (revised edition), by C. H. Cooley. Copyright 1902, 1922 by Charles Scribner's Sons. This and all other quotations from this source are reprinted by permission.

social-interaction process but went into greater detail on the developmental aspects. In contrast to Cooley, who stressed the child's reactions to and feelings about significant others like a parent or nurse, Mead emphasized the cognitive essence of the self-concept and its relationship to society at large. For Mead, the self-concept arises through thinking and being able to take the role of others—seeing oneself as others do.

He described three stages of self-development. In the *preparatory stage* a child might imitate others without really understanding what he or she is doing. The child might "read" a book like daddy does, going through the motions of being in a different role before being able even to appreciate the functions of the activity. Imitation provides the experience of going beyond one's current role.

In the *play stage* children place themselves more directly into others' roles, playing doctor, train engineer, police officer, mommy, daddy, and teacher. The child starts to view itself from the perspectives provided by these new roles, as when teaching a "little boy" to read. At this stage, though, the complexities of the roles are not yet clear to the child. No unified conception of self has emerged. The child shifts quickly and often inconsistently from one role to another, since its own role is ambiguous. Yet, from trying out new roles and perspectives, the child learns to view itself and others in new ways.

The third phase is the *games stage*, in which self-concept development becomes more stable and complete. During games like baseball the child learns to view itself from a number of perspectives simultaneously. In team games, the child must anticipate what teammates as well as opponents are likely to do in a given situation and plan accordingly. The child fits into an intricate social network and comes to appreciate the nuances of being a responsible member of society (Meltzer, 1972).

The composite of other roles that the child perceives, like teammates, is termed the *generalized other*. It is a generalized role or viewpoint of society as perceived by the individual. Through the generalized other, people can plan actions and evaluate their behaviors in a social context. This viewpoint allows people to anticipate how others will react, which in turn affects their own actions. Once this generalized viewpoint is achieved, a person can "conduct himself in an organized, consistent manner" (Meltzer, 1972, p. 10). A person can behave in a socialized way in new situations.

Through imitation, play, games, and the appreciation of the generalized other, people develop a coherent view of themselves that embeds them in the social world. The embedment is complete enough for Mead to remark that "selves can only exist in definite relations to other selves. No hard-and-fast line can be drawn between our own selves and the selves of others, since our own selves exist and enter as such into our experience only insofar as the selves of others exist and enter as such into our experience also" (1934, p. 196). Further, the embedment is due to the social-interaction process:

The self, as that which can be an object to itself, is essentially a social structure, and it arises in social experience. After a self has arisen, it in a certain sense provides for itself its social experiences, and so we can conceive of an absolutely solitary self. But it is impossible to conceive of a self arising outside of social experience. When it has arisen we can think of a person in solitary confinement for the rest of his life, but who still has himself as a companion, and is able to think and to converse with himself as he had communicated with others [p. 140].[2]

From the perspective of symbolic interactionism, then, the genesis of the self-concept is the social-interaction process.[3] Interdependence characterizes social life, and one learns that the reactions of others are contingent on one's own appearance and actions. Significant others provide a basis for viewing ourselves. In addition, through imitation, play, and games, a myriad of social roles can be explored. People view themselves in terms of a generalized social perspective and can imagine the attitudes of others toward them. These attitudes shape the self-concept and provide a basis for altering one's own behavior to influence the social audience.

SOCIAL EXPERIENCE

Some people are offended by the suggestion that the self-concept arises in social interaction and is affected by what others think. They willingly admit that other people probably have had their self-concepts formed and affected this way, but—as for themselves—well, they are more independent than that. Such resistance is understandable. The self, the core of one's being, is sometimes viewed as the last vestige of personal independence in a world that has become oriented toward others. Given this skepticism, it is worth examining some of the evidence that supports the basic hypotheses of symbolic interactionism.

Early Social Interaction

According to symbolic interactionism, the self-concept arises from social experience. It follows that without social interaction any self-concept that exists will be extremely crude and one's interpersonal relations will be hindered. The most direct way of testing such hypotheses

[2]From *Mind, Self, and Society*, by G. H. Mead. Chicago: University of Chicago Press, 1934.

[3]Harry Stack Sullivan (1953), a perceptive neo-Freudian psychiatrist, espoused developmental concepts that are very close to those of Cooley and Mead. He believed that one's personality emerges only in the context of interpersonal relations. Like Cooley, Sullivan was led to conclude that the self-concept developed through relationships with a few significant others. Sullivan believed that people adopt significant others' standards, values, and evaluations as means of minimizing rejection, gaining approval, and maintaining satisfaction and security.

would be to randomly assign newborn infants to either an enriched social interaction experience or a period of social deprivation. For obvious ethical reasons, one cannot conduct such a study with humans—I hope no one would want to. But such studies have been conducted with nonhumans.

Gordon Gallup (1977) reasoned that the self-concept rests on the fundamental ability to recognize and code oneself as a distinct personal entity. If an organism cannot recognize itself, it is difficult to argue that it can have a sense of self; if it does show self-recognition, the basis for a rudimentary self-concept would be present. Gallup investigated self-recognition in chimpanzees and other great apes. He concluded that the great apes do possess a rudimentary self-concept and that it is dramatically affected by social experience. In an initial study, he individually exposed preadolescent chimps to a full-length mirror to see how they would react. For the first two or three days, the chimps reacted to their mirror image as if it were another chimp, bobbing up and down, vocalizing at the reflection, and occasionally making threatening gestures. Later, the chimps began to show signs of self-recognition. They used the mirror to groom parts of their bodies that were outside their normal sight, entertained themselves by blowing bubbles and making faces, and even picked food from their teeth.

Despite these observations, skeptics might have been unconvinced of the chimps' ability for self-recognition. So Gallup anesthetized each of the chimps and painted an odorless, nonirritating bright red dye on parts of their faces that they could not see without a mirror. Because of the anesthesia and the properties of the dye, the chimps would not be able to know that it had been applied unless they saw it in the mirror and knew that the image in the mirror was theirs. After awakening, the chimps were placed in their individual cages, without mirrors, and the researchers counted the number of times they spontaneously touched the dye-marked spots. The mirror was then reintroduced. It was found that, when the chimps could see themselves in the mirror, they touched the spots 25 times more frequently than when the mirror was absent. The chimps spent more time looking into the mirror than they had before being marked with the red dye, and they attempted to smell and examine their fingers after touching the spots. This is convincing evidence for self-recognition in nonhumans.[4]

If self-concept development is dependent on social experience, as symbolic interactionists suppose, then chimps reared in isolation without the possibility of social interaction should have difficulty at the

[4]Gallup and others have found evidence for self-recognition in other great apes such as orangutans but not in other species of monkeys such as spider monkeys, capuchins, macaques, baboons, and gibbons. These other species can learn to use mirrors to manipulate objects and can even turn from a mirror to look directly at an object reflected in it. They just don't seem able to recognize themselves.

mirror recognition task. Gallup (Gallup, McClure, Hill, & Bundy, 1971) raised some chimps in isolation and compared their responses to chimps raised with companions. While the normal chimps seemed to recognize themselves in the mirror, the socially deprived chimps did not.

In another study (Hill, Bundy, Gallup, & McClure, 1970) two isolation-reared chimps who showed no signs of self-recognition were given three months of social experience by being housed in the same cage. In contrast to a chimp that continued in isolation, who remained unable to identify the reflection, the chimps given social experience showed signs of self-recognition ability. At least some of the effects of the social isolation were reversible. This is persuasive evidence of the necessity for social experience in the development of the self-concept.

With the importance of social interaction in mind, Gallup (1977) has speculated about what might happen if an organism capable of self-concept development were reared with members of another species, from whom the animal might learn unusual patterns of behavior and self-identification. Presumably, the animal might come to misidentify itself and see itself as a member of that other species. The data are certainly consistent with this possibility, although conclusive evidence has yet to be amassed. One chimp raised with humans and taught sign language referred to other chimps whom she had seen for the first time as "black bugs." Vicki, another chimp raised in a home with humans, was taught to sort pictures into two piles—human and nonhuman. One day while Vicki was working on this task, her own picture was slipped in with the other photos. When she came to it, Vicki placed it in the pile with the humans!

The evidence from studies of the great apes clearly indicates the importance of social experience in the development of self-recognition ability (see also Meddin, 1979). The rudimentary self-concepts possessed by the great apes seem to require social interaction to develop fully. These results are consistent with correlational studies of humans that indicate that early social experience is a key to the later development of effective interaction patterns (see Mussen, Conger, & Kagan, 1969). Similar experimental studies with nonhuman species indicate that both lack of mother contact and peer isolation produce later behavioral abnormalities (Harlow & Harlow, 1966; Harlow, Harlow, & Suomi, 1971). Social experience is of paramount importance in the development of a normal personality.

Reflected Appraisals

A major assumption of the symbolic-interactionist approach is that people's self-concepts develop as they see themselves reflected in the actions of significant others. Even after the self-concept has formed, others' self-directed actions still should influence what people think of themselves, at least under certain conditions. As Cooley (1902/1922) put it:

> As we see our face, figure, and dress in the glass [mirror], and are interested in them because they are ours, and pleased or otherwise with them according as they do or do not answer to what we should like them to be; so in imagination we see in another's mind some thought of our appearance, manners, aims, deeds, character, friends, and so on, and are variously affected by it [p. 184].

A person's perceptions of the impressions others form about him or her are termed *reflected appraisals*. Reflected appraisals can be based on explicit or implicit information. For example, Grandpa might bring over one of his friends to see his 3-year-old grandson and remark in the child's presence "Look at that build—husky already. And you should see his grip. That boy's gonna make a fine fullback some day; nobody will be able to tackle him."

Hearing the explicit evaluation, the child begins to form self-constructs such as strong and athletic. Implicit information can also be transformed into reflected appraisals. Tacit cues for reflected appraisals can derive from the attentions of others (Does Mother care about me, or does she seem to ignore me?); the tones of others' voices (Is Mother calm or agitated when I'm around?); and the things they don't say (Why doesn't Mother ever say I'm pretty?).

Reflected appraisals do not always correspond perfectly with the actual evaluation another person attempts to convey. A person might misinterpret what another says, particularly if the comment is ambiguous to begin with, and believe that the self-evaluation was more or less favorable than the source intended (see Jacobs, Berscheid, & Walster, 1971). Moreover, explicit and implicit information can sometimes conflict, making it difficult to obtain a clear reflected appraisal. A mother might tell her daughter that she is darling and loved, while the child notices that her mother speaks in an affectionless tone, doesn't look her in the eye, and never hugs her. Confusion can result, as the child has difficulty determining how her mother really feels. Messages may even flatly contradict each other, as when a mother asks her daughter to give her a hug, while her tone of voice clearly tells the daughter to stay away. Such contradictory messages can lead to disorganized behavior patterns later in life of the type exhibited by schizophrenics (Bateson, Jackson, Haley, & Weakland, 1956).

One's parents typically provide the first significant source of personal evaluation through reflected appraisals. One dramatic example of how the reflected appraisals of parents can affect one's self-concept is the story of the boyhood of John Stuart Mill (1806–1873), the British philosopher who made important contributions to psychology, sociology, and economics. James Mill, John's father, was a disciplinarian who structured the boy's education and development strictly. John learned Greek by the age of 3; by 7 he had read Plato, Herodotus, and Xenophon and had begun the study of Latin. By 12 he had finished Virgil, Ovid, Aristotle, Socrates, and Aristophanes; was expert in geometry, algebra, and calculus; had written a Roman history and a history of Holland; and had edited his father's history of India (Heilbroner, 1967). His father's demands were constant. There were no vacations, no play with peers, no "pleasure" reading. James kept up a constant barrage of tests for his son. Even while riding, the boy was forced to memorize signs and aspects of the countryside, on which his father would quiz him later to improve his memory. Through all this, John had no idea that his upbringing was unusual or that he was particularly gifted; his self-evaluations were provided by his father, who treated his accomplishments as unremarkable (Tedeschi & Lindskold, 1976). Only later, when he compared himself with others, did he come to recognize his uniqueness.

Research on Reflected Appraisals. Numerous correlational studies have examined the relationship between people's self-evaluations, how they perceive that others view them, and how those others actually do view them. Miyamoto and Dornbusch (1956) had male and female college students rate themselves on the attributes of intelligence, self-confidence, physical attractiveness, and likableness. The students also rated how several specific friends (either fellow fraternity members, sorority members, or sociology classmates) would rate them on these attributes, and the friends were asked to give ratings of how they felt about each other. Each student was then asked to rate how "most people" would evaluate him or her on each attribute. It was found that people who rated themselves higher believed that their friends and most other people would rate them higher, and they actually did receive higher ratings from the friends. People's self-evaluations and the perceived and actual responses of others clearly covaried.

Of course, people can misperceive the actual evaluations they receive from others and come to believe that the others are more or less positive than they actually are. Thus, symbolic interactionists propose that perceived evaluations (reflected appraisals) are more important in affecting the self-concept than actual evaluations. Miyamoto and Dornbusch found support for this hypothesis in that the students' self-ratings corresponded more closely to the perceived than to the actual responses of others. Finally, symbolic interactionists stress the importance of the generalized other. In this regard, responses to the items dealing with how one is viewed by most other people can be seen as reflected appraisals relevant to the generalized other, and should be closely related to self-ratings. In support of this view, it was found that the subjects' self-ratings corresponded more closely to their perceptions of how most other people felt about them than to the average of subjects' perceptions about how specific individuals felt about them.

Moore (1964) examined the relationships between husbands' and wives' self-descriptions, descriptions of their spouses, and descriptions of how they thought their spouses would describe them. All three variables were related, and self-descriptions varied more closely with perceptions of how the spouse felt about them than with how the spouse actually felt about them. Moore also reasoned that women who worked outside the home should be less affected by their husbands' opinions than women who did not. The former should be exposed to the appraisals of numerous other co-workers, while the latter should be exposed primarily to the appraisals of their husbands. Hence, the husband's appraisal should carry more weight with the latter group than with the former. As predicted, ratings of the husbands' perceived appraisals were more closely related to self-descriptions for those who stayed home than for those who worked outside.

Other studies have produced comparable results and have shown that self-descriptions are correlated with the reflected appraisals of parents (Coopersmith, 1967; Jourard & Remy, 1955), teachers (Quarantelli & Cooper, 1966), and co-workers (Reeder, Donohue, & Biblarz, 1960). The major difficulty with all these studies, though, is that they are correlational. The results show that self-evaluations and reflected appraisals are related to each other, but they don't show that reflected appraisals directly produced corresponding changes in self-evaluations (see Shrauger & Schoeneman, 1979, for a critical review of this literature). Perhaps people's actual abilities produce both their self-evaluations and the evaluations they receive from others, in which case reflected appraisals might have no direct impact on self-evaluations. Perhaps people form their own self-evaluations first, then convince significant others to agree with them. Most probably, each of these alternatives is partially correct.

Experimental studies provide a means of reducing these possibilities by determining whether or not reflected appraisals directly affect self-evaluations. Videbeck (1960) had students in a speech class read poems aloud and then receive evaluative feedback from a "visiting expert" in the communications area. Unbeknown to the students, the feedback they received was actually bogus and unrelated to their performance. Half of the students were randomly assigned to receive a positive evaluation that rated them superior in controlling their voices and conveying meaning, while the other half were rated quite low on these attributes. Subsequently, the students were asked to rate themselves on the specific attributes mentioned in their evaluation from the speech expert, other attributes related to the evaluation they received but not specifically included in it, and still other attributes unrelated to the evaluation but still in the general area of communications (such as adequacy in social conversations).

Videbeck found that the students' self-ratings were significantly affected by the visiting expert's evaluation of them and that their self-ratings were most affected on the items closely related to the evaluation. Those receiving a positive evaluation showed a large positive increase in their self-ratings on attributes specifically related to the appraisal, a moderate increase on attributes relevant to the appraisal, and only a slight increase on attributes unrelated to the appraisal. Those receiving a negative evaluation showed a large decrease in self-ratings on attributes specifically related to the appraisal, a moderate decrease on attributes relevant to the appraisal, and only a slight decrease on attributes unrelated to the appraisal.

Results from this and other experiments (see Backman, Secord, & Peirce, 1963; Bergin, 1962; Gergen, 1965; Haas & Maehr, 1965; Kinch, 1968; Maehr, Mensing, & Nafzger, 1962) indicate the impact that reflected appraisals have on self-evaluations, particularly for those attributes most directly related to the appraisal. Reflected appraisals can produce corresponding changes in the self-concept.

Of course, not all reflected appraisals produce change or equal amounts of change. Evaluations by those we dislike or consider incompetent are usually dismissed or discounted; they produce little or no change in self-evaluations (Bergin, 1962). The reflected appraisals of significant others—those perceived as important, attractive, competent, or powerful—are weighed more heavily. Reflected appraisals also vary in the degree of confidence we have in them. A person might conclude that another individual feels positively toward him or her but be uncertain about how much or even whether the conclusion is justified. Not surprisingly, reflected appraisals are weighed more heavily when one's confidence in them is high (Backman et al., 1963). Thus, reflected appraisals that are given by significant others and perceived as credible have the greatest impact on the self-concept.

At times, discrepancies may arise between one's self-evaluation and the perceived or actual appraisals of others (see Gergen, 1971; Lundgren, 1978; Webster, 1975). Such discrepancies can reduce the likelihood of harmonious interactions with the evaluator, threaten to invalidate one's self-conception, and thus generate stress. Indeed, individuals who exhibit the greatest amounts of stress in their interpersonal relations also are found to have the greatest discrepancies between their self-appraisals and the perceived or actual appraisals of others (Lundgren, 1978).

Reflected appraisals can have significant effects not only on the self-concept but on subsequent behavior patterns. Miller, Brickman, and Bolen (1975) compared the effects of telling children that they do have certain attributes with the effects of telling them that they should have those attributes. When children were told they were good at arithmetic and given letters and medals to reinforce the point, they increased their self-evaluations in mathematics and actually did better on tests. Children who were told they *should* do better in math did not make such gains. When one is told he or she should be better, the reflected appraisal is not "He thinks I'm good at [whatever]" but rather "If he thinks I should be good at [whatever], it must mean that he believes I'm not good at it now."

Everyone chuckles at the naive wishes of the characters in the *Wizard of Oz*—the scarecrow wanted a "brain"; the tin woodsman, a "heart"; the lion, "courage." Even the Wicked Witch of the West could not deter them from their quests. In the end, the pseudo-wizard answered their pleas and gave them the attributes they desired. The scarecrow received a "diploma" that certified his intelligence; the tin woodsman, a "philanthropy award" testifying to his generous character; the lion, a "medal of valor" for courage in the face of extreme adversity. And they were quite content with their newly found attributes. The usual interpretation of the story is that we "find what we want in our own backyards" and don't have to pursue it; the characters had always possessed the attributes they desired. An alternative interpretation is that the characters came to see themselves, accurately or not, through the actions of others. Receiving awards, obtaining trophies, getting medals, being commended or put down—all serve to define social identity, and all have an impact on the self-concept.

Comparative Appraisal

Other people can affect a person's self-judgments without even directing their behaviors toward them. The simple presence of others can influence self-evaluations by affecting one's relative standing. *Comparative appraisal* is the process of evaluating one's own attributes and performances by determining where one stands in relationship to relevant others. Suppose Joan just received a "B" grade in her psychology course. How good a psychology student is she? She might be a "good" student if grades were assigned on the basis of a normal distribution, in which case she would have done better than about two-thirds of the class. She might be "very good," though, if only about 10% of the class received a grade of "B" or better. She might be "very bad" if she was the only one in the class not to receive an "A." By comparing her performance with those of others, she can evaluate the caliber of her work.

Reference groups are the people against whom we compare ourselves (Hyman, 1942). As reference groups change, so do self-evaluations. Jonathan Swift's famous character Gulliver was a man of average height in his own land. On his travels, he became a giant compared to the tiny inhabitants of Lilliput and a midget compared to the huge inhabitants of Brodingnag. Similarly, a budding actress might perceive herself as very glamorous and sophisticated while growing up in her home town. After moving to Hollywood, she might perceive herself as very plain and awkward in comparison to the established stars. Her actual characteristics have not changed, but her standards of comparison have.

Morse and Gergen (1970) dramatically demonstrated the importance of comparative appraisals on self-evaluations. Subjects in their experiment believed that they were applying for a part-time job and reported individually for an interview to determine their suitability. After each applicant completed a self-esteem measure, a "secretary" escorted another "applicant" into the room. The second applicant, who was actually an experimental accomplice, was made to appear to have either socially desirable or undesirable attributes. "Mr. Clean," the desirable applicant, was neatly attired in a business suit, carried an attaché case, which he opened to remove some sharpened pencils, revealing a statistics book and a philosophy book. "Mr. Dirty," the undesirable applicant, wore an old sweat shirt, had no socks, seemed disoriented, and tossed his beaten-up copy of a trashy novel onto a table. Shortly thereafter, the subject was given another questionnaire to fill out that contained a second measure of self-esteem. It was found that subjects' self-esteem decreased in the presence of "Mr. Clean" and increased in the presence of "Mr. Dirty." The attributes of the reference person caused subjects to shift their own self-evaluations. As these results suggest, two people with very similar attributes will form quite different self-evaluations if different reference groups are used for comparison.

Interim Summary

The genesis of the self-concept is the social-interaction process. Early social experience is important to the development of the self-concept and to the effectiveness of later interaction patterns. The reflected appraisals of significant others shape the contents of the self-concept, as people come to see themselves the way significant others seem to. Comparative appraisals further define the self-concept, as our relative standing against people in reference groups provides information about what we are like.

People categorize and evaluate themselves. Through the socialization process, they learn the rules and values of others in society and begin to understand why other people give particular evaluations in particular settings. Once these rules and values have been digested, people can apply them to themselves and make judgments even when no one else is around. Thus, we can imagine a person in complete solitude who still makes self-judgments and feels pride or guilt about his or her actions.

ROLES: THE PARTS WE PLAY

People come to define themselves through social interaction, seeing themselves in part through the eyes of significant others. One of the factors that affect how other people see us and act toward us is the roles we occupy. Some, like the male or female role, we are born into; others are the result of our personal efforts and abilities or lack of them—doctor, lawyer, psychologist. In either case, roles exist apart from the particular individuals who occupy them and can act as social scripts that dictate how we should act.

The word *role* derives from the Latin word *rotula*, the sheet of parchment wrapped around a wooden roller that contained the part that an actor recited on stage. In the theater, roles constrain actors' behavior, at least to some degree. Actors must say certain lines at certain times, engage in specific behaviors at specific moments, work with particular props, coordinate their actions with those of other actors, and, in general, convey to the audience the character of the person they are playing. Within these constraints, of course, actors are free to display their own unique talents, fleshing out the character to give spontaneity and life to the author's words. They might ad-lib on occasion, throwing in or changing lines and dramatizing gestures to bring the character home and touch a responsive chord in the audience. Typically, the better the actor, the better his or her ability to improvise in a way that meets with the audience's approval. But the role still gives direction and purpose to the actor's behaviors, guiding them along a predetermined course.

Role Theory

Role theorists have taken this model and applied it to everyday social behavior. Role theory (see Biddle & Thomas, 1966; Merton, 1957; Sarbin & Allen, 1968; E. J. Thomas, 1968) is a prominent area of study that has been greatly influenced by symbolic interactionism and the dramaturgical approach[5] Just as actors' behaviors are guided by their

[5]The concept of role has been claimed to be "the theoretical point of articulation between psychology and sociology," in that it is "the largest possible research unit within the former discipline and the smallest possible within the latter" (Rommetveit, 1955, p. 31).

roles, people's social behaviors are shaped by the roles they occupy. A role is usually defined in terms of the part an individual plays within a group. Possible roles are numerous: doctor, lawyer, banker, politician, parent, teacher, son, daughter, construction worker, female, male.

Each role carries with it certain perceived and expected behaviors that role occupants enact in social situations. The perceived attributes are easily demonstrated by the stereotypes most people associate with certain roles. Everyone can characterize what a "traditional woman," or "homemaker," is supposed to be like. She should be dedicated to her family, be oriented toward the home rather than a professional career, and be submissive, affectionate, emotional, and skilled at cooking, cleaning, sewing, and so on. To facilitate the adoption of this role, young girls were and often still are cuddled and encouraged to express emotion, given doll sets so that they could gain the "proper" perspective through play, taught how to cook and sew, discouraged from expressing dominant or aggressive behaviors, and so on. Young boys often receive quite different training to encourage behavior patterns that are relevant to the "male" role in society. The expected behaviors that roles carry with them, then, are based on social agreement about what the occupants of certain roles should be like; society encourages and rewards proper role enactment and discourages out-of-role behaviors. People's cognitive scripts for social interactions are based in part on shared beliefs about such role requirements.

The stereotypical attributes associated with particular roles often emerge because of their usefulness to society. For example, bankers would quickly go out of business if they were perceived as unstable, untrustworthy, risk oriented, and poor at mathematics. Hence, stereotypes of bankers include such attributes as conservative, cautious, stable, precise, and good with figures. Society and bankers both benefit if a person with these characteristics takes such a job, or if the person acquires these characteristics quickly after.

Everyone has many roles. A person might be a wife, mother, daughter, teacher, professor, scientist, athlete, and many other things. On occasion the demands of roles may conflict, as in the case of a professor who has her own husband enrolled in a course or the college student who returns home for the holidays to find that his newly acquired independence is not appreciated by his parents. People often shift from one role to another within a brief time. A university faculty member might adopt a "professor" role while at work, maintaining an intellectual aura and seeming emotionally aloof. After work, the professor might shift into a "parent role," shed the dignity that was so carefully cultivated during the day, and gleefully crawl around on all fours with the children. Occasionally people have difficulty shifting out of roles at appropriate times, as when a lawyer greets his or her spouse after work in the tone of voice usually reserved for the jury.

Roles and the Self-Concept

The cumulative impact of one's roles can influence the self-concept and behavior. People typically come to view themselves in terms of the attributes and behavior patterns dictated by their roles (see Kuhn, 1960; Sarbin & Allen, 1968). The roles become internalized as part of the self-concept, providing people with role-related self-constructs and expectations: "A banker should be categorized as conservative and stable." "I should behave in a certain way, and others should treat me in a certain way." Through role enactment, people can "become" the roles they play. In a statement quite reminiscent of William James' discussion of habits (see Chapter 2), Waller (1932) noted:

> That stiff and formal manner in which the young teacher compresses himself every morning when he puts on his collar becomes . . . a plaster cast which at length he cannot loosen. . . . The didactic manner, the authoritative manner, the flat, assured tones of voice that go with them, are bred in the teacher by his dealings in the classroom . . . and these traits are carried over by the teacher into his interpersonal relations [pp. 381–382].

The internalization of a role seems to be greatest when people become "comfortable" in it, when they come to value the benefits that the role supplies and to believe that they can fulfill the role-expectations. An army draftee might initially hate the army and do everything he can to avoid being type-cast as a military man. Of course, his sergeant doesn't take kindly to disobedience or a non-military manner, so he forces the recruit to "shape up." Soon, the young man begins to reap some rewards from his new role. Not only does he escape punishment, but he gets passes to leave the base and finds that the young women in town just adore men in uniform. He then begins to consider all the benefits of army life—free room and board, comradeship, educational opportunities, and even the thought that he is serving his country. He also finds that it is not so hard to fit the army role; he scores well on marksmanship tests and learns new tasks easily. He soon becomes gung ho military.

Of course, if people don't come to value the benefits of the role, or they believe that they can't fulfill its requirements, problems develop. The person is not likely to internalize the role but in many cases tries to escape from its constraints, by leaving the job, for example. It has been found that, when self characteristics are incongruent with the requirements of the role, "role enactment will be poor in terms of appropriateness, effectiveness, and convincingness" (Allen, 1968, p. 205). Such failure further reinforces the belief that one can't play that role. If one's self-constructs and self-efficacy expectations contradict role requirements, escape from the role rather than internalization becomes more likely (see Sarbin & Allen, 1968; E. J. Thomas, 1968).

In sum, roles provide scripts of how we are expected to behave, and these scripts influence our behaviors. Roles thus partially define the identities we establish in social interactions and can influence our self-concepts. In turn, our self-concepts can affect the quality of role enactment and thus affect the degree to which we internalize any aspects of roles that might initially be discrepant with our self-concepts.

THE PUBLIC SELF: SOCIAL IDENTITY

As William James implied, the self-as-known emerges as people associate themselves with the variety of material, bodily, and social aspects of life. Each association is revealing, since each can be used to categorize and evaluate the individual. Thus each association has implications for what the individual is "really like," what he or she deserves from life, how he or she should be treated by others, and how he or she should act. Cooley enlarged the picture by proposing that the self-concept develops from social interaction as people discover that the actions of others reveal, by reflection, something about them and that they can control the actions of others through their own behaviors. Actions have social meanings, and people will consciously or unconsciously control the self-image presented to others in order to achieve certain goals. Mead described the nature of the self-concept further by noting that through play and games people come to view themselves from the standpoint of the generalized other—the amorphous internal presence of society's attitudes and rules. People categorize and evaluate themselves in part according to how their actions are viewed by others and might affect others. Finally, role theorists added that people come to view themselves through the roles they enact in society. The integral relationship between people's self-concepts and social identities is apparent in all of these views.

Social identity is the way a person is defined and regarded in social interaction. Just as situations must be defined by the interacting participants to determine which behaviors are appropriate (see Chapter 2), so people must be defined to clarify what they are and how they will act toward each other. Will one be dominant or submissive? Agreeable or disagreeable? Dependable or flighty? These are just a few of the many questions that must be answered before each person's participation in an interaction can be coordinated with those of others. As Stone (1962, p. 93) says, "Identity establishes what and where the person is in social terms. It is not a substitute word for 'self.' Instead, when one has identity, he is situated—that is, cast in the shape of a social object by the acknowledgement of his participation or membership in social relations." Through one's identity, one becomes part of the social matrix of relationships among people.

Any self-relevant factor that might be noticed by other people has the potential to affect one's identity and has an impact on social relationships. Such factors include, among others, the roles we occupy, such as employer/employee and doctor/patient; our relative status—that is, the evaluations of the roles; public behaviors and the social attributes that describe the behaviors, such as friendly/unfriendly and dominant/submissive; our "background," including ancestors and schools attended; and our publicly observable features, such as fat/thin and handsome/ugly. To the degree that such self-relevant factors affect how people are categorized, evaluated, and treated, they affect social relationships. Many factors that appear on the surface to be irrelevant to social relationships turn out on closer analysis to be quite meaningful. Consider one's hair color. Do you believe that blondes have more fun or that redheads are fiery and emotional? Have you ever dyed your hair, and, if you did, why? Many seemingly unimportant bits of information about people affect how we see and act toward them. On these bits of information our identities rest.

We can draw a distinction between one's identity as perceived by oneself and as perceived by others. One's own perception is equivalent to a theory that the individual has constructed about how he or she is defined and regarded in social interactions. It contains a series of social facts about the person, constructs that the person uses to describe his or her social attributes and behaviors, and beliefs—hypotheses or expectations—about how facts are related to constructs and constructs related to one another. This theory is embedded within the self-concept, which is a larger, more inclusive theory. In one sense, one's perceived identity is similar to James' social self, but it is more inclusive than the latter since many factors that James chose to exclude from the social self, such as physical features, wealth, and accomplishments, have implications for how one is defined and regarded in social relationships. One's identity as it is perceived by others, on the other hand, is simply the theory that they have constructed about how the individual is defined and regarded in social interactions.

A distinction also can be drawn between people's *situated identities*, which are specific to particular interactions with particular others (see Alexander & Lauderdale, 1977), and people's *composite identities*, which are general and which subsume a variety of social interactions with different people. A person can have many situated identities—one for each audience he or she encounters.

Identities are what people attempt to monitor and control in front of real audiences. People's outcomes from interaction are shaped by how they are defined and regarded by others, so people try to control their identities in front of others to control those outcomes. This is the essence of public self-presentation. Through many devices, people attempt to control the facts, constructs, and beliefs that others have about them.

In controlling our own identities, it is often necessary to influence the identities of others. Identities reflect relationships between people. If one person wants to be viewed as a dominant, powerful individual, it is necessary to have someone else assume a more submissive, less powerful posture. If one wants to be viewed as extremely competent, it is necessary that at least some other people are viewed as not having much skill.

People can control the identities of others either by objectively influencing others' behaviors or by subjectively perceiving that others have particular characteristics. In the first category is the phenomenon sociologists have termed *altercasting*: the use of social influence to place another into a particular identity (Weinstein & Deutschberger, 1963). The actor who wants to be viewed as, say, powerful will try in a hundred ways to cause other people to assume submissive postures: bullying them, disparaging their ideas, refusing to follow their suggestions, and so on. If the altercasting is successful and the other person begins to behave submissively, then the actor's own desired identity is established in the relationship.

In the subjective category, actors can control the identities of others simply by perceiving them to have particular attributes, without even trying to alter their behaviors. Actors who want to view themselves as, say, dominant can contemplate social comparisons that make them look good in relation to others. They might think about all of the times that other people blindly conform to the wills of others or how most other people never have an independent thought in their whole lives. By mentally putting other people down, actors elevate themselves on whatever dimension they select. These *selective social comparisons* allow people to conceptualize themselves in desired ways.

To select an identity does not always involve a conscious choice (Child, 1968). People often have certain characteristics activated in an interaction without being fully aware of what is transpiring. Imagine a professor meeting his former mentor at a party. Although, technically speaking, he now has the same status as his old teacher, he still reacts with deference, assuming a subordinate role. At the same time, the former teacher assumes the posture of "superior." Both may fail to realize precisely what is occurring: they are selecting identities that steer their interaction along a particular course. As another example, consider how fat people are often viewed and treated as if they were jovial and good-natured. Soon, the fat person might find himself telling jokes that fit the identity that others have provided. The unconscious selection of identities occurs when a particular cognitive script relevant to an identity is engaged by cues in the situation without the individual's being fully aware of it.

People do not have total control over their identities. Some aspects are difficult or impossible to alter, such as physical characteristics and ancestors. Others, like friendliness or dominance, are more easily controlled. Yet, even when people intentionally attempt to control aspects of their identities, the control is not complete. A particular identity might be met with resistance from those who don't want to accept it or even rejected entirely. A person may try to be dominant, but, if initial dominant gestures are thwarted, she may concede and become more submissive. A couple on their first date might take some time to reach agreement on the role each will assume and how each will behave— Who opens the door? Who picks up the check? Thus, all interactions involve some degree of *identity bargaining*, which is the process of mutual accommodation through which people come to agree on what role each will play in the interaction (Weinstein & Deutschberger, 1963).

Altercasting often comes into play during identity bargaining. An often repeated, sexist example is that of a woman's extracting a confession of love from a man, thus casting him into a particular identity vis-à-vis her. The male finally concedes to the altercast identity, but only after extracting some concession in return—"Of course I love you; now why don't we go to my place?" (Blumstein, 1973). When identity bargaining reaches mutually acceptable conclusions, relationships are likely to thrive; when it fails to, they are likely to terminate (if the parties can extricate themselves).

SELF-AWARENESS AND IMPRESSION MANAGEMENT

Now that we have an understanding of the self and identity, it is time to return to the distinction made at the beginning of the chapter between the *I* and the *Me*. Recall that the *I* is the person as a non-self-conscious acting entity, passive, subjective, acting without conscious attention to itself as an object. The *Me* is the empirical self—the self as known by the individual. The self-concept is our personal representation of the *Me*. Social identity, at least as it is know by us, is our representation of how we believe we are viewed and evaluated in our social relationships.

As the distinction between the *I* and *Me* makes clear, we do not always consciously attend to ourselves as objects, social or otherwise. Sometimes we just act, and we can truthfully assert later that we weren't even thinking about how we looked at the time. We weren't consciously playing a role, protecting our identity, or trying to please an audience. At these moments, caught up in the flow of our activity, we lose personal awareness. Self-presentation in its deliberate, tactical form is the last thing on our minds; we are in an *I* state. At other times, the *Me* gains ascendence. We contemplate what we are like, how we look to real or imagined audiences, and how information in the environment reflects on our status as social objects. These different states have different implications for impression management.

Elaborating James' discussions, Duval and Wicklund (Duval & Wicklund, 1972; Wicklund, 1975) proposed that two types of self-awareness exist: objective and subjective. *Objective self-awareness* corresponds with the *Me* state. "When attention is directed inward and the individual's consciousness is focused on himself, he is the object of his own consciousness—hence, 'objective' self awareness" (Duval & Wicklund, 1972, p. 2). By contrast, *subjective self-awareness* corresponds to the *I* state. "When attention is directed away from himself he is the 'subject' of the consciousness that is directed toward external objects, thus the term 'subjective' self awareness" (p. 2). They proposed that a person can be in only one of these states at any moment, although one's awareness can oscillate rapidly between them.

Research indicates that people's behavior does depend on which state of self-awareness predominates during a particular time (see Carver & Scheier, 1978; Davis & Brock, 1975; Diener & Srull, 1979; Duval & Wicklund, 1972; Federoff & Harvey, 1976; Geller & Shaver,1976; Hull & Levy, 1979; Wicklund, 1975). In order to maximize objective self-awareness in experimental settings, researchers introduce cues that focus subjects' attentions on themselves, such as a mirror, camera, or tape recorder. To produce a state of subjective self-awareness, such cues are purposefully eliminated so that subjects will focus their attention outward.

When people are in a state of objective self-awareness, they become more sensitive to the self-relevant aspects of their environments (Hull & Levy, 1979). They make more self-referent responses—using more *I*'s and *Me*'s in their statements, for example—and organize information from the perspective of its self-relevance. Because of this increased sensitivity to self-relevant information, people in a state of objective self-awareness become more conscious of the evaluative aspects of their actions. They focus on how their actions look to others and show concern for their appearance before real or imagined audiences. They observe socially appropriate standards for conduct more closely. In short, objective self-awareness creates a noticeable social perspective that individuals use to categorize and evaluate themselves (see Diener & Srull, 1979).

It is not yet clear precisely why a state of objective self-awareness produces the effects it does. Duval and Wicklund (1972) suggest that objective self-awareness generates *self-evaluation*—that is, the individual compares his or her actual behavior against ideal standards for conduct and reaches a conclusion about how well he or she is living up to them. This self-evaluation supposedly produces an *affective reaction* of either self-satisfaction or self-dissatisfaction depending on whether one's conduct meets the standards (Wicklund, 1975). Alternatively, Hull and Levy (1979) propose that objective self-awareness in and of itself does not produce a focus of attention on the self and lead to affective reactions. Instead, they suggest that it causes people to interpret and organize information from the standpoint of its self-relevance. It is not, they argue, a naturally self-evaluative and affect-producing state. Thus, Duval and Wicklund emphasize the self-evaluative and motivational properties of the state, while Hull and Levy emphasize its cognitive organizational properties. Perhaps both properties are involved.

What is clear is that, when people are in a state of objective self-awareness, their behavior becomes more socially strategic. They become sensitive to information in the environment that suggests different impression-management alternatives, and they vary their behavior to produce desired effects on others. For instance, people publicly take credit for their successes but publicly blame their failures on factors outside themselves when they are in a state of objective self-awareness (Arkin, Gabrenya, Appelman, & Cochrane, 1979; Federoff & Harvey, 1976). When in a state of subjective self-awareness, people don't exaggerate publicly either their credit or their lack of blame. Similarly, objectively self-aware people are more responsive to the evaluations they receive from others. They react with a stronger negative response to unfavorable feedback and with a stronger positive response to favorable feedback (Fenigstein, 1979). Thus, people's self-presentations are most responsive to making a favorable impression on audiences when a state of objective self-awareness exists.

Some people are chronically more objectively self-aware than others. Some of us spend little time thinking about how we appear to others and how they are evaluating us, while others of us spend a great deal of time in such contemplation. Indeed, there are relatively stable individual differences in the degree to which people are publicly self-conscious (see Fenigstein, 1979). It has been proposed that a "major consequence of self-consciousness is an increased concern with the presentation of self and the reactions of others to that self-presentation" (Fenigstein, 1979, p. 75). Thus, a concern for self-presentation can come about through either situational cues or a personality disposition.

People seem to be conscious of their ongoing self-presentation tactics only when they are in a state of acute or chronic objective self-awareness. It is in this state that people are most likely to focus attention on themselves as social objects and evaluate themselves from the perspective of real or imagined audiences. Their concern with the self-relevant aspects of information allows them consciously and tactically to plan, monitor, and control their actions to create desirable impressions on audiences. The meaningful implications of self-presentation actions can be thought through, and behaviors can be selected from among alternatives to maximize the reward/cost ratio in a given situation. The conscious use of self-presentation tactics seems to depend on being in a state of objective self-awareness. It is during these moments that we are most aware of our places as actors on the stage of life.

This is not to say that impression-management principles are irrelevant when people are in a state of subjective self-awareness. In this state, although people do not explicitly contemplate how their actions reflect on their identities and are not conscious of their own self-presentations, their actions still reflect on their identities. Many of the actions people carry out when in a state of subjective self-awareness reflect patterns of behavior that were successful in comparable situations in the past. Such action patterns are cued by some resemblance between the present situation and the situations in which the habits were developed (see Chapter 2). Part of the reason such habit patterns were successful in the past is that they made a desirable impression on audiences and resulted in a desirable reward/cost ratio. An action that begins as a consciously chosen impression-management tactic can subsequently be used unconsciously when a similar situation is encountered. The habits of social life often have their genesis in favorable impressions created on others.

In sum, people are most aware of the impression-management nature of their actions when they are in a state of objective self-awareness. They consciously select action alternatives for the effect they are likely to have on real or imagined audiences. People's actions seem to be best fitted to a particular situation when they are objectively self-aware. Objective self-awareness usually produces actions that appear to be instances of the conscious use of impression management. Nonetheless, impression-management principles are still relevant when people are subjectively self-aware. Many of the actions people then employ reflect impression-management habits developed over a lifetime. The actions may not be ideally fitted to the specific demands of the situation, since it is likely to differ somewhat from the situations in which the habits were developed. The actions may not have obvious impression-management implications. But many of the habits of social life took their original form because of their success in achieving impression-management goals.

INDIVIDUAL DIFFERENCES IN IMPRESSION MANAGEMENT

It is a commonplace to say that people are not all the same. In identical situations, some people are highly concerned with how they appear to audiences—they are publicly self-conscious—while others seem relatively unconcerned. In addition, some people monitor and control their own actions carefully, considering the impact each gesture is likely to have on an audience, while other people don't seem to pay much attention to such considerations. Some people are good at manipulating others and often able to get their way, while others are ineffective. Such individual differences are the stuff that makes life interesting and somewhat unpredictable. In this section we'll examine some of the most important individual differences that work on impression management has revealed.

Self-Monitoring

Effectively conveying an intended impression to others requires controlling and synchronizing a variety of verbal and nonverbal actions. Words, gestures, intonation, and movements must mesh to form a consistent picture; otherwise, the intended self-presentation breaks into a number of inconsistent parts. The supervisor who tries to appear self-confident, for example, will be laughed at behind her back if her hands tremble and her voice cracks when giving an order. It often escapes people's attention that they are conveying information to audiences that contradicts the impressions they want to create. They concentrate on a few channels of communication, such as the specific words they mean to speak, and ignore others, such as nonverbal actions. Audiences are sensitive to such discrepancies and often look for subtle cues that give the actor away and reveal the "real truth" (Goffman, 1959).

Some individuals are better than others at controlling and synchronizing their expressive behaviors. Actors and politicians are in professions that place a premium on effective self-presentation. For example, Fiorello LaGuardia, the popular mayor of New York, was highly skilled in expression and thus adept at controlling the images he conveyed to others. When giving a speech, he invariably left the impression that he was of the same background as whatever ethnic group he happened to be addressing (Snyder, 1974). Other people, of course, may be poor actors and may have difficulty communicating even the simplest of images.

Mark Snyder (1974) brought attention to individual differences that exist in the ability to monitor and control one's expressive behaviors. He proposed that people differ in their self-monitoring ability. "The self-monitoring individual is one who, out of a concern for social appropriateness, is particularly sensitive to the expression and self-presentation of others in social situations and uses these cues as guidelines for monitoring his own self-presentation" (Snyder, 1974, p. 528). In short, a self-monitoring individual is one who is sensitive to what others want and has the ability to control his or her own actions to present a desired identity.

Snyder developed a self-report scale to measure self-monitoring.

The scale consists of 25 items that tap various facets of self-monitoring ability, including

> (a) a concern for the social appropriateness of one's self-presentation (e.g., "At parties and social gatherings, I do not attempt to do or say things that others will like"); (b) attention to social comparison information as cues to appropriate self-expression (e.g., "When I am uncertain how to act in social situations, I look to the behavior of others for cues"); (c) the ability to control and modify one's self-presentation and expressive behavior (e.g., "I can look anyone in the eye and tell a lie with a straight face [if for the right end]"); (d) the use of this ability in particular situations (e.g., "I may deceive people by being friendly when I really dislike them"); and (e) the extent to which the respondent's expressive behavior and self-presentation is cross situationally consistent or variable (e.g., "In different situations and with different people, I often act like very different persons") [Snyder, 1974, p. 529].

People in professions or groups that are known to be good or poor actors score differently on the scale, attesting to its validity (Snyder, 1974). Dramatic actors score higher than average. In contrast, patients in psychiatric wards score lower than average, suggesting their inability to mesh their own actions with situational demands. Moreover, people who score higher on the scale are perceived differently by their friends. High self-monitors are rated by their peers as more highly skilled at controlling and modifying their social behaviors and emotional expressions to suit the situation (Snyder, 1974). Interestingly, high self-monitors are not perceived by peers as any more or less ingratiating or attractive than low self-monitors.

High self-monitors seem to possess both the *ability* to successfully control their expressive behaviors and the *motivation* to seek out and use cues that indicate what is socially appropriate. As far as ability is concerned, it has been found that high self-monitors are better able to communicate emotions accurately on demand even when they don't feel a particular way (Snyder, 1974). Thus, a high self-monitor can more easily feign being angry, sad, happy, surprised, fearful, or guilty. As far as motivation is concerned, high self-monitors are more attentive to social-comparison information; they look to audiences to provide cues about what they should do in a particular situation (Snyder, 1974). In fact, it has been suggested that high self-monitors "may be habitually more concerned with making accurate predictions about their social environment" (Berscheid, Graziano, Monson, & Dermer, 1976, p. 988). High self-monitors want to know what is happening around them socially; they attend to and utilize the information they find.

This attention to social information is exemplified in a study by Snyder and Monson (1975). They had subjects participate in a videotaped discussion group. Half the subjects were informed that the videotape would be played back to members of the group, thus making the group's reactions to their behavior salient. The remaining subjects were told that the videotape would be played back to other undergraduate students in their classes, thus making their peers' reactions to their behavior salient. People concerned with how audiences react to their behavior should take such information into account and vary their behavior to create the best impression possible. When the group is salient, they should want to appear likable and agreeable, exhibiting a relatively high amount of conformity to the others' opinions. But when their peers are salient, they should want to appear autonomous and independent, exhibiting relatively little conformity to the group members' opinions. High self-monitors did precisely this, conforming when the group was salient and remaining independent when their peers were salient. Low self-monitors did not vary their behavior on the basis of these cues; they exhibited the same moderate amount of conformity or independence irrespective of which audience was salient. Other studies also suggest that high self-monitors are better at controlling their behaviors for impression-management purposes (see Arkin et al., 1979; Miller & Schlenker, 1978). That is, if one tactically considers what behavior is most likely to create the most favorable impression on a particular real audience and then places high and low self-monitors in the situation, the high self-monitors are most likely to behave in the tactical fashion. Thus, not only are high self-monitors more skilled in the arts of impression management, they practice them more.

The high self-monitor's adroitness at fitting social behaviors to appropriate situations has a side effect: high self-monitors are less consistent over time in their behavior than low self-monitors. High self-monitors are constantly adapting their behaviors to the particular situation, thus presenting themselves in different ways, while low self-monitors are more likely to express their private beliefs irrespective of the situation. Low self-monitors exhibit a high correspondence between their private attitudes and their subsequent behaviors, while high self-monitors exhibit little correspondence (Snyder & Swann, 1976; Snyder & Tanke, 1976). Similarly, low self-monitors usually describe themselves in a way consistent with their chronic self-esteem; those with low self-esteem, in a self-deprecating way; and those with high self-esteem, in a self-enhancing way (McCown, 1978). High self-monitors, though, sometimes present themselves in a way that is discrepant with their level of self-esteem if it is to their advantage. Thus, depending on one's values, high self-monitoring can be viewed as a virtue or a vice. On one hand, the high self-monitor is more adaptable in social interactions. But the adaptability often comes at the expense of personal consistency.

Finally, high self-monitors seem better able to spot when other people are using ingratiating tactics (Jones & Baumeister, 1976). Since high self-monitors are more sensitive to social cues and adept at playing to an audience, it should not be too surprising that they are also able to tell when others are doing the same. Interestingly, high self-monitors seem to react more negatively to suspected ingratiators than do low self-monitors (Jones & Baumeister, 1976). Perhaps they dislike in others what they see in themselves.

Needs for Social Approval

Some people care more about receiving the approval of audiences than others do. The predilection to seek approval is measured by the Social Desirability Scale (Crowne & Marlow, 1964). The scale consists of two kinds of statements. The first are statements that people would like to be true about themselves but that are false of almost everyone—for example, "Before voting, I thoroughly investigate the qualifications of all the candidates." "I never hesitate to go out of my way to help someone in trouble." "I'm always willing to admit it when I make a mistake." The second kind are statements that people would like to be false about themselves but that are true of almost everyone—for example, "I sometimes feel resentful when I don't get my way." People who answer the items in the socially approved way instead of by expressing the "truth" are categorized as having high needs to gain social approval.

People who have a high need for social approval seem to be more desirous of being accepted by others and also more fearful that they will be rejected. This combination of hope and fear produces some paradoxical behaviors. On one hand, those who score high in the need for approval conform more in groups, exhibit less overt hostility after they have been insulted, and are less likely to speak dirty words in a situation where they do not seem called for. On the other hand, those in this group spend much of their time alone, do not go out of their way to make friends, are not very conversational, and are not perceived by others as being as friendly (Crowne & Marlowe, 1964). Furthermore, they are not as skilled in conveying interpersonal information accurately. For example, they cannot produce on demand convincing demonstrations that they are happy, sad, and so forth (Zaidel & Mehrabian, 1969). They also seem to be more defensive; they are particularly likely to seek approval after failure by describing themselves in glowing terms (Schneider & Turkat, 1975) or by privately rejecting the negative evaluations of others (Crowne & Marlowe, 1964).

The composite picture of the high-need-for-approval individual is of someone who badly wants to be liked yet lacks the confidence, assertiveness, and skill to make the most of social situations. The same desire to be liked that produces conformity when a person is in a social situation also generates the fear of rejection that drives him or her away from more complete participation with others. "The high-need-for-approval individual has learned that conformity, submission, and the normative anchoring of his behavior entail the fewest risks of social rejection and threats to self-esteem. His self-justification and attempts to validate his own self-worth seem to represent defensive efforts to cope with antici- pated failure" (Crowne & Marlowe, 1964). As one might expect, the need for social approval does not seem strongly related to self-monitoring (Snyder, 1974). Although high self-monitors often want to gain the ap- proval of audiences, they are skilled at social interaction and adept at creating the "right" impression.

Machiavellianism

For centuries Niccolò Machiavelli's name has been associated with the guileful use of power and manipulatory tactics. Machiavelli (1469– 1527) began his career as a minor official in the Florentine government in Italy. When the Medicis rose to power, he was accused of complicity in a plot against the new rulers and banished to the countryside. With time on his hands, impelled by impending poverty and a desire to reenter the political sphere, he turned to writing. *The Prince* (1513/ 1966), his magnum opus on the arts of power, was dedicated to Lorenzo the Magnificent in the hope of winning favor with the Medicis. He did not succeed in accomplishing that goal, but his work has become famous—many would say infamous.

To Machiavelli, the political and interpersonal worlds revolved around the use of power (see also Russell, 1945), which he considered necessary to accomplish any political goal. If right prevailed, it was only because the side that advocated it had more power than its adver- saries. The first and foremost rule for a leader is to achieve and hold power at all costs. Therefore, Machiavelli proposed that political ac- tions should be free of moral considerations. Neither morality nor im- morality should enter into a leader's calculations, because the worth of an action should be judged only in terms of the needs of the state. The end always justifies the means. He went on to assert that a leader should not be "morally good," otherwise he would perish. He must be cunning, for instance, keeping his word only when it is to his advantage to do so.

Since power often depends on the opinions of others and their opinions are shaped by propaganda, it follows that it is necessary to appear to be more virtuous than one's adversary. A leader should dis- guise his amoral character, since to appear unscrupulous is a disadvan- tage. Machiavelli emphasized the importance of this point: "The mob is always impressed by appearances and results; and the world is com- posed of the mob" (p. 64). "All men will see what you seem to be; only a few will know what you are, and those few will not dare oppose the many who have the majesty of the state on their side to defend them" (p. 63). His book is a treatise on the amoral use of power and impression management to serve the ends of a leader.

To many, Machiavelli's precepts are appalling, cynical, and hypocritical—unworthy of credence by a civilized society. (In his defense, he has been viewed as a "disappointed romantic" who was only trying to help his country through a difficult period [Russell, 1945, p. 511].) Yet, there is little doubt that many believe the same sorts of things he did. Even those who castigate him as immoral sometimes find themselves behaving in ways that Machiavelli would have applauded. Indeed, many past and present leaders seem to have taken his advice to heart.

Richard Christie (Christie & Geis, 1968, 1970a) became fascinated with the Machiavellian character and developed a scale to classify people according to the degree to which they accept basic Machiavellian precepts. The scale includes statements taken directly from Machiavelli's writings as well as those that Christie made up: "The best way to handle people is to tell them what they want to hear." "Anyone who completely trusts anyone is asking for trouble." "Never tell anyone the real reason you did something unless it is useful to do so." Interestingly, the items taken directly from *The Prince* did a better job discriminating subjects high in Machiavellianism than the items Christie made up to appeal to his Machiavellian contemporaries.

The Machiavellian character consists of a constellation of attributes. People who score high on the scale are more distrustful of and hostile toward others, and they have a more negative view of people in general. As might be expected, they receive low scores on measures of trustworthiness and altruism, and they tend to stereotype other people on the basis of race. Machiavellians' unflattering views of others also seem to extend to themselves. They are more likely to endorse socially undesirable statements about themselves and score lower on measures of self-esteem. Perhaps Machiavellians simply are more honest about themselves; perhaps they are more cynical in general; perhaps their disparaging view of the world causes them to disrespect themselves. Whatever the cause, Machiavellianism does not seem to be related to any type of clinical psychopathological tendencies.

The Machiavellian character cuts across many types of backgrounds. No relationships have been found between Machiavellianism scores and IQ, education level, or the education or occupation level of one's parents. Nor is Machiavellianism related to being a Republican or a Democrat. However, Machiavellianism is higher among people who come from large urban areas and is quite prevalent in White male college students. It increases with the age of the respondent, exhibiting a noticeable jump during the first year in high school, but decreases as people become much older. The cynicism of many youths may be a factor in the higher Machiavellianism scores around the high school and college years.

Upbringing is an important factor in the development of Machiavellianism. Kraut and Price (1976) found that sixth-grade children whose parents score high on the Machiavellianism scale are more successful at deceiving others, although they are no better or worse at being able to see through other children's attempts at deception. They also found a positive relationship between a father's Machiavellianism score and those of his children.

Machiavellians are more successful in accomplishing their goals in many competitive, achievement-oriented situations. They "have greater success in meeting the demands of American society—including getting ahead in college" (Christie & Geis, 1968, p. 972). Yet this success comes at a price: Machiavellians display higher anxiety than the average person. Managers in one large company also reported greater job strain and less job satisfaction if they scored high on the scale (Gemmill & Heisler, 1972). Their more cynical, critical perspective and lack of trust for superiors and subordinates probably contributes to these feelings. Machiavellian managers also felt that the company permitted them less opportunity for formal control. Machiavellians do not seem to feel confident of their ability to succeed solely through traditional channels, virtues, or solid accomplishments; they may feel compelled to manipulate others in order to achieve their objectives (Solar & Bruehl, 1971).

There is little question about the Machiavellians' success at interpersonal influence. Machiavellians do better than the average person when placed in a competitive situation, such as a bargaining game, where interpersonal influence can affect the outcome (see Christie & Geis, 1970b; Geis, 1970a). In one study, subjects were placed in three-person groups composed of one high on the Machiavellianism scale, one intermediate, and one low (Christie & Geis, 1970b). They then had to bargain about the best way to split $10 between them. Those who scored high took home an average of $5.57; those who scored intermediate took home $3.14; and those who scored low left with a paltry $1.29. In group situations, Machiavellians are the dominant persons, behaving decisively and being sought-after by other members (Geis, 1970b).

Machiavellians are also adept at resisting the influence of others, at least when it is to their advantage to do so (Geis & Christie, 1970). They find ways to circumvent complying with another's requests and persuasion. When the situation calls for it, though, Machiavellians can appear to be quite emotionally attached to others and deferential. Male subjects in one study were instructed to get a female subject to go to a party with them (Blumstein, 1973). The female, meanwhile, was instructed to remain aloof, act as if she were popular, and try to find out whether the man was really the type of person she would like. Males who scored high on the Machiavellianism scale displayed behaviors that appeared to show greater interdependence and bonding between themselves and the female. They were also more deferential and ingratiating, displayed a greater need for help and support, and were quite willing to assume whatever role the female tried to altercast them into. Thus, when the female seemed to want to get her own way, they let her—after all, their goal was to get her to say yes to the date.

Part of the reason for the Machiavellians' success at interpersonal manipulation can be traced to their detached, cognitive orientation toward interpersonal situations. They can coolly calculate and assess strategic and tactical possibilities. Other people, by contrast, often let their emotions get in the way of their success (Geis & Christie, 1970). For example, when people debate an issue that is relatively neutral and uninvolving like the merits of a new postage stamp, those who score low on the Machiavellianism scale do just as well as those who score high. Everyone can approach such issues cool and detached and map out the possibilities. However, when debating an issue about which people really care, like instituting universal military conscription, those who score high on the Machiavellianism scale outperform those who score low (Geis, Weinheimer, & Berger, 1970). Machiavellians can put their personal emotional reactions aside and concentrate on "winning the battle."

Another reason for the Machiavellians' success is their willingness to employ devious tactics that others condemn. Machiavellians are not averse to cheating, lying, or stealing if it is in their best interests (see Bogart, Geis, Levy, & Zimbardo, 1970; Exline, Thibaut, Hickey, & Gumbert, 1970; Geis, Christie, & Nelson, 1970; Harrell & Hartnagel, 1976). The "in their best interests" restriction is important; Machiavellians will not display such socially inappropriate behavior if the potential gains are minimal or if there is a high probability of being caught. Thus, Machiavellians cheat less than the average person when justification is minimal, but much more than average when justification is high (Bogart et al., 1970). Further, when Machiavellians are accused of cheating on a test, they look their interrogator in the eye more while denying their guilt, ultimately confess less to the crime, and tell lies that are rated more plausible by onlookers (Exline et al., 1970).

The detachment, deception, manipulation, and ultimate success of Machiavellians in getting their way in interpersonal interactions begin to take form at an early age. Braginsky (1970) examined the manipulative tactics used by fifth-grade (10 year old) children who were categorized as being high or low in Machiavellianism. To provide the children with the opportunity to employ whatever manipulative skills they had developed, a cover story was concocted. The experimenter pretended to be a home economist employed by a cracker company that was having children taste a new product. Each child was given a cracker to taste. The crackers had actually been soaked in quinine to make them taste bitter. After the child tasted the cracker, the experimenter said "So far no one has eaten very many of these crackers, and I guess you can see why. But it's really important to us to know how these crackers taste after someone has eaten a few of them." She then said that she would pay the child five cents for each cracker the child persuaded a classmate to eat. Machiavellian boys and girls were both quite successful: they got classmates to eat more than twice as many crackers as did the non-Machiavellian children. The Machiavellian children were also quite adept at using lies to persuade their classmates. Boys and girls told different types of lies. Machiavellian boys used more lies of commission; that is, they distorted or twisted information. Machiavellian girls told more lies of omission; that is, they conveniently changed the subject when asked specific, potentially damaging questions by their target. Thus, the girls chose more subtle, evasive tactics than the boys, who met questions head on with untruths. Onlookers rated the Machiavellian children as seeming more honest, comfortable, innocent, effective, and successful than the non-Machiavellian children. The little Machiavellians not only got their way but looked good doing it.

In sum, the Machiavellians' success in interpersonal endeavors seems to be traceable to these dispositional characteristics: ability to initiate and control the structure of interaction; ability to resist social influence when it is to their advantage; orientation toward a detached, cognitive assessment of the situation; and willingness to employ "unethical" methods to achieve goals. As these factors suggest, certain situations are ideally suited for Machiavellians and will result in the greatest difference between their behaviors and those of other people. Machiavellians excel in face-to-face situations where they are permitted some latitude in the types of behaviors they can use and where other people are likely to be distracted by emotional considerations (Geis & Christie, 1970). In situations that do not contain these characteristics, there may be little or no difference between what Machiavellians and other people do and accomplish.

Some of the People Most of the Time and Most of the People Some of the Time

As we've seen, there are individual differences relevant to impression management. It would not be sound, however, to draw from this the conclusion that only certain types of people engage in self-presentation and are concerned about the images they convey to others. In one or another situation, everyone engages in impression management, monitors and controls behaviors, craves approval, or acts in a Machiavellian fashion. True, some people exhibit such patterns much of the time. But what is true for some of the people most of the time is also true for everyone some of the time.

SUMMARY

The self-concept is a theory that people construct about themselves. It helps us maintain a favorable reward/cost ratio in life, organize self-relevant facts and experiences, and perhaps maintain self-esteem. Although the self-concept originally emerges from our experiences, it can also influence subsequent experiences. Our self-constructs (categorizations of ourselves) affect what we notice about ourselves, how we interpret it, how we respond to it, and what we expect to be able to accomplish.

The self-concept develops from social experience. Infants learn that their own actions influence the actions of others and that the actions of others can be directed at them to reflect, as from a looking glass, something about them. Later, children place themselves in the roles of other people and come to view themselves as others might. They anticipate what effect their own behaviors will have on others and how others will categorize and evaluate them. We learn early in life to control our own actions and the impressions they might form on others and, in so doing, to control the outcomes we receive from social life.

Research demonstrates the importance of social experience in influencing the self-concept. From studies of self-recognition in the great apes to studies of how people view themselves and are viewed by others, the evidence consistently points to the conclusion that our self-concepts derive from our social experiences. Our self-appraisals are directly influenced by the reflected appraisals of significant others and by our appraisals of our attributes in comparison to those of others.

Social identity means how people are defined and regarded in interactions. As such, it is a theory we either hold about ourselves (our perceptions of our own identity) or about others (our perceptions of the identities of other people). One's perceptions of one's own identity are part of one's larger self-concept. People attempt to influence the identities they project to others through impression-management tactics. A person who categorizes herself as attractive, friendly, and forceful is likely to behave in ways that convey these impressions. Altercasting means trying to cast another into a particular identity, thus indirectly influencing his or her identity in the relationship. Of course, not all attempts to establish particular identities are successful. By identity bargaining, participants in interactions negotiate the identities each will have.

People are conscious of themselves and their identities when they are in a state of objective self-awareness. They are then most sensitive to self-relevant information, and they categorize and evaluate themselves from a social perspective. In such a state people seem to be most conscious of their self-presentations and seem to use impression management in a deliberate, tactical fashion. At other times, people are subjectively self-aware; they attend to what is happening around them and are less concerned with self-relevant information and evaluation. In such a state it is the unconscious habits of impression management that take over. Some people are more publicly self-conscious than others. These chronic personality differences mean that some people show more concern with how they appear to others.

There are other personality variables that have been studied in the context of impression management: self-monitoring, the need for approval, and Machiavellianism. A self-monitoring individual is one who is sensitive to what others want and has the ability to control his or her actions to present a desired identity. Self-monitors are better actors and are more skillful in the arts of impression management.

People who have high need for approval are desirous of being accepted by others, but they also have a great fear of rejection. Thus, they conform more in groups in the hope of pleasing others but also tend to be defensive and afraid to participate in social interaction. Thus they end up being viewed as less friendly.

Machiavellianism is a personality constellation that describes people who view others as pawns. Machiavellians are distrustful of and hostile toward others. They take a cool, detached view of interactions, not allowing their emotions to interfere with their goals. Machiavellians are very successful in manipulating others and reaching their goals, and they do not hesitate to use tactics such as lying, cheating, and stealing. They are particularly likely to get their way in face-to-face situations where they have some latitude in the types of actions they can employ and where other people are likely to be distracted by emotional and ethical considerations. These personality variables indicate that some people are more concerned with and successful at impression management than others. But what is true of these types most of the time is true of most people some of the time. Sometimes we all feel self-conscious, need social approval, monitor and control our own actions, or act in a Machiavellian fashion.

FOUR

For such is the nature of men that howsoever they may acknowledge many others to be more witty, or more eloquent, or more learned, yet they will hardly believe there be many so wise as themselves.

Thomas Hobbes

Other men's sins are before our eyes; our own are behind our back.

Seneca

Nature has given us pride to spare us the pain of being conscious of our own imperfections.

Duc François de La Rochefoucauld

THE SELF IN SOCIAL INTERACTION: CONSTRUCTING PERSONAL REALITIES THROUGH ASSOCIATION

Commentators on human nature often point out that people think of themselves in ways that maximize their desirable attributes and minimize the rest. We see our good points but not our bad and value our own accomplishments more than similar ones of others. We take credit for our achievements but shift the blame for failures to others or to the situation. We label our own behaviors positively and the same behaviors of others negatively: "I am frugal; he is miserly." In short, people seem to construct personal realities biased in their own favor, sometimes pushing objective reality to its limits in doing so. Hitler, for example, once proclaimed "The work that Christ started but could not finish, I—Adolf Hitler—will conclude" (Toland, 1977, p. 302). In this chapter we'll explore how people select and deal with self-relevant information to influence the images that they form of themselves and convey to others.

NEEDS FOR SELF-ESTEEM

Why do people often seem to bias and control information in self-serving ways? One of the most common answers is that we have a need to maintain or enhance our self-esteem (Hall & Lindzey, 1978; Wells & Marwell, 1976). In other words, people desire to think well of themselves and their actions. To some theorists, these needs create self-serving motivational pressures that "bias" or "distort" people's perceptions and evaluations, of both themselves and others, allowing them to feel superior and worthwhile.

Many theorists have asserted that the need for self-esteem is rooted in innate propensities. William James (1890/1952) believed that self-seeking—the tendency to seek honor, respect, and favorable regard from others, to care for and adorn our bodies, and to accumulate material possessions—was a "fundamental instinctive impulse" and could not be modified easily, if at all. He linked self-seeking to the innate demands of self-preservation. In underscoring the idea that self-seeking was innate rather than acquired to help people get along in the world, James stated: "The noteworthy thing about the desire to be 'recognized' by others is that its strength has so little to do with the worth of the recognition computed in sensational or rational terms" (p. 199). In a similar vein, the personologist Gordon Allport (1937) posited a built-in self-enhancement motive. He noted that people attempt to protect themselves against information that could threaten their self-esteem, and he called the defense of the ego "nature's eldest law" (p. 170).

Since self-evaluations are made relative to other people, many theorists, such as Alfred Adler, the neoFreudian psychotherapist, propose that needs for self-esteem are rooted in even more basic strivings for superiority over others. According to this view, self-evaluation depends on social comparison, and, to occupy a desirable social position, one must evaluate oneself favorably relative to particular other people

(Wells & Marwell, 1976). Such social relativity is quite compatible with symbolic-interactionist views of the nature of the self-concept.

Whether the need for self-esteem is based on innate urgings and primitive emotions is debatable. Such a hypothesis is nearly impossible to test, and the types of phenomena it explains—such as, distorting information or making self-serving statements—can also be explained in other ways. Nonetheless, the idea that the need for self-esteem has an innate basis has captured the fancy of many. It cannot be ruled out.

The Necessity for Self-Respect

Self-esteem enhancement might occur because it plays an instrumental role in establishing effective action patterns. According to psychotherapist Nathaniel Branden (1969),

> Man needs self-respect because he has to act to achieve values—and in order to act, he needs to value the beneficiary of his action. In order to seek values, man must consider himself worthy of enjoying them. In order to fight for his happiness, he must consider himself worthy of happiness [p. 107].

Self-doubt, like other forms of doubt, can lead to a paralysis of action (see Chapter 2). People who deserve nothing will attempt nothing. People who deserve to have the world at their feet just might have it there. Thus, self-esteem enhancement could be a necessary prerequisite for survival.

Personal Control

From a pragmatic perspective, one's goal in life is to function effectively, adopting action patterns that maximize rewards and minimize costs. Beyond simply valuing oneself, a person must also sense an ability to control personal actions and the environment. Beliefs in one's efficacy increase the probability that one will initiate potentially rewarding actions and persevere toward task accomplishment (Bandura, 1974; White, 1959). The necessity for effective control may influence the ways people conceptualize self-relevant events. It has been found that people attribute personal successes to self-relevant factors, such as ability and effort, but attribute personal failures to environmental factors, such as bad luck or task difficulty (see Weary Bradley, 1978). It has been hypothesized that, by doing so, they gain feelings of control over their own outcomes. They continue rewarding activities following a success, or they try again following a failure (Kelley, 1971).

As Harold Kelley (1971) put it,

> Attribution processes are to be understood not only as a means of providing the individual with a veridical view of his world, but as a means of encouraging and maintaining his effective exercise of control in that world. . . . The attributor is not simply an attributor, a seeker after knowledge. His latent goal in gaining knowledge is that of effective management of himself and his environment [p. 22].

The desire for personal control has been demonstrated in numerous attribution studies (Berscheid et al., 1976; Langer, 1975; Miller & Norman, 1975; Wortman, 1976). The necessity for feelings of personal control as prerequisites for action, then, could produce perceptions and attributions that appear to be self-serving and esteem enhancing.

SOCIAL INTERACTION AND IMPRESSION MANAGEMENT

Perceptions and actions that seem self-serving could be due to innate self-esteem needs, the necessity for self-respect, or desire for personal control. But self-serving perceptions and actions might have their genesis in the nature of the social-interaction process. It is on this process that we will concentrate.

Controlling Identities

Social interaction is characterized by interdependence. To function effectively, one must influence the attitudes and behaviors of others, attempting to guide them along the paths one wishes them to take. The identities that people establish affect how they should behave in front of others (the president can behave quite differently around the company than the janitor); how they are treated (a "nice" person is treated differently from an "obnoxious" one); and the outcomes they receive (an expert in business receives more salary, respect, and approval than a novice). Hence, by attempting to influence the impressions of oneself that others form, a person plays a role in affecting his or her social outcomes. The nature of interdependence in social life gives people a potent hedonic reason to establish and control their identities in ways that are in their best interests.

The realities that people construct through public descriptions of their perceptions, feelings, and attributes can affect the identities they establish. A person who can convince others to see her as frugal, not miserly, has a definite advantage over one who cannot. A person who convinces others to credit him for his successes but exonerate him for his failures profits from this interpretation. A person who convinces others that he should legitimately be perceived as the embodiment of

Christ-like attributes possesses power to make demands that would otherwise be unthinkable. Through public descriptions of the traits they possess, the things they are accountable for, and the ways they view the world, people can secure identities that maximize the public esteem in which they are held and the outcomes they receive.

Public Descriptions and Private Perceptions

People can and do control the impressions they create on others through their public descriptions of attributes, behaviors, and events. When people think of impression management, they usually think of outward behaviors, of the things we do to others. The very term *impression management* invokes images of falsehood and dissimulation. Yet, it is reasonable to suggest that a person might inwardly accept responsibility for a failure but tell others that he is really not responsible. Or a person might perceive herself as miserly but tell others she is frugal. In such instances, a person who naively observes the public behavior might conclude that self-serving biases colored the actor's perceptions; yet the actor's private perceptions could hardly be described as biased.

A clear conceptual distinction can thus be made between public descriptions of events and private perceptions of them, and the conditions under which these coincide is open to debate. Some have suggested that, if perceptual distortion to protect self-esteem does occur, there is no clear evidence to indicate it (Ajzen & Fishbein, 1975; Brewer, 1977; Miller & Ross, 1975; Ross, 1977). On the other hand, several researchers who originally doubted the existence of self-serving perceptual biases subsequently conducted well-controlled studies that led them to conclude that such biases do indeed exist (Miller, 1976; Sicoly & Ross, 1977). It is plausible to suggest that private perceptions follow very logical, unbiased patterns while public descriptions of those perceptions are influenced by self-presentational concerns (Forsyth & Schlenker, 1977a). Perhaps what have been called "self-esteem needs" represent nothing more than the desire to maximize social outcomes by controlling one's public esteem. A wide variety of research on attribution can be reinterpreted in terms of self-presentational processes (Weary Bradley, 1978; Weary & Arkin, in press).

On the basis of the research conducted so far, it is difficult to separate private perceptions from public descriptions, so the resolution of this issue awaits future research developments. We do know that people will vary their public descriptions to present themselves to others in desired ways, sometimes telling the truth and sometimes lying. But we do not unequivocally know that people's private perceptions follow a similarly self-serving course. Nonetheless, possible social reasons why self-serving perceptions might occur are worth considering.

Managing the Self-Image

Symbolic interactionists propose that, once people learn and digest the rules that society applies when judging behaviors, they use these "personal standards" to judge their own actions even when no one else is present. The association between doing something "good" and being rewarded, which is learned early, should produce feelings of pride, accomplishment, or virtue when one does something "good" now. This is true even if no one else is watching. The past association between doing something "bad" and being punished should produce feelings of guilt, shame, anxiety, self-doubt, or embarrassment in the same way. The socialization process makes people similar in that, to feel good about oneself, a person must believe that others feel good about him or her—at least the "significant others," living, dead, and imaginary, whom one admires and respects. To believe that one's actions would meet with praise or censure from significant others produces a pleasant or unpleasant internal state, even though no one may have seen the action or ever learn of it. A person alone on a tropical island can still feel pride at saving a crippled bird's life. A person who masters a task when no one else is watching still gains a feeling of accomplishment and wishes that only so-and-so (a significant other) had observed the success. These feelings have been learned over the course of a lifetime of socialization. Naturally, the feelings may be greater when others are watching, but the feelings still exist and can affect behavior.

In this sense, people may be concerned with managing their impressions for themselves as well as for others. Just as people manage the impressions they create on others to maximize their reward/cost ratio, so people may manipulate the images they form of themselves in order to maximize rewarding internal states and minimize punishing ones.

One way of controlling internal states is through selective attention.

> Almost limitless "good" and "bad" information about the self is potentially available (e.g., in the form of memories), depending on where one looks and how one searches. An individual can seek, and usually find, information to support his positive or negative attributes, his successes or failures, almost boundlessly. . . . By means of such selective attention the individual presumably can make himself feel either good or bad, can privately congratulate or condemn himself and, in the extreme, can generate emotions from euphoria to depression [Mischel, Ebbesen, & Zeiss, 1973].

People can also control their internal states by interpreting the information they find in self-enhancing or self-degrading ways to fit their emotional needs. A man who deeply hurt his fiancee by breaking off their engagement might think of himself as having acted rationally in the long-run best interests of both, thereby feeling good about his behavior, or as having acted selfishly and cruelly, thereby feeling bad. Thus, alternative descriptions of one's motives and attributes—different cognitive scripts—can be employed to place the same action or characteristic in different lights.

People can create Walter Mitty fantasy worlds in which a shy, meek individual is transformed into a James Bond character with the world at his feet. The line between private perceptions and public descriptions, between self-esteem and public esteem, may become thinner than is comfortable as fact and fiction merge. As Heider (1958, pp. 120–121) explained, "Since one's idea includes what 'ought to be' and 'what one would like to be' as well as 'what is,' attributions and cognitions are influenced by the mere subjective forces of needs and wishes as well as by the more objective evidence presented in the raw material" of experience. These needs and wishes may largely derive from the exigencies of social life. From an information-processing perspective, there is every reason to believe that people do display perceptual repressions and rationalizations that protect and enhance themselves (Erdelyi, 1974).

Interpreting Reality

The very terms *bias* and *distortion* may be misleading, whether one believes that self-serving biases occur or not. The terms may be rather inaccurate and might best be abandoned or used only in a limited context. Both imply that there is a "true" state of affairs that is somehow "improperly" perceived by an individual for personal reasons. For example, five observers might apply the construct "deceitful" to describe Jeff's behavior, so we assume that, if Jeff describes himself as "tactful," he must somehow be distorting his self-perceptions. Yet, no set of facts can be unequivocally described by only one construct; this point was made in personality theory by George Kelly and in physics by Albert Einstein. Constructs exist in people's minds; they are not tied to specific events or behaviors. Some constructs are better than others because they more adequately explain events or behaviors, but, after we have narrowed the possibilities to several plausible constructs on the basis of the data, the choice among them is often arbitrary. Jeff may be as "correct" as the five observers.

Reality is not so inflexible that it must be perceived in only one way. Behaviors, events, and personal characteristics can be conceptualized in different ways to create different images and impressions. Facts are given meanings by constructs, and one can always apply slightly different constructs to the same facts in order to create the impressions one wants. Two similar executives might both think of themselves as "enterprising and shrewd" and the other as "pushy and selfish." Euphemisms are also employed to change perceptions of one's job, attributes, or actions; the garbage collector becomes the "sanitation engineer" and the office runner becomes the "junior executive trainee." Similarly, a student who succeeds on a course exam finds it easy to locate the cause of the success in personal ability and effort, while one who fails can usually locate external factors that excuse the poor performance.

Some attribution theorists (for example, Bem, 1972) believe that people observe their own and others' behaviors and arrive at logical, unbiased attributions based on the behaviors and the environmental context. But attribution is not a process in which one examines an event and draws one logical, inescapable conclusion. There is never only one attribution to be made about an event or only one construct to be applied to a person. People exercise their option to sort through the attributional possibilities until one or more can be found that best serve self-interests. Is this "distortion," or is it a rather "logical" process itself?

How often have you observed a behavior (your own or another's) but not known how to interpret it? Perhaps you interpreted the behavior one way, then you read that psychologists interpret comparable behaviors as, say, manifesting ego-defense, or insecurity, or a need for achievement, and you suddenly said "That's right, that's what it is." The behavior, of course, hasn't changed, but the interpretation of it becomes "clear." Later you might read a book that interprets the behavior differently (first you read Sigmund Freud, then B. F. Skinner). You might change your original interpretation or stick with the original, depending on which seems to fit the facts best and which has the most intuitive appeal (is compatible with other constructs you hold).

People may employ particular interpretations of their behaviors because these are compatible with their existing constructs and serve their interaction goals and because they have persuaded others that the interpretation is correct. To talk of "distortion" in such cases seems rather strong, but to talk of constructing reality in ways that serve self-interests seems quite appropriate.

The complex relationship between private perceptions and public descriptions is not entirely understood. From a logical social perspective there is every reason to believe that self-serving perceptions occur, although the precise conditions under which they do have yet to be fully explored. Recognizing that no definitive conclusion has been reached about when public descriptions agree with private perceptions, we'll examine how people construct personal realities through descriptions of their perceptions, attributions, and feelings and what factors might affect this process. To do so, we'll have to explore the nature of self-relevant images, the social meanings they convey, and the concerns people have about them.

The Value of Images for the Self-Concept and Social Identity

Self-presentation involves controlling, manipulating, and influencing the images of oneself that are conveyed to others (Goffman, 1959) and—I would add—to oneself as well. Any bit of self-relevant information is potentially revealing and can contribute to the categorization and evaluation of an individual. One's perceived intentions, values, physical characteristics, job, family, abilities, possessions—each conveys an image. An *image* is a mental picture or categorization of an individual. It affects the way one is evaluated, how one has behaved, will behave, and should behave, and how one is treated in social interaction. In short, images describe the individual and how he or she fits into the social matrix. One's self-concept and social identity are composed of numerous interrelated images of oneself; each image is discrete yet part of the whole.

Many images are mutually exclusive; there can be rivalry and conflict between them. This is clearly the case when dealing with opposite sides of the same dimension; one cannot be both friendly and unfriendly at the same moment. It is also the case when it comes to different, but nonetheless related, images. As William James (1890/1952) described it,

> I am often confronted by the necessity of standing by one of my empirical selves [read "images"] and relinquishing the rest. Not that I would not, if I could, be both handsome and fat and well dressed, and a great athlete, and make a million a year, be a wit, a *bon-vivant*, and a lady-killer, as well as a philosopher; a philanthropist, statesman, warrior, and African explorer, as well as a "tone-poet" and saint. But the thing is simply impossible. The millionaire's work would run counter to the saint's; the *bon-vivant* and the philanthropist would trip each other up; the philosopher and the lady-killer could not well keep house in the same tenement of clay. Such different characters may conceivably at the outset of life be alike *possible* to a man. But to make any one of them actual, the rest must more or less be suppressed [pp. 199–200].

Thus, some sets of images go together, while other combinations would strain our credence in the component images. Of course, some people might see particular images as compatible that others see as incompatible (there are more than a few "lady-killer philosophers" lurking about).

As we've seen, any self-relevant image can be expected to produce a particular set of consequences for the individual. People who are seen as competent, loyal, motivated, attractive, and personable can rise quickly in life. Possession of these images allows them to command high salaries, respect, approval from others, and self-satisfaction. People who are seen as incompetent, disloyal, unmotivated, unattractive, and dis-agreeable can hardly expect an abundance of pleasant outcomes. *Each image or image set has a particular expected value to those who are seen as possessing it.* The expected value of an image consists of the subjective worth of the consequences that seem to be associated with possessing the image and the likelihoods that these consequences will occur. More precisely, the expected value of an image is the sum of the values of the consequences perceived as associated with the image, the value of each consequence being multiplied by the perceived probability that it will actually occur if the image is possessed.[1] George, for example, might think that if his boss views him as loyal there is a 60% chance that he will receive the $1000 raise he wants, a 90% chance that his boss will respect him, and an 80% chance that his boss will like him. The ex-pected value of that image is high, and George might try to influence the boss's impressions of his loyalty. The expected value of an image deter-mines its *attractiveness:* images with positive expected values are at-tractive to the individual, and those with negative expected values are unattractive.

Image Attractiveness: Benefits and Liabilities

The consequences of an image can be either positive or negative. Perceived positive consequences are termed *benefits,* and perceived negative consequences, *liabilities.* Benefits and liabilities include (a) outcomes received by acquiring the image and (b) behaviors as-sociated with possessing the image. *Outcomes* are the internal or exter-nal benefits and liabilities, such as money, friendship, respect, ap-proval, self-satisfaction, or anxiety, that one expects to receive by ac-quiring the image. Many images carry mixed outcomes—both benefits and liabilities. For example, an honest person might be trusted by others but also be viewed as gullible. Many criminals are negatively

---

[1]The expected value of an image can be expressed mathematically as

$$I = \sum_{i=1}^{n} b_i e_i$$

where I is the expected value of the image, b is the strength of the person's belief that certain consequences (benefits and liabilities) will be associated with the image, and e is the person's evaluation of each of these consequences (i). For a more complete discussion of decision theory and derivative expected value models in social psychology, see Fishbein and Ajzen (1975) and Lee (1971). Jones and Wortman (1973) proposed an approach to ingratiation that draws on decision theory and hence is similar in some ways to the ideas presented here.

sanctioned for their actions but are admired for their bravado—Jessie James and Bonnie & Clyde, for example.

Images give the holder a certain set of allowable behaviors. These are also consequences of possessing the image, and they comprise its prerogatives and responsibilities. *Prerogatives* are the freedoms enjoyed by acquiring the image. For example, a person with high status in a group is given many prerogatives that those of lower status don't enjoy. He can deviate from group norms with greater impunity, disagree with others without being viewed negatively, walk into a subordinate's office and make himself at home, and so on. *Responsibilities* are the behaviors a person who possesses the image should or should not exhibit. They are limitations on freedom since they require the holder to do some things and refrain from others. A company executive is expected to work hard, be loyal, perform unpleasant chores like firing incompetent employees, and so on.

The prerogatives and responsibilities that accompany particular images have certain worths to the holders. Some people evaluate the responsibilities of being an executive negatively; they don't want to perform such behaviors. Other people relish such responsibilities and evaluate them positively. As another example, many undergraduates don't go to graduate school because they don't want to fulfill its responsibilities, such as a lifetime of hard work and constant study to keep abreast of developments. It has even been found that some people will purposely fail tests to avoid being seen as a success (see Carson, 1969; Jones & Berglas, 1978). When one is seen as successful, one is expected to have future successes. Each success brings on more challenging tasks and more responsibilities. To cut short this spiral, many people fail at the start, avoid creating behavioral expectations that they don't want to fulfill, and thus retain their freedom.

As these examples suggest, the expected value of particular images varies from person to person and from situation to situation. People's personalities interact with situations to affect which consequences are perceived as associated with particular images and the value of those consequences. For example, an image of being wholesome and nice—an asset to Pat Boone's career—might spell the end of Don Rickles' career, since audiences are used to viewing him the opposite way. A college student values being seen as intelligent more than some professional wrestlers do, whose gate receipts can depend on their image as Neanderthal types. It is also true that the student wishes to be viewed as intelligent more by his professors than by seldom-seen acquaintances and that a wrestler might wish his fans and his family to view him in opposite ways. Another common example is the man who wants his wife to view him as coordinated at athletics but who, when it comes to doing household chores, does everything in his power to make her view him as clumsy. If you break enough dishes, his reasoning goes, you might not be asked to help out in the kitchen any more. Thus, the expected value of an image is quite relative; no image has the same attractiveness to all people or even to the same person at all times in all situations.

Claiming Images

People do not simply claim those images that have the highest expected values. If they did, fantasies would dominate realities. People would always view and describe themselves in their most ideal ways, unchecked by facts. Reality provides constraints on how people see and describe themselves. For one thing, people who accurately appraise their own characteristics can make reasoned decisions that maximize their reward/cost ratios. People who have either inflated or deflated views of their characteristics are likely to tackle tasks at which they are doomed to failure or avoid tasks at which they could succeed. Reality thus places a premium on "knowing thyself."

In addition, social reality provides this constraint: people are supposed to be what they claim to be. People are socialized to match their words and their deeds, and we watch others to make sure that they are being truthful. People who are caught in public lies, such as claiming they are something they are not, risk negative sanctions for the attempted deception. People must fulfill the requirements of the images they claim or risk punishment.

Requirements are those characteristics and behaviors which a holder of the image should have or be able to perform in order to claim the image legitimately. A person who claims to be physically attractive should have some such recognizable feature. A student who claims to be a mathematical genius should have done things that substantiate the claim, and he had better not fail a basic algebra test unless he wants to be laughed at. Typically, the more valuable the image is in society, the more stringent are the requirements imposed on those who claim it. Thus, it is more difficult to meet the requirements for calling oneself an M.D. than for calling oneself a garbage collector. People are not entitled to receive the benefits of a valued image until they fulfill or can fulfill its requirements or at least convince their audience—which might include themselves—that those requirements have been or can be met.

A *claim* to an image occurs when people act to associate themselves with it. People can act to claim an image through their self-descriptions and other verbal or nonverbal behaviors or through their attempts to stage a situation that makes others draw a particular conclusion. For example, Tom wants to portray himself as a college football hero. He constantly discusses football with his friends and takes every opportunity to throw in some personal reminiscence about how he won this or that game for the team. He also keeps himself in shape (it's difficult to make others believe one is an ex-football-hero if one's fat-to-muscle ratio is preposterous) and places his trophies and game balls prominently around his house. An image can also be claimed by remaining silent when other people or events associate oneself with it. For example, a friend might remark to another person in Tom's presence that "Tom here was captain of the football team in college and quite an athlete." If Tom fails to refute the remark, he has accepted the image, thereby claiming it.

Challenges are questions that arise about one's legitimate claim to an image—that is, does the person meet the image's requirements? Challenges can come either from other people or from facts. A person who claims to be a policewoman might have other people ask to see her credentials. A person who claims to be an actress might have others ask her what acting jobs she's had. A person who believes he is intelligent has to subsume numerous behaviors under that self-construct's rubric and come up with explanations for any stupid past actions that threaten the image. Life is a constant series of tests in which we are called on to substantiate our claims through personal performance or some other means. When the facts don't seem to fit the claims, people must abandon the image or provide some explanation for the discrepancy sufficient to satisfy the audience—again the audience may include oneself.

Images are *successfully claimed* when they are (a) claimed and not challenged or (b) claimed, and the actor can produce documentation or an explanation that withstands challenge. Since life is a series of tests, it is rare for an image claim to go unchallenged for long. A challenge might not occur during relatively brief encounters with others whom we never expect to see again, such as a stranger on an airplane to whom one might feel free to brag shamelessly. A challenge might not be perceived by a person who had developed the technique of psychological repression to an extreme—such people fail to acknowledge events that challenge the claims they make and hence never question themselves about whether they really are what they say they are. Aside from such exceptions, challenges arise continually.

One implication of continual challenges is that people who really are what they say they are—that is—meet the requirements of the images they claim—will be highly successful in avoiding embarrassing situations. They will also be less anxious, since they don't have to worry about possible challenges nor how they will substantiate their claims. They will also be relatively effective in making decisions about what they can realistically accomplish. People who claim to be what they are not will sooner or later fail to meet a challenge, and their façades will crumble, causing embarrassment and possibly negative social sanctions. They may also experience anxiety about challenges that they know they can't meet. Worse, if they privately believe that they are really something they are not, they are likely to make decisions that fail to maximize their reward/cost ratio, such as tackling tasks at which they can't possibly succeed or avoiding tasks at which they could.

A good "con man"—one who has the gift of persuasion and a convincing set of explanations for discrepancies between his image and reality—might fool others for a long time. He might never be caught. But if enough challenges occur, the odds are that his illegitimate identity will be repudiated sooner or later. Thus, people who meet the requirements for the images they claim are most likely to maintain effective interaction patterns in the long run and experience a greater sense of personal security and satisfaction.

"Be true to yourself." "Don't play a role." "Don't try to be something you're not." "Get in touch with your own self." "Know thyself and act accordingly." These all translate as "Act in ways that make only those claims that can definitely withstand challenges." Claiming to be what one is not, then failing to match one's words with deeds, produces negative reactions in others and usually in oneself.

When an image claim is repudiated because the actor can't fulfill the requirements, he or she loses all the benefits of the image. If an unsuccessful claim is perceived as only a minor error in judgment ("I thought I was an 'A' student but now have to admit I'm only a 'B' student") and is recognized as such by the actor, little harm is done. Although the actor may experience some embarrassment and disappointment, people tend to be forgiving about such minor inaccuracies. But if an unsuccessful claim is perceived as a flagrant attempt to deceive, particularly if to obtain personal gain, the actor is likely to receive severe negative sanctions. People whose claimed images are repudiated might feel extreme embarrassment, shame, or guilt; feel they have failed to live up to their moral code; be ridiculed or ostracized; or be perceived as a liar, as untrustworthy, or as out of touch with reality. If the violation is sufficiently flagrant, they may even be confined to prison (if impersonating a police officer) or a mental hospital (if claiming to be God). Thus, inaccurate and repudiated claims to images can lead to internal and external punishments and to negative sanctions.

We can thus distinguish between the *expected value of an image* and the *expected value of a personal claim to an image.* The former is the expected worth of an image if it is successfully claimed; it is what the person believes it would mean to have the image of being intelligent, sexy, rich, popular, or whatever. Those images that have the highest expected values are our ideal images—the ways we wish we were and would like to be. The *expected value of a personal claim to an image,* though, is the expected worth of what the person believes would happen by claiming the image. To claim to be an expert could produce benefits if the claim were successful, but to claim expertise and have others scoff because the claim can't be substantiated would be costly.

The expected value of a claim to an image, then, consists of three factors: (a) the expected value of the image, (b) the perceived probability that one can successfully claim the image (or its inverse, the perceived probability that the claim will be unsuccessful), and (c) the expected value of the sanctions for an unsuccessful claim, which is usually a negative quantity since such sanctions are aversive for most people. We should expect that if each of the other factors were held constant, the expected value of claiming an image would increase as (a) the expected value of the image increases (for example, the actor believes that the image would impress an audience); (b) the probability of a successful claim increases (for example, the actor believes she can persuade the audience, or she personally knows of no contradictory information and much supporting information); and (c) the expected value of sanctions for an unsuccessful claim decreases (for example, the actor believes that the audience is kind and supportive and will not notice or punish a repudiated claim). More specifically, the expected value of claiming an image is the sum of the following: the probability that the claim will be successful multiplied by the expected value of the image, plus the probability that the claim will be unsuccessful multiplied by the expected value of the sanctions.[2]

It is hypothesized that the expected value of claims to images is what allows us to predict people's relevant behaviors, both in public and in private. People seem to claim those images from mutually exclusive image sets that have the highest expected values for image claims. For the sake of brevity, we will call images that have positive expected values for claims *desirable images;* those with negative expected values for claims we will call *undesirable images.* People claim desirable images and avoid claiming undesirable ones.[3]

[2]The expected value for claiming an image can be expressed mathematically as

$$IC = p(I) + (1 - p)S$$

where IC is the expected value of claiming an image, p is the probability that one can successfully claim the image, I is the expected value of the image, and S is the expected value of the negative sanctions associated with an unsuccessful claim. S can be expressed as

$$S = \sum_{i=1}^{n} (ps_i)(es_i)$$

where ps_i is the probability that a particular sanction will occur and es_i is the value of the sanction. Sanctions can be both external, such as the consequences of being seen as a liar, being reprimanded, or making incorrect decisions and internal, such as the consequences of feeling embarrassed, viewing oneself as a liar, or feeling like a failure.

[3]It is worth noting that this same formulation can be extended to cover *any* of our beliefs, not just ones that are self-relevant. Any belief has a certain *attractiveness* (expected value *if it is true*) to the holder, and it has a certain *perceived probability of being true*. It also has a certain *perceived probability of being false* and, if it is false, a number of *aversive consequences* (the expected value of the negative sanctions for holding and acting on an incorrect belief) could befall the holder. Whether the topic of one's belief is God, a political candidate, or a social issue, the same fundamental concerns apply. People should endorse those beliefs that maximize the expected value for believing a particular thing.

This same formulation should operate in private (without the presence of a real audience) to affect our perceptions and attributions about ourselves and in public (in the presence of a real audience) to affect our self-relevant descriptions. That is, we should find that our private claims of what we are depend on how we fill in each of the values in the equation when we are alone. Our public claims of what we are should depend upon how we fill in each of the values in the equation when we are in the presence of a real audience. People's private self-perceptions are *fundamentally* no different from their public self-descriptions, since both are described by the same basic formula. What is likely to differ between the private and the public are the values that are put into the formula. For instance, a person privately might view a particular image as only moderately valuable (say, +5) but recognize that a salient real audience values it very much (say, +10). She then should be more likely to claim the image in public in order to impress the audience than to use it privately to describe herself to herself. Or a person privately might think that a particular image really describes him (say, with a probability of 80%) but believe that he could never convince a particular real audience that it does (he thinks there is perhaps only a 30% probability that this audience would accept his claim to the image). He then should be more likely to claim the image privately than publicly. In other situations the reverse can be true: a person might value an image more privately than publicly or believe that a real audience is uncritical and likely to accept an image that the person privately believes is false. In still other situations, a person's private and public calculations might correspond perfectly, leaving no difference between private beliefs and public pronouncements.

The formulation above allows predictions of how people think of themselves privately and how they describe themselves publicly, and it indicates when private perceptions and public descriptions are likely to correspond and when not. To the degree that being alone (private), as opposed to being with a particular real audience (public), does not affect how one computes each of the factors in the formulation, private perceptions and public descriptions should correspond; to the degree that the private/public dimension is involved in one's calculation of these factors, private perceptions and public descriptions should differ.

THE SELF-CONCEPT AND IMAGE CLAIMS

It is now time to be more explicit about how the self-concept affects people's claims to images, both privately and publicly. There are at least six ways in which it can do so; in explaining these I will draw on ideas in the previous chapter. First, the self-concept affects people's sensitivity to information—that is, it partly determines what types of things people attend to. People are more likely to notice information that is relevant to one of their self-constructs (Markus, 1977). Once information is noticed, it can be used to guide behavior in the particular situation. For example, a person who views herself as independent rather than conforming should be likely to notice the smallest bit of information relevant to her claim, and then she can deal with it to strengthen or protect her claim to the image. Thus, if she just agreed three times with the opinions expressed by another person, she should notice it and might attempt to support her claim to independence by commenting "Isn't it a coincidence that we happen to have so many similar opinions?" If she did not categorize herself as being at a particular point along the independence/conformity dimension, she might not have noticed the implications of agreeing with the other person. Any claim to an image, private or public, should produce an increased sensitivity to relevant information. Thus, a person who publicly claims to be independent even though she doesn't privately believe it also should be likely to notice relevant information, since she must use it to defend her public claims. Whether people are more sensitive to information when it is claimed privately than only publicly is not yet clear, but it is certainly plausible.

Second, the self-concept affects how people privately interpret information that they do notice. People interpret information in ways that make it more consistent with existing self-constructs, and they tend to resist information that is inconsistent (Markus, 1977). Thus, in the preceding example, the person who viewed herself as independent tried to interpret her actions in a way that made them consistent with her self-construct. The more ambiguous the information is, the more likely it is to be interpreted consistently with existing self-constructs—private image claims—and with existing public claims to images as well. Thus, a person who privately views herself as a conformist but publicly claims to be independent should try to convince others that when she agrees with them it is merely a coincidence. Even though she should not privately believe her explanation, she might be able to convince a real audience of it.

Third, the self-concept affects people's recall of information. People are more likely to recall information that is consistent with their self-constructs (Markus, 1977). The self-concept provides an organizational framework for information, and information that fits into the framework is better integrated and better recalled. Thus, a person who privately categorizes himself as independent should be better able to recall past events that support that image and therefore be better able to withstand challenges to the image. Similarly, once people have publicly claimed a particular image, they should be better able to recall relevant information that is processed after their claim.

Fourth, the self-concept affects the expected value people place on particular images; it affects an image's attractiveness. People tend to overvalue images they believe they possess and undervalue ones they believe they don't possess (Rosenberg, 1968). Thus, a person who views herself as independent will evaluate independence more positively than someone who does not. As we've seen, the attractiveness of a particular image partially determines how likely people are to claim it. All else equal, a person who privately claims a particular image should view it as more desirable and be more likely to claim it publicly.

Fifth, the self-concept affects the probability that people believe they can successfully claim particular images, both privately and publicly. By definition, if an image already is part of a person's self-concept, the person is privately claiming it with some certainty. Going beyond this truism, we can say that people's existing self-concepts play a part in affecting claims to new images. Some images, more general and inclusive than others, subsume numerous specific images. For example, the image of being a good athlete subsumes images that pertain both to attributes (being coordinated) and to achievements (being a good tennis player, baseball player, swimmer). Images have implications for claims to other images that either overlap with them or are wholly or partially subsumed by them. Thus, it is difficult to conceive of a poor athlete who happens to be a superb tennis player, or of a good athlete who would not be good at tennis given sufficient practice. The implications that images have for other images show why William James was correct when he noted that the "millionaire's work would run counter to the saint's."

Images already contained in the self-concept affect people's expectations of whether they can successfully claim other, implied images. People who already claim an image such as being a good athlete should attach a high probability to being able to claim images that are implied but which they may not have thought of before, such as being dexterous or being capable of playing tennis well. Because these new images are implied by the old, we are more likely to believe that they won't be challenged or will at least be able to withstand challenges. All else equal, the higher the perceived probability that a claim will be successful, the greater the likelihood that it will be made. Thus, both private and public claims to new images are influenced by the self-concept via its effects on the perceived probability of making claims successfully.

Sixth, the self-concept affects the expected value of negative sanctions that can be imposed for claiming an image unsuccessfully. Some attributes and qualities (a) make people more or less likely to believe that they will be punished for inaccurately claiming an image and (b) exaggerate or minimize the degree of punishment. For example, a person who views herself as beautiful and likable might underestimate the likelihood that an audience will punish her misbehavior. A person who takes exceptional pride in being viewed as honest by co-workers should refrain from making inaccurate claims because, if he is caught, even their mild disapproval will be devastating. Thus, claims to images are influenced by the self-concept via its effect on the expected value of negative sanctions.

In sum, the self-concept affects image claims in a variety of ways. These range from its affects on the cognitive encoding and organizing of information to its affects on influencing the desirability of particular images.

THE ASSOCIATION PRINCIPLE

People claim desirable images and avoid claiming undesirable ones. Phrased differently, people want to establish their personal association with desirable images and disestablish their personal association with undesirable images. This association principle, as we'll see, describes a wide variety of data about how people shape self-relevant information.

The concept of *personal association* describes the relationship between the individual and the image. When association is high, the person is linked to the image, either possessing it (as in being intelligent); seen as responsible for producing it (as in being responsible for the team's victory); or seen as closely related to it (as in being the great-great-grandson of a couple who came over on the Mayflower). We've seen that images can refer to a wide variety of traits, intentions, values, physical characteristics, possessions, and so on. Some images refer to what a person is (Is she intelligent and friendly?); others refer to events that a person is accountable for (Is he responsible for failing the test or does responsibility lie in the environment?); and still others refer to indirect connections between the person and other people, objects, or entities (Is he really the son of Senator Foghorn?). Association/dissociation incorporates all these relationships.

How one goes about establishing or disestablishing association naturally depends on the type of image involved. Images that describe what a person is involve self-constructs that are dispositional (intelligent, athletic, nice) or physical (attractive, tall, muscular). To establish an association with personal attributes, people claim them through one of the ways we've already described. They try to show why that construct should be legitimately used to describe them. They may present facts to show how these self-constructs fit them. Dissociation requires showing why the attributes don't fit.

Images that involve events are usually products of actions, like making money, receiving particular grades in school, or winning at sports. To establish an association with an event, people attempt to increase their personal responsibility for it, as by indicating that an "A" grade in school was a function of personal effort and ability rather than a lenient teacher. Dissociation involves showing why one is not responsible.

Images that are indirectly connected to the person require establishing some tangential temporal, physical, or psychological similarity with other people or entities ("I was there when Joe DiMaggio hit in his 56th straight game" or "I lived down the street from Robert Redford"). Pointing out such connections or setting the stage so that others notice them (for example, by placing in one's living room a picture of oneself standing next to the President) is enough to create an association.

Two derivations of the association principle are worth noting before we examine some of the phenomena it can be used to explain. First, people want to maximize the association between themselves and desirable images and minimize the association between themselves and undesirable images. This tendency should be greater as the desirability or undesirability of the image increases. Second, people want to maximize the attractiveness and minimize the unattractiveness of images with which they are already associated. Let's explore some of the ways they go about doing so.

Basking in Reflected Glory

People are skillful in turning indirect, tenuous, or nonexistent relationships into manifestations of association. The clearest case is that people bask in reflected glory (Cialdini, Borden, Thorne, Walker, Freeman, & Sloan, 1976; Cialdini & Richardson, in press).

When the New York Yankees win, numerous New Yorkers talk about how "we" won while discussing the sports scene over drinks in a bar. Should the ballplayers lose, though, the cocktail-hour analysts puzzle over how "they" could have blown the game. Sportswriters (see Neft, Johnson, & Cohen, 1976) often comment on the remarkable number of people who claim to have been present in a ballpark when a memorable event occurred—although only 34,320 ticket stubs were collected at the Polo Grounds on October 3, 1951, literally hundreds of thousands of people now claim to have been there when Bobby Thomson hit his famous bottom-of-the-ninth home run to defeat the Brooklyn Dodgers and send the Giants to the World Series. How many times have you heard people (yourself included) mention the time they shook hands with some famous celebrity, or lived down the road from some sports figure, or sat next to a famous actress during dinner? It is common to walk into an office and see a picture of the occupant standing next to a famous politician or author. Dozens of examples of basking in reflected glory (BIRG) should come to mind.

Robert Cialdini and his associates (Cialdini, Borden, Thorne, Walker, Freeman, & Sloan, 1976) conducted three studies to demonstrate the prevalance of the BIRG effect and to explore the conditions under which it is most likely to occur. In their first study, they observed college students around campus on the Mondays following weekend football games that involved the college team. They found that students wore more school-identifying apparel—such as school buttons, jackets, and sweatshirts that displayed the school name, nickname, mascot, or insignia—when the team had won that weekend than when it had lost. No one likes to be associated with a loss, but apparently victory has many claimants.

In a second study, college students were called on the phone by a person who supposedly was taking a poll to see what campus information was known by students. When asked about the performance of the school's football team in a particular game, students used the word *we* more often when they described a team victory than a defeat. This association effect was greatest for those students whose public esteem had been threatened by the caller. To some of the students, the caller indicated that they had answered some questions about campus activities incorrectly and did not seem to know as much as most students; these should have been more concerned about restoring their threatened images than those whose esteem had not been threatened. When asked about the team's performance, these students used the most *we* statements to describe a win, thereby compensating for their initial loss of esteem.

In a third study, Cialdini and his associates again found that students used the pronoun *we* more often when describing a victory than a defeat. In addition, there was a tendency (although only marginally significant) for students to use *we* even more to describe victories if the caller was supposedly unassociated with the school (identified as a member of a "Regional Survey Center") than if the caller might also share in some of the glory of the team by being affiliated with the university (identified as an employee of the "University's Survey Center"). "Insiders" who have an equal claim to the glory might be expected to be less impressed than "Outsiders" with a simple association.

Through their choice of pronouns, clothes, and other symbols, people associate themselves with laudable people and events and dissociate themselves from the bland or disgraceful. Parents often seem to fall victim to this tendency. A proud parent might remark "That's *my* boy," when the child receives a good report card, but, should the poor child misbehave, each parent might turn to the other and say "What's the matter with *your* son?" Association can also be demonstrated by describing an important person with terms that connote familiarity or that reveal information that only an intimate would know. For example, during a party the conversation might turn to discussions of State Senator Ben Jones. Each of the conversants mentions how *Senator Jones*, or just *Jones*, did this or that. But one of them mentions the Senator by his first name, remarking that "Ben has done a hell of a job." Naturally, the other people assume that he must know Senator Jones; otherwise he would never take such liberties.

Cialdini, Borden, Thorne, Walker, Freeman, and Sloan (1976) clearly showed that people will act to establish an association between themselves and desirable images. In a second series of studies, Cialdini and Richardson (in press) examined whether people also act to increase the attractiveness of images with which they are already associated and decrease the attractiveness of rival, alternative images. In their studies, students were approached individually on campus and asked to participate in a survey. The students were first given a brief "creativity test" supposedly of interest to the survey team. Some of the students were randomly given feedback indicating they were below average in creativity; the rest received no feedback. The students who were told they did poorly should have felt a threat to esteem; they were predicted to display more impression management than the others. All students were then told that the survey team was interested in their opinions about various educational institutions and were asked to evaluate either their own Arizona State University or their cross-state rival the University of Arizona. In both studies, a tendency was found for the students who had failed the earlier test to enhance the quality of their own university and to significantly deflate the quality of the rival institution. Cialdini and Richardson refer to these evaluative changes as *basking* (increasing the value of images with which one is already associated) and *blasting* (decreasing the value of rival images).

Why should people seek such indirect association? It is clearly appropriate for a person to note with pride the game-winning home run he hit; he earned the credit. It seems quite another matter for people to note with pride that they were merely there when the home run was hit. Cialdini and his associates believe that association is important because of *evaluative generalization*. People "look similarly upon things that are merely connected to one another, even in relatively trivial ways" (Cialdini & Richardson, in press). People have a tendency to generalize their evaluation of one thing to associated things. If I like John, and John likes George, even without knowing much about George I assume that he is likable. People's tendencies toward perceptual and cognitive harmony allow evaluations to "rub off" on associated people, objects, and events. This is the basis of Heider's (1958) balance theory, an integral part of his approach to the everyday psychology of people.

If you think such simple association isn't a powerful force, consider the era of Senator Joe McCarthy in the early 1950s. People actually lost their jobs simply because they knew others who read communist newspapers, even though these others often read such papers because they were written in their native tongue, not because they were communist sympathizers. Times have not changed dramatically. One study (Wilder, 1978) found that college students expected members of the same discussion group to have beliefs that were more similar to one another's than to those of people at large. Of course, one is likely to say that members often belong to a group because they are similar to one another in many ways. In this case, however, the college student subjects were explicitly told that the "group" they were observing was formed arbitrarily by the experimenter and was meeting for the first time! Thus, simply perceiving people as connected by a tenuous group membership is enough to create such generalization.

THE MUM EFFECT

The royal messengers of old Persia were honored and entertained when they brought the king news of a military victory but put to death upon telling him of a defeat. Although we no longer kill bearers of bad tidings (at least in most places), people still prefer to associate themselves with the communication of good news rather than bad, even when they are not responsible for the event but act only as transmitters of information.

Abraham Tesser and Sidney Rosen (1975) have summarized the results of numerous studies they conducted that demonstrate that people transmit messages that are pleasant for the recipient but avoid transmitting messages that are unpleasant for the recipient. They termed this the "MUM effect," after people's predilections to keep mum about bad news. In exploring why the effect occurs, they found that people don't seem reluctant to transmit bad news because they feel guilty about communicating it (although they do feel some guilt), but because they fear that they will be negatively evaluated by the recipient. Fear of a negative evaluation seemed to occur even though everyone involved understood that the communicators had in no way caused the bad news.

This appears to be an example of the evaluative generalization between people and the things with which they are associated. The bearer of bad tidings perhaps fears being connected in the recipient's mind with the aversive event, to be afraid of a "rub off" effect that will make him or her less attractive. A compounding factor is the possibility that the recipient will perceive the bearer as gloating over his misfortunes; this would further decrease the evaluation. The danger of transmitting bad news is apparently felt by most people and is mentioned explicitly by some when they note that being the bearer of bad tidings often results in being disliked. To combat the effect, people seem to adopt a simple tactic—merely keep mum.

ATTRIBUTION: EGOTISM, BEYOND AND BACK

The old saying "Success has a thousand fathers while failure is an orphan" seems to contain more than a little truth. Everyone wants to be responsible for a success; no one wants to be responsible for a failure. People can be and are held responsible for the products of their actions. Responsibility translates into credit or blame, kudos or censure, depending on whether the product is considered a success or a failure. In life, we constantly attempt to determine what "caused" particular events. These attributions allow us ultimately to level verdicts of responsibility or nonresponsibility. Sorting through the possible attributions that can be made about the causes of events and selecting ones that produce the desired degree of personal responsibility for success or failure is a common phenomenon.

On exam days, students display an ingenious set of descriptions of the teacher, test, and themselves. Those who do poorly lament the obtuse ramblings of the professor during past lectures that would surely have created confusion in an Einstein; they note the unfairness of the exam, the pickiness of the items that failed to reveal their true depth of knowledge, the poor lighting and distractions in the exam room, and the poorly written textbook. Clearly, they knew the material well, but events beyond their control (many of them unjust) kept them from the success they undoubtedly merited. Those who do well display a different pattern. The test was hard, perhaps, but quite fair; the book was clearly written; the professor coherent and in command; and their abilities and efforts accurately and sensitively measured.

Commentators have noted that political figures seem particularly adept at judiciously taking responsibility at the right moment, receiving credit for not only their own actions but those of people around them, capitalizing on the lucky break to give the image of a person who knows how to succeed. Concomitantly, they manage to find the thousand-and-one external factors that would leave them nonresponsible for failures. Michael Korda briefly chronicled the lives of some of history's famous men who gained prominence despite repeated early failures in the political, military, and business realm, including Winston Churchill and George Washington. As Korda noted, these "great failures know how to look the other way at the right moment. . . . They know better than to identify themselves with a losing cause: They may have been the captain of the ship, but not its owner" (1977, p. 213).[4]

It's interesting to notice the attributions that emanate from Washington, D.C., after newsworthy events. If the item, such as a decrease in unemployment or inflation, meets with popular approval, members of both political parties find the cause of the event in the past actions of their own party. Should the opposite occur, such as an increase in unemployment or inflation, pronouncements decry the poor planning and unwise policies of the opposition party. It has been suggested that the Nixon administration tried to shift the blame for all failures, such as the Watergate break-in and ensuing scandal, from Executive actions to such diverse causes as overzealous but well-meaning aides, a vindictive and hostile press, and political enemies; and tried to minimize the consequences through such tactics as calling the break-in a "third-rate burglary" hardly worthy of attention.

Egotism in Attributions

These anecdotal examples suggest that people attempt to control attributions about events in ways that associate them with desirable images (successes) and dissociate them from undesirable images (failures). Research reveals that such association/dissociation does reliably appear.

One early study was conducted by Johnson, Feigenbaum, and Weiby (1964). Educational psychology students served as teachers of mathematics to two 4th-grade boys. On an initial task (learning to multiply by 10), one of the pupils did well and the other did poorly. On a second task (learning to multiply by 20), half of the subjects found that the pupil who had done poorly did well, so that now both of their pupils were successful. The other half of the subjects found that their pupils retained their initial levels, one doing well, the other poorly. Actually, the performance of the pupils was unrelated to the subjects' teaching behaviors, since subjects were randomly assigned to one or the other condition. It was found that subjects who worked with the improving pupil attributed his better performance to their own teaching skills, while those who worked with the constantly poor student attributed his performance to the pupil's poor efforts or lack of intelligence. Thus, simply knowing that improvement occurred produced attributions that seem to be egotistical.

Following up these results, Beckman (1970) similarly found that subjects who taught a pupil who improved his performance over time, first failing and then succeeding, attributed the eventual success to

[4]From *Success! How Every Man and Woman Can Achieve It*, by M. Korda. Copyright 1977 by Success Research Corporation. This and all other quotations from this source are reprinted by permission of Random House, Inc.

themselves. Subjects who simply observed the teacher/pupil interactions, and hence were not ego-involved in the outcome, attributed the success to the characteristics of the child. As compared to these neutral observers, the teacher-subjects' own attributions about the performance seemed quite self-serving.

It has been suggested that results such as these are not caused by self-serving motivational influences, but are simply logical conclusions drawn from the particular combination of people's expectations, efforts, and outcomes in such situations (Bem, 1972; Brewer, 1977; Miller & Ross, 1975; Ross, 1977). Without going into the details of these arguments (you are encouraged to examine these interesting positions on your own), it is enough to say that more recent work seems to cast doubt on their validity as complete explanations of self-serving attributions (Miller, 1976; Ross & Sicoly, 1979; Schlenker & Miller, 1977a; Sicoly & Ross, 1977; Snyder, Stephan, & Rosenfield, 1978; Weary Bradley, 1978). As one example, Fiore Sicoly and Michael Ross (1977) had subjects complete a social-sensitivity test that was ostensibly related to their social perceptiveness and later told them that they did quite well or quite poorly (once again, scores were randomly assigned). When asked to attribute responsibility for their performance, success subjects took more personal responsibility for their outcome than did failure subjects, a result that might appear self-serving but does not of itself refute any of the criticisms made by advocates of the logical-attribution position. Subjects then were given feedback from observers who watched their performance. This feedback was bogus; it was invented to give subjects about the same amount of responsibility that they assigned themselves, slightly more responsibility than they assigned themselves, or slightly less responsibility. Subjects were then asked to rate how accurate the observers were in the way they assigned responsibility.

Supporting the self-interest position, it was found that subjects who succeeded rated the observers' feedback as more accurate when it assigned them more rather than less responsibility. These subjects apparently wanted to be seen as responsible for their succcess and reacted positively to information that further increased their responsibility but derogated information that took responsibility from them. Subjects who failed rated the observers' feedback as more accurate when it assigned them less rather than more responsibility. These subjects seemed to desire minimal responsibility for their apparently poor performance and reacted positively to observers who reinforced that view but negatively to those who contradicted it. Thus, people responded most positively to the feedback when it deviated from their own ratings in a flattering or complimentary direction. In addition, these flattered subjects also rated the confederates as more perceptive, likable, and as having more information on which to make an accurate causal attribution. These findings make the logical-attribution position less tenable, and they indicate that most people do want to appear responsible for success and nonresponsible for failure.

It has even been found that under the worst possible failure conditions, in which the situation was prearranged to suggest to subjects that they were highly responsible for the failure, people seem to be the most egotistical in their attributions (Schlenker & Miller, 1977a; Stevens & Jones, 1976). Logic was compromised in an apparent effort to recoup lost esteem. It is easy to be rational and logical when it comes to making attributions about other people whom one has never met and with whom one is totally uninvolved. It is more difficult to be rational and logical when it comes to making attributions about one's own identity-relevant behaviors. The rational information-processing model appears to work best in the former situation, while egotistical patterns appear to emerge in the latter (Fontaine, 1975).

Task Importance

Not all outcomes are equally valuable to people. Landing a $100 account for the firm doesn't have the implications on performance of closing a multi-million-dollar deal. How a student performs on a practice exam isn't as crucial to her image as how she does on the real thing. Thus, as the importance of the task increases, so should the tendency to engage in self-serving attribution patterns. Task importance should affect the attractiveness of the image and thus increase the association/dissociation effect.

Dale Miller (1976) found support for this hypothesis. Subjects completed a social-sensitivity test and later discovered they did quite well or quite poorly (feedback was bogus). After completing the test but before discovering how well they had supposedly done, the importance of the test was manipulated. Half of the subjects were told that the test was well established and that "many agencies and businesses use people's scores . . . to assist them on client and employee decisions," and high scores were said to be related to "such desirable characteristics as intelligence, personal and marital happiness, and job satisfaction." The remaining subjects were told that the test was new, its "usefulness was still very much in doubt," that it had not yet been found to relate to any important characteristics, and that scores on it could hardly be seen as important or diagnostic. This information was introduced only after subjects completed the test; this was to insure that it did not affect either their expectations of how they would perform or how hard they would work on the test. Miller found that when subjects succeeded they attributed their performance more to their own ability and effort and less to the difficulty of the test or to luck. Further, these self-serving effects were much more pronounced under high- than low-importance conditions.

Egotistical Attributions in Interpersonal Relations

When people work in groups to accomplish a common goal, each of the group members shares, at least to some extent, the responsibility for the outcomes that are generated. Social psychologists often discuss how group members diffuse responsibility among them (see Janis, 1972; Mynatt & Sherman, 1975; Schlenker & Miller, 1977a). People recognize that blame for potentially aversive actions can be spread around to the others in the group, and so they're more likely to take risks and make decisions that they might not be willing to on their own. If a group decision actually does turn out to be a failure, it is not hard for group members to discover ways subtly to shift the blame for the failure to others in the group, thereby minimizing their own accountability. For example, following a financial fiasco caused by a decision of the board of trustees of a college, each member of the board might bemoan the small role he personally played, wish he had influenced the others in the group more than he did, and generally manage to shift attention and blame away from himself and on to specific persons or the group as a whole (Mynatt & Sherman, 1975; Schlenker, Soraci, & McCarthy, 1976).

If a group endeavor turns out to be successful, on the other hand, each group member seems to find ways to infuse responsibility, accenting his or her own prominence in bringing about the accomplishment. Each of the group members proudly takes a bow, and "knows" that without him or her, the group could not have accomplished all that it did. Of course, such infusion of responsibility might create intragroup conflicts. Star players on sports teams frequently clash over who really is essential to continued team success and therefore who deserves the largest salary. Gossip magazines eagerly report the dissensions created in rock bands when each member of the group feels that he or she is the major factor in their success. Just think of the number of actors who have left successful television shows that involved several key characters to venture out on their own because they believed they weren't getting the recognition or salary they deserved. (Many of these have never been heard from again.) Are such reports limited to the dilettantes of show business, sports, and business, or are we all prone to such tendencies?

Studies have revealed comparable patterns of egotism in more mundane group situations (Caine & Schlenker, 1979; Forsyth &

Schlenker, 1977a, 1977b; Medow & Zander, 1965; Mynatt & Sherman, 1975; Schlenker, 1975c; Schlenker & Miller, 1977a, 1977b; Schlenker, Miller, Leary, & McCown, 1979; Schlenker et al., 1976; Snyder, Stephan, & Rosenfield, 1976; Streufert & Streufert, 1969; Wolosin, Sherman, & Till, 1973). As one example, Robert Wolosin, Steven Sherman, and Amnon Till (1973) had pairs of college students participate in a game in which they either had to cooperate to earn money (they could win only when both coordinated their actions and both received the same amount) or had to compete (when one person won, the other lost). After playing, subjects "discovered" that they had won or lost money; in actuality, this feedback was randomly assigned. They were then asked to divide responsibility for their performance among (a) themselves, (b) their partner (or opponent), and (c) the experimental conditions (lighting, noise, task difficulty, luck, and so forth).

In the cooperative situation, subjects attributed responsibility in ways that gave them credit for a success and their partner blame for a failure. Subjects assigned themselves more personal responsibility following a success than a failure. Further, relative to their partners, subjects took a significantly greater amount of responsibility when the pair had succeeded and a slightly lesser amount of responsibility when the pair had failed. Thus, they saw themselves as more responsible than the partner following success, but less responsible than the partner following failure.

In the competitive condition, successful subjects also assigned more responsibility to themselves than they did to their opponents or to environmental influences. This communicated the message that they won because of their superior ability. Consider, however, the case in which you lose when competing against another person. If you assign low responsibility to yourself and high responsibility to your opponent, it might indicate that your opponent is better than you. In competitive situations, it is impossible to blame an opponent for your failure without appearing to be inferior. Subjects in this experiment found a way to avoid giving that impression. After a failure, they stated that the *situation* was most responsible for their performance, with themselves and their opponent much less responsible (they assigned themselves and their opponents equally low responsibility). These attributions suggest that the opponent did not have superior ability; instead, the situation took control and fortuitously allowed the opponent to win. Analogously, in sports, the unfortunate umpires and referees (situational factors) frequently feel the wrath of losing teams.

In competitive situations, people often seem to recognize that their opponent is going to display a pattern of attributions that is likely to disagree with their own interpretation. At the same time, they typically underestimate the degree of disagreement that actually exists between their own attributions and those of the opponent (Snyder et al., 1976).

Fitting the Facts: Reality Constraints That Diminish or Reverse Egotism

Most situations are sufficiently ambiguous that precise allocations of responsibility are arbitrary. It would be convenient for a situation to be so clear that one can say "John's performance was due to 34% skill, 45% effort, 11% luck, and 10% task factors." In fact, no such situations exist, and it is doubtful that psychological science will ever advance to the point where such determinations can be made. Certainly, approximate amounts of responsibility can be allocated. We constantly make judgments about responsibility for consequences, as in a court of law. But, within broad ranges of responsibility attributions, people are free to attempt to control the images they present by judiciously distributing a desirable pattern of responsibility between possible causes.

Personality and situational influences act as constraints that serve to define these ranges. Once again, we find that reality—the facts—act as potential limitations on the amount of responsibility people can claim. There is hardly any point in a football player's claiming 100% responsibility for his team's victory. No one would believe him; he would alienate his teammates, the press, and the public; opposing players would single him out for attention to whittle down his ego; and his own teammates would probably "accidentally" miss blocks at crucial moments, hoping for their opponents to take care of this egomaniac. Egotism that is recognized as such is hardly self-serving. Similarly, the president of a company would find it nearly impossible to deny all responsibility for a decision made at a meeting over which she presided. Thus, she might display "leadership" by accepting responsibility for the fiasco that resulted and then find the 101 ways to shift blame to other members of the group. Hence, the old adage "I accept the responsibility but not the blame, the difference being that people who are to blame lose their jobs." Of course, in such cases individuals do not actually want to "accept the responsibility." They announce responsibility and then present information that indicates that they are really much less responsible than it appears on the surface. They allow the listener to conclude "She really isn't responsible, but it was admirable for her to say she was."

Since claims to images can be refuted by facts, the desirability of an image decreases as it departs from them. No amount of ingenious reasoning can substantiate the claim that one is a genius if one fails every test one takes. Logic can be compromised, but it can't be entirely thrown to the winds without repercussions. Thus, the range of believable attributions that can be made is either limited or increased by present and anticipated information.

A claim to some amount of responsibility should be affected by the attractiveness of that amount, the probability that the claim will be believed, and the expected values of the negative sanctions for an unsuccessful claim. Any factors that affect any of these components should also affect the amount of responsibility people claim for a particular consequence. For example, people with low needs for achievement should not value being seen as highly responsible for a success as much as people with high needs for achievement, so they should display patterns of attributions that are less egotistical (holding all other factors constant). Studies support this hypothesis (Weiner, Frieze, Kukla, Reed, Rest, & Rosenbaum, 1971).

One's "track record"—past performances on comparable tasks—constrains the claims that one can make. If one's past record is exemplary, positive claims can be made about one's ability, expectations of future success, and personal responsibility for any subsequent successes. A person with a history of failure, though, is likely to anticipate future failures, interpret events in terms of failure, and be disbelieved if grand predictions are made about future successes. Simply, one's track record affects one's expectations, interpretations of events, and the perceived probability that one can successfully claim images that depart radically from that record. Thus, it has been found that people with low self-esteem, particularly those who say they are certain of their lack of abilities or who publicly announce that they are likely to fail on an upcoming task, attribute failure to their own lack of ability (see Feather, 1969; Fitch, 1970) and are more likely to reject responsibility for success (see Maracek & Mettee, 1972) compared to people with better track records.

Anticipating future tests on which a public failure is possible is also likely to constrain egotism in attributions. For example, Marlene and Linda both take an exam in a math course; Marlene believes that this is the only exam she'll have to take while Linda believes that the exam is only the first part of a two-part exam, the remainder to be given later in the day. After the exam, they both discover that they received "A" grades. The teacher then asks them how much ability they have in mathematics. Who do you suppose would claim greatest ability: Marlene, who believes she can rest on her laurels from that exam, or Linda, who believes she will have to take another exam in a few hours at which she might do poorly? Studies have shown that people who anticipate taking future tests at which failure is possible are less egotistical in their claims and attributions than are people who do not have to encounter such future tests (Wortman, Costanzo, & Witt, 1973).

Finally, the probability of successfully claiming an attractive amount of responsibility (high following success and low following failure) is affected by the degree to which other people know or might learn of information that could refute the claim. Suppose a student fails the final exam in the fourth psychology course he has taken and schedules an appointment with his professor to see if anything can be done about his grade. Do you think the types of attributions he describes to the professor might depend on whether the professor is aware of the fact that he also failed the first three psychology courses he took? If he knows that the professor is aware of this fact, he cannot readily dismiss responsibility. The data consistently indicate that he does poorly in psychology, so he might plead for mercy. If the student knows that the professor is unaware, however, he might explain that his failure in the course is unique and due to factors beyond his control. He studied hard and feels he has the ability and motivation to succeed, but somehow things just didn't work out right. Maybe it was the fact that he doesn't do as well on multiple-choice questions as on essay exams (or vice-versa, depending on which type of exam was used). People take more personal responsibility for failures when their audience knows about their past failures.

Conversely, if an audience is aware of information that indicates that one has high ability and motivation, they should be quite impressed. One can make egotistical claims and be believed. Yet an even better tactic is available for those with well-known track records of success. Such people can be modest, publicly taking less personal responsibility than the audience is willing to ascribe to them. In this way, they can be seen as competent, successful, and humble, a highly valued attribute in our society. A person who has a track record of success (and thus believes his claims can be substantiated) but believes that the audience is unaware of that track record does not have this option. He should be more egotistical in his claims than the person who believes the audience is already aware of the past successes.

This hypothesis that people should react to success or failure depending on whether the audience knows or does not know of their prior performances has been supported by studies of self-descriptions (Ackerman & Schlenker, 1975; Baumeister & Jones, 1978) and attributions (Frey, 1978). Certain other studies not conducted specifically to test such hypotheses established conditions that were likely to produce reverse egotism (Ross, Bierbrauer, & Polly, 1974) and obtained similar results (see Weary Bradley, 1978). Thus, what one's audience knows affects how one describes attributions of responsibility for a particular set of pleasant or unpleasant consequences.

We thus can see that self-serving attributions that appear to be egotistical are likely to occur only under certain conditions. The first is that people be objectively self-aware or publicly self-conscious (see Chapter 3). That is, they should be attentive to the self-relevance of successes and failures and evaluate themselves from a social perspective. We should expect that objective self-awareness would increase egotism since people in that condition become concerned with how they appear to real or imagined audiences. Indeed, objective self-awareness has been shown to increase egotism in attributions as has making people aware that their responses will be shown to an audience (Weary Bradley, 1978).

The second condition is that the attributions that might be made from the positive or negative outcomes be pertinent to the people's desired identities. The more pertinent the information is, the more likely it is that egotistical patterns will occur. Trivial or invalid successes or failures, for instance, do not produce overly egotistical attributions. Similarly, the more threatening the information is to a person's desired identity (a "D" grade is more threatening to a scholar's identity than a "C" grade), the more he will want to insure that he is viewed as minimally responsible for the outcome. The more glorifying the information is to a person's desired identity (as an "A" is more glorifying to a scholar than a "B"), the more he will want to insure that he is viewed as maximally responsible for the outcome. Of course, if other people already give the scholar credit for the "A," then he can be humble and be seen as both highly responsible and modest.

Third, there should be no pressing reason for the person to be objective about his attributions. There are several reasons why a person might *have* to be objective. The person might be in a situation where it is to her advantage to judge accurately her abilities and accomplishments. A student who is trying to decide whether to spend four years taking difficult pre-medical courses in college should try to find out whether she has the ability to succeed or whether she will be wasting her time and money. The person might be in a situation where present or anticipated information will come to the attention of audiences and clearly refute attributions that contort the truth. When such reasons exist for people to be objective, more objective patterns of attribution are obtained.

Symbolic Gestures to Influence Attributions

People attempt to control attributions through more than just their verbal statements. Some situations simply don't lend themselves to making statements about who did what and what caused what. Consequently, people often use gestures that communicate the attributions they want an audience to make.

For example, a tennis player jumps into position, takes a prodigious swing at the bouncing ball, and either misses it completely or sends it sailing into the net or fence. The actions that follow can be fascinating. The player carefully scrutinizes the strings on the racket (perhaps they caused the mistake), walks over to the spot where the ball bounced and kicks at it (maybe the ball struck a pebble or rough spot on the court), and slams the racket into the ground ("I'm mad at myself; I usually don't miss shots like that and am a much better player than that shot would indicate"). Through symbolic actions, a clear set of attributions can be communicated to an audience, and people become adept at such nonverbal behaviors.

Setting the Stage

The experiments we've explored up until now studied how people attribute responsibility for events that have already occurred. But there is no need to wait for something to happen before doing something about it. People attempt to set the stage for desired attributions about events even before those events occur.

Michael Korda describes businessmen who know how to control information about events in advance to produce the desired impression later.

> Astute power players know just how to create and publicize epic crises in order to get the credit for solving them, and how to predict catastrophes just before announcing good news in order to make the good news sound even better. In fact, if this game is played properly, even *bad* news can be made to sound like a triumph—it's simply necessary to make the predictions so terrible that anything short of bankruptcy will come as a relief [1976, p. 166].[5]

One can even gain a reputation as a "miracle worker" while one's department is losing money if one skillfully sets the stage. In illustrating this, Korda (1976, pp. 166–167) describes a hypothetical case in which you are the head of a department in a large corporation. Suppose it is your educated estimate that your department will be about $200,000 below last year's level. What do you do—sit around and wait for the catastrophe and the axe to fall? Hardly. Korda advises action. Announce that a "catastrophe has struck," that the department will be in the hole at least $400,000, and that "heads are going to roll." Establish that "you are not at fault" (and that it is not your head that will roll) by calling in your staff, mentioning possible betrayals (blaming the catastrophe on others) and reprisals. Next, magnanimously take responsibility for the fiasco (responsibility is all right, blame is not), thereby making yourself seem a leader for standing by your faulty subordinates, and announce to superiors that you will allow yourself to be "made the scapegoat." This dramatic act can be punctuated by handing in your resignation, but only if you're certain the superiors won't accept it. Work hard, sending memos to everyone (thereby making yourself noticed by the appropriate superiors), stay in your office beyond closing time, and see your

[5]From *Power! How To Get It, How To Use It*, by M. Korda. Copyright 1976 by Michael Korda and Paul Gitlin. This and all other quotations from this source are reprinted by permission of Random House, Inc.

superiors as often as is feasible. "The more you involve them, the more *your* problem becomes 'our' problem, and the responsibility for it is spread above you as well as below you" (p. 167). The stage is set, and when you proclaim that the loss is *only* $200,000 you will emerge a hero. Somehow, *you* have managed to *save* the company $200,000!

In Korda's examples of setting the stage, the goal of the actor is to present an unambiguous pattern from which an audience will draw the desired conclusion. An alternative strategy is to set the stage by attempting to fog attributions, so that possible causes of events become lost in the mist. Edward E. Jones and Steven Berglas (1978) describe how people "sometimes do things to *avoid* diagnostic information about (their) own characteristics and capacities" (p. 200). This tactic is most likely to be used by people who are uncertain of their own self-competence, yet want to succeed. Jones and Berglas propose that "an important reason why some people turn to alcohol is to avoid the implications of negative feedback for failure and to enhance the impact of positive feedback for success" (p. 201). By drinking, people usually decrease chances of success. Then, if failure results, it is not necessarily because of poor ability—the bottle can be faulted. If success occurs, the person must surely be a genius; how else could the alcohol have been overcome? The implications of performance are averted, since they only indirectly touch on the person's competence.

Further, the drinker can revel in fantasies of tomorrow's conquests, a common phenomenon in heavy drinkers.

> These fantasies involve thoughts about how successful one will be *when* he breaks the drinking habit or *if* he did. The problem drinker tells himself that he will report for meaningful social measurement when he's good and ready, but typically he never is. The suspected truth is too horrible to risk, and in the meantime he may prosper in fantasies of glorified competence [Jones & Berglas, 1978, p. 203].

The problem, of course, is that such a tactic has a high probability of gaining the actor the label "alcoholic," a pejorative image to most people. But life often involves such "least of evils" choices. Which is less aversive—being seen as an alcoholic or confronting unambiguous information that might confirm one's worst fears of incompetence? Each person must answer the question individually. If the answer is "alcoholic," one can even think of the many famous historical figures with the same label and bask in reflected glory.

Other examples of attributional fogging indicate its prevalence and suggest that it is hardly reserved for only the heavy drinkers among us. Consider the student who parties all night before a big exam, getting little or no sleep. Or the obese adolescent who has no medical cause for his excess weight yet continues to eat. He has no social life, girlfriends or buddies, worries that he lacks the personality to acquire them even if he were of more normal physical proportions, and has arranged things so that he probably never will acquire them. His weight, of course, can always be blamed. Similarly, "the ingratiator who avoids disclosing his true preferences or opinions protects himself from the ultimate implications of rejection as a person. Even if he gets rejected, this isn't so bad if he was 'just trying to be nice,' if he held his true self in reserve" (Jones & Berglas, 1978, p. 201). Failure can be attributed to the ingratiatory role, not oneself. Or consider the insecure student who joins an unusual political or religious group—one whose extreme ideas are rejected by most people in the society; all the better if the group also espouses atypical modes of dress and grooming. Any rejection by society can be blamed on "their" lack of foresight, prejudice, and hypocrisy rather than one's own ideas, work habits, ability, and personality. Naturally, this is not to say that all alcoholics, partiers, obese individuals, ingratiators, and members of extreme groups do what they do only to fog attributions. Attributional fogging, though, may play more than a minor role in a good number of such cases.

SUMMARY

Although the self-concept develops from social interaction, people also attempt to control self-relevant information to influence social interaction and, indirectly, their self-concepts. The most frequently discussed examples of such control are behaviors that seem to be egotistical. Egotistical actions have been explained as due to needs for self-esteem, the necessity for self-respect, needs for personal control, and the nature of social interaction. The line separating private perceptions from public descriptions is sometimes a thin one, as people can selectively attend to and interpret self-relevant information in order to construct personal realities that might fulfill their goals in social life.

In controlling personal realities, images are important. Since we categorize and respond to people on the basis of the images we form of them, images can lead to a particular set of consequences for the holder. As such, images have expected values, and these vary from person to person and situation to situation. Although images with high expected values represent our ideals of what we wish to be like, reality imposes constraints on what we can actually claim about ourselves, both publicly and privately. Images have requirements that a holder is expected to fulfill, and challenges constantly arise that can repudiate claims to attractive images. Repudiated claims can produce negative social sanctions, and they act as checks on people's claims, causing them to avoid claims that are easily recognizable as lies. The images that people actually do claim for themselves, both publicly and privately, seem to be those with the highest expected values for image claims.

People want to associate themselves with desirable images and dissociate themselves from undesirable images. In so doing, they behave in ways that allow them to bask in reflected glory (they associate themselves with admirable people and events) and keep mum when it comes to transmitting bad news to others. Further, people's attributions about the causes of self-relevant events are affected by the quality—good or bad—of the outcomes of those events. In general, people take greater personal responsibility for successes than for failures, attributing success to personal factors such as ability and effort but failure to environmental factors such as bad luck or task difficulty. Although people seem to want more responsibility for success than for failure, reality constraints can produce patterns of attributions that are nonegotistical. These diminished and reversed patterns can be predicted from an impression-management perspective, since the attractiveness of the image, the probability of successfully claiming it, and the expected value of the negative sanctions for an unsuccessful claim all seem to affect how people construct personal realities.

F I V E

Apologies only account for the evil which they cannot alter.

> Benjamin Disraeli

Conscience is the inner voice that warns us someone may be watching.

> H. L. Mencken

PROTECTING THE SELF: IMPRESSION MANAGEMENT IN PREDICAMENTS

No matter how much thought and effort people expend constructing a desirable identity, they still face the task of trying to maintain the identity when confronted with events that threaten it. The occurrence of threatening events is inevitable: people simply can't control all the events that bear on their identities; they can't anticipate all the consequences of their own actions (some of which may be undesirable); and they often succumb to temptations to lie, cheat, steal, or behave in ways inconsistent with the identities they desire to project. Social life is replete with pitfalls, pratfalls, and other identity-threatening predicaments.

Any event that casts aspersions on the lineage, character, conduct, skills, or motives of an actor creates a predicament. Predicaments run the gamut from embarrassing incidents, such as a minor faux pas that makes its perpetrator lose face and appear foolish and unpoised, through being caught in a moderate breach of conduct, such as lying, to being caught in a serious breach, such as a major crime. In all of these cases, the actor's desired identity vis-à-vis a particular audience is threatened. The audience is likely to attribute undesirable characteristics to the actor, and the actor might be negatively sanctioned. To avoid or minimize such negative repercussions, impression-management tactics are used to remedy the situation. The actor might attempt to *account* for the event, using an excuse or justification that could satisfactorily explain it to the audience. Or the actor might *apologize* for the event, trying to show that it should not be taken as an accurate or typical reflection of his or her identity. These *remedial tactics* offer to the actor a means of escaping from the predicament unscathed or at least with as few negative repercussions as possible. In this chapter, we'll explore predicaments—their nature, their ramifications, and the impression-management tactics people use when caught in them.

THE NATURE OF PREDICAMENTS

According to *Webster's New World Dictionary* (1960), a predicament is "a condition or situation, especially one that is dangerous, unpleasant, embarrassing, or, sometimes, comical." The term implies a perplexing and undesirable set of choices and consequences from which it may be difficult to disentangle oneself. From an impression-management perspective, though, we're not concerned with all such undesirable situations, only with ones that specifically bear on an actor's social identity in front of an audience. For our purposes, *predicaments are situations in which events have undesirable implications for the identity-relevant images actors have claimed or desire to claim in front of real or imagined audiences.* To help clarify the nature of predicaments, examine the key words in this definition.

Predicaments arise from events that potentially damage an actor's identity vis-à-vis an audience. An event is a socially meaningful unit of analysis that describes an *action and its consequences.* The event (the action and consequences) can be evaluated somewhere along a positive-to-negative, or good-bad, continuum. For example, a human behavior and its consequences are an event when a person is caught telling a lie that harms others and makes him appear dishonest; when an actor commits a faux pas that surprises others and makes her look foolish; or when a person behaves in a way that makes it appear he is trying to gain the liking of a new acquaintance but ends up being rejected. Most events with which we will be concerned are of human origin—they describe the behavior of a person and its consequences. But events also describe acts of nature; a snowstorm and its consequences are an event. Such events can affect the identities of people, as when the weatherperson is blamed for the blizzard. Such accusations are without "rational" basis, but audiences sometimes make such inferential leaps.

An event has *implications* for the identity of an actor when the actor is perceived as responsible for it. The concept of responsibility is essential in understanding human behavior. When one is responsible for an event, one is answerable for it. People (oneself included) judge one's role in the event and, depending on their verdict, can reward or punish one's behavior. Responsibility serves to channel rewards and punishments to their appropriate destinations in proper amounts (Hart, 1968; Heider, 1958; Turner, 1968). If people are held responsible for praiseworthy (positively valued) events, they are entitled to reap the proper credit; if they are held responsible for blameworthy (negatively valued) events, they should receive appropriate punishment. Responsibility is the adhesive that links an actor to an event and attaches an appropriate sanction to the actor who deserves it.

At the simplest level, actors can be held responsible for an event for two reasons: they are associated with the event because of some connection between them and the action's origin or they engaged in the behavior that led to the consequences. The first is termed *responsibility through global association* (Heider, 1958; Shaw & Sulzer, 1964). At this level, people are held responsible for events they did not directly cause but to which they are seen as connected. For example, an actor can be held responsible for the actions of ancestors (a person is insulted when an audience derogates her ancestors); family (a mother is mortified when her small daughter asks why their hostess is so fat); friends (a person is criticized because of her best friend's unsavory reputation); or group (a student is called a loser because her team lost the big football game). The weatherperson derogated because of the blizzard is likewise only globally associated with that event. Basking-in-reflected-glory and wallowing-in-reflected-obloquy (Chapter 4) are dependent upon this sort of indirect responsibility.

Actors are held more responsible for events when their own actions are seen as having *produced* the consequences (Heider, 1958; Shaw & Sulzer, 1964). The linkage between the actor and the event is then clearer than in the case of global association; the actor, or at least the actor's actions, caused the consequences. Of course, the event may have been an accident, or the actor may have been forced to do what he did and hence may not be totally responsible for the event. Audiences therefore make adjustments in the degree to which they hold actors responsible, depending on the circumstances. The more personally responsible an actor appears to be for an event, the greater are the implications for the actor's identity.

The implications of an event are *undesirable* whenever they appear to contradict the images the actor has claimed or desires to claim, given the situation and the real or imagined audience. Because of the event, the actor's claim to desirable images is challenged or repudiated, and he or she is associated with undesirable images. Keep in mind that the desirability of a particular image varies from person to person and from situation to situation for the same person (see Chapter 4). Thus, a person who claims to be unintelligent but honest would not confront a predicament if an event occurred that made her appear to be unintelligent, but would confront one if an event occurred that made her appear to be dishonest. Similarly, a person might brag to the members of his gang about the amount of money he stole from people he mugged, since by so doing he expects to win approval from the gang members. But should the person be accused by the police of such an act, he should prefer to deny it and maintain an identity as a law-abiding citizen. The two audiences, gang members and police, have different values and will reward or punish different acts. Therefore, different identities should be maximally desirable in front of each. In front of the gang, no predicament exists; in fact, the mugger should want to take credit for the act and maximally associate himself with it. In front of the police, a predicament exists; the mugger should want to avoid blame for the act and maximally dissociate himself from it.

As these examples indicate, a predicament is created by undesirable events irrespective of whether an actor *has claimed* a particular set of images or simply *desires to claim* them. Examples from the former category are numerous—there are many occasions on which people claim to be one thing but subsequently confront contradictory events. Perhaps the most common instance is when one's performance doesn't measure up to projected claims, as when a student claims to be attractive but is soundly rejected by a prospective date; a self-described scholar fails an exam that most people pass; a proper host belches loudly at a formal dinner party; or a minister unthinkingly swears when a door slams on her foot. Such events throw doubt on the actor's veracity, judgment, character, skills, conduct, or motives, and are unanticipated by an audience that believed the actor's original claims. The unanticipated nature of the event momentarily disrupts the ongoing interaction. The impression created by the event, if uncorrected, can result in a lowered evaluation of the actor.

When such situations cause an actor to become flustered or feel ill-at-ease, they are referred to as *embarrassing incidents*. These are one of the traumas of everyday social interaction that can sidetrack or even derail the most perfectly planned performances. Since embarrassment is a common occurrence with important interpersonal implications, the topic has received a great deal of attention from psychologists and sociologists (Goffman, 1959, 1967; Gross & Stone, 1964; Modigliani, 1968, 1971; Sattler, 1963, 1965, 1966; Weinberg, 1968). According to Goffman (1967, pp. 107–108), embarrassment occurs whenever the "facts at hand threaten to discredit the assumptions a participant finds he has projected about his identity." The actor becomes visibly flustered and unpoised. He or she might fumble, stutter, turn crimson, and speak in an unusual quivering pitch, groping for what to do and say next. Unless some way is found to regain poise, the predicament can turn from bad to worse, since the actor might acquire a reputation for being socially unskilled. As Goffman (1967, pp. 101–102) suggested, "to appear flustered, in our society at least, is considered evidence of weakness, inferiority, low status, moral guilt, defeat, and other unenviable attributes." He goes on to note that children are often intentionally placed in embarrassing predicaments by teasing adults in order to train them to develop poise in difficult situations. Those who learn the lesson well develop a flexible behavioral repertoire that will serve them in the years ahead. It should be added that the ability to extricate oneself from a predicament, be it caused by an embarrassing incident or by something else, is a socially valued and admired skill.

There are also numerous occasions when an actor desires to claim publicly a particular set of images because of the fear of punishment for failing to do so. These situations occur when an audience has the power to require the actor to adopt a particular identity and to punish actions that breach the identity. If the actor perceives that such an audience is making an accusation that a breach occurred, a predicament exists. The following examples illustrate: a child is accused by his mother of lying; a student is accused by an instructor of cheating on an exam; a woman is accused by a merchant of shoplifting; a man is arrested by the police for robbery. The child is required by parents to be truthful; the student is required by the instructor to be honest; and the woman and man are required by society to be law-abiding. Breaches of these required images can be sanctioned by the agents responsible for enforcing them. Even if an actor is not guilty of the alleged transgression, the public accusation and portent of punishment still create a predicament. It may be easier to escape the predicament when one is not guilty, but escape is necessary nevertheless.

Predicaments that involve transgressions usually generate efforts on the part of the accused to present the required identity while being observed by the audience. The accused may not privately believe that he or she is truthful, honest, or whatever but will publicly appear to be these things when the powerful audience is present. As always, the desirability of a required set of images in a particular situation must be compared to the desirability of alternative image sets before precise predictions can be made about what any person will do publicly. However, in such transgression situations, the portent of punishment causes most people to try to project the required images while under the scrutiny of the audience.

Predicaments occur before *real or imagined audiences*. Symbolic interactionism proposes that people evaluate themselves as social objects by using a social frame of reference, conjuring imagined significant others who serve as judges of attributes and conduct (see Chapter 3). A real audience does not have to be present for an individual to experience some of the negative repercussions of a predicament. Through the socialization process, people internalize particular standards, construct a self-concept, and become aware of what particular groups of other people require them to be. When events occur that breach important aspects of the individual's identity or self concept, *internal distress* is aroused. Depending on the situation, the actor in the predicament labels this distress embarrassment, shame, humiliation, guilt, disappointment, or anxiety.

One form of internal distress is the anxiety created by the fear of detection and punishment following transgressions (such as lying, cheating, and stealing). As children, people learn to associate transgression with punishment; when subsequent transgressions occur, anxiety is generated (Aronfreed, 1961). Even when it is objectively clear that no one was around to witness the transgression, there is still the annoying feeling that, somehow, others will discover it. As Walster, Walster, and Berscheid (1978, p. 22) point out, this is really not so surprising. "As children, when we were certain that our harmdoing was not observed by anyone, we were often startled to find out that our sophisticated parents 'somehow' discerned even our best concealed acts. And, even if they didn't, God did." This form of distress represents what the cynical newspaperman H. L. Mencken referred to when he commented that "Conscience is the inner voice that warns us someone may be watching." Even individuals who privately experience no remorse or guilt over transgressions (because they don't privately accept the required images and standards, for example) should experience anxiety when contemplating how disapproving audiences would react. The actors should imaginatively rehearse what they would say to such audiences if they happened to be apprehended.

A second form of internal distress might occur when predicament-creating events contradict important aspects of an actor's self-images (Aronson, 1968; Carson, 1969; Walster et al., 1978). In such cases, additional internal distress might exist when the actor evaluates himself from the perspective of an imagined audience. For example, a devout minister who unthinkingly swears would feel ashamed and embarrassed when contemplating the deed. A student who privately claims (expects) to do well in a course feels foolish upon receiving a failing grade. Likewise, a person who succumbs to temptation and lies, cheats, steals, or performs some other transgression that violates a self-image experiences guilt. In each case, these negative repercussions occur whether a real audience is present or an imagined audience is evoked. Thus, social predicaments do exist in "private"—private, that is, in that no other live human being need be present. All that is required is an *imagined audience that prompts attention to the self as a social object* (Duval & Wicklund, 1972; Wicklund, 1975).[1]

In general, the repercussions of predicaments are greater in front of real audiences than imagined ones. For instance, the swearing minister should be even more mortified if a group of parishioners overheard than if they did not. In the latter case, the only aversive consequences are self-generated; in the former, he confronts both self-generated punishment and whatever might be meted out by parishioners through their disapproval and lowered evaluation. Thus, predicaments have their greatest repercussions when they occur in the presence of real audiences, but they still affect the actor even when they occur only in the presence of imagined ones. Predicaments are a *social* phenomenon, but they are not just a *public* phenomenon.

The above definition of a predicament encompasses a wide variety of topics that, on the surface, might appear to be dissimilar. Predicaments include such phenomena as making an embarrassing faux pas or mistake (Modigliani, 1968, 1971); receiving a negative interpersonal evaluation after attempting to project attractive qualities to others (S. C. Jones, 1973; Mettee & Aronson, 1974); receiving "failing" feedback on personality or intelligence tests after trying to project an image of success (Modigliani, 1971; Shrauger, 1975); and being accused of transgressions of social, moral, or legal rules (Schlenker, 1978; Schlenker et al., in press; Schlenker & Schlenker, 1975; Walster et al., 1978). A great deal of research has been conducted on each of these topics. Yet the topics have typically been viewed as distinct research areas. From an impression-management perspective, these topics and others have the common element of placing actors in social predicaments where their projected or desired identities are threatened by

---

[1]One sidelight to the present discussion concerns the interpretations that have been placed on Goffman's propositions about embarrassment. Goffman proposed that embarrassment "occurs in clear-cut relation to the real *or imagined* presence of others" (1967, p. 98, italics added). He went on to discuss embarrassment in terms of the social implications of losing face in front of *an audience*, by which he seems to have meant a real or imagined audience. However, some researchers have interpreted Goffman as saying or implying that a loss of face can only occur in front of a *live* audience and that the loss of face is relegated only to a *specific* setting (Apsler, 1975; Modigliani, 1968, 1971). These interpretations do not follow from a dramaturgical approach rooted in symbolic interactionism.

events. To minimize the negative repercussions of such a threat, impression-management activities follow.

The Severity of Predicaments

Predicaments range in severity from minor embarrassing incidents that are quickly forgotten by all parties to major events that permanently damage one's identity. The severity of a predicament is primarily affected by two factors: (1) the *undesirability of the event* that precipitated it and (2) the actor's apparent *responsibility* for the event. *The more undesirable the event is and the more responsible the actor appears to be for it, the more severe the predicament is.*

Events are undesirable to the degree that they are negatively evaluated because they contradict projected or required images. For example, cheating, breaking one's word, lying, hurting others, and appearing foolish are negatively evaluated by most people. The more negative the evaluation, the more undesirable the event. Thus, a person accused of lying confronts a less severe predicament if the lie "wasn't so bad," say, telling a "white lie" to get out of a date than if the lie produced a great deal of damage—lying to con a widow out of her life's savings, for example.

An actor's responsibility for an event can range from zero to 100%. If the actor is not responsible in any way, then no predicament exists no matter how undesirable the event is. However, as one's apparent responsibility for an undesirable event increases, so does the severity of the predicament. As we'll explore more fully later, responsibility is usually low for events with which one is only globally associated, higher for events in which one's own actions produce unforeseen or accidental consequences, and highest for events in which one appears to have freely and purposefully acted to produce the primary consequences associated with the action (Heider, 1958; Shaw & Sulzer, 1964). Thus, holding the consequences constant, predicaments created by accidents (the actor could not control his actions and therefore produced the consequences, as when one slips and spills coffee on someone), and mistakes (the actor intends to produce one consequence but unfortunately produces another, as when one intends to pour coffee into someone's cup, but pours it into the other's lap) are less severe than ones created by intentional acts.

The more severe a predicament is, the greater the negative repercussions for an actor. The actor should experience greater internal distress such as anxiety and guilt, receive greater negative sanctions from audiences, and produce greater damage to his or her identity—thereby adversely affecting relationships with the audience. Studies indicate that people do react more negatively to hypothetical actors when the actors are more responsible for an undesirable event and when the event involves high-magnitude negative consequences (Shaw & Reitan, 1969; Shaw & Tremble, 1971).

Further, the more severe the predicament is, the more far reaching the negative repercussions are. A minor predicament is likely to be quickly forgotten by audiences; an actor's embarrassment or chagrin is likely to be confined to the specific situation. But severe predicaments receive greater attention. Descriptions of severe predicaments are likely to be spread by word of mouth from one audience to another. They might be written up in newspapers or comprise part of one's personnel record in a company. The stigma created by severe predicaments (for example, a criminal record) can stick with one through life. Thus, the effects of severe predicaments are not confined to specific settings and a specific audience. As we'll explore more fully shortly, the more severe the predicament is, the more aversive it is for the actor and the more motivated the actor should be to try to reduce or eliminate the negative repercussions through impression management.

Avoiding and Concealing Predicaments

Given the negative repercussions of predicaments, people should attempt to avoid them if at all possible. Failing that, as when an embarrassing accident occurs or one succumbs to temptation and breaks rules, actors should attempt to conceal the predicament from other people. People will go to great lengths to "maintain face" in front of real audiences (Goffman, 1959, 1967).

Research demonstrates that people will sacrifice monetary payoffs in order to minimize public embarrassment (Brown, 1968; Brown, 1970; Brown & Garland, 1971; Garland & Brown, 1972). To illustrate, Brown (1970) had college students perform either an embarrassing or nonembarrassing task. For the embarrassing task, the students were instructed to "suck, bite, and lick" a rubber pacifier, supposedly for the purpose of forming a sensory impression of it; doing this is certainly not in keeping with the image most college students would wish to present to others. For the nonembarrassing task, the students merely had to "touch and feel" a rubber soldier with their hands. After performing the task, the subjects were told that they would have to describe their feelings during the task to a panel of classmates who were in another room (the classmates supposedly did not see them actually perform the task). They were given the option of communicating their description to the panel in one of several ways, and they would make a larger or smaller amount of money depending on the method they selected. They could talk directly to the panel while a videotape was being made of their speech, for which they would receive $1.50; make a videotape of their speech that would be shown to the panel ($1.00); make an audio-tape of their speech ($.50); or write a descriptive statement without signing their name ($0.00). In addition, each subject was told either that the audience knew what the payoff schedule was and hence could tell that they would be sacrificing money if they selected one of the more anonymous mediums or that the audience was unaware of the payoff schedule.

It was found that subjects sacrificed the greatest amount of money—that is, selected one of the more anonymous mediums for transmitting their descriptions—when the task was embarrassing *and* the audience did not know the costs of the sacrifice. If the task was not embarrassing or if the audience knew they would be giving up money, subjects sacrificed less and selected one of the more public mediums. When asked why they made the sacrifice, the "embarrassed" subjects stated that the major reason was fear of "looking foolish," "silly," or "ridiculous" in public. People will incur costs to "cover up" an embarrassing incident, thereby looking as good to their audiences as they can. In a second study, Brown (1970) found that subjects who were embarrassed made greater monetary sacrifices if they believed the panel of classmates would be acting as "evaluators" rather than "non-evaluators." As people become more concerned that their public identities are being evaluated by an audience, they seem to increase their attempts to conceal the details of embarrassing incidents.

In other studies (Brown & Garland, 1971; Garland & Brown, 1972), it was found that college students likewise sacrificed monetary payments in order to minimize the amount of time they spent singing before an audience. The sacrifices were greater when (a) the subjects believed they were incompetent singers and hence would be more embarrassed; (b) their audience was comprised of excellent singers who might be more negative in their judgments; and (c) their audience was comprised of friends rather than strangers. These studies clearly support Goffman's (1967) proposition that embarrassment is an aversive state that people try to avoid. Further, they support the hypothesis that the greater the potential loss of face, the greater the sacrifice incurred to avoid it.

A common occurrence in social life is the attempt to conceal identity-threatening events from real audiences who might disapprove. The misbehaving child tries to hide a transgression from parents; the cheater on an exam tries to give the appearance of doing anything but cheating; the criminal attempts to hide from the police. One study of how people attempt to conceal identity-threatening information from others was conducted by Lewittes and Simmons (1975). These researchers unobtrusively observed the behaviors of college males at the campus bookstore, comparing the behaviors of those who purchased sexually oriented magazines such as *Playboy*, *Penthouse*, and *Oui* with the behaviors of those who purchased more "reputable" magazines such as *Time* and *Newsweek*. Despite contemporary society's more liberal attitudes toward sex, there are still many people who, for whatever reasons, would prefer not to publicize the fact they buy and read sexy magazines. It was found that the purchasers of the sexy magazines (a) more frequently requested a bag to place the magazine in and (b) more frequently bought other goods besides the magazine. The bag, of course, hides the purchase from public attention once the buyer leaves the check-out stand. By making other purchases, the males may have been attempting to show that they weren't the sort of people who would come into the store *only* to buy the sexy magazines. Further, by making other purchases, the males assured themselves of getting a bag without having to ask for it. (Naturally, the desirability of any particular image depends on the specific situation, audience, and actor. Thus, men on airplanes sometimes display a copy of *Playboy* or *Penthouse* to the stewardesses, conveying the impression that they are receptive to certain sorts of interaction.)

REMEDIAL BEHAVIOR

When predicaments occur, as they inevitably do despite one's best efforts to avoid or conceal them, actors confront a variety of possible negative repercussions. They might experience internal distress, negative sanctions, or a damaged identity that could adversely affect their relationship with the audience and other audiences who learn of the predicament. It is proposed that *actors in predicaments will engage in behavior designed to reduce the potential negative repercussions and maximize their expected reward/cost ratios* as best they can, given the nature of the predicament. The more severe the predicament, the greater is the motivation for such behavior.

Retreat: Hiding Away until the Storm Passes

Confronting the ominous repercussions of a predicament is not a pleasant experience. It is particularly aversive as the severity of the predicament increases and one's perceived ability to be able to deal successfully with the predicament decreases. Under such conditions, a normal reaction is to try to flee from the situation, escaping from any real audience who might be present and retreating to a place of relative safety. Thus, a debutante who is mortified when her wig falls off during the most gala festivity of the year and who can think of nothing to say to remedy the predicament might run from the crowded room. A criminal might turn and run at the sight of the police, believing that being apprehended would bring conviction. For the debutante, retreat brings the opportunity to regain composure outside the sight of the real audience; for the criminal, retreat brings the opportunity to maintain freedom a bit longer.

Signs of mild retreat occur in most embarrassing incidents. People who are embarrassed usually lower or avert their eyes (Modigliani, 1971). Thus removing the audience from the actor's visual field perhaps helps the actor regain composure. (It also suggests the ostrich-like response: "If I can't see the audience, perhaps they can't see me.") Another means of retreating while physically staying on the scene is to faint. It used to be acceptable in Western society for women to faint when confronted with embarrassing incidents and other predicaments. When in a faint, one cannot be expected to deal with the audience.

A flight response, then, can be to an actor's advantage when the expected negative repercussions are great, one's expectations of successfully dealing with the predicament are low, and there is a reasonable chance of escape, either temporarily to regain one's composure or permanently. Under these conditions, flight is most likely. However, in most situations a flight response is not to the actor's advantage. In fact, it can turn the predicament from bad to worse. Most people normally have to confront the audience again anyway, so retreat simply postpones the inevitable. In addition, the actor's reputation is likely to be ruined. The actor appears unpoised and socially unskilled. Flight also makes an actor who is accused of a transgression appear to be even more guilty than he or she may have first appeared; innocent people are not expected to run. If the actor is finally apprehended, he or she is likely to find it even more difficult than it was initially to remedy the predicament. Sooner or later, a remedial tactic must be employed.

Remedial Tactics: The Fix

Remedial tactics are impression-management activities that attempt to deal with the predicament, offering the audience, real or imagined, an explanation of it or an apology for it that can place the actor and the event in a different perspective. By so doing, the actor attempts to minimize the negative repercussions of the predicament.

Goffman (1971) notes that remedial tactics can be best understood if it is assumed that "the actor and those who witness him can imagine . . . one or more 'worst possible readings,' that is, interpretations of the act [read *event*] that maximize either its offensiveness to others or its defaming implications for the actor himself" (p. 108).[2] Given the facts available to the audience, what is the worst conclusion they might draw about the actor and the predicament? Impression-management activities can be employed to block worst-case readings and reduce the severity of the predicament to the best reading one can expect to manage successfully.

The possibility for a worst-case interpretation explains why audiences are sometimes surprised when an actor goes on and on attempting to explain or apologize for an incident. The audience might see no real need for the actor's apparent concern, but the actor takes no chances. As Oliver Wendell Holmes bluntly put it in a more restricted realm "Apology is only egotism wrong side out. Nine times out of ten the first thing a man's companion knows of his short-comings, is from his apology." From the actor's perspective, however, the expected value of assuming the worst and being wrong is usually less negative than the expected value of assuming the best and being wrong.

For the moment, we will not be concerned with the "truth" of a particular remedial tactic—that is, whether it accurately describes the event according to some "objective" standards or even accurately describes the actor's private beliefs and feelings. What we will be concerned with are the types of remedial tactics that can be employed, their interpersonal functions, and the conditions under which they will most likely be used.

There are at least two general, somewhat overlapping, classes of remedial tactics: *accounts* and *apologies*. Accounts are explanations of the predicament-creating event, while apologies are admissions of blame coupled with an attempt to be pardoned.

ACCOUNTS

Accounts are *explanations* of a predicament-creating event *designed to minimize the apparent severity of the predicament*. The actor provides a more acceptable or satisfactory explanation of the event than that contained in a worst-case reading. Recall that the severity of a predicament is determined by the undesirability of an event and the actor's responsibility for it. Accounts are aimed at precisely these two elements. Through accounts, the actor tries to influence the audience's views about the event or his responsibility for it. If successful, an account will minimize or eliminate the apparent severity of the predicament. The actor thereby decreases the potential for negative repercussions.

[2]From *Relations in Public: Microstudies of the Public Order*, by Erving Goffman. © 1971 by Erving Goffman. (New York: Basic Books, Inc., 1971.) This and all other quotations from this source are reprinted by permission.

The study of accounts can be traced to several convergent lines of thought in psychology, sociology, and philosophy. The seminal work of John Dewey (1922, 1939) on the nature of motivation is one. Dewey argued that what we term a "motive" is really only a linguistic statement that arises after an action already has occurred—motives do not produce action; they explain or account for it. A motive statement serves to influence how other people, and ultimately the actor himself, interpret the actor's reasons for behaving the way he did. The sociologist C. W. Mills (1940) expanded Dewey's treatment of motives, arguing that motive statements are needed only after unexpected actions that cause an audience to question the propriety of an actor's intentions and character. From a different perspective, the philosopher J. L. Austin (1961/1970, 1962/1975) published an essay in 1957 entitled "A Plea for Excuses." In it, he analyzed the nature and functions of excuses and justifications, concluding that they are not merely descriptions of an event or an actor's role in it but, rather, attempts to defend oneself against accusations that one has done something bad or untoward. Legal philosophers have shown considerable interest in the types of defenses provided by these accounting tactics (Hart, 1968). Virtually all of these sources seem to have influenced the work of Scott and Lyman (1968), who provide an insightful and delightfully readable sociological analysis of accounting in everyday life. Goffman's (1971) discussion of remedial interchanges is also highly recommended to interested readers.

There are three basic forms of accounts: *defenses of innocence, excuses,* and *justifications.*[3] *Defenses of innocence* are attempts by actors to show that they had nothing to do with the supposed event; either it didn't occur or they were in no way responsible for it. Such defenses completely dissociate the actor from the alleged event and offer the potential for total exoneration. *Excuses* are attempts by actors to minimize their responsibility for predicament-creating events, although in so doing the actors tacitly or explicitly admit that an undesirable event did occur and they had some role in it. For example, a soldier might admit to having killed, but explain that he was under orders and hence not fully responsible (Scott & Lyman, 1968). The accounts by Nazi war criminal Adolf Eichmann during the Nuremberg trials following World War II and U.S. Army Lt. William Calley during the Viet Nam war illustrate the use of excuses to explain mass carnage. *Justifications* are attempts by actors to minimize or deny the undesirable nature of a

---

[3]It should be noted that disagreements exist about how accounting tactics should be subcategorized. D'Arcy (1963) proposes a framework based on three factors: (a) *qualifying circumstances,* which are the necessary conditions that must exist before any responsibility can be assigned to an actor, (b) *specifying circumstances,* which are the conditions that permit an action to be labeled one way rather than another, and (c) *quantifying circumstances,* which determine the amount of commendation or condemnation that should occur.

predicament-creating event, although in so doing the actors tacitly or explicitly admit that an event did occur and they have some responsibility for it. For example, a soldier may acknowledge having killed but justify it by noting that "they," the enemy, fully deserved such a fate and that he should be commended for such laudable service to his country (Scott & Lyman, 1968).

Defenses of Innocence

Defenses of innocence construct a barrier between the actor and the alleged undesirable event that the actor hopes will be impenetrable. If the audience accepts them as representing the truth, the actor is totally exonerated and appears to have been wrongly accused in the first place. This is a most fortuitous state of affairs for actors who confront predicaments, since the attempted dissociation between the actor and the alleged event is complete. However, the use of such defenses is limited to certain situations, to be seen below, because the audience usually has to be almost completely mistaken about the accusation in the first place. If the audience actually observed the alleged undesirable event, yet still makes the accusation, the chances of their being completely mistaken are greatly reduced, the chances of their accepting the actor's defense of innocence, likewise.

One type of defense is a *defense of nonoccurrence*. Here the actor tries to show that the event under consideration did not occur. An example is a plot often used in mystery stories. An individual is accused of some crime, say a murder, but is later able to convince the accusers that no murder took place. The alleged victim may have died of suicide or stroke. He might not even be deceased, having left false clues behind to make it appear as if a murder occurred while he was really skipping the country and hiding his identity. In any case, the alleged undesirable event did not take place, and the accused is exonerated. Some of the defaming accusations often confronted by actors can likewise be argued to be either fabrications or misconstruals of what "really" occurred.

A second type of defense is a *defense of noncausation*. Here the fact that an undesirable event occurred is not challenged, but the accused actor attempts to show that he or she was in no way responsible for it. In essence, the actor pleads "I didn't do it." An actor accused of a murder might argue that she was actually miles away at the time of the incident and produce an alibi to "prove" it. Or, accused of breaking a lamp, a child might point a finger at the dog. A married person might explain that, despite rumors to the contrary, he wasn't the one seen entering the motel. If the audience accepts that the actor is completely nonresponsible, the actor is exonerated.

There are, however, complications to defenses of noncausation. Even if the actor "didn't do it," he or she still might be held indirectly or globally responsible. First, causality can involve long, complex links between an origin and a consequence. It may not be enough to demonstrate that you didn't perform *the* act that produced the undesirable effect; you may have to show that you didn't commit any act that was in any way causally related to the effect. Thus, the accused in a murder case who was miles away at the time of the act might be charged with paying someone to commit it or conspiring with the person who did commit it. The child may have to prove that although the dog knocked over the lamp, she wasn't running around the room teasing and chasing the dog. The causal linkage becomes even more complex in the case of a scientist whose theory led to the invention of a weapon of mass carnage. As the old ditty goes, the loss of a war can be blamed on a blacksmith who didn't have the necessary nail for a horse's shoe.

Many such indirect linkages are formally recognized and sanctioned by law. For instance, parents can be held legally responsible for some of the actions of their children, as when a child damages the property of another. The parents, presumably, are charged with the task of bringing their children up "properly"; if they fail, they are responsible. (This presumed failure of parents partially explains why parents are so easily embarrassed, and defensive, when their children misbehave in public.) As another example, many states hold an individual responsible for all repercussions of any felony he or she commits. A person can be accused of murder if during an armed robbery a police officer trying to make the arrest accidentally kills a bystander. The criminal is held legally responsible, since without the precipitating felony no death would have occurred.

Defenses of noncausation gradually fade into mere excuses as the indirect linkage becomes stronger. A plea of "I didn't do it" is not enough to produce exoneration if the audience charges indirect causation. The actor still appears to be at least partially responsible. Nonetheless, indirect, and hence shared, responsibility is better than total, personal, direct causality. The actor may at least be able to reduce some of the negative repercussions of the predicament.

A second, perhaps more disconcerting consideration is that people are often held responsible at least to some degree for undesirable events they can not be said to have even indirectly caused. This is *global responsibility*, the lowest level of responsibility that can be assigned. It occurs when people are only tenuously connected to some event (Heider, 1958). For example, it is not uncommon for a person of the Jewish faith to be asked why "you people" killed Jesus Christ or for a person to be persecuted because of his parents' failure to legalize their union. Even the statement "I had nothing to do with it" is not enough to satisfy some audiences. Again, however, fewer negative repercussions usually occur when an actor is able to reduce responsibility from the worst possible level to the level of global association.

Excuses

Excuses permit actors to admit that an undesirable event occurred, that their own actions in some way caused the consequences, but that they are not really as responsible for the event as it might appear. Thus, excuses are an attempt to reduce one's responsibility from the worst possible level to the lowest level possible in the situation. As responsibility declines, so do the negative repercussions for the actor. Excuses are exemplified by the declaration "I did it, but I (couldn't help it) (was forced to do it) (didn't know what I was doing)."

To demonstrate how responsibility can be reduced, it is instructive to examine the worst possible case from the actor's standpoint—that in which responsibility is maximal. People are held maximally responsible for events when they appear to have *freely* and *intentionally* acted to produce the major consequences under consideration; that is, they could *foresee* the consequences, they *tried* to bring them about, and they were *not under pressure* from circumstances that share some of the responsibility for the event (Heider, 1958; Shaw & Sulzer, 1964). For example, a defendant in a murder case is held most responsible (and faces the most severe sentence) if it can be shown that she planned the deed for a period of time, was mentally capable of foreseeing the consequences of the act, and was not under unusual duress. In this case, responsibility is squarely on the shoulders of the actor. She cannot claim that the murder was a mistake ("I thought the victim was a burglar"), an accident ("I was cleaning the gun and it went off"), or the result of forces beyond her control ("I was under the influence of drugs"). Under such conditions, audiences (oneself included) are maximally confident that the event reveals something about the actor's motives, character, and disposition (Jones & Davis, 1965). Since the event itself is undesirable, they attribute malicious motives to the actor and assume that she is a "bad" person, the type to commit such transgressions habitually. Maximal responsibility results in the event's having maximal impact on one's identity, and it makes one maximally deserving of punishment.

Excuses are designed to reduce responsibility from this maximal level to the lowest feasible amount given what the circumstances will allow the audience to accept. In contrast to defenses of innocence, excuses merely mitigate responsibility; they normally don't eliminate it. As Austin (1961/1970) put it:

Few excuses get us out of it completely: the average excuse, in a poor situation, gets us only out of the fire into the frying pan—but still, of course, any frying pan in a fire. If I have broken your dish or romance, maybe the best defense I can find will be clumsiness [p. 177].

Unforeseen Consequences. To reduce responsibility, actors can argue that, although the act and its undesirable consequences occurred, the actor either *could not possibly have foreseen* or *merely did not foresee* the consequences. The strongest of such pleas is that the actor could not have foreseen what happened and hence could not reasonably have been expected to do anything other than what he or she did. The actor may have caused the consequences, but cannot be said to have acted improperly; without foreseeing, there can be no intent. The accused actor normally adds that if he had foreseen what happened he never would have done it. If accepted by the audience, pleas of this strong type normally produce attributions of the lowest amount of responsibility that can be assigned to an actor given that he or she actually performed the act that led to the consequences.

Explanations that an event was an accident or mistake can involve excuses of this strong type. Actors can claim that they had no voluntary control over a particular act. A host who spills a drink on a guest can cite an involuntary muscle cramp; a driver who causes an accident can plead that she suffered a stroke and could not have helped it. Alternatively, an actor can admit to having control over actions but absolutely no way of reasonably foreseeing or averting the consequences. For example, a woman walking on a crowded beach who loses the top of her bathing suit can explain that its fasteners had a hidden defect, or a driver who hits a pedestrian can explain that the pedestrian ran out from between parked trucks. Many embarrassing incidents, such as an inopportune belch or a malapropism, can be excused by this type of explanation.

A weaker excuse is an explanation that, although the consequences might have been and perhaps should have been foreseen, one didn't foresee them. Either through ignorance, carelessness, or stupidity, one went ahead and produced the undesirable result. An actor might shoot at a target, miss, and accidentally hit a child. Although this actor can be described as negligent, stupid, or morally weak, we could not necessarily say that he was a malicious or cold-blooded killer. Similarly, an embarrassing incident can be excused through an explanation of unforeseen consequences, as when one is looking off in the distance and trips or neglects to zip up before leaving the bathroom. Actors who employ this type of excuse still risk some negative repercussions, but these are usually not as undesirable as those implied by the worst-case interpretation. This type of excuse does not reduce responsibility to the level of complete unforeseeability, but it does reduce it below that of the maximal level (Heider, 1958; Shaw & Sulzer, 1964).

In many situations, excuses fall somewhere between the strong and weak versions of unforeseen consequences, where there may be doubts in the minds of both actor and audience about whether the consequences were unforeseeable or just unforeseen. Could the actor have been expected to take precautions to avert the consequences? If the answer is no, the event is unforeseeable; if yes, it was merely unforeseen.

Extenuating Circumstances. A second major category of excuse is actors' explanations that they performed the act but that *extenuating circumstances* existed. These circumstances shift some of the responsibility for the event from the actor to causes that may have affected the actor's behavior or its consequences. These additional factors allow the actor to claim reduced freedom of decision or reduced competence at the time of the event. The actor thereby appears to have had less than the "normal" amount of choice in performing the act, given the circumstances. Such explanations are based on a variety of factors: "I couldn't help it, I was drunk . . . stoned . . . coerced . . . under strain . . . mentally ill . . . untrained . . . possessed by demons . . . too turned on to stop . . . tired . . . threatened . . . a victim of an impoverished environment," and so on. These circumstances vary in their effectiveness in excusing the actor, depending on the situation, the reputation of the actor, and the audience (Goffman, 1971; Scott & Lyman, 1968). The actor can rarely emerge from the predicament unscathed after using such an excuse, but at least responsibility is shared with another possible cause of the event.

Scapegoating is a frequently used excuse that locates the extenuating circumstances in the actions of others (Scott & Lyman, 1968). Minority groups are often used as scapegoats and blamed for the problems of a country—for example, Jews in Germany prior to World War II and Blacks in the United States. Similarly, a person accused of killing another argues that the victim precipitated the incident. A student who is flunking out of college can blame the unfortunate state of affairs on a romance, a distraction that makes it impossible to study. A mother might explain to her questioning friends that her son hasn't gone further in life because his wife doesn't encourage him enough (or allows him to be lazy). The *diffusion of responsibility* (Mynatt & Sherman, 1975), in which people in groups share responsibility among themselves and thereby claim minimal responsibility for any negative consequences caused by the group's decisions, is a similar type of account (see Chapter 4).

Acts that are particularly heinous, such as bizarre murders, are often difficult for audiences to comprehend. In such a context, excuses that cite overpowering extenuating circumstances can be particularly effective. Audiences are often willing to accept that no normal human being could have done such a despicable thing unless something was "wrong" with him or her. Depending on the culture, such excuses might cite witchcraft, possession by demons, or mental illness to explain the behavior (Goffman, 1971). David Berkowitz, the notorious "Son of Sam," was the object of New York City's greatest man-hunt in history after killing six young people and wounding seven others in nighttime stalks. When finally apprehended in 1977, he explained that he killed because he was commanded to do so by a voice that spoke to him through a neighbor's dog. At different times during police questioning, he variously termed his master, the person represented by the voice, as a man who lived 6000 years ago; the devil; and a neighbor, Sam Carr. He proclaimed of the voice "He told me to kill" and said of the killings that "it was commanded" ("'Son of Sam' Suspect," 1977). At the same time, he had perfect recall of the murders, often correcting police on details during interrogations. In some cultures, Berkowitz's account of the reasons for his behavior would be accepted as a factual description of the influence of the devil. In our culture, his account was taken as an indication of mental illness. (Interestingly, Berkowitz later admitted to having invented his tales of satanic possession ["Berkowitz Admits," 1979].) He stated "There were no real demons, no talking dogs, no satanic henchmen. I made it all up via my wild imagination so as to find some form of justification for my criminal acts against society." He had been declared mentally incompetent by the court prior to this statement, and this judgment has not been reversed.)

The degree to which any such explanation is considered mitigating by an audience is influenced by the commonly accepted beliefs of people in the particular society or subgroup. It is one thing for people in Western society to accept mental illness as a plausible explanation for murder; it is another to excuse a murder because of the influence of television, something to which we are all exposed. The defense attorney for Ronald Zamora, a 15-year-old Miami, Florida, youth accused of robbing and killing an elderly neighbor, argued that the boy was insane by virtue of "TV intoxication." A constant diet of violent television programs allegedly made him unable to distinguish fact from fantasy; to Zamora, the defense argued, the act of killing the neighbor was just another scene out of a TV show such as *Kojak*. The defense failed; Zamora was convicted in 1977.

Thus, excuses allow an actor to admit some responsibility for an undesirable event while concomitantly explaining the event in a way that reduces responsibility below the worst-case interpretation. We'll examine some of the research on excuses shortly.

Justifications

Justifications allow an actor to admit some responsibility for an undesirable event but minimize or deny its undesirability. If the justification is accepted by the audience, the severity of the predicament is attenuated. Skillful actors can even transform a potentially undesirable event from something negative to something positive; then, instead of feeling guilt or embarrassment they can take pride in being responsible for it. Undesirable events can be justified in at least three, somewhat overlapping, ways: (1) directly minimizing the negativity of the event; (2) comparing the event with similar ones that other people have been responsible for but for which they were not punished; and (3) embedding the incident in the context of higher, more desirable goals that permit or even require the event under the given conditions. These three types can be used separately or in combination.

Direct Minimization. In this first type of justification, actors attempt directly to minimize the negativity of the event. The event is described as less (or not at all) harmful, untoward, bad, costly, important, improper, meaningful, significant, offensive, or whatever, than it might appear from a worst-case reading. For example, in transgression situations, a mugger argues that the victim wasn't hurt too badly; a student who cheats explains that it didn't affect anyone else's grade; a child points out that the broken lamp was old and needed replacement anyway; a defendant asserts that the crime is a victimless one. In other types of situations, a businessperson describes an embarrassing faux pas as a minor flub not worthy of comment; a self-described honor student passes off the test she failed as invalid; a disappointed Romeo derogates a date's intelligence and explains that he didn't like her anyway.

When the undesirable event involves harm to others, people can try to justify it directly by contending that the *victim* was insignificant. This is done by noting characteristics of the injured party that make it permissible to harm him. It might be explained that the victim was only a Nazi, criminal, Communist, prostitute, Black, Jew, or whatever. Each society and subgroup within a society usually has a list of the types of people who can be "justifiably" mistreated because they are supposed to be inferior, unworthy, potentially dangerous, unimportant, or simply not the kinds of people that "decent" citizens should be concerned about (Scott & Lyman, 1968). Thus, it is argued that no real damage is done by harming them, and the event emerges as being less negative in its consequences. Whether the victim experienced pain is irrelevant if the victim is immaterial to begin with. Animals have usually been afforded this inferior status. Mistreating, injuring, or even killing an animal is often dismissed by the comment that it was only a dog, cat, insect, or whatever. Note that justifying an event by this means does not require asserting that the victim instigated an attack on the actor—which would involve a plea of self-defense—or that the actor was trying to save or protect society by ridding it of the victim—which would involve appeals to higher goals (see below). It can include these elements, but it does not have to. Simply, this justification pleads that the event itself is not negative because harming such a person (or animal) is no real harm at all.

Justification through Comparison. The second type of justification is more indirect than the first; it depends on social comparison processes. These allow the actor to try to minimize the undesirability of the event by comparing his or her own situation with those of others who do the same thing or worse but are not punished. It is exemplified by statements such as "others do worse things," or "everybody does it" (Scott & Lyman, 1968). The implication is that if everybody does it it must be reasonably normal or acceptable. In addition, the actor usually asserts or implies that to single him or her out for punishment when everyone else is getting off the hook is most unfair. The tables are thereby turned on the accusing audience and they are put in the position of having to explain why they would consider punishing the actor. The actor can even go on to assert or imply that, since everyone does it, the criterion for labeling the event "bad" is in need of revision. For example, a person accused of the possession of marijuana can cite statistics on the large proportion of the population who light up, note that the vast majority of these individuals are never apprehended by the police, and argue that the laws underlying the accusation are unfair or unwise. Similarly, people who are caught in a predicament because they receive identity-threatening information can exaggerate the degree to which others would receive the same type of information in the same setting. For example, research indicates that subjects who take a test and are later told that their performance indicated that they possess an undesirable attribute such as latent homosexuality later assert that most other people possess the same characteristic (Bramel, 1962, 1963; Holmes, 1978; Steiner, 1968).

Justifications through Higher Goals. Finally, undesirable events can be justified by embedding the event under a larger set of values and goals that are either admirable or acceptable. The following exemplify the tactic: a dentist justifies giving painful injections of novocaine to patients by explaining that he or she is saving them greater pain in the long run; parents inform their children that they are punishing them "for their own good;" a liar explains that the lie was actually to benefit the victim; a terrorist explains that bombing deaths of civilians are in the cause of freedom; killing during wartime is justified by each side by citing the positive goals for which it is fighting. Actors who employ such justifications may even admit that if the event is taken out of the context in which it occurred, the act and its consequences are bad. However, they assert that *in* the context, the event is not negative; usually, it is asserted to be positive. In other words, although one vignette in a cognitive script (as one frame in a comic strip) might be evaluated negatively if judged in isolation, the overall effect of the script is judged desirable (see Chapter 2). Thus, higher goals and more important values can be brought to bear to justify events and transform the potentially heinous into the meritorious.

The Use of Accounting Tactics: Remedying Predicaments

As predicaments increase in severity, people should become more likely to employ an accounting tactic, thereby giving them an opportunity to avoid a worst-case reading and reduce or eliminate the potential repercussions from the audience. Accounting tactics are ideal for this task, since they permit actors to *explain* the undesirable event. Actors can present their side of things, proffering an alternative interpretation to the way an audience might view the "reality" of the situation. If the audience accepts the actor's account, the severity of the predicament and the negative repercussions are attenuated.

In addition, *as predicaments increase in severity, actors should use accounting tactics in a more extreme way.* That is, the discrepancy between a worst-case reading and the actor's account must become greater if the actor is to reduce significantly the negative repercussions. For example, people should deny more responsibility for a very undesirable event than they do for an only *slightly* undesirable event. The greater the harm to another, the more likely the actor should be to justify it by saying that the victim deserved it.

Research from a number of areas supports these hypotheses. Brock and Buss (1962) examined people's reactions after they harmed another person. College student subjects in the experiment were given the task of teaching a partner a series of problems by delivering an electric shock to him or her each time a mistake was made. Actually, the partner was a confederate of the experimenter who made a predetermined number of errors on the task so that the subjects would have to deliver shock. Before the task began, the subjects were given either high or low choice in deciding whether to continue. Subjects in the high-choice condition should feel more responsible for delivering shocks to the confederate than subjects in the low-choice condition; at the very least, the former subjects should believe that their audience will hold them more responsible and hence have a more negative worst-case reading of their actions. In addition, each subject was told the level of shock to administer: low range (mild shock, minimal harm) or high range (painful shock, greater harm).

It was found that subjects in the high-choice condition justified their shocking behavior by minimizing their reports of how painful the shocks were; they underestimated the degree to which they harmed the partner. The subjects in the low-choice condition, on the other hand, increased their reports of how painful the shocks were. Since the latter subjects had been told they had little or no choice about their behavior, their actions were excused by being in a low-choice condition; they could then legitimately blame the experimenter.

In addition, subjects in the high-harm condition insisted that they were under more of an obligation to the experimenter to administer shocks than subjects in the low-harm condition. Thus, subjects who did the greatest harm also seemed to account for their behavior by exaggerating the degree to which they were pressured to deliver shock by the experimenter, thereby excusing their actions even further. Similar results were found by Brock and Buss (1964).

Such results are not confined to a single domain. For example, suppose an actor tells a lie that causes another person to be misled and hurt. How will the actor react? Numerous studies have been conducted to investigate this question, and they provide strong support for the accounting hypotheses. Hoyt, Henley, and Collins (1972) had college student subjects write an essay that strongly and convincingly argued that "toothbrushing is a habit fraught with danger to one's health." These essays were supposedly going to be used by a research group in a project being conducted in surrounding junior high schools. The expected consequences of the essays were manipulated by making half of the subjects believe they might be doing a great deal of damage and the other half believe they would be doing no damage at all. The former subjects were told that their essays would be used to convince junior high school students not to brush their teeth, or at least to brush them less! It was explained that a six-month follow-up on these students should reveal "that the students who read the don't brush essays will suffer more cavities and dental problems." (Actually, the essays were never used to convince anyone.) The remaining subjects were told that their essays would merely be used as part of a classroom demonstration and should have no effect whatsoever on the junior high students. Prior to writing the essay, subjects were also given either high choice about proceeding (stressing their decision to help and their *choosing* to help) or low choice (telling them "What you are going to do is . . ."). (Interestingly, only one out of 77 subjects refused to write the essay; most students will agree to perform such a task when asked by an authoritative and respected researcher.) After completing the essays, subjects were asked to give their opinions about a number of medically-related topics, including the merits of toothbrushing.

From an image-maintenance perspective, we should expect that subjects in the low-consequences condition would not regard their situation as much of a predicament. After all, no particularly undesirable event occurred. True, they wrote an essay that endorsed a topic they privately disagreed with, but the act had no real consequences that could affect them or anyone else. Hence, we should not expect them to interpret the situation as a predicament or to go out of their way to try to account for their actions.

Subjects in the high-consequences condition *do* confront a predicament. They did something they believed would harm other people—and junior high students at that! They should attempt to account for their undesirable action. Subjects who were given no choice about writing the essay have a ready-made excuse for their behavior. If they had no choice, as the experimenter implied, they had little responsibility; the undesirable consequences are not their fault. Subjects with high choice, on the other hand, cannot similarly excuse their actions, since it was made clear that they did have the option of not writing the essays. The use of excuses is blocked for them by the nature of the situation. Their only alternative is to *justify* the behavior. In this case, if they explained that toothbrushing is not really all that healthy and that toothpastes may contain harmful chemicals and abrasives, their actions would appear to be less harmful than they might on a worst-case reading. This is precisely what was found in the study. The only subjects who showed significant attitude change—that is, expressed opinions that were less favorable toward toothbrushing and toothpastes than other students—were those who were given high choice *and* who believed their actions would have high consequences.

Interestingly, if people in a situation like this can find an audience who will excuse their actions, they do not justify their behavior. In a similar study, Riess and Schlenker (1977) had subjects write anti-toothbrushing speeches that they believed would have high consequences. Before doing so, subjects were given either high or low choice about proceeding. However, after finishing the speech, some of the subjects discovered that a majority of a group of students who observed the situation through a one-way mirror felt that they had little or no choice in acting the way they did; other subjects discovered that the majority believed they had relatively high choice. In this situation, the only subjects who *justified* their actions by expressing more unfavorable opinions about toothpastes were those who were given high choice initially *and* who discovered their audience also believed that they had high choice. For these subjects, an excuse wouldn't work, so they had to employ a justification. However, subjects who initially had high choice but were told that the audience thought they had little choice did not significantly justify their act; they apparently accepted the excuse provided by the audience.

A wide variety of other research, exploring numerous topics, likewise indicates that, when people appear to be responsible for undesirable events, they employ excuses (Modigliani, 1971; Mynatt & Sherman, 1975; Walster et al., 1978) and/or justifications (Calder, Ross, & Insko, 1973; Cialdini, Kenrick, & Hoerig, 1976; Collins & Hoyt, 1972; Davis & Jones, 1960; Gaes, Kalle, & Tedeschi, 1978; Glass, 1964; Modigliani, 1971; Mynatt & Sherman, 1975; Schlenker et al., in press; Walster et al., 1978). Further, such accounting tactics are employed whether the undesirable event is created by a *transgression* that harms others, as in studies where subjects lie or deliver shocks, or by some other undesirable event that threatens one's projected identity. A few further examples from research will be useful in illustrating the range of accounting.

To begin, it is worth keeping in mind that most people—certainly the college students who comprise the vast majority of the subject population for psychological research—hold a reasonably favorable opinion of themselves and most of their attributes. During experiments, where they know that they are being evaluated by a psychologist researcher, they are on their best behavior, trying to project an identity that contains socially approved images like appearing intelligent, competent, attractive, and so on (Rosenberg, 1965). The experimenter usually knows little or nothing about their past, and their expected interaction with the experimenter is brief. So, unless something happens during the study to give the experimenter *consistent and valid* evidence of one or more of their relative frailties or failings, they should attempt to project a positive identity in most respects.[4] If an isolated event occurs during the study to contradict this positive self-presentation, subjects should try to account for it. They can cite numerous possible excuses or justifications for the potentially undesirable isolated event.

For example, Modigliani (1971) had subjects take a test in which they publicly failed in front of not only the experimenter but some other subjects as well. It was found that the more embarrassed the subjects were—and hence the more concerned with how they appeared to the others—the more accounting they did when later interacting with the audience. Subjects did such things as minimize the importance of the failure, cite excuses for the performance, like "Fluorescent lights really affect my concentration," introduce redeeming or self-enhancing information that might compensate for the failure, like "I'm usually much better at these types of tasks," fish for reassurance, and defensively change the subject. Since they were obviously responsible for the undesirable event, they tried to remedy the predicament and save face.

In a slightly different vein, Mynatt and Sherman (1975) had sub-

[4]Conditions can be arranged in laboratory studies that make it difficult or impossible for subjects to significantly excuse or justify an undesirable event. For example, conditions can be arranged so that subjects receive consistent failing grades on a variety of tests that purportedly measure the same ability (see Dutton, 1972). In such instances, subjects do not dispute the information. Instead, they act in ways that indicate they really do lack the ability in question. The consistent negative information serves as a reality check that holds self-presentations within the bounds of what might be credible to the audience (experimenter). If the subjects disputed such consistent negative information, they would appear to be quite irrational and egotistical. Therefore, they accept it.

jects serve as advisors, either alone or in a group with two others, to another person (actually a confederate) who worked on a series of problems. The situation was rigged so that the confederate took the subjects' advice on 80% of the trials and ended up doing either quite well or quite poorly. Giving advice to someone else, who takes it and then fails abominably, should create a predicament. Indeed, the subjects accounted for their advisee's loss when they were subsequently asked for their perceptions. When subjects were part of a group of advisors, they accurately reported how often their advice was taken, believed they had influenced the advisee's decisions, recognized that the advisee had done poorly, but *denied personal responsibility* for what occurred. They excused the undesirable event by blaming it partly on the other members of the advising team. When subjects worked alone as the advisor, they did not directly deny personal responsibility; after all, they were the only advisor. However, they did *indirectly excuse* their behavior by saying that they had little influence on the advisee and by reporting that the advisee took their advice only 56% of the time (it was really 80%); in addition, they *justified* the event by rating the advisee's outcomes as not too bad. Many similar studies of how people deny their responsibility for failing outcomes (see Chapter 4) can also be interpreted in terms of accounting.

In sum, an impressive variety of research demonstrates, under controlled conditions, that people do employ accounting tactics when confronted with a predicament.[5] The more severe the predicament, the more accounting they seem to do. The necessity for explaining undesirable events for which one appears to be responsible is a byproduct of social life.

The Use of Accounting Tactics:
Selecting an Explanation

Excuses and justifications are not mutually exclusive classes; they overlap. People often combine excuses and justifications in attempts to reduce both responsibility and the undesirability of the event. There is rarely, if ever, only one tactic or combination of accounting tactics that will effectively extricate an actor from a predicament. This usually

[5]Other traditional research areas not normally interpreted from an impression-management perspective can also be interpreted in terms of accounting. For example, people who receive failing feedback on personality or intelligence tests typically derogate the test's validity (Eagly, 1967; Schlenker & Miller, 1977a), thus justifying the failure by making it seem unimportant or nondiagnostic. Similarly, people who receive unfavorable interpersonal evaluations typically derogate and dislike the evaluator (S. C. Jones, 1973; Mettee & Aronson, 1974), thus justifying the event by making it seem less meaningful. Receiving a negative evaluation from someone you dislike or feel is stupid is less threatening than receiving one from someone you like or feel is intelligent.

makes it difficult to predict exactly how a particular actor will respond in a particular situation. Nonetheless, some general hypotheses about the factors that affect the selection of accounting tactics can be offered.

First, people seem to *select the accounting tactic they believe maximizes their expected reward/cost ratio in the situation.* If an actor believes a particular account won't work—that is, won't be accepted by the audience—it won't be used. Given the choice between two possible explanations of an event, people will select the one that offers the greatest potential for eliminating the most negative repercussions. Such expectations are affected by a complex interaction of factors related to the actor (desired identity, reputation vis-à-vis the audience, personality characteristics, verbal skills, goals), the audience (their identities, what they appear to know about the actor and the incident), and the situation (the type and magnitude of the undesirable incident).

At first glance, the above proposition seems to suggest that people will do and say anything to escape from predicaments irrespective of what the "truth really is." Although there is certainly an element of accuracy in such an interpretation, it does not do justice to the complexities of social life. Explanations of any event are held in check by reality constraints (see Chapter 4); there are limitations on the degree to which people can contradict consensually accepted facts and still be believed by an audience. An account will not be effective in convincing an audience, and hence will have a low expected reward/cost ratio, unless it is fitted to the situation. That is, the account should appear to take into consideration (1) the gravity of the situation; (2) the facts that are known about the situation by the audience; and (3) the prevailing beliefs the audience has about such situations as represented by the values and beliefs of the particular society or subgroup. These factors all act as *reality constraints* that prevent actors from "distorting the facts" beyond what audiences can accept and fit into their existing cognitive scripts. Hence, it is hypothesized that *people will choose accounts that they believe are fitted to the situation as it appears to be known by the audience.*

Let us first see why accounts must be fitted to the gravity of the situation in order to be effective (Austin, 1961/1970; Goffman, 1971; Scott & Lyman, 1968). The excuse "I forgot what time it was" is usually effective in explaining why one was embarrassingly late for a party. It will not work for a doctor whose patient died in the emergency room while waiting for the doctor's arrival. The justification "It didn't really matter" might be expected to explain why one ran over a frog; it should not be expected to explain why one ran over a child. People are expected to regard certain offenses more seriously than others and therefore to take extra precautions to prevent them. If it appears from the account that the actor did not do so, the account will be rejected by the audience (oneself included).

Second, accounts should be fitted to the facts that are known about the event by the audience. The justification "I didn't hurt him much" might work if the victim later turned up with only a small bruise; it would not work if the victim was found bloody and quite dead. Accounts can only be pushed so far before the concepts they contain no longer fit the accepted facts, and they are rejected by the audience (oneself included).

Third, accounts should fit the prevailing ideas in a particular society or subgroup; otherwise the audience will have difficulty accepting the account at face value (Scott & Lyman, 1968). Unless accounts are fitted to prevailing beliefs, the audience will not be able to integrate them into their existing cognitive scripts about the world. For example, most people in Western society dismiss accounts that try to excuse behavior by blaming the event on witchcraft, demonic possession, commands by voices from the beyond, and so on. Such "causes" for behavior are simply not believed by the average person. Therefore, the account is rejected on face value. (Of course, in some other cultures, usually termed "primitive," such accounts would be accepted as describing the "truth.") The only way one of the above accounts will be accepted in Western society is that the audience translates it into an account that they can view as plausible. For example, blaming one's behavior on witchcraft could be translated by the audience as symptomatic of the actor's mental illness. Mental illness is a widely accepted "cause" for aberrant behavior in Western society. Interestingly, if an actor intends to try to excuse behavior by accounting for it as a sign of mental illness, he or she is better off employing some other outlandish account that demands such translation by the audience. People who confront a serious predicament, such as being charged with a murder, and simply say "I couldn't help it; I'm mentally ill" are seen as too rational and calculating to be believed. This "Catch 22" is also part of our prevailing cultural beliefs.

Negotiating. An initial account is not necessarily a final product that the audience must accept or reject. Accounts are often *negotiated* by the actor and real audience until a final product acceptable to both is arrived at (Scott & Lyman, 1968; Scheff, 1968). That is, the actor suggests one explanation for the situation; the audience responds by modifying it greatly or slightly; the actor rejoins; and so forth until a finished product emerges. For example, a student who fails a test might explain to the instructor that a number of distressing events occurred in his life that interfered with his studying, including breaking up with his girlfriend. The instructor, thinking that the student is only lazy, doesn't accept this excuse and counters with the assertion that the same thing probably happened to other students in the class who nonetheless managed to find the time to study. The student rejoins in some way to make the account more credible, such as pointing out that, since he and the young woman were going to be married in two weeks, his trauma was much greater than that of other students who appear to be in the same boat. The instructor has many ways to respond to this elaborated excuse. The process goes on until either the negotiations are broken off or mutual accord is reached. In this sense, the "truth" of a situation— "the" explanation for it that is accepted by people—comes from a process of negotiation and consensual agreement about the meaning and cause of particular events. In science, "truth" is determined by consensual agreement of trained scientists who interpret what the "facts" mean. Similarly, in everyday life, "truth" is decided by consensual agreement of the people who are involved with interpreting an event.

Real audiences do not assist actors only by negotiating accounts with them; they frequently provide initial accounts (Scott & Lyman, 1968). For example, a member of the audience might help an actor out of an embarrassing situation by making some light comment and tossing in a justifying remark such as, "Oh, that happens to all of us on occasion." The audience thereby informs the actor that they don't regard the event as particularly undesirable and won't hold it against him or her. The actor's identity is preserved, and the interaction can proceed, much to everyone's advantage. Indeed, people who are skillful at helping others preserve their identity soon gain reputations as kind, pleasant, and quick-witted.

As the severity of a predicament increases, though, real audiences should become less willing to assist actors *with accounts that are in the self-interests of the actor.* For example, few people are interested in helping a cheater, liar, or murderer explain his or her actions in a way that gets the actor off the hook. True, they might be willing to offer an explanation of the actor's behavior, but the explanation should more closely resemble a worst-case than a best-case reading. It is therefore hypothesized that, as the severity of a predicament increases, actors will be assisted by others only to the extent to which the actor and the others are linked in their outcomes; that is, what happens to the actor has ramifications for the identity and outcomes of the other. The greater the association between the actor and the other, the more likely the latter should be to offer an account for the actor that resembles what the actor would prefer to say for himself or herself. For example, relatives, friends, members of the same group or club, and people the actor has paid for help, such as an attorney, are all closely linked in the minds of others and in their outcomes. What happens to one has ramifications for the others. Therefore, as predicaments increase in severity, one should expect people who are closely linked to be more likely to assist one another with accounts, thereby defending their own identities.

APOLOGIES

The second major class of remedial tactics is the apology. In an apology, actors *admit blameworthiness* for an undesirable event, but concomitantly *attempt to obtain a pardon* or reduce the negative repercussions from real or imagined audiences. *Apologies are designed to convince the audience that the undesirable event should not be considered a fair representation of what the actor is "really like" as a person.* That is, the actor contends that the undesirable images that would be applied to him or her if a worst-case reading of the event were made should not be applied, because those images do not represent what he or she is like.

In order to accomplish this goal in situations where the undesirable event appears to have been caused by one's own actions, blame must be attached to a "self" that no longer exists or has changed sufficiently that audiences do not need to be concerned about a repeat of the offense. Thus, a current "good" self is split off from the past "bad" self that was responsible for the undesirable event. Such self-splitting is contained in *all* apologies. Goffman (1971, p. 113) describes an apology as "a gesture through which an individual splits himself into two parts, the part that is guilty of an offense and the part that dissociates itself from the delict and affirms a belief in the offended rule." The "good" self attempts to continue beyond the undesirable event; the "bad" self is left behind, discredited and vilified by the actor. The actor thus displays evidence of rehabilitation and vows that he or she can once again be counted on as a worthy social participant.

In situations in which the undesirable event was not caused by one's own actions, but in which one might be held responsible nonetheless, an analogous sort of "splitting" is required. In this case, though, the actor attempts to dissociate himself as much as possible from the apparent causal origin of the event. Thus, the daughter of a convicted murderer apologizes for her mother's onerous deed or a father apologizes to the teacher for his son's misbehavior. In so doing, the actor attempts to convey the impression that although he or she can be held blameworthy *in some sense* (global responsibility) for the undesirable event, it cannot be taken as an accurate reflection of what he or she is like.

It is important to distinguish between an expression of sympathy and an apology. The words "I'm sorry" can mean either. One can say "I'm sorry" to comfort a friend whose parent has just died (sympathy) or to apologize to a relative of a person one has killed. For an apology to be used, a predicament must exist for the actor. That is, a worst-case reading of the undesirable event must bestow at least some responsibility on the actor.

An apology, at least in its fullest form, contains the following elements: (1) an expression of guilt, remorse, embarrassment, or chagrin; (2) clarification that one recognizes what the appropriate conduct should have been and sympathizes with the application of negative sanctions for such a rule violation; (3) rejection of the inappropriate conduct and disparagement of the "bad" self that misbehaved; (4) espousal of the appropriate conduct and a vow to behave appropriately; and (5) the performance of penance and an offer to compensate the victim (Goffman, 1971). The more of these elements that any given apology contains, the more rehabilitated the actor will appear to be— provided, of course, that the actor is viewed by the audience as sincere.

The Function of Apologies

The elements of an apology gain their effectiveness by performing two interrelated functions: they attempt to *redress the past* and they extend a *promise of more desirable conduct in the future.* If the audience is convinced of the sincerity of an apology that performs these functions, they no longer have to be concerned about the undesirable event nor the actor who was responsible for it. To punish such an actor further would perform only one function—revenge. Although revenge itself can be a very satisfying reason for punishing someone, the punishment cannot change the actor any more than the actor has supposedly already been changed.

In order to redress the past, the actor must pay some penalty for the undesirable event. The penalty can be in suffering mental, physical, or economic hardships or in compensating victims of the undesirable event. Several of the elements of an apology perform these functions. Expressions of guilt, remorse, or embarrassment communicate how terribly the actor supposedly feels about the incident and how much he or she is suffering inside. A skillful actor might even express guilt to the point where the audience concludes he or she has experienced unbearable self-inflicted agonies. The audience is thus left to conclude that no further punishment is needed to teach the actor a lesson. Similarly, castigation of the "bad" self serves to inform audiences that one recognizes the misconduct and is self-imposing punishment. Self-castigation is the self-inflicted counterpart of being punished by receiving social disapproval.

Self-castigation has another value that might not be readily apparent. According to Goffman (1971)

> were others to do to him what he is willing to do to himself, he might be obliged to feel affronted and to engage in retaliatory action to sustain his moral worth and autonomy. And he can overstate or overplay the case against himself, thereby giving the others the task of cutting the self-derogation short . . . [p. 113].

Finally, offering to make restitution allows the audience to conclude that all will be made right with the victim. If victims are adequately compensated, the actor will have done the best he or she could to redress the damage (see Walster et al., 1978).

Full apologies also extend a promise of more acceptable future conduct on the part of the actor. Through the elements of his apology the actor indicates that he knows what he should and should not do, agrees with the audience that negative sanctions should be imposed for misconduct, implies that he will accept such punishment both now and in the future, affirms his intention to behave properly, and shows evidence (such as guilt) of the ability and willingness to punish himself and make restitution (Goffman, 1971). Thus, the actor tries to provide evidence that he will henceforth do a better job of monitoring and controlling his own behavior. He has internalized all the facets that other people require in a "properly socialized" individual.

When audiences are satisfied that the actor has redressed the past and extended a believable promise of acceptable future conduct, they pronounce him or her rehabilitated; a pardon is granted. If the apology fails in performing these two functions, it will be rejected by the audience; the actor is then negatively sanctioned. Research does indicate that people who express remorse for their misconduct, appear to have suffered punishment, and attempt to compensate their victims are viewed more favorably and are given less severe negative sanctions than are those who do not perform such repentent acts (Austin, Walster, & Utne, 1976; Bramel, Taub, & Blum, 1968; Kalven & Zeisel, 1966; Walster et al., 1978). Further, studies indicate that juries are more lenient toward defendants who show repentence and claim to have suffered (Austin et al., 1976; Kalven & Zeisel, 1966; Walster et al., 1978).

The Use of Apologies

Apologies, at least in mild versions, are used in perfunctory and ritualized ways in everyday social interactions (Goffman, 1971). Minor breaches of conduct are invariably followed by a rapid, unthinking "I'm sorry" or "Pardon me." This ritual allows minor predicaments to be passed over quickly and forgotten by the interactants. In such minor predicaments, the offending event is so inconsequential that it is best to have it resolved with the least effort on everyone's part. The apology ritual serves this function. Even though the actor does admit blame, who cares?

As predicaments increase in severity, the event cannot be taken so lightly. It is one thing to mention an inopportune subject during dinner; it is another to be caught stealing the silverware. More severe predicaments receive greater attention from both the actor and the audience.

Apologies, which always involve the admission of at least some blame, must then be considered more carefully by the actor before being proffered. Apologies offer at best a pardon; the actor is forgiven by the audience. They do not offer a not-guilty verdict, as do some accounts (for example, defenses of innocence, excuses that allow verdicts of not guilty by reason of insanity, and justifications that appeal to acceptable higher goals). If an actor expects to escape from all the negative repercussions of a severe predicament, an apology is not the best tactic.

It follows that apologies are most likely to be used by actors when (1) they do not mind admitting blame for an undesirable event because the repercussions are trivial or (2) irrespective of how undesirable the event is, they believe that it is extremely unlikely that a guilty verdict can be avoided. At the present time, no research has been conducted that bears on these hypotheses.

Apologies and accounts represent conceptually separate classes of remedial tactics, but the two classes overlap in large part in that they can often be used together. An actor can both admit blame through an apology and attempt to excuse or justify the undesirable event. Thus, people often say "I'm sorry. It was my fault. [Apology] But it was an accident. [Excuse] Oh, I'm glad you weren't hurt very much. [Justification]" Thus, people combine remedial tactics in whatever ways they believe will allow them to *maximize their expected reward/cost ratio, given the nature of the predicament.* Naturally, not all apologies and accounts can be combined; some types are mutually exclusive. An actor cannot both plead blamelessness through a defense of innocence and accept blame through an apology. At least an actor cannot do so if he or she expects the audience to believe the remedial attempt.

In sum, apologies offer an actor the opportunity to accept blame for a predicament while at the same time attempting to reduce the negative repercussions by exhibiting credible evidence of rehabilitation. If successful, an apology allows the actor to leave the undesirable event behind and present a reformed identity to the audience.

THE PRIVATE AND THE PUBLIC: TRUTH AND DECEPTION

What people privately believe about themselves and events may or may not differ from what they publicly say about themselves and events. People sometimes tell the "truth," at least as they see it, so that their public statements correspond with their private beliefs. Sometimes they lie, tailoring their public statements to maximize their expected reward/cost ratio from a particular real audience even though the statements depart radically from their private beliefs. As we saw in Chapter 4, whether any particular public statement corresponds with private beliefs depends on whether being in the presence of a particular real audience differentially affects the expected values of the public versus the private claims. A person might privately believe something because she thinks it more accurately describes the "facts" as she knows them and will therefore maximize her expected reward/cost ratio in the long run. But she might publicly say something else because she believes it will be accepted by the real audience and offers her the potential for greater rewards or fewer punishments in that specific situation.

Interaction between Beliefs and Statements

Private beliefs and public statements should be regarded as conceptually separate at any particular moment; they are not the same. Yet they can influence one another. One's private beliefs can affect one's later public statements, and one's public statements can affect one's later private beliefs.

First, and perhaps most obviously, one's private beliefs about oneself and an event can influence one's public statements. Suppose a person harms another and privately feels extremely responsible. This actor, let's say, has a strong moral upbringing, believes that harming others under any conditions is quite wrong, and thinks she might have been able to avert the harm had she tried hard enough. An audience who actually observed the incident, though, independently concludes that she was acting only in self-defense; she was completely justified in what she did. When she describes the incident to the audience, much to their surprise, she apologizes profusely and takes a larger amount of responsibility than they would have assigned her. In this case, her own private beliefs have caused her to view the event more negatively than an "average" audience did, made her overestimate the degree to which they would blame her, and made her expect that the audience would have accepted nothing less than the full apology she gave. Thus, one's private beliefs about oneself and an event affect (1) expectations that one can successfully use a particular remedial tactic, (2) the expected value of the tactic if it is used successfully, and (3) the expected value of the negative sanctions that would be mediated by the audience if the remedial tactic fails.

A less obvious, more intriguing assertion is that *people's public descriptions of themselves and events can (under certain conditions) affect what they later come to believe privately.* For example, an actor might account for a predicament in a way that she expects will be acceptable to the audience and will minimize negative repercussions. Later, she comes to believe privately the excuse or justification that she gave, even though it might differ somewhat from her initial beliefs about the incident. Or an actor might apologize for a predicament, overemphasizing his own guilt in order to win the sympathy of the audience, and later come to believe that his "bad" self was really more blameworthy than he might have initially thought. In either case, the actor has *internalized* her or his public statements, coming to believe privately that they accurately describe the "facts" of the incident. In short, the actor accepts the public statements as "true."[6]

Conditions Affecting Internalization

Naturally, people do not internalize all public statements. They sometimes regard their statements as "necessary" deceptions or even "self-serving" lies and never come privately to believe them. Actors' own cognitive scripts can be stretched only so far by the "facts" before they no longer can incorporate the event. Under what conditions might internalization occur? Unfortunately, there is relatively little research on this question, since most of the studies that have examined people's behavior in predicaments have used measures that make it difficult or impossible clearly to separate public statements from genuine reflections of private beliefs. Nonetheless, some hypotheses can be tentatively offered.

First, of course, a person must deliver an account of his actions or

[6]A number of theorists have suggested for one reason or another that people do come to internalize their public statements (Abelson, Aronson, McGuire, Newcomb, Rosenberg, & Tannenbaum, 1968; Bem, 1972; Collins & Hoyt, 1972; Fazio, Zanna, & Cooper, 1977; Festinger, 1957). Two of the leading approaches to internalization are dissonance theory (Festinger, 1957) and self-perception theory (Bem, 1972). According to the original version of dissonance theory, people are assumed to experience dissonance, an aversive motivational state, whenever they hold two conflicting cognitions, such as "I believe *X*" and "I said not-*X*." People are hypothesized to reduce the dissonance, and one way is to change their private beliefs to bring them in line with their behaviors. Thus they would privately believe "not-*X*." Subsequent revisions of dissonance theory have proposed that conflicting cognitions generate dissonance primarily when cognitions contradict important aspects of one's self-image; thus, people should experience dissonance when they hold cognitions such as "I am a moral person who doesn't tell lies" and "I just told a lie" (Aronson, 1968). Other theorists further revised the concept to propose that people experience dissonance only when they feel personally responsible for producing aversive consequences (Collins & Hoyt, 1972). Self-perception theory, on the other hand, does not assume the existence of aversive motivational states. Instead, people are hypothesized to infer their attitudes from their behaviors under conditions where possible external causes of the behavior are not apparent. Thus, a person who said "not-*X*" would come to believe that the statement reflects his private beliefs so long as no salient environmental pressure for the statement seemed to exist. Many, though not all, of the specific predictions made by dissonance theory also are made by the self-presentation approach to accounting described in this chapter. Recent versions of dissonance theory can be viewed as a special case of the more general self-presentation approach (Schlenker, 1978; Schlenker et al., in press).

an apology for his actions to a real or imagined audience (oneself included). As we've seen, remedial tactics are used primarily under conditions such as appearing to be responsible for an undesirable event. Thus, an important antecedent of internalization is the existence of conditions that precipitate the use of a remedial tactic. But such conditions are not sufficient for a remedial tactic to be privately believed. The actor still might label his statements as self-serving lies.

Second, people's remedial tactics should be only slightly-to-moderately discrepant with their initial private beliefs about themselves and the event. If people's statements differ greatly from their initial beliefs, they are likely to code any public statements as self-serving deceptions designed only to fool a real audience. For example, a child who breaks the cookie jar might tell her mother that the dog did it while privately knowing full well that the dog wasn't even in the room. In this case, the child should not internalize the account, since it contradicts the facts too flagrantly. Instead, the child should label the account as a lie and privately recognize that she was really responsible. Experiments that have found suggestions of internalization seem to have used procedures that minimize the likelihood that subjects' accounts would be privately labeled as a lie (Collins & Hoyt, 1972), while those that have found no internalization seem to have used procedures that maximize the likelihood that subjects would privately label their account as a lie (Gaes et al., 1978; Schlenker et al., in press). Thus, public accounts that blatantly contradict private beliefs should not be internalized.

Notice that the above hypothesis does not suggest that people privately label a public account as a "lie" but later come to believe it. Just the opposite is predicted: if people do label a public account as a lie, they will not internalize it. *Any factor that prevents the actor from labeling the public statement a "lie" should maximize the likelihood of internalization.* This is the reason why blatant discrepancies between public statements and initial private beliefs should not be internalized—they are easily labeled as lies. Several other factors also should prevent such labeling. If a *knowledgeable* audience *who knows most of the details of the event* accepts the actor's account as truthful, the actor should be likely to internalize it. Even though the account might not perfectly reflect the actor's initial private beliefs, the audience's acceptance makes the actor think that the account accurately describes the situation. In contrast, if a nonsignificant audience (say, composed of people the actor thought were stupid or uncritical) or an audience the actor felt was unaware of the details of the event indicated that they accepted the account, little or no internalization should occur. Instead, the actor should simply conclude that he fooled this particular audience but he could not fool another audience composed of more significant or knowledgeable others.

Sorting through Accounts

In many real-life situations there is ambiguity about whether or not a public account accurately describes an event. For example, when a predicament occurs most actors can think of several possible ways to "explain" it. They might privately favor one interpretation over another, but they have some doubt. When confronted by an audience, though, the actors offer the account that has the greatest expected value for minimizing the negative repercussions of the predicament. If the account is successful in front of a significant audience, the actors come to believe that it, rather than one of the other readings of the predicament, is the "truth." In one sense, then, we might cynically conclude that people have a proclivity for self-deception; they tend to believe privately things that reflect more favorably on themselves. Yet, in another sense, reality is not so clearly defined that we can pronounce judgments of absolute truth and falsehood. Sorting through the possible accounts and accepting one that seems to describe the facts while concomitantly maximizing one's expected reward/cost ratio is a very rational, logical process.

People "try out" desired interpretations of situations on others, searching optimistically for one that will present the situation in a positive light and be accepted by an audience (oneself included). "Facts" can be selected and interpreted in many ways, and people often confront situations where they are just not sure why they behaved in a particular way or why things happened as they did. It is not all that unusual for people to be honestly perplexed about why they did something. They consider in their own minds several possible "causes" of their behavior, but they just don't know which one or ones is "really" the truth. In such situations, a desired interpretation can be proffered to an audience, and, if they accept it, it increases the actor's confidence that the interpretation is correct. People search for reassuring truths. It is the best of all possible worlds where an explanation can be found that presents the "facts" in a positive light and is also "true." The search typically takes the form of selectively explaining the details of an incident from the perspective of the actor, replete with comforting interpretations of the actor's motivation. An assertion is then made, and a question for the audience is tagged on at the end, such as "I was doing the right thing, wasn't I?" or "I couldn't really have helped it, could I?" or "It wasn't really such a bad thing to do, was it?" If a significant audience (family, friends, so-called experts) concurs with the actor's suggestion, the "truthfulness" of the assertion is increased in the actor's mind.

In this regard, it can be added that when an audience says "That person is rationalizing" the judgment is in the eye of the beholder. Audiences form judgments about how accurately actors' descriptions of undesirable events correspond with the facts as the audience sees them.

If an actor's account seems self-serving and to depart from the facts as the audience sees them, and if the audience thinks that the actor believes what he says, the audience concludes that the actor is *rationalizing*. A different audience may or may not pronounce the same judgment.

ACCLAIMING: THE OTHER SIDE OF THE COIN

Before leaving the topic of predicaments, a related phenomenon should be briefly mentioned. There are many occasions in life where a *desirable event* occurs—that is, one that is positively evaluated. A child might generously share her playthings with another, or a person might contribute to a worthy charity or complete a difficult task. In a thousand different ways, people can appear to be responsible for a potentially praiseworthy occurrence. Appearing to be responsible for desirable events has its rewards. People then experience feelings of pride or accomplishment, they enhance their identities, and they stand some chance of being positively sanctioned by real audiences. The repercussions of desirable events are decidedly positive. Naturally, the more responsible a person appears to be for the event and the more desirable the event is, the greater the magnitude of the positive repercussions.

In order to increase their expected reward/cost ratio following desirable events, people should attempt to insure that a "best-case reading" occurs. That is, out of the possible ways the incident can be interpreted or explained, they should prefer to apply the one that maximizes the desirable implications for their identity. Such a reading would maximize (1) their apparent responsibility for the desirable event and (2) the desirability of the event. People should prefer to avoid readings of the event that do not accomplish these objectives.

For example, a person who contributed money to charity should prefer the audience to attribute his action to the fact that he believed in the worthy cause and acted only out of this motive. He should prefer to avoid less favorable attributions that lessen his responsibility, such as "He did it to get a plaque in his honor" or "He was pressured into it by the canvasser" or "He did it merely because it is expected of those in his social position." In each case, an extenuating circumstance exists that allows responsibility to be shared with other factors besides his beneficent motives. Maximum responsibility, remember, exists when a person appears to have freely and purposefully behaved to produce the primary consequences associated with the event and did not engage in the behavior because of external pressure, accident, or to achieve associated consequences. To the degree that a desirable event permits such an interpretation, actors should apply it. At the very least, they should attempt to maximize however much responsibility they can be assigned, given the nature of the situation.

Similarly, people should attempt to maximize the desirability of the event itself (the action or its consequences). For instance, a child who shares his toys with a playmate should attempt to convey the impression that the toys are valuable ones and not simply old ones that he might have thrown away anyway. The more desirable the toys appear to be, the more credit due the child for sharing them.

Such situations can hardly be termed predicaments. No identity-threatening event occurs, and no accounting tactics are needed to "explain" the event. (The term *accounting* has been used to refer exclusively to explanations following *undesirable* events. See Goffman, 1971; Scott & Lyman, 1968.) Yet, impression-management tactics are used in such situations in a manner complementary to the way they are employed in predicaments. Just as people can be said to use accounting tactics following undesirable events, they can be said to use *acclaiming* tactics following desirable events. Acclaiming tactics are designed to explain a desirable event in a way that maximizes the desirable implications for the actor. To do so, people use *entitlings*, which maximize their responsibility for the event, and *enhancements*, which maximize the desirability of the event itself. These are the counterparts of the accounting tactics of excuses and justifications, respectively.

People do use acclaiming tactics when circumstances appear to deprive them of credit for desirable events (Goldman & Schlenker, 1977; Schlenker & Riess, 1979; Schlenker & Schlenker, 1975). Schlenker and Schlenker (1975) had subjects commit themselves to do something that was potentially desirable—say very complimentary things about another person who was listening to the evaluation. The subjects privately felt that the other person was only about average, but their complimentary evaluation should have made the other person feel good and hence was a potentially desirable gesture. The commitment to deliver the evaluation was obtained under one of two conditions: either the subjects were told that they could choose to do it if they wanted, but they didn't have to (they had a choice) or they were told that they had been randomly assigned to deliver the compliment (they had no choice). In addition, some of the subjects were led to believe that they later would interact with the other person, who would be told about how they came to deliver the evaluation; the others were led to believe that they would not see or talk to the other person again. It was expected that subjects would be most strongly motivated to try to receive credit for their compliment when circumstances appeared to deny them responsibility for the deed (when they had no choice) and when they had the opportunity to interact with the other person, who could then respond favorably. Subjects would not need to use an exaggerated acclaiming tactic if either they were not going to interact with the other person (and hence could not receive any credit) or they already appeared to be responsible for the compliment (they were given a free choice about delivering it). This is precisely what was found when subjects were given the opportunity to express their "real" feelings about the other person. Subjects who appeared to be nonresponsible for the compliment and who later would meet the other person expressed very positive attitudes toward her. By expressing such favorable attitudes, they made it appear that they sincerely meant the nice things they said earlier. In contrast, subjects who either were already responsible for the compliment or who would not meet the other person again did not express such extremely favorable opinions; they had no reason to exaggerate their statements.

According to the Association Principle (see Chapter 4), people act to establish (or maximize) their association with desirable images and act to disestablish (or minimize) their association with undesirable ones. Further, they maximize the attractiveness and minimize the unattractiveness of the images with which they are already associated. Acclaiming and accounting are impression-management tactics that serve precisely these functions.

SUMMARY

Predicaments are situations in which events have undesirable implications for the identity-relevant images actors have claimed or desire to claim in front of real or imagined audiences. Predicaments range from embarrassing incidents, where an event appears to contradict the image an actor has projected to others, to transgressions, where an event appears to break moral, legal, or social rules that the actor is required to obey. When predicaments occur, actors confront numerous negative repercussions, including feelings of guilt or anxiety, an adversely affected identity, and the possibility of receiving punishments (negative sanctions) from real audiences who observe or learn of it. The more severe the predicament—that is, the greater the actor's apparent responsibility and the more undesirable the event—the greater the potential negative repercussions.

In order to reduce or eliminate the negative repercussions, actors employ one or more remedial tactics. Remedial tactics are impression-management activities that attempt to deal with the predicament. The actor can account for it, offering an explanation that contains an excuse ("I am less responsible than it otherwise might appear") or a justification ("The event is less undesirable than it otherwise might appear"). Or the actor can apologize for it, accepting the blame for the incident but attaching the blame to a "bad" self that is not really representative of what the actor is normally like as a person. Both tactics provide actors with an escape route from predicaments or, at the very least, a way of minimizing the aversive consequences of predicaments.

The other side of the coin is events that have desirable implications for the images people have claimed or desire to claim in front of real or imagined audiences. People want to associate themselves with such events, and they use acclaiming tactics to do so. Acclaiming tactics are attempts to explain a desirable event in a way that maximizes the desirable implications for the actor. To do this, people use entitlings, which maximize their responsibility for the event, and enhancements, which maximize the apparent desirability of the event itself.

PART THREE

THE LINES

The construction of identity is an artful pursuit: a nuance here, a gesture there, a word or phrase turned this way instead of that. The verbal and nonverbal lines that people use to create particular impressions on audiences can be as creative and subtle as the work of a master poet or as dreadful as a piece of bad art. In Part III, we'll explore how people construct identities through verbal and nonverbal impression-management tactics. The first two chapters consider the *verbal modes* of impression management. We'll examine how people use *verbal self-descriptions* and examine such matters as when people are modest rather than braggart about themselves and how their self-descriptions are affected by the values and expectations of other (Chapter 6). We'll explore the use of *attitude expressions* — the way attitude statements are used to create particular impressions on real or imagined audiences (Chapter 7). The next two chapters examine the *nonverbal modes* of impression management. We'll explore how people employ body language, paralanguage, and space to create particular impressions (Chapter 8). Then we'll consider how personal appearance, props, and scenery are used for impression-management purposes (Chapter 9).

Much of the material in the first nine chapters describes how people go about constructing and protecting socially desirable identities, trying to be perceived as competent, attractive, likable, and so forth. Yet many people maintain identities that are not socially desirable, as in the case of people who present themselves as mentally incompetent, anti-social, violent, or threatening. To dispel any notions that impression management involves only the portrayal of socially acceptable attributes, Chapter 10 explores some of the reasons people have for constructing socially undesirable identities and considers some of the impression-management tactics they use in doing so.

S I X

Great modesty often hides great Merit.
Benjamin Franklin

Praise yourself daringly; something always sticks.
Francis Bacon

The more you speak of yourself, the more likely you are to lie.
Johann Georg von Zimmerman

THE ART OF IMPRESSION MANAGEMENT: SELF-DESCRIPTIONS

People function as their own advertising and public relations firms. Some have better "products" to sell than others, and some are better salespersons than others, but their goals are similar—to achieve profits in the marketplace of social life. They release advertisements about themselves that consist of explicit or implied claims about what they are like and what they have done and can do. Of course, some of these claims are more accurate than others. Some advertising appeals take the subtle, low-key approach, underestimating the product's virtues in the hopes of building credibility. Others take the hard-sell approach, claiming more than they know is true in the hopes of making at least some of the claims stick in the audiences' minds. Packaging (like clothes and hairstyles) and product claims (self-descriptions) are selected to appeal to appropriate segments of the market—particular groups of real or imagined significant others. Some products are tailored for an audience from the business community and are packaged in blue pin-striped suits with product claims that might appeal to those who like Wall Street and golf. Others are tailored for appeal to the opposite sex and include sporting sexy clothes and sophisticated conversation. Still others are tailored for the counterculture, with dress and ways of talking that manage the impression of not caring about impressions. Impression management is, in part, the art of self-advertisement to particular audiences.

In this chapter, we'll explore how people use self-descriptive statements in the course of presenting themselves to audiences. Self-descriptive statements are verbal or written expressions of attitudes, beliefs, and facts about oneself. As a rule, they are the most direct and least subtle way of laying claims to particular sets of images. It is often difficult to slip self-descriptive statements into conversations. Unless they are introduced in appropriate contexts, actors risk appearing self-centered or egotistical. For this reason, people usually go out of their way when meeting new acquaintances to ask them about themselves, and they hope that the acquaintances reciprocate. People are usually delighted when an audience requests self-descriptions, since they are then free to introduce pertinent information for identity construction. Much of the small talk in our lives consists of self-relevant descriptions and communication of attitudes that form the foundation of each participant's identity. In addition, some people are remarkably adept at turning conversations in appropriate directions so that they can introduce self-descriptions. In a hundred different ways, people manage to bring their desirable attributes to the attention of their audiences.

We'll begin our examination of self-descriptions with the most sycophantic sort of self-relevant statements—ingratiatory ones. We can then work back from this solely audience-oriented tactic to ones that are less illicit but nonetheless strategic.

INGRATIATION THROUGH SELF-DESCRIPTIONS

The most universally disapproved subarea of impression management is *ingratiation*. The mere mention of the term brings to mind a variety of pejorative meanings. To be called an ingratiator is to have one's credibility as a social interactant challenged. Ingratiation implies deceit—playing to the audience and giving them what they want to hear. The ingratiator's goal is to be seen as attractive, and nothing else. To return to the advertising analogy, ingratiation is a form of self-advertising in which claims are made only to gain purchasers, not necessarily to convey accurate information. A credibility gap (the current euphemism for lying) develops because the audience cannot place any trust in the words of the ingratiator. A mitigating word: these harsh statements paint in black and white a picture that is more often found in shades of grey. At its extreme, ingratiation does involve such unabashedly offensive aspects. Yet in common practice it can appear quite different.

Edward E. Jones (Jones, 1964, 1965; Jones & Wortman, 1973) pioneered the study of *ingratiation*, which he defined as "a class of strategic behaviors illicitly designed to influence a particular other person concerning the attractiveness of one's personal qualities" (Jones & Wortman, 1973, p. 2).[1] To increase attractiveness, the ingratiator manipulates "the attributions made by the target person" about himself or herself. Naturally, the ingratiator's "personal resources and the setting in which he finds himself may dictate the particular attributions sought after. He may seek attraction by attempting to elicit attributions of friendliness, or perceptiveness, or integrity, while avoiding attributions of ulterior motivation" (p. 3). In other words, the job of the ingratiator is to discover what the audience finds attractive in an individual and then give it to them.

Jones describes four modes of ingratiation: (1) *complimentary other enhancement*, or flattery, designed to accent the strengths and virtues of the other, thereby making oneself seem perceptive, intelligent, discriminating, and quite likable; (2) *opinion conformity*, or agreeing with the opinions of the other, thereby making oneself seem similar, perceptive, intelligent, and so forth; (3) *rendering favors*—people who do nice things are likely to be viewed as considerate, caring, and friendly; and (4) *attractive self-presentations or self-descriptions*—explicitly presenting oneself in ways designed to claim images the other will find attractive. All of these tactics allow ingratiators to claim, directly or indirectly, particular sets of images designed to be attractive to targets. In this chapter, we'll concentrate primarily on the last tactic, self-presentation through self-descriptions; we'll take up the others in Chapter 7.

Jones believes that ingratiating actions are illicit and deceitful because they go beyond what people consider to be "legitimate" types of behaviors in interpersonal relations. Although ingratiators seem to be publicly accepting a social contract that states that they will act out an

---

[1]From *Ingratiation: An Attributional Approach*, by E. E. Jones and C. Wortman. Copyright 1973 by General Learning Press. This and all other quotations from this source are reprinted by permission of the Silver Burdett Company.

appropriate identity during the encounter and help the other person do the same, they are really concerned with doing only one thing—making themselves appear attractive, and thus benefitting only themselves. In the process, ingratiators' actions often involve dissimulation.

Ingratiation and Impression Management

Ingratiation is a distinct subarea of the more general area of impression management. It stands out because of these aspects: (1) its single goal of gaining attractiveness, (2) its emphasis on pleasing others, (3) the salience of short-run personal profit like getting a job or raise, and (4) the strong possibility that a discrepancy exists between privately held beliefs and publicly endorsed statements. Of course, impression management in general can involve many other goals aside from simply being viewed as attractive by others and pleasing them. Actors can attempt to be viewed as powerful irrespective of their attractiveness to an audience. They can attempt to project images that are consistent with their self-images irrespective of how the audience responds. For example, an idealistic and highly scrupled dissident might try to insure that everything she does projects images that are true to her personal beliefs. Impression management goals are varied, and being seen as attractive is only one of them. Further, as the example of the dissident implies, impression management does not necessarily involve either an illicit set of behaviors, an emphasis on short-run personal profit, or a discrepancy between public and private images. People often work as hard or harder to attain consistency between their public and private images as they might to lie in order to impress an audience. In addition, they can attempt to present themselves in ways that make them attractive to specific others without necessarily violating "legitimate" social contracts. A woman in love with a man might try to insure that the images she projects to him display only love and admiration, and in so doing she is hardly attempting to benefit only herself or to disregard his feelings. Thus, ingratiation is set apart from other areas of impression management by its myopic focus. Ingratiating behaviors are predictable via the equations underlying the Association Principle. Ingratiators simply weight the elements that constitute a desirable image heavily in favor of what they think their immediate audience wants, believes, and will do rather than what they want, believe, and can do.

The distinction between ingratiation and other forms of impression management is usually more blurred than it might appear on the surface. Everyone is guided by self-interest, and everyone compromises at least slightly in front of an audience. There are numerous situations in life in which it is in one's best interests to be positively evaluated by others. A door-to-door salesman recognizes that the customer's first

impression will usually make or break the sale; a man who meets his
fiancée's parents for the first time knows that the impression he leaves
could affect his marital future. However, it is rarely crystal clear that
one is playing to an audience *only* to increase attractiveness. Degrees of
wanting to be attractive shade into one another so gradually that one
must draw an arbitrary line to separate them.

The distinction further blurs in that ingratiation need not involve
intentional effort. Jones and Wortman (1973, p. 50) contend that ingratiating behaviors "are rarely the result of conscious or deliberate
planning." Such actions are well ingrained and habitual.

> Through a long and complex socialization process, the average person
> develops deeply imbedded reaction tendencies that are triggered by set-
> tings of differential resources or power. Most of the time . . . the
> attraction-seeking response is relatively automatic or unthinking. Alterna-
> tives of utter openness and candor are not even considered as the depen-
> dent person nods, smiles, agrees, or compliments [p. 51].

Motives for Ingratiating

Why would people ingratiate? Jones believes that people do so to
enhance their own *actual power* in a relationship, thereby reducing their
dependence on the other. In most instances where ingratiation is clear-
cut there is a real power differential between the ingratiator and the
audience. The audience possesses the ability to reward or punish the
ingratiator more than vice-versa. It is true that *inter*dependence exists
in all interactions; the outcomes people receive depend on the interplay
between their own behaviors and the behaviors of others. Some relationships, however, are more one-sided than others, and feelings of *dependence* are generated in the less powerful individual. To reduce the
dependence and the power differential, ingratiators attempt to make
themselves more attractive to the other. If the powerful party comes to
like the ingratiator, it becomes more difficult to harm or punish the
latter, and the powerful party is more likely to dispense rewarding
outcomes.

People who occupy positions of lower power often resort to ingratiation and lying, since they have few alternative ways of attempting
to influence the more powerful party (Tedeschi, Schlenker, & Bonoma,
1973). Employees in a large company are limited in the types of influence they can exert. They usually lack the material resources to use
threats or promises with any effectiveness, and their persuasive appeals
often fall on deaf ears because they lack prestige in the powerful party's
eyes. They can exert influence, though, by manipulating and controlling
information through ingratiation and outright lies. Less powerful persons in bargaining games have been found to lie more about critical

information than do more powerful persons, and they frequently deceive the more powerful into settling for agreements that are worse than the latter could otherwise have achieved (Fischer, 1969).

When people apply for jobs they often resort to ingratiation and lying about their backgrounds. In his insightful analysis *The Organization Man*, William Whyte, Jr. (1956) recommended lying on personnel tests to increase one's chances of getting a job and gaining promotions. Whyte attempts to justify the tactic by arguing that large organizations stifle creativity and individuality and that the best (only) way to fight back in such a repressive atmosphere is to control the information the corporation receives about you. The morality of the tactic can be debated, and potential risks exist for those who use it. But it is used. Goldstein (1971) checked the job application forms of 111 people who applied for positions as nurse's aides in a large group of nursing homes by comparing their answers against their prior employers' records. In 57% of the cases, job applicants overestimated both the duration of time they spent on their past job and their previous salaries.

Playing to the Audience's Values

To study how people behave in ingratiation situations, experiments have been conducted that simulate the pressures an ingratiator is likely to face. In one of the first such studies, Jones, Gergen, and Davis (1962) told college student subjects that they would be interviewed by another person. Some of the subjects were instructed to "just be themselves" during the interview: "Present yourself . . . as you actually see yourself and try not to over-emphasize your good points or to play up your failings" (p. 5). Other subjects were given an ingratiation goal. They were asked to imagine that they were interviewing for a very attractive opportunity, a fellowship that would pay all their expenses abroad during the summer, and that the interviewer would play a major role in determining who got the fellowship. Since they would undoubtedly want to impress the interviewer in such a situation, their goal was to "try to figure out what kind of person the interviewer probably likes and then act like such a person . . . even though it does not accurately reflect the picture you have of yourself"(pp. 5–6). During the interview, subjects were asked specific forced-choice questions about themselves and had to respond with self-ratings that could vary from positive to negative. In this study and in several similar ones (Gergen, 1965; Schneider & Eustis, 1972; Schneider, Eustis, Manzolati, Miller, & Gordon, 1971), subjects who were given the ingratiation instructions described themselves more positively to the interviewer than did those who were told to be accurate—they exaggerated their strengths and minimized their weaknesses.

Not all ingratiation situations call for self-enhancing presentations. Some audiences prefer people who are loyal, compatible, and
modest to those who are independent, competent, and egotistical. Some
employers even prefer docile "yes-men." Other audiences (or the same
audiences in different situations) prefer getting a job done even at the
cost of associating with people they personally dislike. People are sensitive to such audience preferences. To illustrate, Gergen and Taylor
(1969) led Navy ROTC cadets to believe that they would be interacting
in a situation that emphasized either their decision-making ability and
task competence or their ability to interact successfully and get along.
When describing themselves to one another to get acquainted before the
task, subjects in the condition that stressed competence presented
themselves in a self-enhancing manner, thereby projecting competence
and self-confidence. Those in the situation that stressed compatibility,
though, presented themselves in a more self-demeaning, modest fashion. This was particularly true of low-status subjects who would not be
in charge of leading the pair and hence were the most dependent; high-
status subjects were less affected by the situational pressures.

People also are likely to present themselves differently to a powerful audience than to a group of peers. An employee might use self-
enhancement to impress the boss, but five minutes later use modesty
when discussing the same topic with a co-worker, thereby seeming
competent to the former and compatible to the latter. Students employ
similar strategies depending on whether they are interacting with a
teacher or a classmate. Hendricks and Brickman (1974) had students in
a college class write down their grade expectations for the course and
led them to believe that either a teacher or a fellow student would be
looking at it. When presenting themselves to the teacher, students used
self-enhancement by overestimating their expected grade (compared to
their actual grade-point-average in other classes); when presenting to a
fellow student, they were fairly accurate.

High- and low-status people confront different impression-
management tasks when trying to make themselves compatible with
one another. They have different concerns about balancing their likableness against their power and authority. To examine the tactics
people use in such situations, Jones, Gergen, and Jones (1963) paired
high- and low-status Navy ROTC cadets and led them to believe that
they would be working together. In order to get to know one another
better they were given the opportunity to describe themselves using a
variety of self-attribute rating scales. Subjects either were told that it
was very important for them to be compatible and were requested to try
to get their partners to like them or were told that it was very important
for them to be accurate about themselves. The high-status subjects
should be concerned with maintaining their dominance in the situation
and so should want to present themselves very positively on important

attributes. In fact, they always described themselves more positively on attributes they felt were important in the situation. However, when they were told to be compatible, they became more modest in their self-ratings compared to those who were told to be accurate, particularly lowering their self-descriptions on the unimportant attributes. Thus, when compatibility was stressed, the high-status subjects emphasized some of their frailties, but primarily on the attributes that would not damage their overall power. Analogously, powerful people often take the opportunity to joke with subordinates and reveal some of their weaknesses, but they usually make sure that the jokes are limited to trivial matters that will not undermine their authority.

Low-status people confront a different task. They don't want to be viewed as upstarts or threats to those in power, so they should try to avoid highly positive claims to important attributes that might make them appear as if they were challenging their superiors. At the same time, they don't want to appear too self-demeaning, or they might be viewed as incompetents. The low-status subjects in this study resolved their dilemma in fine fashion. When told to be accurate, they presented themselves more positively on the important than unimportant attributes, being almost as positive about themselves as the high-status people. But when told to be compatible, they abandoned their positive claims to the important attributes and became more modest, while at the same time increasing the favorability of their claims to the unimportant attributes. Thus, the low-status subjects mixed their self-presentations with nonthreatening modesty on the items that might challenge their superiors and with self-aggrandizement on the items that wouldn't.

Ingratiators can become so focused on making themselves attractive to others that they miss opportunities to maximize their profits. Imagine someone with a legitimate grievance against his employer. Is it better to be polite and pleading, thereby not offending anyone, or aggressive and threatening, with the risk that superiors will react negatively? One study (Rosen & Jerdee, 1975) assessed the reactions of bank managers to two types of grievance letters purportedly written by subordinates. Aggressive, threatening letters were better received than polite, pleading ones. If people have *legitimate* complaints, they are often better off being assertive than submissive; deference can be an ineffective strategy under conditions where a superior expects people to stand up for their rights.

The Ingratiator's Dilemma

Ingratiators face a complex challenge. At the same time that they attempt to convince the target that they possess attractive qualities, they must avoid creating suspicion that they are exaggerating, lying, or only out to make an impression. This is quite a dilemma because it is precisely in situations where self-serving presentations are most profitable that the audience is most likely to be skeptical of what the ingratiator says and least likely to believe the self-presentation (Jones, Davis, & Gergen, 1961; Kraut, 1978). How do ingratiators try to make a favorable impression while not having the audience discount the performance?

People in ingratiation situations seem to resolve the dilemma by adopting complex strategies that mix self-aggrandizement on the qualities that count most (those the audience is likely to find most attractive) with modesty and self-demeaning statements on the qualities that are less important. They thereby make a favorable impression while concomitantly building up their credibility in the audience's eyes. The probability of successfully claiming a mixed set of positive and negative images is higher than claiming a set that contains nothing but the positive. Stires and Jones (1969) hypothesized that people will employ such a balancing tactic in situations where it is clear that the target is fully aware of his power over the ingratiator and thus realizes that the ingratiator has something to gain by making a favorable impression. This is the normal situation ingratiators encounter. However, there are some situations in which the target might be unaware of the potential benefits to the ingratiator if the latter makes a favorable impression. Perhaps the target is unaware of his own power or believes that the ingratiator doesn't recognize who he is. Stires and Jones hypothesized that in such situations ingratiators should take advantage of the target's naiveté and present themselves in a uniformly self-enhancing fashion.

To test these hypotheses, they placed some subjects in a situation where they could receive better outcomes if they impressed a powerful target, while other subjects' outcomes were not dependent on the target. The dependent subjects were further divided into those who were told that the target was fully aware of his power over their outcomes and those who were told that the target was unaware that his evaluation would affect the subjects, even though it would. When subjects later described themselves to the target, those who were dependent presented themselves more positively on *competence-relevant* items than did those who were nondependent. Thus, all of the dependent subjects tried to impress the powerful person with their task-related abilities. In addition, dependent subjects who believed the powerful target was unaware of his own power also presented themselves more positively on *social qualities* which were a matter of reputation (like being popular, interesting, and socially sensitive). Subjects who believed that the target knew of his own power didn't risk such uniform self-enhancement. Instead, they presented themselves more accurately on the social items and no higher than the nondependent people. When confronting the ingratiator's dilemma, people do seem to balance their self-presentations to mix the good with the bad and maintain overall credibility. But when people believe that a powerful audience will not be suspicious of ingratiation, they present themselves aggrandizingly on a variety of attributes.

The Line Blurs: "Natural Ingratiation"

Social life is such that most people most of the time want others to like them. People usually act in congenial ways, avoid hurting others' feelings, avoid arguments by minimizing opinion differences, and, in general, act in ways that promote friendship (Homans, 1974). Given this normal state of affairs, would people who are specifically told to get others to like them behave any differently from people who aren't given any specific instructions? Kahn and Young (1973) sought to find out. They paired male and female college students and had them converse for fifteen minutes, during which time their verbal behaviors were carefully recorded by the experimenters. Prior to their conversation, one member of each pair either (a) was told to make the other like him/her as much as possible, (b) was told to make the other dislike him/her as much as possible, or (c) was given no instructions other than that the pair would be talking. The subjects in the ingratiation condition and the no-instructions condition behaved similarly on each of ten measures (for example, they displayed positive self-descriptions, opinion agreement, and flattery), never differing from one another. The only differences that were found between the three conditions occurred for those in the group who were told to make themselves be disliked. They disagreed more with the other's opinions, made more debasing comments about the other, and engaged in less friendly conversation than did the subjects in the other two conditions.

There are many differences between this study and the ones described earlier which found large effects from the ingratiation instructions. Specifically, (a) subjects in this study were not highly dependent on one another; (b) they were not asked specific questions about themselves that allowed self-ratings (it can be difficult to slip highly positive self-descriptions into a conversation), and (c) subjects in the control condition were given no instructions, while subjects in the control conditions of most of the other studies were told to be "accurate" about themselves (being told to behave normally and being told to be fully accurate about oneself are probably quite different instructional sets). Nonetheless, these results do suggest that in many natural situations people set out to become liked whether told to or not. The line between ingratiation and normal behavior is often hard to distinguish.

The major reason that the line is difficult to distinguish is that the label "ingratiation" assumes that an actor has a particular motive—

illicitly attempting to be attractive. The same set of behaviors—making positive statements about oneself, complimenting another person, agreeing with another's opinion, or doing favors for others—may or may not involve ingratiation. The thing that distinguishes the ingratiator from a charming, honest, desirable individual is the *motive that we assume he had for behaving as he did.* If we, as observers, feel his motive was illicit, we label his actions as ingratiation and condemn him with the label of ingratiator. He can make the same judgment about himself by asking himself why he was trying to be liked. If he attributes his behavior to an ulterior motive, he should feel that he has ingratiated; if not, he should feel that his behavior was pure. Ingratiation, then, is in the eye of the beholder, at least to some extent, since it is a label that we apply when we conclude that an individual had an illicit motive for attempting to be liked.

PLAYING OFF THE AUDIENCE

As people's dependence in a relationship decreases, the temptation to allow the audience's values to override their own also decreases. Their own values enter more heavily into the calculation of what constitutes attractive images; that is, they behave more in accord with what they personally deem to be attractive than with what an audience deems attractive. Audiences, though, are rarely, if ever, totally ignored. People's beliefs about what the audience admires, the likelihood of claiming particular images in front of the audience, and the types and certainty of negative sanctions that would be administered for unsuccessful claims usually affect their self-presentations. Further, the audience's behaviors in the situation are likely to modify the plans that people formulate for achieving their goals in the interaction. They might have to counter an attempt by the audience to altercast them (see Chapter 3); they might rely on the audience's actions to determine appropriate behaviors in the situation; and they might use the audience for social comparison when evaluating themselves.

Matching

People often employ a matching tactic in social interactions, matching their own self-presentations to those offered by the audience. Lord Chesterfield (Earl of Chesterfield, 1774/1901, p. 139) employed the technique with great skill: "With the men I was Proteus, and assumed every shape to please them all: among the gay, I was the gayest; among the grave, the gravest . . ." The technique has fallen into disrepute in modern times, at least when it is noticed, and numerous politicians have been chided by their opponents for trying to be all things to all people. Most modern presidents have felt the sting of such criticism. Contemporary politicians often appear to be guided more by public opinion polls than by inalienable convictions. One could equate these tactics with abandoning one's principles in the pursuit of personal gain. But the tactic can also be justified. Paul of Tarsus, who had a dominant role in the founding of the early Christian church, both used and justified it. In the First Epistle to the Corinthians he stated "And unto the Jews I became as a Jew, that I might gain the Jews . . . to the weak I was weak, that I might gain the weak: I am made all things to all men, that I might by all means save some." Further, "Give none offense, . . . even as I please all men in all things, not seeking mine own profit, but the profit of many, that they may be saved."

People use matching tactics in their everyday interactions. To demonstrate the tactic, Gergen and Wishnov (1965) paired subjects with partners and told them that they would be exchanging personal information in order to get to know one another. When they received their partner's self-ratings, they found that the partner was either quite egotistical (highly positive self-ratings), quite humble (low self-ratings), or about average. When subsequently describing themselves to their partner, subjects became more positive about themselves to the egotistical partner and more negative about themselves to the humble partner. Schneider and Eustis (1972) similarly found that subjects matched the boastful or modest behaviors of others, and the matching effect was strongest when they were told to make as good an impression as they could on their partner.

Several explanations for the matching effect have been offered. Gergen and Wishnov suggested that people become more positive when presenting to egotistical others in order to maintain a position of relative power. If they present themselves as humble or average, the egotistical partner would be able to assume the dominant role in the pair. Schneider and Eustis suggested that people watch the self-presentations of others in order to decide what behavior is appropriate and permissible in the particular situation. It is also possible that subjects are trying to impress the other person by seeming similar to him or her—people like those who are similar to themselves. Finally, matching might be based in part on the avoidance of negative feelings arising from social comparison. As Cooley (1902/1922, p. 184) said, "We are ashamed to seem evasive in the presence of a straightforward man, cowardly in the presence of a brave one . . . ." To avoid such feelings, people might match the self-presentations of others to resolve any disparity in social comparison that might otherwise leave them feeling bad.

By definition, matching establishes similarity between interactants. If both are friendly, self-confident, optimistic, and strong, their chances for a mutually satisfactory relationship are increased. Interpersonal difficulties can result when people don't match the behaviors of others, particularly when one party attempts to establish a dominant position relative to the other. Two people who are strong, aggressive, and of high status can get along quite well, and they frequently prefer each other's company to that of "inferiors." Should one attempt to be stronger, more aggressive, and of higher status than the other, discord results. The target of the power move is then faced with the choice of resisting or allowing himself to be altercast into relative submissiveness. If the target allows himself to be altercast, the relationship can again proceed smoothly with both participants agreeing on who each will be. But if the target resists, a spiral of one-upmanship can occur as each tries to gain ascendency and avoid being cast into a submissive role.

All interpersonal acts involve some degree of attempted altercasting. A person who displays friendship is inviting friendly behaviors in return, and a person who displays dominance is inviting submissiveness (Carson, 1969). The altercasting aspect often goes unnoticed, but becomes both salient and offensive when it involves the attempt to place others into identities they don't want. Davis and Schmidt (1977) argue that what we mean by an "obnoxious" person is simply someone who tries to impose on other people "selves" the others don't want to assume. We label people "nice," though, when they refrain from imposing unwanted selves on others and especially when they bend over backwards to show others that the identities into which they have been cast are ones they really wanted all along. On her popular television show, Mary Tyler Moore was the epitome of the nice person, while Phyllis Lindstrom was the epitome of the obnoxious. Both types have advantages and disadvantages. The obnoxious often get their way at the expense of being liked, while the nice are liked but often fail to get what they want. A person who combines the best of both is labeled "charismatic." The epitome is the charismatic political leader who convinces constituents that they are getting what they really want while actually giving them what he or she really wants.

Fulfilling Stereotypes

Interactions transpire smoothly when the participants know what to expect from one another. Smooth interactions are predicated on the abilities of participants to assume identities that others recognize and accept as the basis for their interpersonal behavior. Such expectations about the identities of others are derived in part from the participants' stereotypes. *Stereotypes* are *generalized images of others* that are based on group characteristics and not necessarily on the specific individual qualities of the other. Roles (such as banker or teacher), group memberships (such as Nazi or Socialist), and ethnic background (such as Italian or Jew) generate stereotypes of what a particular other person is like even before we know anything else about that person. Stereotypes are embedded in particular cognitive scripts. When a stereotypical attribute is noticed, it engages the entire script and causes people to make inferences that go beyond the data at hand. People infer that the other person has a particular set of additional characteristics and that he or she is likely to behave in certain ways.

According to Goffman (1959), people are more likely to have successful and smoothly flowing interactions if they behave in ways that fulfill the stereotypes of the audience. Every participant in an interaction employs stereotypes, at least to some extent, as a basis for deciding how to act and anticipating what the others are likely to do. When expectations based on stereotypes are violated, the interaction is disrupted, at least momentarily. The surprised party awkwardly gropes for the appropriate things to do and say, not knowing quite how to respond. Stereotypes provide a basis for regulating smooth and predictable interactions, and fulfilling stereotypes publicly can lead to rewards.

When actors claim images that contradict stereotypes, at least some negative consequences occur. Not only is the interaction disrupted, but the violator is likely to be disliked, censored, and, if the contradiction is sufficiently flagrant, even physically punished. The benefits of acting in accord with stereotypes are an added advantage to members of groups whose stereotypes are predominantly socially desirable, such as those of White Anglo-Saxon Protestant males. Stereotypes are a problem for members of groups whose stereotypes are predominantly loaded with unattractive images. They face a conundrum: conform to the stereotypes and associate oneself with many unattractive images or contradict the stereotypes and risk disapproval.

Stereotypes based on sex roles can be used to illustrate the benefits and liabilities attached to fulfilling and contradicting stereotypes. For centuries, women have had to deal with stereotypes of the female role. The traditional stereotype of women is being dependent, submissive, noncompetitive, weak, helpless, illogical, and emotional (Heath & Gurwitz, 1977). In contrast, the male stereotype is being independent, aggressive, competitive, strong, logical, competent, and unemotional. Early suffragettes who fought against these stereotypes and marched in protest of the treatment of women in Western society were jeered, criticized, and sometimes jailed. People are penalized when their behavior contradicts sex roles. Men who behave in passive and dependent ways and women who behave in aggressive and assertive ways are both viewed by the average audience as less popular and less well adjusted than are people who conform to traditional sex stereotypes (Costrich,

Feinstein, Kidder, Maracek, & Pascale, 1975). Women in business today often confront conflicting stereotypes, some formed by the traditional role of women in society and others by the role of the aggressive businessperson (Korda, 1976, 1977). Business women who conform to the traditional role meet their audience's stereotypes of women but usually fail to advance since they lack the attributes of a successful businessperson. Those who conform to the aggressive business role are often greeted with hostility from males whose stereotypes about women are shattered; the result can be a failure to advance. Many women walk a fine line between conforming to traditional roles just enough to generate liking while concomitantly displaying enough assertiveness and independence to advance in the organization. Despite a changing society, the female stereotype survives (as does the male stereotype) and affects how people are evaluated and treated.

Heath and Gurwitz (1977) examined how college students react to peers who conform to or deviate from traditional sex stereotypes. The male and female subjects who participated were initially categorized as being unfavorable or favorable toward women's liberation (that is, the favorable group took a positive attitude toward women's rights and role in society). The subjects then worked alongside several other people on a series of anagram tests. One of the people in each group was a male or female confederate of the experimenter who made several prearranged self-deprecating ("I'm too dumb to do these"), neutral ("I've seen these types of puzzles before"), or bragging ("I'm really good at them") comments. When asked later to evaluate the confederate, it was found that subjects who were unfavorable toward women's liberation most liked the confederate whose behavior conformed to the traditional role. They most liked the female who was self-deprecating and the male who either bragged or was neutral. Subjects who were favorable toward women's liberation, on the other hand, displayed different preferences. They liked men who were self-deprecating more than men who bragged or were neutral. They preferred the neutral female most, the deprecating female next, and the bragging female least. Apparently, at least a portion of the traditional female stereotype is retained even by those with more liberal attitudes.

People often purposefully conform to others' stereotypes of them, at least the stereotypes of desirable others. Zanna and Pack (1975) asked female subjects to characterize themselves to a male partner. The partner was either desirable or undesirable as a potential date and had previously indicated that his stereotype of the ideal woman was either very close to that of the traditional female or the opposite. When the partner was undesirable, the females' self-descriptions and behaviors were unaffected by his ideal stereotypes. But when the partner was desirable, the females' self-presentations conformed to what they believed he admired in a woman. Clearly, the desirability of a stereotyped image is affected by the significance and values of the audience.

Members of minority groups also confront the problem of stereotypes. Stereotypes of Blacks have included such images as stupid, ignorant, physically dirty, unreliable, lazy, talkative, happy-go-lucky, musical, and pleasure-loving (Katz & Braley, 1933; Schlenker, Bonoma, Hutchinson, & Burns, 1976). These stereotypes were further reinforced in movies of the 1930s and 1940s that portrayed Blacks as ignorantly shuffling and dancing their way through life. In the past, many Blacks intentionally fulfilled the stereotypes of whites in order to avoid punishment and keep the few benefits they received. When alone among themselves, though, they commented on the public deception. Bernard Wolfe (quoted in Messinger, Sampson, & Towne, 1962) noted in 1950 that, being seldom out of view of white audiences, "Negroes in our culture spend most of their lives 'on.' . . . Every Negro is to some extent a performer." However, when "relaxing among themselves," Negroes "mock the 'type' personalities they are obliged to assume when they're 'on'." Members of any group whose stereotypes are predominantly unattractive are likely to behave similarly, at least until an organized social movement occurs that is devoted to changing the stereotypes.

Cries for Black Power in the 1960s were accompanied by demands for the recognition of a black cultural heritage that contained *attractive* images of which blacks could be proud. The Women's Liberation Movement of the 1970s contained similar demands. A large part of each quest for social change was devoted to changing the group's stereotypes in order to free group members from unattractive images. By changing the stereotypes, group members change how they are typically viewed, expected to behave, and treated by society.

It is often hypothesized that people need a clear sense of identification with an ethnic or majority culture in order to enjoy feelings of personal security and well being (Driedger, 1976). I would suggest instead that people desire a clear sense of identification with an ethnic or majority culture *whose stereotypes predominantly include attractive images*. Through such identification, people obtain instantaneous recognition as having attractive qualities, and the recognition will shape the outcomes they receive.

Uniqueness: Standing Apart

Identification as a member of particular groups is a fact of social life. But under normal conditions, no one wants to be seen only as a part of a group, without any unique individual characteristics. (An exception occurs when standing out generates a high potential for punishment, such as in a concentration camp.) Many personality theorists hypothesize that people require a sense of individual uniqueness to allow them to stand out from members of both their own groups and other groups (Fromm, 1955; Horney, 1937; Maslow, 1968). People want to feel as if they have special attributes or gifts that distinguish them from the crowd, provided those qualities are reasonably attractive in their own right. In impression-management terms, claiming such attractive special qualities also allows a claim to the image of uniqueness. Being unable to make any claims to special attributes makes one appear to be ordinary, common, or mediocre—highly unattractive images. People often go to surprising lengths to be able to claim uniqueness. Just flip through Guinness' *Book of World Records* and you can't help being amazed at some of the things that people will do to get their names publicized as being the best at something.

Research demonstrates that people will attempt to show their uniqueness. Although most people are flattered to discover that they are similar to others whom they respect and admire, few people want to discover that they are only average. When college students are given fictitious test results indicating that they are very similar to the average person, they feel upset, and they attempt to assert their dissimilarity (Fromkin, 1968). Students who are told that their opinions on a number of important topics are not unique subsequently display nonconformity to emphasize their uniqueness (Duval, 1972). When children are asked to describe themselves by listing their characteristics, they focus on things that differentiate them from their classmates (McGuire, McGuire, Child, & Fujioka, 1978; McGuire & Padawer-Singer, 1976). For example, children are more likely to mention their age if they are 6 months older or younger than their classmates, their hair color, eye color, and weight if these are atypical, and their ethnic group if they are in a social minority in their schools. McGuire suggests that people spontaneously mention such characteristics because they are the most informative things about them.

People do not seek uniqueness at any and all cost. Uniqueness can shade into deviance and make the actor the target of aggression and rejection (Fromkin, 1970). Consequently, people usually adopt a balancing strategy of showing their numerous similarities with their audiences while going on to point out the attributes which allow them to claim the image of uniqueness. What of the person who, by consensus, seems to be average or common on most attributes, unable to claim superior intelligence, beauty, happiness, and so on? For such people, there is always the opportunity to break the world record for eating persimmon seeds, or doing hand stands, or staying awake while knitting giraffe scarves, or . . . .

Self-Disclosure:
Revealing Frailties in Exchange for Intimacy

Another way in which people play off audiences is attempting to regulate the relative quality and quantity of personal information each individual knows about the other. This comes under the rubric of self-disclosure. *Self-disclosure* is defined as "any information about himself which Person A communicates verbally to a Person B" (Cozby, 1973, p. 73). Nonverbal behavior is sometimes included in the definition (Chaikin & Derlega, 1974). Although the information can be either positive or negative, most theoretical and research interest has focused on the negative. Negative information is information normally not revealed in relationships, since it usually implies unattractive images; frequently it can be kept hidden from public view unless the actor decides to disclose it. It might include the revelation of an embarrassing personal incident or habit, feelings of jealousy and envy in situations where admiration is preached, "wicked" thoughts, and so on. The area of self-disclosure has traditionally been studied with an eye toward the things that constitute a "healthy personality" (Jourard, 1964, 1968). It is often assumed that unless a person discloses to at least one other human being, the development of a healthy personality is blocked. Failing to disclose cuts people off from others and causes them to be ignorant of others' needs. Without disclosure, relationships presumably can't proceed to any depth or intimacy. A person who won't disclose is pictured as isolated, unknown, and therefore unloved (Jourard, 1964).

Self-disclosure can also be viewed from a very different angle—strategic self-presentation in social life. Regulating self-disclosure, particularly of information that would not otherwise be revealed to an audience, is a way of controlling how one appears in social interaction (Jones & Archer, 1976; Jones & Wortman, 1973; Tedeschi & Lindskold, 1976). Simmel (1964, p. 307) observed that "obviously, all relations which people have to one another are based on their knowing something about one another." By controlling the information, people can control the interaction. Self-disclosure can have three major purposes in strategic interaction: (1) controlling the level of intimacy and trust in the relationship; (2) influencing the amount the actor learns about the other; and (3) affecting relative power in the relationship.

There is a curvilinear relationship between the intimacy of self-disclosure and how much the discloser is liked and trusted by the target (Cozby, 1973). People who hold back and reveal little are usually seen as disliking and distrusting the target, and they are disliked and distrusted in return. At the other extreme, people who gush forth highly intimate and revealing personal details are usually seen as aberrant, even sick, for violating the norms of appropriateness; they are disliked and distrusted as well. People who reveal moderate amounts are liked and trusted the most. They are appropriately intimate; they demonstrate that they trust, respect, and like the target; and they may even hit upon many interpersonal similarities as a consequence of the revelations. They are neither cold, standoffish, nor superficial; nor are they fanatical in their revelation of things best reserved for the privacy of their bedroom, an alley, or a confessional.

Moderate amounts of self-disclosure produce reciprocation. The target then feels respected, trusted with some personal secrets, and liked; it is normal in such situations to reciprocate with a comparable amount of self-disclosure (Cozby, 1973). Through their own self-disclosure, actors can therefore discover information about others that an audience might otherwise keep hidden. It would not be surprising if many people actually fabricated information about themselves to use for self-disclosure purposes when their goals were really to give the impression of intimacy and to discover personal information about the other. No research, however, has examined this possibility.

There are dangers of self-disclosure. By revealing negative personal information, the actor risks the possibility that the audience will spread the "gossip" or use it against him. Ultimately, the actor's power can be decreased. People in leadership positions often advise against allowing subordinates to get "too close," since closeness diminishes their respect and power by going beyond the bounds of what is appropriate for a dominant-submissive relationship. Leaders often prefer to maintain a mystique rather than risk being seen as equal. In his book *Power* Michael Korda (1976, p. 302) lists as one of the major rules of power, "never reveal all of yourself to other people, hold something back in reserve so that people are never quite sure if they really know you." He goes on to note that the idea is not to be secretive; "It's more a question of remaining slightly mysterious, as if one were always capable of doing something surprising and unexpected. Most people are so predictable and reveal so much of themselves that a person who isn't and who doesn't automatically acquires a kind of power" (p. 302).

THE PRESSURES OF SUCCESS AND FAILURE

Self-presentations cannot ignore reality—the reality of one's frailties, limitations, and failures. Presenting oneself to others is a commitment to live up to the identity that is claimed and to do nothing that could place that identity in doubt. When public information repudiates a self-presentation, the actor's credibility as a viable social participant is threatened. Unless some acceptable explanation for the discrepancy can be found, the actor gains a reputation for being deceptive. The more people speak about themselves, the greater the risk that some of the images they claim will be repudiated by events. Not surprisingly, people who make public announcements of their expectations of personal performance feel less comfortable and more aroused than those who don't, and this is increasingly true as their predictions depart from what they privately believe they can accomplish (Archibald, 1971).

Although people want to claim attractive images, any factor that decreases the likelihood of a successful claim should constrain self-presentations. When publicly known past or anticipated events càn invalidate a particular self-presentation, people should present a public image that is consistent with their self-perceptions of what they can actually claim. But when surrounding events portend no threat to self-presentations, individuals have the freedom to present themselves as positively as possible. Their self-enhancement is limited only by their perceived ability to *act* the part they are presenting, not by their actually *being* the part.

Following up this line of reasoning, Schlenker (1975a) tested the hypothesis that people present themselves in a self-enhancing way when public information cannot threaten their self-presentations, but present themselves accurately (consistently with what they privately believe about themselves) when public information threatens to invalidate a self-enhancing presentation. He had subjects take a battery of tests that supposedly measured "aspects of social and nonsocial intelligence" and led them to believe that at a subsequent session they would be working as part of a four-person group on a similar set of tests. At the subsequent session, one-third of the subjects were given no feedback about how they had performed on the individual tests, one-third were given bogus scores that indicated they had done extremely well, and one-third were given bogus scores that indicated they had done very poorly. The subjects who received the bogus scores were also told that since the tests they would be working on as part of the group were quite similar to those they took earlier, they could probably expect to perform personally at about the same level. In addition, the procedure for the upcoming group testing situation was described in such a way that subjects believed either that their performance in the group would be completely anonymous so that only they would know how they did or that their performance would be made known to the other group members. Under the guise of getting to know one another better before beginning the group task, subjects completed a questionnaire that assessed their self-descriptions and which they believed would be shown to the other people in the group.

As predicted, it was found that when subjects believed that their upcoming performance would be public knowledge, and hence could invalidate a too-boastful self-presentational stance, they were cautious to claim no greater competency than they expected to demonstrate in the group. The people who expected failure presented themselves as relatively incompetent, while the people who expected success presented themselves as quite competent. However, when subjects believed that their upcoming performance would be completely anonymous and could not invalidate their self-presentations, they described themselves as quite competent irrespective of whether they privately expected to succeed or fail. After all, if they failed, no one would know. It is often said that politicians are more concerned with whether their images will "work" than with whether their images are truthful. Judging from the self-presentations of these college students, politicians are not the only ones who ask the question "Will it play in Peoria?"

The more difficult it is for the audience to check the veracity of a self-presentation, the more likely people are to self-aggrandize. For example, as people get older they often enlarge on the achievements of their youth to the point where minor successes turn into major conquests. The man who was a third-string football player in high school might tell his children that he was the star of the team; the woman who played understudy to a minor character in a high school play might tell her children that she once dazzled the audience in her starring role. Such claims are difficult to check, even more so since the person can no longer be called on to give the performance in question. A fifty-year-old man usually can't be expected to go out and be a football star again. Similarly, fishermen can be counted on to describe the ones that got away as bigger than the ones they caught.

People often attempt to "test the waters" in advance of their self-presentations, trying to discover what their audiences know and don't know about them and what the audiences are likely to believe and disbelieve. When people are first introduced at a party, and one of them says "Oh, I've heard about you" the other invariably comes back with "Nothing bad I trust" or "Really, who mentioned me?" or some other statement that probes for information about the reputation that has preceded them.

People with past histories of failure encounter social pressures to present themselves in ways that are consistent with their actual lack of skills. Some audiences might already know of their deficiencies and hence cannot be misled by self-enhancing claims. Other audiences might not currently know of the deficiencies but could be expected to learn of them. The actors might doubt their abilities to pass future tests in front of that audience or might expect the audience to learn of deficiencies from people who already know about them. If one's deficiencies cannot be hidden from public view, there is no point to giving a self-enhancing presentation that is going to be repudiated.

The same thing can be said of any unattractive image people believe they possess, be it an ugly nose, obesity, or stupidity. If it is public knowledge, one is better off admitting it than denying it. People often point out highly visible deficiencies to their audiences before the audiences can comment on them. Thus, a person might make herself the butt of her own jokes about her ugly features. She believes the audience will notice them anyway, and it usually hurts less to mention visible faults and to joke about them than to wait for the audience to say the same things. She will be seen as ugly anyway, but through her jokes she might compensate somewhat and gain the reputation of a person with a sense of humor. By mentioning faults that will soon become public knowledge (1) one increases one's credibility ("she is the type of person who admits faults and doesn't try to hide or alibi them"); (2) one can gain a reputation for self-insight ("she knows herself"); and (3) the audience is forewarned about possible events that could affect their outcomes. As an example of the last, a person who is a terrible tennis player and has just been invited to play doubles with a new acquaintance might warn him of his inability. If the partner still agrees to play, and they lose, the partner can't blame the actor for misleading him—responsibility for the defeat is shared. Although the actor comes across as a poor tennis player, which was expected anyway, at least he is honest about his own inabilities; this increases his credibility in other areas. If the actor experiences a streak of beginner's luck and the team wins, he can take bows for both his ability and his modesty. When people expect to fail publicly, predicting failure is the best tactic. If failure results, the actor is at least credible; if success occurs, the actor is not only successful, but modest.

Unattractive Images:
Balancing Reality against the Desire for Approval

Reality constraints pressure people to present themselves consistently with their beliefs about their actual attributes. At the same time, however, failure produces high needs for approval. People with low self-esteem, who typically have had consistent past failures, are more desirous than people with high self-esteem to receive approval from others (S. C. Jones, 1973; Mettee & Aronson, 1974). They are more gratified when accepted by others and more disenchanted when rejected. Consequently, people who experience recent failure should want to take advantage of any opportunity that may arise to obtain approval. They should present themselves in ways specifically designed to impress the audience favorably and to gain approval, at least to the degree that they can do so without contradicting information the audience has about them.

Research supports the hypothesis that people who have experienced recent failure present themselves in an aggrandizing fashion when they have an opportunity to obtain approval from an audience *and* their self-presentations are not contradicted by publicly known facts. Schneider (1969) gave subjects bogus feedback on a paper-and-pencil "social sensitivity" test to indicate that they either did very well or very poorly. They were then given the opportunity to describe themselves to an interviewer who would make an independent assessment of their social sensitivity. The stage was set so that subjects could describe themselves very positively without fear of contradiction by the prior scores. First, subjects were told that the interview technique seemed to tap aspects of social sensitivity that were not picked up by the paper-and-pencil test. Subjects thus could claim to be socially sensitive, but in ways that were unmeasured by the prior test. Second, the questionnaire that was to be completed for the interviewer requested that subjects rate themselves on a wide variety of self-descriptive attributes (such as well adjusted in general and hard to warm up to) that were largely unrelated to social sensitivity. With the stage set, subjects were told either that the interviewer would later give them his evaluation or that the interviewer's evaluation would be completely confidential and would not be revealed to them. The former group thus had the opportunity to receive approval if they impressed the interviewer; the latter group had no such chance.

Schneider found that those subjects who failed presented themselves more positively to the interviewer when they expected to receive an evaluation than when they did not. In fact, the subjects who failed and expected to receive an evaluation presented themselves even more positively than subjects who succeeded and expected an evaluation. These approval-hungry people used self-praise when confronted by the opportunity to receive social feedback. Similar results have been obtained in several other studies (Ackerman & Schlenker, 1975; Baumeister & Jones, 1978; Miller & Schlenker, 1978; Schneider & Turkat, 1975). The only types of people who have been found not to display such a quest for approval following failure are those who have both high self-esteem and low chronic needs for approval (Schneider & Turkat, 1975). They instead present themselves humbly after a failure and don't engage in the defensive, audience-oriented behaviors shown by most other people.

Failure usually seems to arouse high needs for social approval that are translated into aggrandizing self-presentations when possible. In most situations in life, however, publicly known failures are likely to contradict at least some self-enhancing presentations. Thus, at the same time people who fail are pushed to gain approval, they are held back in some areas by reality constraints. The most direct means of resolving this frustrating dilemma is by balancing one's self-presentations—being accurate about oneself on dimensions that would be contradicted by publicly known facts but self-aggrandizing on dimensions that would not be contradicted. For example, everyone knows at least one person who has a reputation of being a failure, yet spends most of the time talking about himself as if he had the greatest list of accomplishments ever seen. Oh, he will admit to the "few" faults about which the audience certainly knows, thus introducing the necessary amount of self-demeaning behavior, but tries to compensate for it by his grandiose claims to other attributes.

Baumeister and Jones (1978) tested and supported the hypothesis that people who fail present themselves in a self-demeaning manner on attributes that are relevant to a publicly known failure but compensate by enhancing their self-presentations on attributes for which the failure is irrelevant. After receiving bogus failure feedback on a personality inventory, subjects were led to believe either that their poor scores were completely confidential and unknown to both the experimenter and another person with whom they would later interact or that their scores were known by both the experimenter and the other person. Since it is less threatening to fail privately than to fail and have an audience discover it (Modigliani, 1971), the public failure should arouse the highest needs for social approval and the greatest attempt to compensate through self-aggrandizement. Subjects were given an opportunity to describe themselves to the other person on some attributes that were directly related to the profile and others that were unrelated. It was found that subjects whose poor scores were public knowledge presented themselves in a self-deprecating (consistent) way on the related attributes but were self-aggrandizing on the unrelated ones. Subjects whose poor scores were confidential did not display such compensation and presented themselves more favorably on the related attributes than subjects in the public condition. Ackerman and Schlenker (1975) similarly found that public failure generates the greatest needs for social approval and self-enhancement.

Attractive Images: Modesty versus Self-Aggrandizement

Modesty is an attractive image. People who are known to be successful but who slightly underplay their strengths and refrain from constantly talking about themselves seem secure, nondefensive, well-adjusted, and pleasant. They don't directly offend others through braggartly, egotistical, or threatening claims. Thus, they are likely to gain social approval and avoid disapproval. Although modesty might be ineffective in some situations where aggressiveness and confrontation are valued, most of the time it is in people's self-interests to acquire an image of humility.

People must have something to be modest about for modesty to be effective in impressing others. Modesty can only be claimed when people possess some attractive images like expertise or beauty and then underplay them. If people believe that their audiences know or will shortly come to know that they possess, say, expertise, they can afford to be modest. Since their expertise is already established, they can devote their tactical efforts to acquiring other desirable images. Thus, through modesty, the people can impress the audience with both their expertise and humility as well as avoid any risk of disapproval for bragging. If, however, people believe that the audience doesn't know or won't learn of their expertise independently of their self-presentation, they can't afford to be modest. If they underplay their expertise, the audience might take them at their words and conclude that they are incompetent or insecure. They will lose on both counts, being seen as neither expert nor humble. In such cases, people who want to make a favorable impression on an audience are left with no alternative except self-enhancement. If they want the audience to know, they have to tell them.

Ackerman and Schlenker (1975) tested the hypothesis that, following success, people will present themselves modestly if they believe the audience will learn of their success but self-aggrandizingly if they believe the audience will not. Subjects were given bogus success feedback on a test and then led to expect an interview with a person who either would or would not see their test scores. As predicted, people were modest when the audience would learn of their scores but self-enhancing when the audience would not. Baumeister and Jones (1978) reported comparable results. It has also been found that people are more likely to employ modesty when they expect to receive an explicit evaluation from their audience than when they don't (Schneider, 1969). Successful people who expect to receive social feedback appear to take no chances on offending their audience by appearing to be bragging.

As these studies show, self-enhancement is the tactic chosen by most people to impress an audience that is unaware of their strengths. Modesty is the tactic chosen by people to impress an audience that is already familiar with their strengths. People can, of course, overdo modesty by presenting themselves so far below the level of their actual attributes that they appear to be sickeningly sweet or insecure and unaware of their own strengths. They might even be seen as attempting to mislead an audience if they drastically underestimate their ability. For example, the professional hustler informs people that he is just average or perhaps a beginner at poker, pool, tennis, golf, or whatever. He then proceeds to clean up when the gullible audience bets heavily on the outcomes of his games. Audiences usually punish hustlers for their illicit attempts at personal profit. People react negatively to actors who drastically underestimate their ability and then do well (Brickman & Seligman, 1974). On the other hand, people admire actors who say they will do something and then are able to pull it off. Thus, modesty can be a very effective tactic for impressing audiences who are already familiar with one's strengths, but it is best used in moderation.

As a final note on the competing pressures that exist for people with either attractive or unattractive images, it is worth comparing the self-presentations of those who have recently succeeded with those who have failed. People who succeed present themselves more favorably than those who fail when their self-presentations can be checked by the audience against relevant facts (Baumeister & Jones, 1978; Miller & Schlenker, 1978; Schlenker, 1975a). However, there is a unique set of conditions under which people who fail actually present themselves more favorably than those who succeed. When a publicly known performance on an important test is irrelevant to a self-description and people have an opportunity to interact with or receive an evaluation from the aware audience, they present themselves more positively following failure than success (the conclusion is based on a comparison of the results of Ackerman & Schlenker, 1975; Baumeister & Jones, 1978; Schlenker, 1975a; and Schneider, 1969). The successful people can afford to be modest and thus acquire images of success and humility. The failing people have lost face in public and therefore have high needs for approval. They should be willing to run the risk of being seen as braggarts in order to gain approval, and the facts won't directly contradict a braggartly self-presentation.

People who know that their audience already gives them credit for possessing an attractive attribute have an additional tactic at their disposal: they can point out to the audience all of the obstacles that they had to overcome on their way to success. Drawing attention to the inordinate impediments that they rose above makes their accomplishments seem all the more magnificent. People who accomplish some goal despite factors that would otherwise make the goal difficult to obtain are seen by audiences as being particularly talented or motivated (Jones & Davis, 1965). There is little chance that their accomplishments will be misattributed by the audience to causes outside the actor, such as luck. For example, Helen Keller's achievements are rightfully viewed as all the more remarkable because she transcended her physical handicaps through her own ability and perseverance.

Since audiences take obstacles into account when making attributions about an actor, it should not be surprising that actors use such predilections of their audiences in order to create the most desirable impression possible. For example, the businesswoman who has just landed an important account for her firm can tell her employer about the difficulties she encountered: the client was initially disposed to sign with another firm; the client was in a bad mood after an uncomfortable airplane trip; the client had to leave town on an early afternoon flight so she had only a few short hours to make the sale. But despite these problems, she succeeded. The employer is left to conclude that she *must* be a superb salesperson. Similarly, how often have you heard an older person tell a younger one about how tough things were back in the old days? The older person had to walk to school, study by candlelight, fight his way to the top, and so on. Yet, through ability and fortitude, he conquered. The younger person, in contrast, has things easy—so easy that his accomplishments do not appear to be as much a function of his own ability and motivation in the older person's eyes. To the latter, the younger person didn't rise above the situation; the situation handed him his success.

Of course, if an audience does not already recognize that a person possesses an attractive attribute, then mentioning obstacles is self-defeating. For example, if you were being interviewed by a prospective employer who was seeking the most competent person possible, it would make little sense to tell the employer about all of the obstacles you faced in life. The employer might conclude that, because of the obstacles, you probably had a difficult time acquiring necessary skills and might not be as competent as other people. Instead, people who believe their audience is unsure about their desirable attributes are more likely to disclose information that suggests that they *do* have the attributes and withhold information about obstacles. People disclose obstacles only *after* they are sure that an audience has given them credit for an accomplishment (or will give them credit in the near future). In a role-play study, Quattrone and Jones (1978) found support for this hypothesis. Subjects said that they would mention interfering obstacles when an audience already gave them credit for a positive attribute, but that they would mention facilitating, noninterfering factors when the audience's opinion of them was still in doubt.

The "modesty tactic" and the "obstacle tactic" are variations on a common theme. In both cases, people are recognized (or believe they will be recognized) by an audience as possessing some desirable characteristic—that is, they have achieved (or believe they will achieve) the goal of favorably impressing the audience. With that goal secured, they then can concentrate on a new goal—being viewed either as possessing the additional desirable attribute of humility or as particularly talented and motivated in overcoming relevant obstacles.

INTERNALIZING SELF-PRESENTATIONS: WHEN IS SAYING BELIEVING?

People's proclivities for "self-deception" are legion. Demosthenes stated "Nothing is so easy as to deceive one's self, for what we wish we readily believe." Benjamin Franklin echoed "It's the easiest thing in the World for a Man to deceive himself." Is self-deception as easy as these sages suggest? Can exaggerated self-presentations that start with the goal of impressing an audience end up being privately believed?

Earlier, we found that people do come to internalize role attributes when they become comfortable in a role; that is, they come to value the rewards that the role generates and believe they can successfully perform the required role behaviors (see Chapter 3). An insecure businessperson, for example, becomes more assertive after promotion to an executive role as she finds that she enjoys and can handle the position. We also found that people sometimes internalize their remedial tactics (accounts and apologies) when they are in predicaments (see Chapter 5). The internalization of a remedial tactic is most likely to occur when cues in the situation prevent people's labeling their tactic as a lie, such as when an account is accepted by a significant and knowledgeable audience and the account does not blatantly contradict the facts as known by the actor. These lines of thought lead us to expect that people's public self-descriptions also can become internalized to produce changes in the self-concept.

Research examining the internalization of self-descriptions has focused on the effects of social reinforcement, such as whether a self-description results in the approval or disapproval of the audience. In the first such study, Jones, Gergen, and Davis (1962) had female subjects describe themselves to an interviewer under one of two goal conditions. Subjects either were given ingratiation instructions and told to make "a special effort to create a favorable impression" or were given accuracy instructions and told to be "completely candid and honest" in their self-description. During the interview, the subjects did translate their goals into the expected behaviors: those in the ingratiation condition described themselves more positively than did those in the accuracy condition. After the interview, subjects were told either that they had made a favorable impression on the interviewer or that they had made an unfavorable impression. When later asked how accurate they had been in their self-descriptions, those who received the favorable feedback stated that their self-descriptions were more accurate than did those who received the unfavorable feedback. Whether or not they had inflated their self-descriptions in order to obtain approval made no difference. In either case, a presentation that received approval was described as more accurate than one that did not. In fact, subjects who ingratiated and received approval stated that they were accurate more than did subjects who were accurate but received disapproval. These results suggest that enhanced self-presentations do become believed if they result in social rewards. Keep in mind, however, that we cannot be certain that subjects' *reports* of how accurate they were actually corresponded to their *private beliefs* about accuracy.

To determine if such results generalize to a different type of reinforcement situation and to a different way of measuring subjects' beliefs, Gergen (1965) had females again describe themselves to an interviewer. Some were given ingratiation instructions while others were "encouraged to be honest and natural." The interviewer reinforced some of the subjects during the interview by saying things such as "Yes, I would agree" or "very good" whenever they described themselves very positively; other subjects received no reinforcement during the interview. After the interview, subjects described themselves to another person to determine if their self-descriptions had changed from their initial levels. They also completed a self-esteem questionnaire to determine if their general levels of self-esteem had been altered. The results showed that, after the interview, subjects described themselves more positively and obtained higher self-esteem scores if they had been reinforced. Whether subjects had ingratiated or sought to be accurate did not make a difference so long as reinforcement had been forthcoming. Both reinforced groups were later more positive about themselves than the subjects who were accurate but not reinforced.

There are at least two reasons why such effects might occur (Jones & Wortman, 1973). First, people may come to believe that they actually have the attributes for which they were reinforced. They may have accepted the feedback as truthful and "forgot" about the fact that they enhanced their self-descriptions to get the approval. As Jones (1964, p. 67) put it, "persons tend to exaggerate the perceived representativeness or felt sincerity of any performance which elicits approval." Or, as Samuel Johnson remarked, "Every man willingly gives value to the praise which he receives and considers the sentence passed in his favor as a sentence of discernment." Second, people may raise their self-esteem whenever they believe they have successfully accomplished a task. In the above studies, subjects were given a task—obtain approval—and some of them did it. In most self-presentation situations these forces operate together to produce what appears to be some internalization of an exaggerated self-presentation. As Jones and Wortman (1973, p. 49) note, self-enhancement usually will "elicit positive feedback from others, even though the others may not really be taken in by the self-enhancing claims. As a consequence of making self-enhancing claims, then, an individual is likely to develop an overly positive picture of himself."

There are upper limits to such effects—reality does impose constraints on what people really can internalize. It has been found that, if people blatantly exaggerate their self-presentations far beyond what they know could possibly be true, such internalization does not occur (Schneider, unpublished, described in Jones & Wortman, 1973, pp. 48–49; Upshaw & Yates, 1968). They can still feel successful at having accomplished their goal and increase their general self-esteem slightly, but they don't seem to internalize the specific things they say about themselves. However, if they exaggerate only moderately, internalization does seem to occur (Schneider, unpublished). They accept the moderately exaggerated self-descriptions as sincere self-presentations.

The word sincere derives from the Latin word for "without wax" and goes back to the days of ancient Rome when craftsmen covered cracks and defects in statues with wax. Analogously, a sincere self-presentation can be viewed as one which contains no "cracks" or "defects" that would indicate that the actor cannot meet the requirements of the images he or she claims. To obtain a broader hypothetical view of when internalization occurs, let's pursue this line of reasoning to its logical conclusion. Recall (from Chapter 4) that the desirability of an image increases as the expected worth of claiming it (the probability that it can be successfully claimed times its expected value) exceeds the expected costs of unsuccessfully doing so (the probability that it cannot be claimed times the expected value of the sanctions). People are presumed to select from mutually exclusive sets of images those that have the greatest desirability.

People are presumed to use the same formulation in determining both private claims like self-beliefs and public claims like self-descriptions, although the private and public might differ in their outcomes. For example, people privately might believe they can "fool" one particular audience by describing themselves more positively than they really believe they are. However, they also might believe they could not fool several other audiences who are perhaps more critical or who know personal information about the actors that would contradict their claims. In the former case, no cracks would be publicly revealed in a highly favorable self-presentation; in the latter cases, cracks would be revealed because the people believe they actually can't meet all of the requirements of the images. Thus, these people are likely to describe themselves favorably in front of the gullible audience but not in front of the others. If the people gave the performance in front of the gullible audience and received approval, we should expect that they would feel good momentarily for getting what they wanted, but we should not expect that they would revise their private beliefs about themselves. After all, they still believe that there are many other audiences who would not be as gullible. However, suppose, for whatever reason, that they gave the performance in front of one of the nongullible audiences and still received approval—this could be an indication that they were wrong about themselves. No cracks were revealed. Their performances met all of the requirements for claiming those images. When people receive approval from credible, significant others (and all of the audiences in the experiments described above were such esteemed people), they revise upward their private beliefs of being able successfully to claim the images contained in their performances. They come to believe that they *do* meet the requirements for those images, at least more so than they did previously. Another way of putting this is the way we did when describing roles—people come to believe that they can successfully perform the required role or image behaviors.

Just as not all types of audience will produce the internalization of self-presentations, so too, not all types of approval are likely to produce internalization. The approval must indicate that the actor *meets the requirements for successfully claiming a particular image.* For example, a professional actor might receive standing ovations for his brilliant performance of *King Lear.* Virtually all actors correctly interpret the approval as indicating that they are good at performing the role, not that they meet the requirements for being King Lear. (A few might misattribute the audience's applause and come to believe that they are King Lear, but such instances are rare.) Analogously, when everyday actors give blatantly exaggerated performances, they do not interpret any approval they receive as indicating they really are what they profess to be, just that they are good at performing a role. But if their performances are only somewhat exaggerated, and they receive approval that suggests that the audience grants them the relevant attributes, they should conclude that they really are what they said they were.

SUMMARY

Verbal self-descriptions are the most direct and least subtle way of laying claims to particular sets of images. Through them, people can carve out the types of identities that they want and believe they can sustain in social interactions. At the extreme, people can use self-descriptions for ingratiation purposes, hoping to increase their attractiveness in the eyes of others in order to maximize their own power and external profits in the relationship. Ingratiation tactics are often described as deceitful means of increasing one's power, in which the ingratiator substitutes the target's values for his or her own. In practice, however, interactions are usually replete with attempts to increase one's attractiveness, so the line between ingratiation and other types of self-presentation often blurs. People usually increase the positivity of their self-presentations in ingratiation situations, although they will balance their self-presentations by being self-enhancing about some claims and self-demeaning about others when conveying differential status or attempting to prove their sincerity.

Ingratiation involves playing *to* an audience. In most interactions, people play *off* an audience, using the audience's actions as signposts to modify their own plans about the type of identity that is most desirable in the relationship. People play off audiences by (a) matching the audience's self-presentations; (b) fulfilling the audience's stereotypes; (c) displaying an image of attractive uniqueness; and (d) varying their relative self-disclosures.

Reality places constraints on self-presentations. People claim only those images that they can reasonably hope to sustain in their interactions. Although people will behave in a self-aggrandizing fashion when no public information contradicts their self-presentations, they concede to the demands of reality and present themselves in a more self-demeaning fashion when there is a strong possibility that an audience knows or will know information that could challenge or refute their claims. People who privately believe they possess numerous unattractive images are caught in a dilemma: they desire approval but must balance their desire against the likelihood that public information will invalidate self-enhancement. People who privately believe they possess numerous attractive images have full advantage of the techniques of modesty and self-aggrandizement. If they believe their audience already knows of their positive attributes, they present themselves modestly, while if they believe their audience is uninformed, they present themselves aggrandizingly.

Self-presentations are not only effective in fooling an audience; they also often deceive the actor as well. People use the responses of an audience as one guide for determining what they can legitimately claim about themselves. Approving, reinforcing audiences generally cause actors to internalize their self-enhancing presentations irrespective of whether or not they have publicly distorted what they privately believe about themselves, provided that the distortion is not too blatant.

SEVEN

Flattery is telling the other man precisely what he thinks of himself.

Dale Carnegie

THE ART OF
IMPRESSION MANAGEMENT:
ATTITUDE AND
BELIEF EXPRESSIONS

The word *attitude* came into the English language in 1710 and was originally used as a technical term in art and design to refer to the posture, stance, and physical disposition of a figure in space (Fleming, 1967). A statue, for example, was said to display an attitude toward the surrounding environment that expressed what the figure was supposed to be doing and feeling. The word still retains this original idea of expressing an orientation with respect to something.

By 1725, the meaning of the word had expanded to include another aspect that is still very much with us: a *theatrical* element. Attitude came to signify the feelings conveyed by a living person, whose words, posture, and orientation *impressed onlookers as being adapted to a particular course of action.* It was said that the "most skillful exemplar of living attitudes was a professional actor" (Fleming, p. 292). The professional actor struck calculated poses to impress upon the audience the nature and goals of the particular character being portrayed. If successful, the audience had no doubt about the identity and motivation of the character. The sagacious Dr. Samuel Johnson, offering advice as to how actors should behave, believed that "an actor of merit does not *feel* his part at all. In the measure that he is on top of his craft, his attitudes on the stage do not represent even a momentary lapse of calculation" (Fleming, p. 293). The professional actor should attend continually to the impressions he might be making on an audience and control those impressions with every ounce of skill. Current schools of acting give slightly different advice to aspiring professionals, recommending that to play a role successfully one must feel it and become it. Behaviors then follow with a natural, and one hopes convincing, sincerity. Despite this difference in emphasis, both schools of thespian thought agree on the ultimate goal: to convey to the audience the full depth and breadth of the character being portrayed. The audience must recognize how the character is related to the other characters and to the environment, and acceptable continuity must be maintained from the past through the present to the future. The actor's identity and goals should strike an appreciative chord in the audience. Analogously, in everyday life, people use attitude expressions in order to manage the impressions that real or imagined audiences form of the characters they play.

ATTITUDES AND BELIEFS

In social-scientific usage, attitude is an intrapersonal concept describing an individual's feelings about some aspect of himself or the world. It is defined as the amount of positive or negative affect a person feels toward a particular psychological object or event (Kiesler, Collins, & Miller, 1969). In other words, it is the degree of liking or disliking one feels toward something. People hold attitudes about objects (a painting, a car), issues (taxation rates, freedom of speech), events (the Middle East crises), other people (an employer, a co-worker), and themselves. Most social scientists distinguish between attitudes and *beliefs*, attitudes being expressions of what people *feel* about a particular psychological object or event and beliefs being expressions of what they *think* about it. Beliefs are hypotheses about the attributes of the psychological object or event. For instance, a person might say "I think John is intelligent, trustworthy, witty, and kind" (beliefs) and also say "I like John" (attitude). Thus, beliefs describe the images people associate with the object or event, and attitudes describe how people evaluate those images.

Expressions of attitudes and beliefs usually occur in the context of real or imagined social interactions. Since attitudes and beliefs express the individual's relationship with some aspect of the (usually) social environment, they should be theoretically viewed in the context of social interaction. Like any other behavior, attitudes and beliefs are functional in that they are used to accomplish certain goals (Katz, 1960). Through attitudes and beliefs, people achieve a coherent view of the environment, make predictions about what is likely to occur, and make decisions to maximize their reward/cost ratios. For instance, believing that John is trustworthy, intelligent, and kind and liking him might prompt you to loan him money in time of need. To the degree that your beliefs are accurate, you should be repaid, perhaps with interest, and you have probably secured a loyal friend. To the degree your beliefs are inaccurate, you might never see your money again.

Attitudes and beliefs are also functional in that they partially define people's social identities. Like any other behavior, attitude and belief expressions convey particular images of actors to themselves and to others. Through them, people reveal information about themselves and their relationships with others. Attitudes and beliefs can reveal at least five types of information. First, they can reveal the actor's positive or negative orientation toward a social setting and other interactants. An actor might comment "What a great party. I'm really enjoying the company, and the hostess has been marvelous." The actor thereby conveys enjoyment and a positive outlook rather than boredom and a negative outlook. The actor might then be seen as gracious, well-mannered, friendly, and pleasant. Second, they can reveal the actor's desired role in the interaction. An actor can communicate dominance by expressing beliefs that place other people in a subservient role. Third, attitudes and beliefs can associate the actor with particular groups or types of people. Political beliefs associate actors with liberals or conservatives; attitudes toward particular types of music associate actors with classical enthusiasts, rock-and-roll buffs, and so on. Fourth, audiences often make inferences about actors' personalities on the basis of their attitudes and beliefs. Actors who like to read a lot are stereotyped as intellectual and introverted. Social scientists also make inferences about people's personalities on the basis of their attitudes and beliefs. A particular set of beliefs is presumed to be associated with an authoritarian personality; other sets of beliefs are presumed to distinguish cognitively simple people from the cognitively complex. Finally, attitudes and beliefs can be used by actors to explain the reasons or motives behind their own and others' actions. People can communicate the reasons why an event occurred, such as why they behaved a particular way, by referring to attitudes and beliefs about the event. For instance, a person can explain why he took a particular job by describing his attitudes and beliefs about it ("The boss seems friendly, the employees seem competent and satisfied, and the company seems to be growing rapidly; thus, I like the atmosphere and people, I should be happy, and I should have plenty of opportunity for advancement"). Similarly, people's accounts of undesirable events (see Chapter 5) are replete with attitude and belief expressions ("I cheated on the exam because I didn't believe it would harm anyone else's grade, I dislike the instructor and don't think that she grades fairly, and I have to pass this course in order to graduate on time").

Since attitudes and beliefs usually exist in a matrix of real or imagined social interactions, people can control the information revealed through them for impression-management purposes (Schlenker, 1978). People can publicly and privately express attitudes and beliefs that are designed to claim desirable images and disclaim undesirable ones. A person who thinks of herself as gracious compliments the hostess, thereby demonstrating the proper outlook on that social setting; a person who thinks of himself as an intellectual memorizes facts and figures about world issues and then displays his acumen through properly justified beliefs; a person who wants to be seen as liberal reads up on the appropriate beliefs and expresses them to acquaintances. Naturally, beliefs and attitudes that are expressed publicly do not have to correspond with private thoughts and feelings. People might flatter others or conform to others' opinions only to make a favorable impression, and not because they really believe any of the things they are saying. As always, the degree to which public expressions correspond to private ones depends on the degree of disparity between the desirability of public and private claims (see Chapter 4).

In this chapter, we'll explore how people use attitude and belief expressions for impression-management purposes. Although the impression-management approach described in previous chapters can be employed to integrate a wide variety of material on attitudes and beliefs, we'll concentrate on only four major research areas that have received the greatest amount of attention from social scientists. First, we'll examine how people attempt to match their words and deeds in order to appear consistent and avoid the unpleasing appearance of inconsistency. Second, we'll consider the use of complimentary attitude and belief statements to flatter others and win their favor. Third, we'll explore how people use impression management in order to appear attitudinally similar or dissimilar to their audiences. Finally, we'll show how people respond in persuasive situations to convey the impression of either likableness or autonomy.

CONSISTENCY: MATCHING WORDS AND DEEDS

The norms of Western society encourage consistency and punish inconsistency. People are expected *not* to say one thing while doing another, *not* to express contradictory beliefs, and *not* to endorse two diametrically opposed positions in front of the same audience. Inconsistency breeds unpredictability, and people who are unpredictable are disliked and punished (Gergen & Jones, 1963). To the degree that others are inconsistent, people cannot know how to interact effectively with them. An unstable, changeable person forces people to modify their beliefs about him continuously until they eventually tire of his charade and abandon him for others who make life more predictable and pleasant. As Gergen (1968, p. 300) wrote, "it is simply less taxing and perhaps less anxiety-provoking if the social environment is not in constant and capricious flux. . . . On a broad social level one might even say that social order is to some extent dependent on consistent behavioral patterns among members of a society." Consistency between words and deeds serves an important social function. It allows people to "participate in organized social life with good confidence that others will do what they say they will do. . . . Every man is under compulsion to keep his promises, and to make his acts correspond with his verbal expressions. He constantly watches others to see that they do likewise" (Dollard, 1949, p. 624).

Some theorists (Abelson et al., 1968; Festinger, 1957; Heider, 1958) have even proposed that people have *needs* for cognitive consistency. These needs, which might be derived from innate proclivities or from social learning, motivate people to organize their attitudes and beliefs into consistent patterns and to reduce or eliminate inconsistencies in their cognitive structures. The existence of such needs is subject to debate (Greenwald & Ronis, 1978; Kelman & Baron, 1974; Schlenker, Forsyth, Leary, & Miller, in press; Schlenker & Schlenker, 1975; Tedeschi, Schlenker, & Bonoma, 1971). Irrespective of whether or not people have psychological needs to be consistent, however, there is little doubt that the appearance of consistency usually leads to social reward, while the appearance of inconsistency usually leads to social punishment.

Given the benefits of consistency and the liabilities of inconsistency, people manage the impressions they convey to others in order to establish an image of consistency (Tedeschi et al., 1971). When situations arise that challenge claims to consistency, people usually attempt to refute or explain away the questioning information. For example, a newspaper columnist might raise an apparent inconsistency between what a politician is saying now and what he said a month ago. The politician might proceed to explain that (1) the writer was not listening closely and apparently did not understand what he just said, since it was perfectly consistent with the earlier statement; (2) the writer has his facts wrong, since the politician did not actually say what was earlier attributed to him; or (3) the inconsistency is apparent and not real, once one gets down to the real core of the ideas being conveyed. Thus, the politician attempts to show the absence of inconsistency by changing or denying the interpretation placed on either the present statement or the earlier one or attempts to explain why the statements are really not inconsistent with one another even though they were correctly interpreted. Only if all else fails would the politician usually admit that there was an inconsistency. He could then attempt to save face by saying "Everyone must grow and change with the times. I'm smarter today than I was yesterday. I believe I was wrong then but am correct now." The danger with such a tactic is that, once people admit to having been wrong in the past, the audience might conclude that they are also wrong now. If the politician is verbally adroit and sufficiently skilled in logic, he might be able to avert this conclusion and turn the liability of an inconsistency into an asset. Thus, he might try to leave the admirable impression of personal growth, constant attention to new evidence, and the ability to change with the times.

People avoid admitting inconsistencies. Research indicates that people who have changed their attitudes about an issue, after persuasion, for example, later deny that any inconsistency exists. They even go so far as to insist that they have not changed their attitudes at all (Bem & McConnell, 1970; Goethals & Reckman, 1973). When asked what their prior position on the issue was, subjects state that it *was* exactly the position they *currently* favor (even though a change actually did take place). At present, research has not unequivocally answered whether subjects fail to notice their own inconsistency, are taken in by their own statements and convince themselves that they really are consistent, or recognize the inconsistency but state they were consistent purely for the benefit of impressing the audience. Some theorists argue that people privately recognize their own inconsistencies but publicly deny them in order to impress an audience (Gaes et al., 1978). According to this view, an image of consistency is *only* a public impression-management tactic. The theoretical position advanced here, however, is that both public and private impression management are involved. People indeed display a great deal of public impression management, but these actions can also be accompanied by internalization (the actor comes to believe his or her own words) *under appropriate conditions* (see Chapters 5 and 6).

Capitalizing on Consistency

People's predilections to appear consistent can be turned against them. If people can be made to commit themselves to a particular stance, they then experience pressure to behave consistently with that stance, sometimes having to do things they otherwise might wish not to in order to avoid the appearance of inconsistency. A *commitment* is a social promise that one intends to pursue a particular course of action, and promises are supposed to be followed by deeds. A freely made commitment is hypothesized to anchor people's beliefs, making them resistant to change (Kiesler, 1971). Skilled impression managers, such as salespersons and politicians, often capitalize on the consistency principle by getting others to appear to commit themselves freely to a particular stance, and then reap profits at the expense of the committed party.

One such tactic frequently used in business is the *low-ball technique* (Cialdini, Cacioppo, Bassett, & Miller, 1978). The technique, exemplified by the tactics of new-car dealers, involves getting a customer to make an active decision to purchase a particular car for a relatively low price. The low price is the initial "hook." The customer fills out the necessary forms and the salesperson takes them to the boss for a final check and approval. After a few minutes, the salesperson returns and apologetically explains that the boss refused to permit the sale. Whenever possible the boss is made the heavy, thereby shifting responsibility for the bad news and reducing the chance that the salesperson would appear to be breaking his or her word. The salesperson might say that the boss pointed out that they would be losing money for such a low price or that an expensive extra the customer wanted was left out of the calculation of the price. Naturally, the customer can still purchase the car, but the price would have to be increased, sometimes substantially. Quite frequently, the customer ends up buying the car for the new, higher price. The customer has become committed to go through with the purchase, and so long as the explanation for the higher price appears to be reasonable, the customer follows up the initial commitment to buy. The tactic is likely to fail if the customer does not feel that an initial commitment has been made or if the explanation for the new price is unreasonable, thereby making the customer conclude that the salesperson broke a promise. But skilled salespersons usually take pains to avoid these possibilities. Cialdini and his associates (1978) demonstrated the effectiveness of the low-ball technique in getting people to follow through on freely made initial commitments even after the costs of doing so are later increased.

Another popular tactic that capitalizes on the consistency principle is the *foot-in-the-door technique*. It involves getting a person to comply to an initial small request and subsequently making a *slightly differ-*

ent larger request. The seller gets a foot in the door, so to speak, by making the buyer commit himself to doing something simple, something he is unlikely to refuse to do. This makes the buyer appear cooperative, the sort of person who does certain types of things. Then follows a larger "payoff" request, the one the seller really cared about all along. For example, a representative for a charity might initially ask a couple to place a small, innocuous decal supporting the charity on their front window, something most people will agree to do. Later, he or another representative might ask the couple to place a large, perhaps ugly, sign on their front lawn. It has been found that people who have agreed to the initial minor request are more likely to comply to the later major one (Freedman & Fraser, 1966).

The foot-in-the-door technique is best illustrated by the tactics of many encyclopedia salespersons. Under their company's supervision, the salespersons memorize prepared scripts to the point where they can repeat them while appearing to be spontaneously conversing. The scripts usually begin with the salesperson identifying himself and engaging in friendly chit-chat designed to make a favorable first impression. Additionally, the opening usually contains a key question or two designed to give the salesperson a rough idea of the likelihood of making a sale to the particular customer. "Do you have any children?" Families with children are more likely to make a purchase, and those without are best passed by unless they express real interest. The salesperson then asks a gradated series of innocuous questions carefully designed to secure affirmative responses. "Are you concerned about the education of your children?" "Do you believe an encyclopedia could be beneficial to your children?" Virtually everyone says yes, and the process of committing the customer to a sale has begun. Once such a pattern of agreement has started, it is difficult to stop later.

Some companies have the salesperson lead the customer to believe he or she might qualify to receive a free set of encyclopedias to advertise the product in the neighborhood. Customers are then asked another series of committing questions that are difficult to answer negatively. "If you were given a free set, you wouldn't place it in the garage or in your closet or under your bed, would you? You can understand that we wouldn't want it hidden since the set is being given for promotional reasons. If your friends notice and ask you about your set, you would tell them about it, wouldn't you?" The escalation proceeds until the salesperson gets close to the clincher. "Of course, the company expects that people who are given a free set will care enough about it to keep it updated over the years. Keeping it updated would simply be a sign on your part to indicate that you are the type of educationally concerned family we are looking for. You are, aren't you?" The customers are thus challenged to *prove themselves* to the salesperson, and they agree that they are the "right" sort of person. To say "no" now would be to refute everything said up to this point; the customer would appear incredibly inconsistent.

The clincher comes when it is explained that keeping the set updated amounts to buying a yearly yearbook service, sometimes at inflated prices, which costs roughly what the encyclopedia itself plus the service might cost under regular conditions. To make the introduction of payment seem less offensive, the salesperson usually throws in a line like "You can see, can't you, that the cost of this service amounts to only about the cost of your daily newspaper, and look at how much more you are getting." At this point in the script, customers who have agreed to everything else usually feel painted into a corner. The appearance of consistency becomes their downfall—that is, if they did not really want to buy the encyclopedia. People familiar with such routines can short-circuit the approach and have some fun at the same time by saying "no" to one of the early questions, such as "Do you care about education?" The look of amazement on the salesperson's face and the flustered groping for how to respond usually more than make up for any momentary uneasiness you might feel by giving such a socially undesirable response.

In most situations, people maximize their reward/cost ratios by appearing to be consistent. The appearance of consistency, though, is not desirable for all people in all situations. For example, a person who does not really want to buy an encyclopedia is better off in the long run by refusing purchase even at the expense of appearing inconsistent. At the moment of purchase, however, the customer has been caught up in the excitement of owning the particular item and has been gently led along to agree; it is only after the salesperson has left that the long-run costs of the purchase become obvious. This is one of the reasons behind relatively new laws allowing customers who have purchased a product from a door-to-door salesperson to cancel the contract without obligation within three days of the sale.

In still other situations, people can actually maximize their rewards (as opposed to the above case of minimizing their costs) by appearing to be inconsistent. For example, some people attempt to build an image of inconsistency and unpredictability to make themselves feared. Members of violent street gangs often find that inconsistency is a more desirable image than consistency because they then seem unstable, irrational, and likely to fulfill any threat they make, even if it means injuring themselves. Opponents are likely to back down and give in to the demands of such an "irrational" individual. A milder version of the tactic sometimes occurs in bargaining situations, where negotiators attempt to influence their opponents to make concessions that could not be achieved by rational or persuasive means (Tedeschi et al., 1973). The image of inconsistency is often desirable in a conflict.

It is to almost everyone's advantage *occasionally* to seem inconsistent. People can become so predictable that they are boring (Bramel, 1969). For instance, a man who is tired of the old routine, concerned that his life has degenerated into tediousness and worried that his wife is losing interest in him, might try new, exciting things he has never done before. He hopes thereby to break the pattern of his humdrum existence, acquire a lifestyle with which he is more satisfied, and save his marriage. Thus, on occasion, a little inconsistency can be enjoyable, profitable, and a desirable image. As Ralph Waldo Emerson put it, a foolish consistency is the hobgoblin of little minds.

EXPRESSING ATTITUDES TOWARD OTHERS: APPRECIATION AND FLATTERY

Most social situations are structured to favor the exchange of rewards rather than costs (Homans, 1974). People usually try to be pleasant, cooperative, and appealing because by so doing they establish a harmonious basis for interaction and provide an atmosphere that supports the exchange of rewards. One of the more pleasing types of rewards people can receive is to learn that they are favorably regarded by others. Not surprisingly, when people are called upon to say something about another person who is present, they usually stress the positive and avoid the negative. Harmony is thereby maintained and the recipient of the evaluation feels good. For instance, people who are conversing for the first time find ways to slip positive comments about their partners into the interaction and avoid saying negative things, and they do so to the same degree irrespective of whether they are told prior to the interaction to behave naturally or to try their best to be liked (Kahn & Young, 1973). Similarly, when people expect to be evaluated by others, they evaluate the others more positively than they otherwise might, thereby initiating a tit-for-tat exchange of favorable sentiments (Baron, 1974).

The usual nature of social interaction thus accentuates the positive and minimizes the negative. As the old dictum goes, "If you can't say something nice, don't say anything at all." The advice contains more than an element of truth. People who express positive attitudes and beliefs about almost anything—other people, movies, politics—are liked more than those who are always negative (Folkes & Sears, 1977). The former are seen as optimists rather than pessimists, appreciative instead of ungrateful, and they make for pleasant and reassuring company. Further, someone who puts down other people and things in front of you is likely to do the same thing to you as soon as your back is turned.

People are particularly fond of others who say positive things about them. They like those who like them, think highly of those who think highly of them, welcome compliments, but abhor criticism. We are all sufficiently vain to want to savor the fruits of appreciation. Hearing that we are held in positive regard makes us expect future rewards from the compliment-giver and want to reward him or her in return.

Thus, expressing positive attitudes about another person can produce a multitude of advantages. Actors who sincerely like another person can tell him so, make him feel good, gain favorable regard in return, facilitate harmonious interactions, and achieve the associated images and rewards that being liked by others can bring. As with any other type of public statement, however, compliments carry responsibilities. People who state they admire and like another person are expected to show it with deeds should the need arise. They might be called upon to help the other, to stick up for the other, and to avoid doing or saying things that might cast doubt on their earlier words. Further, public statements should be reasonably accurate, or negative consequences might occur. An actor whose praise for another is outrageously inaccurate can be sanctioned; she might be viewed as out of touch with reality or as an ingratiator whose praise was only self-serving. People therefore have to balance the expected gains from expressing particular attitudes toward others against the expected costs. This usually means that in making comments about others (particularly when those others are present) people try to be as positive as they can without either appearing inaccurate or committing themselves to responsibilities they don't want to assume.

Beyond Appreciation and into Flattery

The tendency to accentuate the positive and minimize the negative when expressing attitudes and beliefs about someone to his or her face is a well-ingrained habit of social life. People often go beyond what they privately believe and feel about another person and make overly praising statements. When they are perceived as doing so for personal gain, we call them flatterers.

Flattery is an ingratiation mode that seeks to exploit the target's vanities. A flatterer emphasizes, plays up, and positively distorts the strengths and virtues of the target while concomitantly ignoring, underplaying, and denying the target's weaknesses and vices. As with all ingratiation tactics, the goal of the flatterer is to make a favorable impression on the target and thereby increase his or her own power in the relationship (Jones & Wortman, 1973). The flatterer seeks personal rewards at the expense of social rules. Flattery, by definition, is a lie; it is a statement the actor does not privately believe. In addition, the flatterer usually has no intention of fulfilling the obligations his or her words create. The flatterer does not intend to help the target in time of need, refrain from disparaging the target in front of a different audience, and so on. Thus, flatterers offer a commodity (praise) that appears on the surface to be valuable but which is actually quite worthless.

As we saw with other ingratiation modes (Chapter 6), the line between sincere appreciation and flattery is clear only at the extremes or in theory. In practice, appreciation often fades imperceptibly into flattery; it is a label we apply when we attribute illicit motives to an actor. People normally focus on the positive and ignore the negative about others when interacting. They might even exaggerate slightly, but they usually try to avoid stepping over the line that would make audiences label them as flatterers. Dale Carnegie (1940), whose book *How to Win Friends and Influence People* stayed atop the *New York Times* Bestseller List for an all-time record of ten years, provides a perfect illustration of trying to be positive while avoiding being seen as a flatterer. He advised that you should be "hearty in your approbation and lavish in your praise" of others (p. 39). However, he was quick to say "No! No! No! I am not suggesting flattery!" These hearty approbations and lavish praises should be in the form of appreciation for the other. What is the "difference between appreciation and flattery? . . . One is sincere and the other insincere. One comes from the heart out; the other from the teeth out. One is unselfish; the other selfish. One is universally admired; the other is universally condemned" (p. 39). Of course, the whole point of his book is to instruct people on how to win friends and exert influence, which can reasonably be argued as being selfish goals, but no matter. Ultimately, his advice seems to translate as follows: it is highly recommended that you praise others, but don't say things that are so farfetched as to contain not even an element of truth or that commit you to doing things you will not do. For instance, he recommends that people figure out the good points of another person and then play them to the hilt, emphasizing these things while ignoring bad points. People then can even feel good about the truthfulness of their own actions. Indeed, people can invariably find something good to say about anyone. People can even employ the strategy depicted by Shakespeare in *Julius Caesar* (Act II, Scene III): "But when I tell him he hates flatterers, He says he does; being then most flattered." Thus, the line between flattery and appreciation is often a matter of opinion, since it depends upon a judgment about the motives of the actor.

Flattery can even be justified as a normally harmless, well intentioned action designed to benefit the other. Lord Chesterfield (1694–1773), an English statesman and man of letters, advised using flattery to gain friends and power. But he carefully justified and qualified his advice.

> Do not mistake me and think that I mean to recommend to you abject and criminal flatteries: no; flatter nobody's vices or crimes: on the contrary, abhor and discourage them. But if a man has a mind to be thought wiser, and a woman handsomer than they really are, their error is a comfortable one to themselves, and an innocent one with regard to other people; and I would rather make them my friends, by indulging them than my enemies, by endeavoring . . . to undeceive them [Earl of Chesterfield, 1774/1901, p. 28].

People could debate for hours the ethics of flattery and the point at which appreciation turns into flattery. But there is little doubt that flattery, lavish praise, and sincere appreciation are employed with some frequency in everyday social life.

Flattery Can Be Effective

Research has shown that flattery can be effective in causing the target to reciprocate with more positive evaluations of the flatterer than would otherwise occur, and, in many cases, with more material rewards. As one example, Kipnis and Vanderveer (1971) investigated how supervisors treat subordinates in a simulated business situation. Each supervisor was told that he would be in charge of four workers who would be manufacturing products on an assembly line. The behaviors of the workers were simulated by the experimenters in order to control both the worker's productivity and the types of notes sent to the supervisor. One of the workers always performed at a superior level, while two always performed at an average level. One of these two average workers sent ingratiating, flattering notes, commenting that he could be counted on for help, would speed up his work if necessary, and that the supervisor seemed to be a "real nice guy." The other average worker did not resort to ingratiation. The fourth worker's performance varied in different conditions from poor to average.

It was found that the ingratiator succeeded in influencing the attitudes and, to some extent, the behaviors of the supervisors. The superior worker always received the greatest pay raises. However, the ingratiator often received more than the other average worker whose performance was identical. Thirty per cent of the supervisors gave higher pay raises to the ingratiating than to the noningratiating worker; 60% gave them equal raises; and only 10% gave the ingratiator less. Further, the ingratiator received a higher final performance evaluation than did the other average worker. In fact, the ingratiator received as high an evaluation as did the superior worker! This high final evaluation may have paid off over a longer period in getting the ingratiators even better raises than the ones the others received.

Increasing the Effectiveness of Compliments

Surprisingly, there has been virtually no research specifically examining the conditions under which people are most likely to *use* praise and flattery or the types of target attributes they are likely to stress when they do. However, there has been a great deal of research examining how people *respond* to praise and flattery when others use them (Jones & Wortman, 1973; S. C. Jones, 1973; Mettee & Aronson, 1974). We know at least some of the conditions under which people respond less favorably to praise than they otherwise might. Given this information, four maximally effective complimenting tactics follow for actors who are interested in making the most favorable impression on others.

First, actors should attempt to be perceived as sincerely meaning what they say and lacking ulterior motives. Compliments that seem to the target to be motivated by ulterior purposes are less effective than those that are seen as sincere (Dickoff, 1961; Jones & Wortman, 1973; Mettee & Aronson, 1974). For instance, it is counterproductive to compliment one's employer and then immediately follow with a request for a raise or to praise a date's intelligence and then point to the bedroom. There are numerous devices actors can use to convey sincerity. For example, they can separate the compliment in time from any attempt to secure a reward, thus trying to show that the compliment is not contingent upon an extrinsic reward. They can attempt to display the appropriate enthusiasm in their voices and admiring looks on their faces when delivering the compliment. They can compliment the target to a third person when they know that the target can overhear the conversation. The target is then likely to conclude that the compliment must be sincere, since it did not seem to be meant for his or her ears. Better yet, actors can compliment the target to a third party who can be counted on to repeat it to the target. A man might praise a woman he admires to her best friend, hoping that her friend will relay the praise to the object of his affections.

Second, to be maximally effective actors should try to compliment targets on attributes the latter find highly attractive, believe they might possess, but are uncertain they actually possess. This strategic prescription is drawn from several lines of reasoning (Berscheid & Walster, 1978; E. E. Jones & Wortman, 1973; Mettee & Aronson, 1974). On the one hand, actors should avoid complimenting targets on attributes the latter know they don't possess. People who are convinced they lack a particular attribute don't respond in a highly favorable fashion when someone praises them on it (S. C. Jones & Schneider, 1968; Regan, 1976). They might doubt the sincerity or motives of the source, feel uncomfortable because they know they can't substantiate a claim to the attribute, and be afraid of looking foolish if they accept the compliment and it turns out to have been meant as a joke. Implausible compliments are to be avoided. Finck (1902, p. 245) similarly advised people who wish to succeed in their romantic adventures to avoid compliments that are radical departures from the facts. "It is useless to try to convince a woman with an ugly mouth or nose that these features are not ugly. She knows they are ugly, as well as Rubenstein [a famed pianist] knows when he strikes a wrong note."

On the other hand, targets who are certain they possess an attractive attribute have probably been complimented on it numerous times already. One more compliment added to this backlog is hardly special or ego-boosting; it may receive a less than enthusiastic response. Further, actors who deliver such "obvious" compliments do not demonstrate any real depth of perception; they only notice what everyone else notices. Indeed, people who are secure in their positive beliefs about themselves do not respond as favorably to global compliments as do people who are insecure (Hewitt & Goldman, 1974). As Finck (p. 245) put it, "The most common mistake of lovers is to compliment a woman on her most conspicuous points of beauty. This has very much the same effect as telling Rubenstein he is a wonderful pianist." Both are well aware of their obvious strengths. Lord Chesterfield (Earl of Chesterfield, 1774/1901, p. 27) advised "Very ugly or very beautiful women . . . should be flattered on their understanding, and mediocre ones on their beauty."

Most people seem to recognize intuitively that flattery is most effective when they avoid gross inaccuracy but also say something the target wants to hear. One of the more common "lines" teenage males use on females when attempting to entice them is to tell them that they have beautiful eyes ("Knowing 'Lines'," 1977). They can't find anything else to say; there's nothing special about the girl that attracts them; yet the girl often feels deeply flattered. Some sex education researchers suggest that teenage pregnancies could be dramatically decreased if girls became better able to identify "lines" and thus were better able to distinguish genuine appreciation from the selfish use of flattery.

Third, actors can increase the impact of their compliments if they appear to be perceptive and discerning. Actors who indiscriminately spread compliments to all comers cheapen the worth of what they say (Blau, 1964; Homans, 1974). As in economics, commodities that are readily available to anyone have little value; commodities that are scarce are sought after. A supervisor, for instance, should not compliment employees on every little thing they do, irrespective of how well or poorly they do it, or his or her opinions will be worthless. Similarly, flatterers are most effective when it appears that they reserve their compliments for those who really merit them (Jones & Wortman, 1973; Mettee & Aronson, 1974). People who flatter everyone please no one.

The appear-to-be-discerning tactic is often used successfully in dating relationships. People who appear willing to go out with anyone, dispense their favors to anyone, and be pleased with anyone seem to be desperate, unperceptive, lacking in confidence, and having little to offer on a competitive market. They cheapen their own worth. Like the toys a spoiled child receives merely for the asking, they might be momentary fun during times of boredom but do not rank as cherished possessions. On the other hand, people who appear to be discerning offer more of a challenge. They seem to be perceptive and difficult to win and to have much to offer in a competitive market. People who are able to win their favors appreciate the effort it may have taken; they feel special. Like a toy a child finally obtains after saving money for weeks, they are treated as cherished possessions. Economic principles of scarcity and demand extend to the evaluation of people in interpersonal relationships.

Research supports the effectiveness of playing (or being) hard to get. Walster, Walster, Piliavin, and Schmidt (1973) found that male college students prefer women who are selectively hard-to-get over ones who are either easy-to-get or uniformly hard-to-get. The selectively hard-to-get woman was one who had earlier indicated that she did not particularly care for several other males as prospective dates, but did seem to care about the male subject. Thus, she appeared to be discerning, yet left the impression that she was not completely out of reach. The male subjects probably felt quite complimented and quite special. The uniformly hard-to-get woman was one who had earlier indicated that she did not particularly care for any of the males who were offered as potential dates, including the subject. Thus, she may have appeared to be stuck up, difficult or impossible to win, completely out of reach, or indiscriminately disliking everyone. The easy-to-get woman was one who had earlier indicated that she liked all of the males who were offered as potential dates, including the subject. Such an undiscerning person does not emerge as a valuable commodity. This research suggests that the most effective tactic for increasing one's worth as a social participant is to appear to be discriminating but balance it with some attention to the target to make him or her feel special and believe that there is some possibility of ultimately gaining favor. The tactic applies to any area of interpersonal relations, not just dating, and stands as a minor qualification of the general rule that people are usually better off stating positive attitudes than negative.

Fourth, actors should phrase their compliments with sufficient precision that the target, particularly one with low self-esteem, does not misinterpret them. People with low self-esteem often interpret ambiguous compliments as veiled disparagements, while people with high self-esteem interpret ambiguous compliments as praise (Jacobs, Berscheid, & Walster, 1971). Skillful impression managers should be sensitive to the likely interpretations of the target and adjust the precision of compliments accordingly.

The four tactics above have been shown to be effective in increasing the positive impact of compliments. Unfortunately, no research has been conducted to determine if people actually do use these tactics when confronted with a particular target and situation. It seems likely, however, that most individuals quickly learn in life the probable reactions of people to particular types of compliments. When they encounter a situation in which they want to deliver a compliment, they probably consciously or unconsciously adjust their behaviors to derive the maximum impact possible.

Indirect Complimentary Gestures

There are numerous indirect methods of delivering compliments that don't rely on explicit verbal praise. Any action that suggests that the target is respected, approved, admired, and liked can be effective in demonstrating complimentary attitudes. The list of possible actions is numerous. One can imitate the target's behavior (remember that "imitation is the sincerest form of flattery"), seek the target out and pay attention to him or her, ask the target's advice or aid, do favors for the target (rendering favors is listed as an ingratiation mode by E. E. Jones & Wortman, 1973), bring the target gifts on no special occasion, accede to the target's preferences (go to a movie she wants to see rather than insisting on one you prefer), address the target by name or an appropriate title, talk about things that interest the target, and so on. Elaborating on a few of these tactics, Dale Carnegie bluntly advised

> Remember that the man you are talking to is a hundred times more interested in himself and his wants and his problems than he is in you and your problems. His toothache means more to him than a famine in China that kills a million people. . . . Think of that the next time you start a conversation [1940, p. 93].

As the master politician Benjamin Disraeli put it, "Talk to a man about himself and he will listen for hours."

Carnegie also advised "Remember that a man's name is to him the sweetest and most important sound in any language" (p. 84). In order to personalize the way you greet others, it is recommended that you take careful note of the names of people to whom you are introduced, surreptitiously writing the names down if necessary, and memorize them for future reference. By greeting someone by name, you demonstrate that he or she is sufficiently important to you to be remembered. It has been found that people who address others by name during conversations are liked more than those who don't (Kleinke, Staneski, & Weaver, 1972; Staneski, Kleinke, & Meeker, 1973). An exception that these studies found occurs when the name-user is highly dependent upon the other and uses the other's name frequently in a conversation. Name-users are then perceived as being insincere, phony, and incompetent. Thus, people should avoid going overboard and saturating a conversation with a powerful person's name, or else they appear sycophantic.

ATTITUDE SIMILARITY: TO AGREE OR NOT TO AGREE

Whenever people interact, they discover areas of agreement and disagreement; they learn where they are similar and dissimilar. Learning that another person shares many of one's attitudes and beliefs is normally rewarding. The certainty of one's opinions on particular issues might be reinforced through finding an ally who holds similar views, thereby increasing one's feelings of having formed the correct beliefs (Byrne, 1971). One also discovers common likes and dislikes, interests, topics of conversation, and preferences for things to do together, like golf, dancing, and watching movies. Similarity reduces interpersonal tension and disagreement (Newcomb, 1953). Discovering that another person is similar leads one to expect and to have mutually rewarding encounters with him or her (Tedeschi et al., 1973).

For these and other reasons, people display markedly greater liking for those whose attitudes and beliefs are similar to their own (Berscheid & Walster, 1978; Byrne, 1971). Numerous studies have led to the conclusion that there is normally a *direct* relationship between the proportion of similar attitudes two people share and their liking for one another (see Byrne, 1971). People whose attitudes are similar to one's own are not only better liked than dissimilar others; they are also perceived as more intelligent, more knowledgeable, better adjusted, and more moral (Byrne, 1971). There is little doubt that in most situations actors create a more favorable impression and reap greater benefits from their audiences if they are perceived as attitudinally similar. For example, similarity is directly related to teachers' chances of being hired by high school principals, loan applicants' chances of receiving a loan from business students playing the role of loan officers, and defendants' chances of being acquitted or being given a more lenient sentence by simulated jurors (see Byrne, 1971).

Either consciously or through the habits developed in social exigencies, people capitalize on the advantages of being seen as attitudinally similar. One of the most common tendencies during conversations is for the participants' opinions to converge, becoming more similar to one another's (Newcomb, 1953). People overplay areas of agreement and underplay areas of disagreement. Public speakers often try to include in their speeches at least some opinions they believe their audience already endorses. Doing this increases the audience's liking for the speaker and makes them more receptive to arguments on issues with which they might disagree (Berscheid & Walster, 1969). Politicians employ the tactic frequently, filling their speeches with clichés and opinions designed to appeal to the audience they are currently addressing. The tendency to show similarity is so habitual that people display it even when told to be completely accurate about their own views. For example, politically moderate students who were given accuracy instructions prior to delivering a speech nevertheless became more conservative in front of a conservative audience and more liberal in front of a liberal one (Newtson & Czerlinsky, 1974). Managing the impression of attitude similarity has its tactical advantages in social interaction. When advantages exist, people normally shift their behavior to reap the profits.

Ingratiation and Opinion Conformity

Opinion conformity can be employed as an ingratiation mode to extract rewards from powerful others (Jones, 1964; Jones & Wortman, 1973). Nearly all people, given that they are highly motivated to obtain a particular set of outcomes and are highly dependent upon a particular other person to obtain them, are likely to engage in the slavish "yes man" type of behavior so stereotypically associated with the junior executive. Numerous studies indicate that people employ tactical opinion conformity to influence a powerful audience (Davis & Florquist, 1965; E. E. Jones et al., 1965; E. E. Jones et al., 1963; R. G. Jones & Jones, 1964). These studies support the ingratiation hypothesis that as people are made more dependent upon a target the use of opinion conformity increases. When people coincidentally happen to hold exactly the same opinions as a powerful audience, they not only state these similar opinions but increase their reported confidence in their correctness (R. G. Jones & Jones, 1964). Thus, they go beyond their typical stance and emphasize their certainty of the truth of what they (and their superiors) say. Opinion conformity is particularly high when the audience is an emotional, irritable, punitive individual with a great deal of power over an actor's outcomes (Davis & Florquist, 1965). People don't want to take even the slightest risk of annoying such a person. The sycophancy and obedience of Hitler's subordinates is understandable (although not excusable) given his power and his reputation for uncontrolled, irrational outbursts.

In most situations it is very reasonable to assume that people will reward those they like. However, on occasion an exception might occur.

An extreme case would be an employer who prefers to hire people he personally *dislikes* because he has found that such people have worked out best for the company in the past. They do their jobs well, don't get hung up on personal relationships, and, if they don't work out, are easy to fire. Job applicants who are apprised of these preferences should attempt to make themselves disliked by the employer (given, of course, that they want such a job). After all, the purpose of gaining the approval of others is to obtain other rewards, not to obtain approval for its own sake. If the contingencies for rewards are changed from the normal emphasis on liking to an emphasis on disliking, impression-management behaviors should follow suit.

Jellison and Gentry (1978) found support for this hypothesis in a study that parallels the example above. Subjects were asked to play the role of a job applicant and were forewarned that the interviewer who decided on the candidates usually hired either those he personally liked or those he personally disliked. They were also given information about the interviewer's attitudes on several topics that were included in a personnel selection test. When they later took the personnel test, the subjects conformed to the interviewer's opinions when they believed he hired people he liked but expressed dissimilar opinions when they believed he hired people he disliked. Impression-management behaviors are sensitive to shifts in audience preferences.

A similar, though less unusual, situation occurs when an audience seems to minimize the importance of likableness in favor of other attributes. For example, most of the time people are judged on both their likableness and their competence. Some audiences weight likableness as more important than competence when judging others; other audiences do the reverse; and still other audiences weight them about equally. If a powerful audience favors people who are likable, compatible, and able to get along, dependent actors should take advantage of these preferences and conform to these opinions, thereby demonstrating their compatibility. If, however, a powerful audience favors those who are competent irrespective of their compatibility, dependent actors should take advantage of these biases and speak their own minds. Indeed, E. E. Jones, Gergen, Gumpert, and Thibaut (1965) found that college student subjects display the greatest opinion conformity to a work supervisor when the latter preferred compatibility rather than work competence. This result was obtained so long as the supervisor had some personal flexibility and control over the outcomes the subjects would receive.

As these studies show, people will attempt to create the impression on audiences that best satisfies their own goals in the interaction. In most situations, although certainly not all, people therefore conform to the opinions of others in order to manage the impressions of similarity and likableness.

Avoiding Sheer Sycophancy

Sooner or later audiences tire of people who agree with them on everything. People can become so similar and predictable that they become boring. There is no longer a challenge, an opportunity for growth, or a contribution made by the other. The dyad merges into a single unit. When two people agree about everything, one of them is superfluous. Marriages, for example, are often as threatened by boredom as by conflict. Similarly, most superiors eventually realize that employees who agree with them on everything are rather indiscriminating individuals whose contribution to the organization is questionable. Thus, sooner or later it is in people's self-interests to stick up for their own beliefs even at the expense of appearing to be dissimilar on some topics.

In situations of high dependence, less powerful people draw a line between employing sufficient opinion conformity to generate a potentially rewarding degree of attraction and so much conformity as to leave doubts in the audience's mind about their usefulness, ulterior motives, independence, and competence. Dependent people therefore try to present themselves as highly similar to their audience, but not so similar that it appears they have not got a mind of their own. E. E. Jones, Gergen, and Jones (1963) found that people who are attempting to be compatible with another do display a high degree of opinion conformity. But they balance this conformity with independence on issues that are likely to create the most favorable impression on their audience. In their study, high-status ROTC cadets interacted with low-status cadets. The high-status subjects should have desired to maintain their relative power. So when they were specifically attempting to increase their compatibility, the high-status subjects conformed to their low-status partner's opinions on issues that were largely irrelevant to their interaction, thereby displaying attitude similarity. But they remained independent on issues that were directly relevant to the interaction, thereby maintaining their autonomy and relative power. Thus, they balanced their opinion statements such that they appeared to be both powerful and compatible. When low-status people were under pressure to be compatible, however, they adopted a different balance. They should have wanted to make themselves compatible on topics that mattered most in the relationship, thereby seeming compatible and nonthreatening. But they should have desired to display at least a modicum of independence, and the best place to do this was on topics that mattered less. As predicted, low-status people displayed opinion conformity on relevant issues but displayed independence on irrelevant ones. The ability to draw the line between overdone conformity and repugnant independence is often the difference between successful people who achieve their goals in life and unsuccessful ones who gain reputations as failures.

Audience Reactions to Agreeable versus Disagreeable Actors

Audiences can never know for certain what is inside an actor's mind. Actors who agree with the opinions of another person might be honestly expressing their private beliefs, which coincidentally happen to be similar to the other's, or they might be publicly conforming even though they privately disagree. Further, actors might conform to the opinions of another because they are cooperative, friendly, agreeable people, or because they are devious, manipulative sorts. Audiences may not be able to get inside actors' minds, but they nonetheless make attributions about the actors' intentions, motives, goals, and personalities based on what they can observe on the surface. Attribution theory (Heider, 1958; E. E. Jones & Davis, 1965; Kelley, 1967) specifies some of the factors people take into account when making inferences about others.

Two such factors are the specific actions of the actor and the context of the situation in which they occur. When actors encounter high-dependence situations, where external pressures to ingratiate exist, and then display high opinion agreement, audiences attribute the agreement to devious motives instead of truthful or cooperative intentions. The perils of using opinion agreement in high-dependence situations are illustrated in a study by E. E. Jones, Jones, and Gergen (1963). Observer-subjects watched an interaction between two people, one of whom (the actor) was either dependent or nondependent on the other (the target) and who either continually agreed with the target's opinions or agreed only on occasion. When the actor was dependent on the target, he was less favorably evaluated by the observers if he agreed continually than if he agreed only on occasion. The combination of continual agreement and high dependence caused the observers to like him less and view him as less candid and more self-promotive. In addition, when the actor agreed only on occasion, he was liked more when dependence was high than low. People who resist conformity when the pressures are great seem to be given extra credit by observers for maintaining their autonomy. Interestingly, the observers predicted that the target of the dependent and highly agreeable actor would be taken in more by the ingratiation attempt than they were, expecting the target to like that actor more than they did. The observers thus implied that, although they saw through the ingratiation attempt, the target probably would not. A later study produced similar, although much weaker, results (Jones, Stires, Shaver, & Harris, 1968).

People differ in their values and in their sensitivity to whether others are likely to be using ingratiation. For example, high self-monitors, who are motivated to impress others and adept at controlling their own behavior for *public* impression-management purposes (Snyder, 1974), seem to be particularly attuned to whether others are doing the same. E. E. Jones and Baumeister (1976) categorized subjects as either high or low self-monitors and had them observe an interaction. In it, an actor continually agreed with a target's position or remained autonomous, and the observer-subjects learned that the actor had been told he would receive a payment if he either made the target like him or made the target respect him. If an actor wanted to distort his own opinions simply to impress the target, he should agree with the target when trying to be liked and remain autonomously disagreeable when trying to be respected.

Jones and Baumeister found that the low self-monitors were relatively unaffected by the motivational context of the situation, apparently accepting the actor's behavior at face value. They rated the agreeable actor more favorably than the autonomous actor irrespective of whether he might have been motivated to be liked or to be respected. However, the high self-monitors' evaluations of the actor were affected by the context. They derogated the agreeable actor when he was motivated to be liked and derogated the autonomous actor when he was motivated to be respected. They preferred the actor to resist situational pressure, to agree despite trying to be respected or remain autonomous despite trying to be liked. It is unclear precisely why the low self-monitors were not affected by the situational context while high self-monitors were. Perhaps the low self-monitors failed to recognize the particular combination of opinions and motivational context that were in the actor's self-interests, or perhaps they recognized it but were willing to give the actor the benefit of any doubt. On the other hand, perhaps the high self-monitors are generally better able to detect public impression management, or perhaps they are no better able to detect it *accurately* but are simply more likely to project their own tendencies onto others in any situation that even resembles one that calls for a particular public impression-management tactic. Future research is needed to resolve these questions.

As the above studies indicate, actors take a risk when they attempt to impress an audience under conditions in which the audience is most likely to attribute manipulative motives to them. If they are too obvious in their behavior, their attempt could boomerang. People are able to place themselves in the role of others, though, and anticipate how their audiences are likely to respond. They then can adjust their own behaviors to maximize the likelihood of creating the type of impression they desire. For example, when the chances of being viewed as an in-gratiator are greatest, actors might subtly attempt to throw the audience off the track by disagreeing with the target on some minor points, while slavishly agreeing on the major ones. As E. E. Jones and Wortman (1973, p. 27) observe, with just "a pinch of disagreement here and a dash of criticism there, the ingratiator may win favor precisely in those conditions where dependence is most obvious and extreme."

Attitude Similarity and Politics

It is in the self-interests of politicians to be viewed by their constituents as attitudinally similar. Voters do not cast ballots for candidates they believe will oppose issues they favor or favor issues they oppose. Attitude similarity also generates liking, and liking usually translates into votes. Some politicians may resist succumbing to such pressures and state their unadulterated opinions irrespective of the attitudes of their audiences. Such candidates may even be respected for their autonomy. But they are not likely to be elected unless a majority of voters coincidentally share similar beliefs on the important issues or at least don't disagree so strongly as to react negatively. More commonly, politicians tailor their attitude statements on issues to take into account the opinions of voters. Just as anyone else, they are influenced by the views of their audiences. The tailoring does not necessarily involve deception (although it sometimes does), but it certainly involves public impression management.

Three tactics in particular are used with some frequency. First, candidates can adopt positions that are known to be favored by their constituents and then maintain these positions irrespective of the attitudes of the particular audience they happen to be addressing. For example, a candidate may adopt a position that opinion polls show a majority of her constituents favor and then endorse that position even in front of minority groups who oppose it. Second, candidates can state their attitudes in slightly different ways to different audiences, thereby appearing to be more similar to each audience than they may actually be. Third, candidates can attempt to be as vague as possible about their specific opinions while endorsing general platitudinous statements, thereby trying to offend as few voters as possible while hoping that voters will read into their statements whatever they want to hear. These tactics are not mutually exclusive and can be complementary. Naturally, they are not the exclusive domain of politicians. We all use them from time to time.

Richard Nixon's 1968 Presidential campaign can be used to illustrate the tactics, since it has been analyzed in more detail for public impression management than perhaps any other campaign in history (McGinniss, 1970). The attitudes of voters in different parts of the country were gathered by public opinion polls. Campaign strategists then provided advice about how Nixon should be positioned to appeal to the particular groups addressed. At the outset, some groups were written off. Nixon's strategists recognized that he would lose the Black vote, so they made little or no attempt to appeal to Black voters. Nixon's opinions on issues were tailored to appeal primarily to those groups he had a reasonable chance of winning.

Different television commercials were made up for different parts of the country, each focusing on issues of greatest local concern. Often the statements Nixon made about an issue varied slightly from state to state. Thus, "a question about law and order might evoke one response in New England and a slightly different one in the South. Nothing big enough to make headlines, just a subtle twist of inflection, or the presence of a frown or gesture when a certain phrase was spoken" (McGinniss, p. 59).[1] Nixon's advertising advisors also attempted to match entertainers who were willing to give public endorsements of Nixon with particular audiences who would most admire and be persuaded by the entertainer. For example, one of the advisors felt that movie star John Wayne would be particularly effective in selling Nixon in the South, adding that Wayne "might sound bad to people in New York, but he sounds great to the schmucks we're trying to reach . . . down there along the Yahoo Belt. If I had the time I'd check to see in what areas *The Green Berets* [a Wayne movie] was held over and I'd play a special series" of his spots there (p. 127). Thus, both the communicators and the communications were tailored to show similarity to particular audiences.

Nixon's advertising advisors were particularly proud of a series of montage commercials. In them, Nixon's voice was heard in the background giving a stock speech that said as little as possible about specific issues. Television viewers saw only a series of still photographs depicting scenes such as crime in the street, U. S. soldiers in Vietnam, wheat fields in the heartland, and the sun shining on the faces of playful children. The particular stills included in each montage were varied somewhat from area to area; for example, crime in the street stills were featured in big cities. The stills were carefully coordinated to the specific words spoken by Nixon to create just the right impression, allowing viewers to draw from the combination whatever they most desired. Viewers were helped along in their interpretation by the meticulous effort put into the matching. An original version of one commercial that was modified before airing had Nixon saying "most of the soldiers who died to keep us free" while picturing a Black soldier. The slide was pulled, and one with a White soldier was substituted

[1]From *The Selling of the President 1968,* by J. McGinniss. Copyright © 1969 by Joemac, Inc. This and all other quotations from this source are reprinted by permission of Simon & Schuster, a Division of Gulf & Western Corporation. Published in the British Commonwealth by Sterling Lord Agency.

because Nixon's ad men were afraid that the combination might be interpreted by some people as endorsing claims by Blacks that the draft was unfair to them (McGinniss, p. 95).

The advertising strategists believed that the montage approach was the perfect solution to two of their concerns. First, the advisors gave voters little credit for intelligence. According to one, "Most national issues today are so complicated, so difficult to understand and have opinions on that they either intimidate or, more often, bore the average viewer" (p. 39). The montage approach made no demands on viewers. Second, as another of the advertising men said, a "problem we've had . . . is Nixon himself. He says such incredible pap. In fact, the radical-ness of [the montage] approach is in the fact of creating an image with-out actually saying anything" (p. 116). The advisor continued "He's created an image of himself through cornball sunsets and WASP-y faces and no one remembers what he says. Which is gobbledy-gook anyway, of course. But . . . the images stick" (p. 117).

Attitudes as Associators: When Similarity Is Undesirable

People gain reputations based on the company they keep. Those who associate with attractive others can bask in reflected glory; those who associate with unattractive others wallow in reflected obloquy. When two people are known to hold similar attitudes and beliefs, they are associated together in the minds of the audiences. A person who states conservative political attitudes becomes linked in audiences' minds to other conservatives; a person who likes disco music is linked with other advocates of the sound. Even if the actors are unacquainted, the audiences still associate them and usually believe that if they did know one another they would like each other. People who anticipate the associations their audiences are likely to make can control their attitude statements in order to associate themselves with desirable images and dissociate themselves from undesirable ones.

People do manage their impressions through attitude statements in order to control the associations made by audiences. Cooper and Jones (1969) found that, when another person was pleasant and attrac-tive, subjects publicly stated attitudes that were quite similar to those endorsed by the other, thereby displaying similarity and association. However, when the other person was obnoxious and unattractive, sub-jects publicly expressed attitudes that were opposite to those endorsed by the other, thereby displaying dissimilarity and dissociation. Thus, people shift their attitude statements to create the desired types of as-sociations and dissociations. In a comparable vein, when another per-son is described as mentally ill, people report liking the other *less* the more similar his attitudes appear to be to their own (Novak & Lerner, 1968). Thus, they attempt to establish dissociation by expressing unfavorable attitudes toward an undesirable individual who otherwise might appear to be similar. This is one of the few exceptions to the similarity-breeds-liking rule (Berscheid & Walster, 1978).

PERSUASION: IMPRESSION MANAGEMENT UNDER TARGET PRESSURE

In most ingratiation situations, the targets do not explicitly do or say anything to indicate they are trying to get the actor to agree with them. The actor, however, consciously or unconsciously appreciates the pressure arising from his situation of high dependence and agrees with the targets' opinions in order to create a favorable impression. An observer who is *unaware* of the situational context of high dependence would see no pressure being directly applied to the actor by the target. Such an observer would be likely to conclude that an agreeable ingratiator is simply a friendly sort of individual who has much in common with the target. Of course, this is precisely the attribution the ingratiator wants to create in both observers and targets.

People often confront a different sort of situation when another individual explicitly attempts to persuade them to agree. The pressure to agree is then obvious to all parties, and can affect the attributions people make about actors who subsequently agree rather than disagree with the persuader's opinions. Interestingly, the persuader and uninvolved observers usually form diametrically opposed impressions of agreeable actors in persuasion situations.

Western society places high value on being independent, autonomous, and internally controlled. Autonomy is an attractive image for most people in most situations. Actors who resist agreement with a person who has obviously persuasive intentions should be viewed as autonomous, self-confident, and able to stick up for their own views. Observers should like and respect them. However, actors who agree with a persuader appear to have succumbed to the pressure. They appear to be easily influenced, manipulable, lacking in confidence, and unintelligent; they should be liked and respected less by observers than actors who resist the pressure.

The persuader, by contrast, has a different perspective. Actors who remain independent in the face of his persuasion have frustrated his goals and made him look and feel ineffective and uninfluential. They display attitude dissimilarity and perhaps cause the persuader to question the correctness of his own beliefs. The persuader should derogate autonomous actors following his unsuccessful influence attempt. He should dislike them and defensively view them as unintelligent. If he said that they were likable and intelligent it would imply that his own beliefs were incorrect, that he was ineffective, or both. Actors who agree with his opinions following the persuasion, on the other hand, have allowed him to achieve his goals and made him look and feel effective, influential, and intelligent; and they display attitude similarity. The persuader should respond favorably to agreeable actors, liking them and viewing them as intelligent. If he said they were dislikable and unintelligent it would imply that *anyone* could have had equal influence over such a manipulable person.

In a series of studies, Cialdini and his associates (Braver, Linder, Corwin, & Cialdini, 1977; Cialdini, 1971; Cialdini, Braver, & Lewis, 1974; Cialdini & Mirels, 1976) supported the above reasoning. They found that observers of a persuasion situation form a more favorable impression of actors who don't yield than those who yield; the former were regarded as more intelligent and liked more than the latter. Persuaders, however, form a more favorable impression of actors who yield than those who don't; the former were regarded as more intelligent and liked more than the latter. Further, the effect occurs *only* for persuaders who have a high sense of personal control (Cialdini & Mirels, 1976). Such people believe they can influence the environment, and they should be the most frustrated when their persuasion attempts meet with resistance and the most concerned about appearing to lose control.

Managing Impressions
for the Persuader or the Observers

People are aware of the fact that they generally create a more favorable impression on observers when they resist a persuader's attempt at influence but create a more favorable impression on the persuader when they yield. Subjects who were asked to imagine themselves in a persuasive situation accurately predicted how they would be regarded by both observers and the persuader depending on whether or not they yielded to the influence (Braver et al., 1977). Given that people can accurately anticipate how different audiences are likely to respond, it follows that when they encounter a persuasion situation they will either yield or remain autonomous depending on whom they want to impress. If they are attempting to impress a group of observers they should remain autonomous and resist. But if they are attempting to impress the persuader, they should yield.

To test this hypothesis, Braver and his associates (1977) exposed subjects to a persuasive speech while an observer watched. After listening to the speech, the subjects were asked to state their opinions aloud either to (1) the persuader only, (2) the observer only, (3) both the persuader and the observer, or (4) neither. As predicted, subjects yielded most when only the persuader was present, thus acting in a way that usually creates a favorable impression on persuaders. They yielded less when both the persuader and the observer were present, thus compromising between complete autonomy and total yielding to maximize the favorableness of the impressions both audiences would draw. They yielded least when only the observer was present or when neither the observer nor the persuader was present. People are quite adept at placing themselves in the positions of others and then conveying the types of attitude information most likely to impress them.

Some people are more motivated to impress others and more sensitive to what will impress them than are others. High self-monitors, for example, are more attuned to social cues that indicate acceptable behavior and are more motivated to make favorable impressions on their audiences than are low self-monitors (Snyder, 1974). It follows that high self-monitors should be particularly influenced by the likely preferences of their audience and should readily shift their own attitude statements in order to create a desirable impression. In support of this hypothesis, Snyder and Monson (1975) found that high self-monitors conform to the opinions of other members of a discussion group when only the other group members are present, thereby trying to impress them. But they conform less when told that the proceedings of their discussion group would be videotaped and shown to other students at their school, thus attempting to impress these uninvolved observers with their autonomy. Low self-monitors did not vary their opinions depending on the audience. Instead, they remained relatively autonomous, consistent with their private beliefs, in either context.

Reactance: Maintaining Autonomy under Threat

Autonomy is a desirable image for some people all of the time and for others some of the time. As we've seen, autonomy is culturally valued. People who stand up for their beliefs in the face of pressure, particularly when the pressure is seen as illegitimate or unreasonable, are liked more by observers than those who yield. In addition, an image of autonomy increases its possessor's *relative power* in social interactions. People who resist influence demonstrate that they cannot be persuaded, threatened, bullied, enticed, or altercast into positions they dislike. As their ability to resist increases, the influencer's relative power vis-à-vis them decreases. People who give in to influence attempts are viewed as less powerful than those who resist (Tedeschi et al., 1973). The more arbitrary or illegitimate an influence attempt seems and the more detrimental compliance is to the actor's best interests, the more costly compliance becomes, immediately and in the long run. Actors who comply to arbitrary and detrimental influence attempts gain reputations as powerless pushovers. Once a compliant person gains a reputation of powerlessness, he or she becomes the target of continual future influence attempts (Tedeschi et al., 1971, 1973). The skinny young man on the beach has sand kicked in his face by the bullies who want to show off their "power;" the girl with a "reputation" becomes the target of every male who is only out for a fun evening. Autonomy is a highly desirable image to convey to an influencer when relative power is salient in the situation.

Children are notorious for attempting to "try out" their own power in the social world by resisting the influence attempts of parents. A child told to eat her spinach can be counted on to refuse. If, however, she had been told not to eat the spinach, she would probably gobble it down as soon as her parents' backs were turned. As we get older, we make more careful discriminations between reasonable influence attempts, which are accommodative in intent, and unreasonable ones, which are designed primarily to benefit the influencer at the expense of the target. Unreasonable influence attempts are more likely to be resisted (Tedeschi et al., 1973).

Reactance is a psychological concept that describes a motivational state induced in people when their freedom to behave or think the way they want is threatened or eliminated (Brehm, 1966, 1972). Once reactance occurs, people are hypothesized to attempt to reestablish their freedom. Attempts to reassert freedom can involve (1) resisting or attacking the threatening agent, such as by making counterthreats, using force, derogating the agent, or simply not complying and (2) increasing one's personal evaluation of the freedoms that are threatened or eliminated and decreasing one's evaluation of what the agent wants one to do. For example, a high school student who is contemplating how to spend the evening might be told by her father that she must study tonight rather than go to a dance. Reacting against the attempt, she might insult her father, insist that the dance will be great (although earlier in the day she thought it might be only OK) and insist that she hates studying (although earlier in the day she didn't mind it that much).

The purpose of reactance is to reassert one's own power and control when freedoms are threatened or eliminated. To do so, it is often necessary to exaggerate one's resistance, giving a dramatized performance that leaves no doubt in the minds of real or imagined audiences about where one stands. Thus, resistance often goes beyond mere noncompliance, and can become an active attempt to assert power and control. For example, during a conversation about politics you might be told by another person that you *must* agree with him. In response to this rude, pushy character, you might take a more extreme stance on the issue than you normally do both to dissociate yourself from his views and to display resistance clearly. People do shift their attitude statements to become more polarized following such demands by others (Worchel & Brehm, 1970).

Reactance occurs with greater magnitude as (1) the importance of the threatened or eliminated freedoms increases (Brehm, 1972); (2) the number of threatened or eliminated freedoms increases (Brehm, 1972); (3) the threat is perceived as more arbitrary, illegitimate, or unreasonable (Grabitz-Gniech, 1971); (4) the threatener is less attractive (Dickenberger & Grabitz-Gniech, 1971); and (5) the actor places higher value on self-reliance and autonomy as self-images (Grabitz-Gniech, 1971). Thus, reactance is *highly* dramatized when a self-reliant actor has numerous important freedoms arbitrarily threatened by a nonsignificant other. These are precisely the conditions where impression management is most needed to project an autonomous image and establish relative power.

Anticipatory Attitude Shifts: Impression Management prior to Persuasion

People are often persuaded to change their attitudes on particular topics by the cogent arguments of significant others, and they often react against persuasion by becoming more extreme against the arbitrary arguments of nonsignificant others. What may be more surprising, however, is that people often give the appearance of attitude change even *before* they hear a persuasive speech, engage in a conversation, or debate with others. Numerous studies have shown that people who expect to encounter an influence situation shift their attitudes prior to entering the situation (Cialdini, Levy, Herman, & Evenbeck, 1973; Cialdini, Levy, Herman, Kozlowski, & Petty, 1976; Cooper & Jones, 1970; Deaux, 1968, 1972; Gaes & Tedeschi, 1978; Hass, 1975; Hass & Mann, 1976; McGuire & Millman, 1965; Snyder & Swann, 1976). Anticipatory attitude shifts only occur when people anticipate some evaluation-laden influence situation in which attitudes will be open to scrutiny by an audience. For instance, simply knowing that other people, even experts, disagree with one's own views (Cooper & Jones, 1970; Hass & Mann, 1976) or that one will not be called upon to defend one's own position (Deaux, 1972) does not produce a shift. These *anticipatory attitude shifts* are used to satisfy impression-management goals during the forthcoming interaction.

Three types of anticipatory attitude shifts occur. First, people can shift their attitudes toward the position that will be advocated by the other(s). For instance, people who believe they will be exposed to a persuasive speech from an expert can shift their reported attitudes in the direction of the position to be endorsed by the expert (Deaux, 1972;

McGuire & Millman, 1965). By shifting their own position prior even to hearing the speech, people minimize the magnitude of apparent disagreement and minimize the amount they might change after listening to the persuasive arguments. They thereby *enter* the situation appearing to be more similar to the expert than they actually are and can *leave* the situation after the influence attempt appearing to be more consistent and less influenceable than they might otherwise appear.

Second, people can shift their attitudes toward a more moderate or neutral stance on whatever issue they expect an encounter. People who adopt a moderate position on an issue gain several impression-management advantages (Cialdini et al., 1973). They look more broad-minded and rational than they might if they took an extreme stance, and they obtain maximal flexibility later. From a middle-of-the-road stance, people can shift to either side of the issue and defend each with some credibility, concomitantly avoiding the appearance of inconsistency. It is difficult to suffer major or embarrassing defeats when one is defending a moderate stance on an issue that has reasonable arguments on both sides. Politicians thrive on moderation.

Third, people can shift their attitudes to become more extreme in the direction of the position they originally favored—a polarization effect. People who are deeply involved with and concerned about a particular issue should want to avoid weakening their own position before they even encounter a threat (Cialdini, Levy, Herman, Kozlowski, & Petty, 1976). Instead, they should want to demonstrate that they are committed to a particular position and will fight to defend it. The appearance of commitment might even intimidate their opponent into backing down or at the very least establish that they are the type of people who can make a decision and stick to their guns.

Which of these types of shifts occurs depends on the desirability of the alternative images to actors given their personal goals, audience, and the situation. When people believe they will encounter an expert who might dazzle them with her acumen, they display an anticipatory shift in the direction of the expert's position (McGuire & Millman, 1965). Moderation shifts are most likely to occur when people anticipate a discussion with peers about a topic that is of relatively little personal importance to them (Cialdini, Levy, Herman, Kozlowski, & Petty, 1976). Under such conditions, people are most concerned with adopting a defensible position that provides them the greatest amount of subsequent flexibility. Polarization shifts are most likely to occur when people expect a discussion with peers on a topic about which they feel strongly and which they believe they can defend (Cialdini, Levy, Herman, Kozlowski, & Petty, 1976). Under such conditions, they appear decisive and involved, and they might place the opponent on the defensive.

Anticipatory attitude shifts do not reflect genuine attitude change. Instead, they represent strategic movements in attitude statements that are designed to convey a desirable impression to an audience. To illustrate, people who are told to expect a persuasive encounter but later told that the encounter had to be canceled revert to their original position on the issue (Cialdini et al., 1973; Cialdini, Levy, Herman, Kozlowski, & Petty, 1976; Hass & Mann, 1976). If anticipatory shifts reflected real attitude change, people's attitudes should have remained at their "new" position rather than snapping back to their original position. Cialdini, Levy, Herman, Kozlowski, and Petty (1976) liken these shifts to what happens when an elastic band is stretched under pressure, only to return to its original form when the pressure is removed. Most of our everyday social interactions seem to involve such strategic shifts rather than any enduring changes in attitudes.

Strategic jockeying to maintain a desirable impression may sometimes be quite conscious and deliberate. More often, perhaps, people do not even attend to the fact that they are shifting their attitudes when confronted with particular audiences. Cialdini, Levy, Herman, and Evenbeck (1973) suggest that, although anticipatory shifts "appear to be strategic and purposeful, they do not seem to be conscious maneuvers. . . . It may well be . . . that these shifts are highly learned responses which are triggered automatically by the expectation of certain kinds of interaction" (p. 106). The habits of impression management permeate social life.

SUMMARY

In one of its earliest English usages, the word *attitude* was applied to the images conveyed by professional actors as they attempted to impress audiences with the natures of the characters they played. Actors' attitudes on the stage represented calculated postures and movements with only one intent—conveying the appropriate impressions of their thoughts, feelings, and goals. In contemporary usage, *attitude* refers to a more private set of feelings that are intrapersonal. Yet attitudes and beliefs still usually occur in the context of real or imagined social interactions and reveal identity-relevant information to audiences. People shift or change their attitudes and beliefs in order to create desirable impressions on real or imagined audiences.

Once people freely commit themselves to particular attitude positions they are under social compulsion to behave consistently in the future. Consistency gives actors a desirable degree of predictability and trustworthiness, and it generates liking and respect. People usually attempt to appear consistent even if it means denying that they have changed or altered their attitudes over time. People's predilections to appear consistent are often turned against them by skilled impression managers who gently pressure them to commit themselves to a particular stance and then paint them into a corner, profiting at their expense.

Attitude and belief expressions can be used strategically to flatter targets and to show similarity to them. Both flattery and opinion conformity are ingratiation tactics used to create a favorable impression on a target; both tactics usually produce increased liking for the actor. When used in a subtle fashion, these tactics can succeed in maximizing actors' reward/cost ratios even in situations of high dependence. The desirability of appearing likable, however, is sometimes overwhelmed by the desirability of appearing autonomous and relatively powerful, so in some situations people derogate or disagree with their audiences instead of complimenting and going along with them.

Persuasion situations confront actors with the decision of yielding to the influence of others or resisting and maintaining autonomy. Persuaders usually form a more favorable impression of actors who yield to their influence than of those who resist, while uninvolved observers of the interaction usually form a more favorable impression of actors who resist rather than yield. Whether people yield or resist depends on a combination of the actor's goals, desired public images, the situational context, and the audience.

EIGHT

A man may have a resounding title, a great position of
authority, money, influence, but if we notice that his
hands are constantly fidgeting on his desk, that he
can't look us in the eye, that he crosses and uncrosses
his legs as if suffering from a bad itch in the crotch
and that when the phone rings, he can't make up his
mind whether to pick it up or ignore it, we can then, I
think, safely conclude that he is not a man of power.

Michael Korda

NONVERBAL BEHAVIOR
AND
IMPRESSION MANAGEMENT

A picture is worth a thousand words. When face-to-face we get the
complete moving picture. We see the look in their eyes, the expression
on their faces, the way their bodies lean, how closely they are willing to
approach, the way they sit, the tenseness or relaxedness of their gestures. We hear the tones of their voices and the speed of their speech. We
may not even be conscious at the time of the impact this information

has on our overall impressions, but there is no doubt that it plays a major role in shaping our views of others. The other person's "style" comes through to form images that can mean more than the specific words he or she speaks.

People skilled in the arts of impression management can make dramatic nonverbal impressions on their audiences. A striking example is General George Patton, one of the dominant military figures of World War II. Patton recognized the importance of controlling nonverbal activities to create the impressions he desired. He practiced his "war face," a stern and demanding visage of determination, in front of a mirror for hours to prepare himself for addressing his men. He wanted to appear dynamic, dedicated, powerful, self-confident, brave. He showed constant concern for even the small details of his public appearance: his ivory-handled pistols in their holsters set off an immaculately brushed uniform with polished brass and boots. He developed hypotheses about what attributes soldiers would most respect in their commander and acted accordingly. For example, he was careful about when he went to and departed from the front lines. "By day he would go forward by road and return in the evening, often at twilight and indeed sometimes after dark in a small liaison plane, his theory being that a commander should always be seen going to the front but never coming away from it" (Essame, 1974, p. 208). The image of Patton riding in a jeep to the battlefront, ivory-handled pistols gleaming in the sunlight, was indelibly impressed in the minds of his men, indeed, of the whole country. He was so successful in creating a public image as "old blood and guts" that "no commander in World War Two succeeded more effectively in impressing his own personality on the officers and men under his command. . . . Indeed, many actually developed some of his idiosyncrasies and mannerisms. It was even said that he had created the Third Army in his own image" (Essame, 1974, p. 208). Actions speak louder than words, and the skilled impression manager has a field day creating and projecting desired images through nonverbal activities.

TYPES OF NONVERBAL BEHAVIOR

In this chapter we'll explore impression management and nonverbal behavior. Three general classes of nonverbal behaviors have received considerable attention from social scientists: *body language*, *space use*, and *paralanguage.*

Body language refers to the encoding (sending) and decoding (receiving) of messages based on cues from body position, such as posture and facial expression, and body movement, such as gestures and changes in facial expression.[1] Communication through body language is currently a popular topic. Like the signs in front of nationwide hamburger stands that advertise the number of patties relished by patrons, the cover on the 22nd printing of Julius Fast's (1971) *Body Language* proclaims in large type that over 2,500,000 copies have been sold. The cover depicts a seated woman, and buzzing around her are questions like "Does her body say that she's a loose woman?" "Does her body say that she's a manipulator?" "Does her body say that she's lonely?" The curious newsstand browser who looks at the back cover is greeted with the further tantalizing assertion that "Your body doesn't know how to lie." The promise is held out to readers that they will be able to see through the staged performances of others and might even learn how to stage their own performances more effectively. Although scintillating, the claims—as we shall see—are exaggerated.

Space use pertains to the encoding and decoding of messages on the basis of interpersonal distancing behaviors (like standing close to or far from another person), seating arrangements (like sitting across from or adjacent to another person at a table), and territorial claims (like claiming a particular room as one's own).[2] We often take space for granted until an acquaintance comes too close during a conversation or a date doesn't come close enough, a roommate places his or her possessions on "our" side of the room, or a fellow employee moves into a bigger office than the one we occupy. Space then becomes salient as we contemplate its ramifications for liking and power. Erving Goffman (1971, p. 28) notes that "at the center of social organization is the concept of claims" to particular spaces and territories, ranging from claims to a particular amount of breathing room (personal space) surrounding the body to claims of the possession of land areas. People have to position themselves at certain distances from others when interacting; select places to stand, sit, and place their possessions; and take at least temporary jurisdiction of particular areas such as a table or room. When they do, they communicate something. These are inescapable facts of social life: space use affects impression formation and people use space for impression-management purposes.

Paralanguage refers to the encoding and decoding of spoken in-

[1]The science of body movement, termed *kinesics* (Birdwhistell, 1970), assumes that basic units of movement can be analyzed to determine the messages they express.

[2]The study of personal space and territory is a burgeoning area of social science. The anthropologist Edward T. Hall's (1959, 1966) seminal work on how space and distance function in interpersonal relationships and the cultural differences that exist in the use of space is highly recommended reading. Hall coined the term *proxemics* to describe the study of distancing behaviors. Social psychologists such as Robert Sommer (1969, 1972, 1974) are investigating *personal space*, which is the "envelope" of space he assumes surrounds the human body, a sort of invisible bubble people carry around with them. Sociologists such as Goffman (1963a, 1971) and Lyman and Scott (1967) have explored how social norms regulate territory use in human societies. Space use is no longer the neglected area of social science that it once was.

formation that is not contained in the denotative meanings of the specific words. These include meanings conveyed through tone of voice, the rapidity of speech, and hesitations and pauses. Professional "actors have long known the nuances of vocal tone and pacing; psychologists are just adding this cue to their understanding of the theater of social interaction" (Weitz, 1974, p. 97).

Nonverbal Behavior in Context

People usually don't have to attend consciously to the messages conveyed through nonverbal behaviors. Our responses are so well ingrained that we encode and decode automatically, often forming impressions of others without even realizing which specific behavior produced our response and often using a particular nonverbal action through habit. There are individual differences, though, both in the degree to which people are sensitive to cues in the social setting that indicate appropriate behaviors and in the degree to which they can monitor and control their own nonverbal expressive actions on the basis of those cues (Snyder, 1974). Professional actors, for instance, find it easier than the average person to communicate subtle feelings through nonverbal behaviors.

Further, some situations focus greater attention on nonverbal behaviors than do others. People seem to concentrate more on nonverbal channels to the extent that (a) accurate information about a person is valuable and (b) there are reasons to believe that such information can't or won't be explicitly expressed verbally or otherwise. During a job interview or first date, for example, people are usually on their best behavior, so we look for nonverbal cues that might suggest an inconsistency to determine how they really feel. During court trials, knowledge of the jurors' attitudes and feelings can be quite useful to lawyers, yet such information can't be directly obtained once the trial is underway. Consequently, some lawyers hire social scientists skilled in the science of nonverbal behavior to study and interpret for them the actions of the jurors. Professional poker players carefully attend to the smallest details of the other players' behaviors to obtain cues about the strength of their hands (Mehrabian, 1971a). A good player might notice that, whenever an opponent smiles a certain way, raises his eyebrows, or holds the cards a few inches further away from his chest than usual, he's bluffing. At the same time, the skilled player closely monitors his own actions to insure that no comparable personal cues are being received by other observant players.

The task of encoding and decoding nonverbal messages would be quite easy if a particular action expressed one and only one thing; all we'd need is a simple codebook. There are at least two reasons why it is not so easy. First, all behaviors occur in some context, and the context can alter their meaning. The same hand gesture can mean different things depending on whether the actor is smiling or gritting her teeth or whether she is in the midst of a heated argument or a playful exchange.

In addition, the meanings conveyed by most nonverbal behaviors are subject to wide cultural and social-group variations. Although the communication of strong emotions (anger, happiness) through facial expressions and voice tones is similar across cultures (Ekman & Friesen, 1975; Weitz, 1974), most other nonverbal messages have fluid meanings. Some cultures show respect by looking down, as in Western Africa, Japan, Puerto Rico, and Mexico, while others show respect by being visually attentive, as in the United States (Henley, 1977). People from the so-called contact cultures, such as Arabs, Latin Americans, and Southern Europeans, stand closer to one another when interacting and have higher levels of interpersonal gaze than people from the noncontact cultures, such as North Americans and Northern Europeans (Argyle, 1976; Henley, 1977). A person who is unfamiliar with these normative differences might misinterpret the nonverbal messages of someone from a different culture. A nonverbal action that would succeed in creating a desired impression on members of one's own social group might backfire when employed against a member of a group that has different norms and beliefs.

These problems are less severe than they might appear on the surface, since people do interpret actions in a context and, within a particular social group, share similar interpretations of actions. Children receive explicit indoctrination into the norms and rules for nonverbal behavior that exist in their group, even when they don't take formal deportment lessons. "Sit up straight and don't walk with stooped shoulders" (you don't want to be seen as a slouch). "Keep your elbows off the table" (it's bad manners). "Look me in the eyes" (or I'll think you're lying). "Don't smile when I'm scolding you" (expressions should be appropriate to the situation). "Come closer when you talk to me" (or I'll think you don't like me). The military bearing—head up, shoulders straight, stomach in, chest out—is held up to young boys in middle-class American homes as an exemplary posture. Adolescent girls quickly come to appreciate the nuances of movement: "If you walk like that, people will think you're a tramp." Through such exhortations and through observing the nonverbal actions of others, children learn which nonverbal actions are associated with which images in their social group. Given this set of beliefs about nonverbal meanings, people can interpret the actions of others and attempt to control their own to convey desirable images.

Nonverbal actions can be used by actors to express themselves symbolically on the two major dimensions of interpersonal behavior: power and evaluation. These two dimensions are present in both the nonverbal and verbal realms (Exline, 1971; Henley, 1977; LaFrance & Mayo, 1978; Mehrabian, 1972). The *power dimension* is the vertical hierarchy that exists in social relationships: some people are "superiors" by virtue of being dominant, upper-class, rich, and competent (knowledge can be power); while others are "inferiors" by virtue of being submissive, lower-class, poor, and incompetent. The *evaluative dimension* is the degree of liking versus disliking felt toward another. Nonverbal behaviors can be coded according to the amount of dominance/submission and liking/disliking they express, given the particular context and social norms.

We'll now examine the nonverbal behaviors that people associate with power and evaluation—at least in the United States where much of the research has been done—and how people go about managing their impressions. Keep in mind that any behavior that can be used to convey a particular image, such as powerful, can also be used in reverse to convey the opposite image, if that image is more desirable for an actor in the particular situation. As always, we'll make use of the Association Principle. People attempt to claim (in this case, through nonverbal behaviors) desirable images and to disclaim undesirable images.

NONVERBAL COMMUNICATION AND POWER

Body Language and Power

The body exudes messages about dominance and submissiveness. People often believe they can tell at a glance whether a politician is capable of holding office, a military person capable of leading, or a business person able to pull off the important deals. Bearing, posture, facial expression, hand and foot movements—all convey messages about power and affect the impact actors have on their audiences.

Research indicates that specific body postures and movements are associated with perceptions of power (see Henley, 1977; Kleinke, 1975; LaFrance & Mayo, 1978; Mehrabian, 1971a; Weitz, 1974). People, at least in the U. S., are perceived as being more dominant and having higher status when (1) their bodies are relaxed rather than tense; (2) their posture is erect and tall rather than slumped; (3) their movements are dynamic, brisk, and purposeful rather than slow, strained, and meaningless; (4) their hands are occupied with the palms not exposed to the audience, as in a hands-on-hips position, rather than with palms upturned, which connotes begging; (5) their hands and feet are not trembling or twitching nervously; (6) their gaze is steady and direct, rather than hesitant and seemingly afraid to make eye contact; (7) their eyebrows are lowered rather than raised; and (8) they initiate touch rather than allow themselves to be touched.

Posture. Moderate body relaxation is viewed as an indicant of power (Mehrabian, 1971a). In part, moderate relaxation suggests that the actor is unafraid of the audience and has the self-confidence not to be constantly on guard. In addition, powerful people are given behavioral prerogatives not afforded those of less power. They can move freely and don't have to assume the rigid, obedient posture of subordinates. A case in point is the military, where the officers move around to inspect the people in the ranks, who stare straight ahead with bodies rigid and faces blank. When interacting with real or imagined others of high status, people assume a less relaxed body posture and orient their heads and bodies directly toward the other, signifying attention and deference.

Although powerful individuals are more relaxed, they also seem to maintain more erect postures. For one thing, erect postures avoid the slumped over and hunched down look of defeat (Henley, 1977). For another, erect postures give a person a height advantage, and height is associated with power. Taller people are viewed as more dominant than shorter people, and leaders are generally taller than their subordinates (Stodgill, 1974). In every Presidential election in the United States between 1900 and 1968 the taller of the two candidates won (Nixon's defeat of McGovern, who was slightly taller, broke the string). It has even been found that people overestimate the height of people with high status and underestimate the height of people with low status (Dannenmaier & Thumin, 1964). Thus, people are frequently surprised to discover how "short" some movie stars, sports figures, and politicians turn out to be when they see them up close.

To take advantage of the correlation between height and power, people who want to be viewed as powerful

> may elevate their bodies in some way . . . such as standing up to emphasize a point, or . . . towering over seated persons while lecturing them. The chin-up position, particularly seen in the military style . . . may be a form of elevation, a way to appear to look down on others when one doesn't have the elevation from height alone [Henley, 1977, p. 128].

People often go beyond posture and movement tactics to increase their height further. Elevator and platform shoes give people a few added inches. Judges gain height by towering over the courtroom from their benches. Nelson Rockefeller had a special desk that contained pull-out steps. If for some reason he wanted to address a group of people in his office he would stride up the steps and stand on the top of his desk (Henley, 1977, p. 59). An interesting height game was played in one of

Charlie Chaplin's classic movies, *The Great Dictator*. Hitler (played by Chaplin) and Mussolini were seated next to one another getting shaves in a barber shop. Each attempted to increase his own dominance and assert superiority, but, given their seated positions, the only way they could do so was to elevate their chairs. Both furiously attempted to jack up their seats until ultimately they reached the ceiling and plummeted to the floor.

Even when sitting, a slouch should be avoided by those desiring to be seen as powerful. In an important meeting, people should avoid low, comfortable chairs that virtually force them to slouch and should select instead a higher straight-back chair (Korda, 1976). Clasping one's hands behind the head with the elbows extended to the sides also seems to be a popular dominance posture. It allows a person to be tall and erect while also suggesting relaxation.

The Energy Look. Research has shown that people in leadership positions are more self-confident and assertive and have greater motivation and drive than the average person (Stodgill, 1974). It would seem to follow that people who move and gesture in a dynamic, brisk, purposeful fashion would be perceived as more powerful than those who move slowly and gesture too little or too much (which might be viewed as nervousness). Korda (1977, p. 73) similarly suggests that people who want to look successful should display the "Energy Look:" move with the head up, chest out, back straight, and arms in motion. In short, you should look "as if you were on your way to do something, rather than moping along as if you had nothing to do. Most successful people walk at a fast, purposeful pace, even if they're only on the way to the bathroom or water cooler" (p. 73). Movement for the sake of movement, though, loses its effectiveness. Hyperactivity and walking about during conversations are signs of stress (Mehrabian, 1971a). Movements with no apparent purpose make the actor appear disorganized and unable to deal with the situation, and they drain energy that could be more appropriately channeled into goal-directed actions. Some psychiatric patients move about in an overly agitated fashion, and their timing and synchronization of nonverbal behaviors is off (LaFrance & Mayo, 1978), leaving the overall appearance of powerlessness and incompetence. Despite relatively little relevant research, it seems plausible to hypothesize that dynamic, purposeful movements are seen as more powerful than listless or purposeless movements.

Hands and Feet. Hands and feet can be incredibly useful appendages, but during social interactions there are numerous occasions when people just don't seem to know what to do with them. Hands droop nervously or twitch on a cigarette, rubber band, or paper clip. Many people anxiously twirl their hair into little knotted curls or run their fingers through their hair in an aimless fashion that upsets any hairstyle they started out with. Feet dangle, swing, twitch, jiggle, pump up and down, and otherwise render noncredible any appearance of self-confidence and security the actor may be trying to present to the audience. In general, it seems that steady hands and feet, coupled with purposeful action, lead to perceptions of power, while nervousness and purposelessness lead to perceptions of powerlessness (Henley, 1977; Mehrabian, 1972).

A posture that is adopted by many professionals is the seated hand-to-chin position, which occupies the hand and gives the appearance of partially supporting the head. The position suggests thoughtfulness and evaluation, as if the actor were in the capacity of a judge (Henley, 1977). In one study (Spiegel & Machotka, 1974), subjects were shown drawings of individuals in different body positions. It was found that in the hands-on-hips position individuals were evaluated as dominant and "bossy;" when the palms of the hands were exposed to the audience with the hands forward the individual was seen as cold, weak, and effeminate. Gestures were rated as dominant and action-oriented.

Korda (1976, 1977) presents numerous anecdotes about how people in business seem to control their hand and foot movements to create impressions appropriate to their goals. "Watch an executive in action, talking over a problem. He sits back, one leg crossed over the other, apparently self-assured and relaxed. At the moment when the discussion becomes serious and difficult, he will almost always uncross his legs, place both feet on the ground, and lean forward with his hands on his knees, assuming his position of maximum power" (1976, p. 208). The self-confidence and relaxation displayed by the initial legs-crossed position become transformed into an erect, sturdy confrontation stance. Korda (1976) believes that

> our feet give us away; they swing back and forth, showing impatience or doubt; we tuck them out of sight under the chair in moments of timidity or fear; we place them solidly before us to indicate that we're not going to budge or change our minds; we turn the toes toward each other in a position of maidenly deference when talking to a very powerful person, and place them far apart, with the toes pointing outward at a forty-five degree angle to show our contemptuous superiority [p. 208].

These suggestive observations have yet to receive empirical testing.

Politicians generally develop dominant gestures as means of showing their self-confidence, power, and, sometimes, distinctiveness. Winston Churchill's gesture of fingers-forming-victory-sign is exemplary. Impersonators usually have no difficulty finding distinctive gestures that can be used to satirize prominent individuals. In some cases, people will intentionally "try out" dominant gestures to improve their image. Mixed results often occur. A case in point is former President

Gerald Ford. In January of 1975, before he delivered a State-of-the-Union address on television, he hired consultants to give him an image of being a "decisive, honest and effective head of state" (Henley, 1977, p. 124). It seemed imperative for Ford to improve his image at the time: he was handpicked for the Presidency by a disgraced President; he sometimes appeared awkward, tripping or banging his head getting out of aircraft; he had a tendency to "misspeak," once commenting that he "watched" something on the radio; and jokes about his ability were making the rounds, including such gems as Lyndon Johnson's "Jerry Ford played football without a helmet."

Columnist Joseph Kraft (quoted in Henley, 1977) chronicled Ford's attempt.

> Mr. Ford appeared on television Monday night with two aides serving up documents—the perfect picture of a working President. He gestured to show forcefulness and walked about to demonstrate energy. The setting for the production was the White House library—the one place in the world most calculated to unsay the widespread public impression that Mr. Ford is not very bright [p. 125].

Unfortunately for Ford, the attempt was not highly successful. The setting seemed too staged and questions were raised about whether Ford's lack of verbal skills may have undermined the dramatic and forceful gestures he employed.

People can and do use gestures that are "not their own," but they must seem "natural" to be successful. In Ford's case, contradictions were present between his gestures and his verbal alacrity. Challenges to the image he wanted to present were contained in his other actions, and the desired image self-destructed. If such inconsistencies can be hidden from view, if actions can be coordinated to present a united front, there is little reason why gestures and other nonverbal behaviors can't be employed. Ultimately, a person's self-concept seems to change as the images generated by actions produce rewards and the actor comes to believe those images can be successfully claimed (see Chapters 5 and 6). Such advice is contained in military publications. *The Armed Forces Officer* (1965), a Department of Defense publication distributed to officers in all branches of the military, advises that as far as being a leader is concerned "It is good . . . to look the part, not only because of the effect on others, but because from out of the effort made to *look it*, one may in time come to *be it*" (p. 70). If people believe they can successfully claim an attractive image, they will come to incorporate that image into their self-concepts. In cases such as Mr. Ford's, though, public reactions suggested that the image he wanted could not be successfully claimed.

The Face and Eyes. In the animal kingdom, facial expressions function as threats, regulate aggressive encounters, and serve to maintain dominance hierarchies (Exline, 1971). Visual images of power are often more important in settling disputes between animals than size or strength alone: "The victor is ordinarily the animal who puts on the more intimidating show" (Brown, 1965, p. 20). In humans, facial expressions similarly function as indicants of power. The face receives the most visual attention from others during encounters and seems to stand out over other nonverbal cues in superior/subordinate relationships (Ekman & Friesen, 1969; Exline, 1971; Mehrabian, 1971a).

The position of the eyebrows is related to perceptions of power. Raised eyebrows are characteristic of surprise, fear, and retreat in all cultures, and thus should be associated with submission; aggressors display lowered brows, suggesting dominance. Indeed, when subjects are shown photographs of faces with the eyebrows in either a raised or lowered position, they rate raised eyebrows as less dominant (Keating, Mazur, & Segall, 1977).

Staring eyes can exude power. Throughout folklore and literature, the eyes purportedly mirror the soul, and staring eyes have been associated with dominance and evil. Dracula supposedly froze his victims with an intimidating hypnotic stare. Rasputin's eyes had the "look" of dominance. People with the "evil eye" are avoided because they are purported to have the power to create all manner of hardship and misfortune. A steady and direct gaze is one of the most universal aspects of threat displays in humans and animals (Exline, 1971). Looking down, never looking directly at another is a universal sign of appeasement and submission. People are said to be "afraid to look him in the eye," and we even lower our heads when defeated. When people are embarrassed, they avoid eye contact with others (Modigliani, 1971). People who look straight ahead rather than downward are perceived as more alert, secure, active, and receptive (Tankard, 1970). Shifty, blinking eyes and refusing to make eye contact are not for those desiring a look of power.

Richard Nixon was sensitive to the importance of eye contact in building his image (McGinniss, 1970, p. 3). While taping campaign speeches for television, Nixon ordered that no one be in his direct line of vision or moving about the studio; otherwise, he might divert his glance and shift his eyes. He had all timing cues (like the number of seconds left in the taping) given directly under the lens of the camera for the same reason. Further, recognizing that a passive facial expression would undermine the image, he ordered that he be alerted a couple of seconds before the camera came on so that he wouldn't be caught in a "frozen" expression.

Although the ability to initiate and hold eye contact is a sign of power, continually looking at another person creates the impression that one is dependent. Both apes and humans show greater visual attentiveness toward their superiors than their inferiors; the higher one's status, the less one has to look at others (Exline, 1971). During discussions, less powerful members of a dyad spend more time looking at more powerful members than vice-versa (Exline, Ellyson, & Long, 1975). This is particularly true when an individual is listening rather than speaking; people show high attentiveness when a more powerful person speaks. Correlational data indicate that ROTC officers who spend the most time looking at subordinates during interactions receive the lowest leadership performance ratings (Exline et al., 1975). Although hardly conclusive, these results suggest that too much visual attentiveness undermines perceptions of power and leadership ability. Thus, powerful people should use a nonshifting, direct gaze and a stare to establish dominance but shouldn't spend too much time visually attending to others, particularly when listening.

Staring is aversive. During confrontations, a steady stare can make others back down *or* become more antagonistic. Children practice games of dominance to perfect their power skills, and a staring game is one of the most common; the first child to break eye contact is the loser and must assume at least temporarily a submissive role in the relationship. Ellsworth and Carlsmith (1973) demonstrated the aversive aspect of staring. In their study, subjects believed they were delivering electric shocks to another person, who was actually an experimental accomplice. Subjects shocked the confederate more when he looked directly at them than when he looked away, suggesting that the subjects were attempting to "persuade" the confederate to avert his glance by punishing his stares. However, if the confederate never looked away and maintained a constant gaze at the subjects prior to the times when shock could be administered, those who had been previously angered eventually reduced the amount of shock they gave. Since they apparently couldn't get the person to avert his gaze, they perhaps hoped that reducing the amount of shock would terminate his stare. Alternatively, they may have simply "backed down" from the direct confrontation brought about by the confederate's continual stare.

In the movie *Cool Hand Luke*, the prison guard who was Paul Newman's antagonist wore silver reflecting sunglasses, allowing him to see while hiding his eyes from scrutiny. His ability to see while keeping part of himself unknown to the audience added to his aura of power. In *Jaws*, suspense and terror were built to a crescendo by keeping the shark hidden from view until late in the picture; scenes were shot from the shark's perspective of seeing and closing in on its victims. The danger of the beast and its power were hidden from its victims until too late. The ability to see but not be seen is associated with power and dominance; it is used to advantage in novels and movies and by skilled impression managers. Being seen but not being able to see, in contrast, is associated with inferiority and powerlessness. Paranoid schizophrenics often mention overpowering feelings of being watched by unseen enemies. We all at one time or another experience feelings that "people are looking at us," of having our privacy invaded when there is nothing we can do about it—we have lost control, at least for the moment.

People prefer to see but not be seen when power is a salient dimension. Jellison and Ickes (1974) led some subjects to expect a competitive interaction in which they should want to minimize their opponent's power while maximizing their own. As predicted, it was found that in the competitive situation subjects preferred to be able to see the opponent but did not want the opponent to be able to see them. Other subjects were led to expect a cooperative interaction. In cooperative encounters, people should want to maximize both their own power and their partners' in order to increase the likelihood that they could jointly profit. As predicted, in the cooperative situation subjects preferred both to see and be seen by their partners. Clearly, visual knowledge is power, and people take steps to share it with or deny it to others depending upon their goals in interaction.

Touch. Touch is associated with warmth, closeness, caring, and intimacy. But touch, particularly the initiation of touch, can become a symbol of power when used in situations where one of the actors wants to make power differences salient. Goffman (1967) suggested that people higher up the status hierarchy can initiate touching those below them, while subordinates rarely touch superiors without some type of invitation. A doctor can touch a patient, and an employer can place his or her hand on the shoulder of a worker, but not vice versa. The power connotation seems to arise from the fact that touch can also be an aggressive action. It is an invasion of one's personal space, a gesture that suggests that one has the right or power to intrude physically on others. Lyndon Johnson was a master of touch as a dominance tactic (Korda, 1976, p. 268). Johnson would "squeeze his subordinates' knees, punch them, stab his finger in their stomach, and generally use every physical means to show just who had the power."

Henley (1977, pp. 102–107) summarizes three unpublished studies (the first and third by her and the second by Thomas Cannon) that suggest that people do use and interpret touch in terms of power. In the first study, observational data obtained from a number of public settings showed that males touched females more than vice-versa; older people touched younger ones more than vice-versa; and people with higher socioeconomic status touched those with lower socioeconomic status more than vice-versa. Henley interprets these findings in terms of the "status connotation of touching."

The second and third studies involved giving respondents questionnaires that asked how often they touched or had been touched by people from higher, lower, and the same status groupings (Cannon study) and whether they believed that other people were likely to touch them in certain specific situations (Henley). People reported touching those of higher status much less than being touched by them, while they reported touching those of lower status more than being touched by them; touching and receiving touch were about equal among peers. People also reported that others were likely to touch them when the others were giving advice, giving orders, and trying to persuade them—all situations in which a dominance/submission relationship is salient. Though the latter two studies merely report what people *think* would happen in different situations, not what *actually* happens, the findings do indicate that the power aspects of touch are salient to people.

SPACE AND POWER

Many animal species, including some insects, fish, and birds and most mammals, stake out territories—areas they mark for occupation and defend against intruders from outside their family or social unit (Ardrey, 1966; Brown, 1965; Hall, 1966; Maier & Maier, 1970). In so doing, members of a species are distributed over the available terrain in ways that seem to make the best use of food supplies and other natural resources. Territoriality minimizes overcrowding and regulates fighting behavior. The size and desirability of an animal's territory are usually proportional to its place in the dominance hierarchy. The higher its status, the greater the size and desirability of its territory and the more areas within a shared territory it is allowed to enter. Power and space use are associated in the animal kingdom.

For humans, too, space is "the prerogative of the rich and the powerful" (Henley, 1977, p. 30). The rich live on palatial estates; the poor are crowded into slums. Dominant street gangs in cities claim the best and biggest "turf." People with high status even take up more space with their signatures than those of low status (Zweigenhaft, 1970). The relationship between space and power is salient even for young children, who build forts and clubhouses and defend them from invasion from unwanted outsiders.

Research (see Henley, 1977; Mehrabian, 1972; Riess, 1977; Sommer, 1969) indicates that space behaviors that increase perceptions of power include (1) having larger personal spaces and territories, such as homes and offices; (2) freely moving into and exerting control in other people's spaces and territories—appearing to be "at home," for example, in another's office; and (3) taking seating positions that provide visual prominence, such as at the head of a table.

Powerful people both take and are granted more space than their less powerful counterparts. More powerful people have larger offices within companies and business organizations (Durand, 1977). Parents often feel free to walk into their children's rooms, but prohibit the children from taking similar liberties. Males, who are usually accorded higher status than females in our society, get larger spaces than females in the home. They more frequently have their own special room and chair, and when a female does get a special room in the house it is usually less desirable, offering less privacy than the male's (Henley, 1977). Males even take up more space on large, open beaches than do females, keeping greater distances between themselves and others (Edney & Jordan-Edney, 1974). Masculine markers such as a man's jacket and briefcase are more effective in reserving or holding space at a table when the occupant temporarily leaves than are feminine markers such as a woman's lace-trimmed jacket and flowered bookbag (Shaffer & Sadowski, 1975).

We grant people with high status more personal space than we do those with low status, remaining at greater distances from them when interacting (Mehrabian, 1972). Providing high status people with larger spaces seems to be part of what we do to show deference and respect. As another aspect of showing deference, we usually allow higher status people to call the shots in a relationship, letting them decide, and then signal, if they want to become more familiar (Mehrabian, 1971a). A supervisor might indicate that it is all right to call her by her first name, for example, or generally act more approachable. If the higher status person wishes to terminate the period of familiarity—for example, if another employee walks into the room and the supervisor wants to reestablish a clear power differential—steps are taken to induce the original deferential behaviors. The person with high status might give an icy stare or a verbal reminder that the two are not equals.

One of the prerogatives of power is the right to intrude on other people's space and territory, often appropriating it for personal use. People who engage in such behaviors, by touching others' property without invitation for example, are rated by onlookers as more dominant than those who don't (Spiegel & Machotka, 1974). The connotations of freely moving about in other people's territories were demonstrated in a study in which films were made of a man working at his desk (described in Sommer, 1969, p. 19). After a few moments, a second man knocked on the door and entered the office. People who watched the films rated the visitor as being the least subordinate when he entered the room and walked directly to the occupant's desk to begin a conversation, more subordinate when he walked halfway across the room and then stopped to converse, and most subordinate when he entered the room but stopped just inside the door. Clearly, freedom of movement is associated with power. The room's occupant was viewed as being more dominant when he took longer to respond to the second man's knock. Being able to inconvenience others, then, by making them wait or for other reasons feel uncomfortable, is a sign of power (Korda, 1976, 1977).

People usually feel more comfortable on their own "turf"—in their own homes or offices, for example—and are more confident in their ability to control this space than are visitors. The occupant of a room in a college dormitory sees the room as more pleasant and private than do visitors and is perceived by the visitor as being more "at home" (Edney, 1975). Furthermore, occupants of a room report feeling less controlled by others than do visitors to their rooms. During confrontations, such as contract negotiations or debates, people usually are more successful when the encounter occurs in their own territory. Martindale (1971) had students play the role of opposition lawyers in a simulated court case and held the negotiations for the case's outcome in the dormitory room of one or the other of each pair of participants. He found that the case was usually won by the student in whose room the negotiation was held. It is no wonder that street gangs, athletic teams, lawyers, businessmen, and politicians generally prefer their own turf, field, or office for confrontations. Similarly, animals usually emerge victorious when a fight is held within their own territory (Maier & Maier, 1970).

The feelings of confidence when in one's own territory can be traced to several causes. First, people who are on their own turf are more familiar with the surroundings; they know all the details of the turf and can use them to advantage. For example, a baseball player is usually able to judge at what angle a long fly ball will bounce off the outfield wall of his home field but might have difficulty judging a comparable hit in an opponent's park. Second, people can set up their own turf to their own advantage by determining or modifying the original layout or by judiciously placing props. Baseball parks are often modified to take advantage of the skills of the hometeam by changing the height of the chalk foul lines to aid or impede bunting or by drying out or watering down the infield to make ground balls harder or easier to field. In offices, the occupant has personal files, secretaries, calculators, prearranged seating arrangements, and a wide array of props with which to convey desired impressions. The visitor lacks such stage-setting ability. Third, norms of courtesy dictate that people respect the rights, property, and space of others. The things we can do in our own home, such as taking our shoes off, walking around in our underwear, and selecting any channel on the television normally cannot be done in the homes of others. These factors put a territory's occupant at a decided advantage over visitors.

Overcoming such factors—triumphing on another's turf—is accomplished only by the strongest. Korda (1976, p. 164), commenting on power in the business world, observes that "Many powerful people, particularly the aggressive ones, *prefer* to go to other people's offices, since they are then invading the other person's turf." The invader then engages in maneuvers to show who has control of that space. He starts by sitting down and putting his feet up on the desk of the room's occupant. He may then employ such power tactics as "using objects as ashtrays when that's obviously not what they were intended for, giving orders to someone else's secretary, spilling coffee, and even lying down on someone else's carpet to do back exercises when the other person is seated at his or her desk" (p. 164). The object of this space-use game is to convey the "impression that you believe his office belongs to you" (p. 164). If successful, there can be no doubt about who is most powerful.

Seating Arrangements

The furniture arrangement in a room involves more than just the aesthetics of interior decoration. Seating arrangements affect the amount of communication that occurs, who talks to whom, how much each person talks, and who seems to be dominant (see Shaw, 1976). You can easily observe such phenomena at any party or gathering. People who occupy central places and seats dominate conversations, while those whose seats are on the periphery of the room are left out of the discussions. The choice of table style is important, since certain styles accentuate power differences among those present while others minimize differences. Legend has it that King Arthur selected a round table because he didn't want status distinctions to affect the meetings of his knights. A more recent example comes from the White House. Mamie Eisenhower enjoyed the status of being First Lady. She used rectangular tables in the White House dining room with President Eisenhower at one end of a table and herself at the other. Jacqueline Kennedy preferred a more egalitarian atmosphere and more relaxed conversations, so she had the rectangular tables replaced with round ones.

A head-of-the-table position at a rectangular table is clearly associated with power. People usually reserve the head spot of the table for the highest-status member of the group (Lott & Sommer, 1967). People with higher status usually take the head spot when given the opportunity, and people who sit at the head spot are most often recognized by others as the leader of the group (Strodtbeck & Hook, 1961). Even if seats are randomly assigned around a rectangular table, people at the head spots act more like leaders and later report feelings of being more of a leader than the people at the sides (Howells & Becker, 1962; Pellegrini, 1971). People assigned to the head spots talk more and are talked to more (Hare & Bales, 1963) and are rated by the group as more talkative, persuasive, dominant, self-confident, and intelligent than those on the sides (Pellegrini, 1971).

Naturally, people who want to be viewed as powerful should attempt to claim a head spot if they have the opportunity, while those who want to minimize their power in the group should attempt to claim one of the side spots. In support of this impression-management hypothesis, one study found that people who scored high on a personality measure of dominance and hence who should want to establish an image of dominance in the group took the head spot more frequently than low scorers (Hare & Bales, 1963). At the other extreme, people who scored high on a measure of anxiety avoided the head spot more often than those who were low on anxiety (Hare & Bales, 1963). A high anxiety score can be viewed as a self-effacing self-presentational stance (Carson, 1969), since the individual is reporting that he or she gets upset easily, worries a lot, and often can't cope with problems. Such an individual should rate dominance as a less desirable image than a person who scores low on an anxiety scale and hence should avoid dominant nonverbal behaviors.

Skilled impression managers in all walks of life capitalize on the association between dominance and the head spot at a table. Korda (1976) noted the phenomenon in the business world.

> Board-room tables . . . are almost never round, since it is necessary to have a very precise gradation of power, and above all, imperative that the most important person, usually the chairman, should sit at the end next to the window, with his back to it, while the second most important person, usually the president or chief executive officer, should sit to his right. If the latter sits at the opposite end of the table (playing "mother," so to speak, in dining-table terms) he not only has the sun in his eyes, but is almost always placing himself in an adversary position vis-á-vis the chairman [p. 236].

Korda's observation about the confrontation nature of two powerful people sitting at opposite ends of a table is congruent with research on the types of seating arrangements people prefer for various kinds of tasks. Sommer (1969) has found that people associate face-to-face seating arrangements across a rectangular table with competition and confrontation. Cooperation is associated with side-by-side arrangements and conversations are associated with sitting corner-to-corner on one of the ends or sitting across from one another at the sides. Thus, if two potential adversaries place themselves in a competitive seating arrangement, they are likely to find their conflict exacerbated. If they want to work out their differences and minimize the likelihood of a confrontation, they would be better advised to use a seating arrangement that is associated with cooperation or conversation. Skilled impression managers can use seating arrangements, whether at home, on dates, in school, or in the office, to facilitate their goals in an interaction.

Students appear to be quite adept in employing classroom seating arrangements to facilitate their goals—either to be prominent in the class and active in discussions or to withdraw and minimize their participation. In the usual row-and-column seating arrangements of classrooms, instructors spend about 68% of the time in the front center of the room and spend more time talking to and looking at students who are seated in the front center (Adams, 1969; Sommer, 1969). Students who enjoy the class, enjoy discussions in general, or want the instructor to notice and remember them when it comes time to assign grades should be expected to select seats (if they have a choice) in the front center. Those who want to avoid prominence should avoid such seats. In actuality, students who want to participate more in class discussions do pick seats that give them visual prominence—the front center of the room in a row-and-column classroom or directly across from the instructor when a class has a rectangular seminar table (Koneya, 1976; Sommer, 1967a, 1967b, 1969).

PARALANGUAGE AND POWER

Paralanguage is the music, not the lyrics. Just as we judge some musical arrangements to be more powerful and dynamic than others, so we make judgments about the power and dynamism of speakers based on the sound of their speech (see Kleinke, 1975; LaFrance & Mayo, 1978; Weitz, 1974). An image of power can be communicated to an audience through paralanguage in several ways. When people are anxious and lacking in confidence, they speak with lower volume and exhibit more speech disturbances, such as stuttering, omitting portions of a word or sentence, failing to complete a sentence, and taking longer pauses between words and sentences—seeming to grope for the correct word but to be unable to find it (see Kleinke, 1975). People who are self-confident do not display such awkward paralanguage. Of course, audiences notice cues that suggest that the speaker is anxious or lacking in confidence. Speakers who exhibit signs of stress and low confidence, like stuttering, making slips of the tongue, repeating and correcting themselves, taking longer pauses, and using a high number of "ahs" and "uhs," are viewed as more incompetent than those who exhibit fewer such signs (see Kleinke, 1975; Miller, Maruyama, Beaber, & Valone, 1976).

People attempting to be viewed as confident, truthful, and powerful should avoid such signs of stress in the voice. Most people seem to recognize this fact and try to control such cues. In one study, subjects were asked to deliver a speech as persuasively as they could to a particular audience. Compared to subjects who were asked to give a neutral speech, the persuaders talked faster and with more volume and intonation (Mehrabian & Williams, 1969). One close friend of mine, a college professor, asked me to point out to him every time he interrupted his own speech with "ahs" and "uhs." He said he was trying to eliminate such signs of doubt and insecurity from his speech. People in many fields record their voices and play them back to correct "mistakes" or go to speech specialists to improve their paralinguistic performances. King George VI of England, father of Queen Elizabeth, was quite shy and exhibited a noticeable stammer when he spoke on the radio or in public. Embarrassed by his speech problem and concerned about how he sounded to his subjects, he took intensive daily speech lessons from specialists, eventually reducing but not entirely solving the problem (Lacey, 1977).

There are powerful and powerless styles of speech, the result of both paralanguage and the use of specific types of words (Erickson, Lind, Johnson, & O'Barr, 1978). The powerless style of speech includes, among other things, the use of questioning voice tones (raising one's voice at the end of a declarative sentence as if asking a question); speech hesitations like "uh," "ah," and "you know"; using hedging phrases like "kinda," "I think," and "I guess," as if unwilling to make a strong assertion; and using polite phrases such as "please," and "thank you." Powerful styles of speech lack most of these features and thereby give the speaker the appearance of being straightforward. People with high status and social power employ the powerful styles of speech, while people with low status and little social power employ the powerless styles (Erickson et al., 1978). Powerful people don't beg or plead; they demand and assume—in their word choices, voice tones, and un-interrupted, goal-directed style.

The powerful style of speech is quite effective in persuading others. Erickson et al. (1978) had college student subjects either listen to or read the testimony of witnesses in a simulated courtroom case. The content of the testimony was identical in both cases, but was expressed in the powerful style for some of the subjects and the powerless style for others. It was found that irrespective of whether subjects read or heard the testimony they rated the witness as more *credible* (convincing, trustworthy, and competent) and as more *potent and attractive* (strong, powerful, active, intelligent, and likable) when the powerful style was used.

Particular types of speech evoke stereotypes in listeners: black dialect, Brooklyn accent, French accent, New Jersey accent, British accent. From the way a person talks, we categorize him or her as upper- or lower-class, Black or White, sophisticated or not. The accent or speech type classifies the actor as part of a particular group, and once we have made that association we attach all the other stereotypical attributes of the group to the person. Many people try to acquire the accent or speech type of a group they admire, irrespective of any actual association with the group. An aspiring actor might take language lessons to sound like David Niven or Maurice Chevalier. A nouveau riche socialite who had been reared in the slums might take diction lessons to try to sound as if she grew up on Nob Hill. The plot of George Bernard Shaw's play *Pygmalion*, the basis for the successful musical *My Fair Lady*, revolved around diction specialist Dr. Henry Higgins' transformation of a lower-class cockney wench, Eliza Doolittle, into a lady who could pass for royalty amongst the socialites of England.

SELF-EFFACING NONVERBAL BEHAVIORS: THE LOOK OF WEAKNESS

Experience teaches us that particular nonverbal behaviors are associated with degrees of dominance or submission in our social groups. Armed with such ingrained knowledge, we can display behaviors appropriate to the images we find desirable. When most people discuss power, they talk about how one can acquire it; power is generally viewed as an attractive image. Books about power—how to get it and how to convince others you have it—make best-seller lists. It is hard to imagine a book about powerlessness—how to get and how to convince others you have it—selling many copies. Yet for many people powerlessness, or at least relative submission, is a desirable image.

An extreme case can be found in the area of mental illness. Many mental patients hold a self-conception of incompetence and powerlessness and are motivated to act in ways that convey these images (Chapter 10). Studies of the nonverbal behaviors of schizophrenics and depressives support the hypothesis that their body language and space use convey impressions of powerlessness and incompetence (see LaFrance & Mayo, 1978; Sommer, 1969). People diagnosed as depressives display averted gaze, engage in little eye contact, constantly look down, and droop their heads and mouths. Each of these behaviors communicates fatigue and submission. People diagnosed as schizophrenic evidence withdrawal and isolation. They engage in little eye contact, display little movement, and take seating positions with low visual accessibility. At the extreme, catatonic schizophrenics display long periods of total immobility, sitting rigidly in a corner with a blank expression for hours on end. These nonverbal actions, although noncommunicative in the normal sense, send out the overriding impression of powerlessness.

The more usual cases of presentations of submissiveness are far from these extremes. In numerous relationships, people encounter others who simply are higher in status, competence, or power than they are, and self-presentations of *relative* submissiveness are appropriate. In organizational hierarchies such as the military, even the generals are accountable to someone and must engage in appropriate deference behaviors in their superior's presence, irrespective of how powerful they are with respect to the rest of the organization. To do otherwise is to risk confrontation and a high likelihood of reprimand. When in the presence of superiors, the appropriate deference is in part conveyed through nonverbal behaviors, such as more rigid postures and greater visual attentiveness to the other.

Nancy Henley (1977) has rigorously documented the treatise that women and minority group members engage in nonverbal behaviors that are associated with relative submissiveness. These nonverbal actions support the stereotypes of majority group members, producing reactions on their parts that further reinforce the submissive claims (see Chapter 6). The resulting spiral can bind the individual in a trap of powerlessness.

NONVERBAL BEHAVIOR AND LIKING

You walk into a restaurant and see two couples seated in different booths waiting for their food to arrive. The man and woman who comprise the first couple are separated by the table between them, but they are directly facing each other, leaning their bodies slightly forward as if they wanted to get closer, and their hands meet in the center of the table. Their eyes are in constant contact, and smiles are on their faces. Each looks quite content. The second couple is of a different appearance. The man is leaning slightly backward, away from the table and from his companion, with his shoulders touching the booth behind him. His posture is slumped, his facial expression signals boredom, and his eyes are looking down, reading the children's games printed on the menu. The woman is also leaning backward, with her arms crossed tightly in front of her. Her eyes wander around the room, seemingly watching the waitresses deliver food to nearby tables. If you were asked to give an opinion about how the members of each couple seem to feel about each other, you would probably have little difficulty.

The nonverbal behaviors of the first couple signal liking, closeness, and the desire to approach. There is *high immediacy* in their relationship (Mehrabian, 1971a). Nonverbal behaviors associated with high immediacy include maintaining smaller interpersonal distances, leaning the body slightly toward the other, touching the other or reaching out as if to touch, orienting the head and body directly toward the other or turning to place oneself in the face-to-face position, and looking at the other (Mehrabian, 1971a). All of these show involvement with and interest in the other. The nonverbal behaviors of the second couple suggest the desire to avoid each other (at least at this moment); their actions signal indifference and lack of involvement. There is *low immediacy* in their relationship. People adopt high-immediacy nonverbal behaviors toward persons they like and low-immediacy nonverbal behaviors toward those they don't like (Mehrabian, 1971a). In addition, people seem to engage in high-immediacy nonverbal behaviors when they want to be viewed as showing interest in and liking the other, and they engage in low-immediacy nonverbal behaviors when they want to be viewed as showing lack of interest or dislike.

There are numerous occasions when people closely monitor their nonverbal actions to make the "right" impression—to impress a date, her parents, and friends; to impress a prospective or current employer; to impress a client; to make some special person feel "extra" needed. If we show interest, involvement, and liking, we expect others to recipro-cate; at the minimum we expect them to be sufficiently flattered by our interest that they increase their liking for us.

An alternative strategy people use to increase an audience's attrac-tion toward them is to claim images that they have reason to believe the audience likes in a person. Many high school males practice the walk and movement of the school's football players, hoping to deceive females into believing that they are on the team (Fast, 1971). The tactic seems to succeed in a good number of cases. The college male often believes that females admire intellectual, studious types. So he buys himself a pipe and a tweed jacket with elbow patches and constantly walks around with books under his arm, gazing off into the distance as if contemplating life's mysteries. The tactical variations on this strategy are almost endless.

Thus, when people contemplate nonverbal strategies to increase their attractiveness in the eyes of others, two major ones come to mind: (1) people can show the other that they care, are interested in, and like him or her and (2) people can claim images—sexy, intellectual, athletic, or whatever—that they believe the audience already admires and likes. Actually, these strategies are quite similar; they are part of the same primary strategy of impression management. People act to establish an association between themselves and desirable images, while dissociat-ing themselves from undesirable ones—the Association Principle. In the case of the first strategy above, people show high immediacy toward others partially because they might honestly feel it and partially be-cause they believe it will make the other feel good or impress him or her. In either event, people are claiming an image—being attracted to the other. In the case of the second strategy, people are claiming other images, some of which they may honestly believe they possess and others of which they may not.

Virtually all the research on nonverbal communication and liking has focused on questions that are at least indirectly relevant to the first strategy—the communication of liking itself. Virtually no research has been done on the second strategy, and much is needed. We'll turn now to what little research is available.

The Nonverbal Communication of Liking

Research (see Exline, 1971; Kleinke, 1975; LaFrance & Mayo, 1978; Mehrabian, 1971a, 1971b, 1972; Weitz, 1974) indicates that nonverbal behaviors associated with the expression of liking and positive affect include (1) closer interpersonal distances; (2) touching; (3) forward lean during encounters; (4) body and head orientations that directly face the audience; (5) moderate body relaxation; (6) "open" body positions with arms unfolded and legs uncrossed (for females but not for males); (7) eye contact; (8) positive facial expressions exemplified by a smile; (9) affirmative head nods; (10) moderate amounts of gesturing and animation; and (11) pleasant and supportive paralanguage that shows signs of interest in what the other is saying, such as "mmmmh."

People want to be near those they like and away from those they don't. Not surprisingly, closer distances, touching one another, and slight forward lean during interactions are closely related to liking. Numerous studies have found that people stand and sit closer to those they like than to strangers and those they don't and that they perceive those who approach them more closely as liking them more. Forward lean of the body when interacting reduces interpersonal distance ever so slightly compared with leaning backward, but it is a sign of approach —of being drawn to the other as if he or she were a magnet. Leaning slightly backward suggests repulsion.

Humanists view touch as exemplary of a natural and healthy bonding between people. We touch others to express tenderness, affection, openness, and closeness. The encounter group movement focused on learning how to communicate feelings to others; it relied heavily on touch as the basic mechanism of communication. A gentle touch does suggest immediacy and liking, at least in most contexts (Mehrabian, 1971a). It is both used by people and seen by observers as an expression of affection.

Body openness seems to be a way people communicate the desire to be approached. Females who sit in "open" body positions, with their arms in their laps and their legs uncrossed with feet planted on the ground are viewed as more pleasant and likable by both males and other females than females who sit in "closed" body positions, with their arms folded and their legs crossed (Mehrabian, 1968). The openness of body position seems to make less of a difference when males are evaluated. The more cocoon-like look of the closed position perhaps suggests to observers that the female is withdrawing, trying to be left alone by others, with the result that observers respond more negatively. It has also been found that when attempting to persuade others communicators produce more attitude change in their audiences when they sit in open rather than closed positions (McGinley, LeFevre, & Mc-

Ginley, 1975). Unfortunately, since only female persuaders and female audiences were used in this study it is unclear whether comparable results would be obtained for males or mixed-sex pairings. At the very least, though, open positions are associated with positive evaluations of females. There is probably an upper boundary on the phenomenon, since body openness can sometimes be so extreme that it exceeds the norms for appropriate behaviors in the situation and leads to negative reactions from onlookers (Kleinke, 1975).

People can show interest and attentiveness to others through direct body and head orientations, eye contact, and smiling. People are seen as expressing more positive feelings and are evaluated more positively when they orient their head and body directly toward the audience rather than turning the head and body slightly to one side; the position of the head in particular is crucial (Mehrabian, 1971a, 1972). If a person has her head angled away when talking, as if looking off in the distance to find something more interesting to do, people's attraction for her decreases.

The eyes universally symbolize affect. The look in another's eyes can signal the start of a romance or the end of one. As the poet's mirror to the soul, the eyes express and intensify the affect present in a relationship. Not surprisingly, it has been found that length of eye contact is greater between friends than nonfriends (Exline, 1971; Russo, 1975); greater in couples with more enduring relationships than more transient ones (Thayer & Schiff, 1974); and greater for couples who say they are more rather than less in love (Rubin, 1970).

A smile is a sign of friendship, pleasure, and approach. It is the most easily recognizable facial sign when greeting others (LaFrance & Mayo, 1978). The importance of a smile in making a positive impression on others has not been underestimated by salespersons and politicians. Dale Carnegie (1940) cites the simple prescription—SMILE—as one of his six rules of how to make people like you, and he devotes an entire chapter just to smiling! "Actions speak louder than words, and a smile says, 'I like you. You make me happy. I am glad to see you'" (p. 72). Smiling can accomplish the goal of being liked. It has been found that a person who leans forward and smiles is seen as warmer and produces greater responsiveness on the part of the audience than one who leans away and doesn't smile (Reece & Whitman, 1962). A person who smiles and makes eye contact is liked much more by an audience than one who doesn't, even though the audience later can't describe exactly what it was that made them feel the way they did (Holstein, Goldstein, & Bem, 1971).

An insincere, mechanical grin, though, might not fool anyone; the stereotypical example is the smile seemingly drawn on the face of a Miss America contestant. For this reason, Carnegie (1940) stresses that smiles should seem authentic and should express the feeling that you are happy inside. What, then, if you don't feel like smiling? Carnegie says "force yourself to smile" (p. 74). By way of explaining the apparent contradiction, he notes that if people smile they may soon come to feel happy, and the insincere smile will turn into a sincere one. He advises salespersons to whistle a happy tune, think of all the things they have to be thankful for, and hum themselves into a good mood before entering a client's office. After psyching themselves up, they can enter smiling.

Trying to Be Liked

When people are attempting to get others to like them, they use a greater number of nonverbal high-immediacy behaviors. Rosenfeld (1965) told female students that during the course of the experiment they would be interacting with another person. Subjects also were told either that their goal should be to make the other person like them or that their goal was to avoid friendship. It was found that those who were seeking friendship placed their chairs closer to the other than did those who were avoiding friendship.

In a second, more thorough study, Rosenfeld (1966) instructed subjects either to try to make another person like them or to try to make the other realize that they had no interest in being friends (without coming right out and hurting the other's feelings). Same-sexed pairs of subjects then conversed for five minutes, during which time their behaviors were observed and recorded. It was found that females smiled and gesticulated more when seeking friendship than when avoiding it. Males, in contrast, did not differentially smile or gesticulate, but did use more affirmative head nods when seeking than avoiding friendship. Both males and females showed more verbal attentiveness to the other (saying "um-humm" and "really"), talked more frequently, and talked for longer times when they were seeking than avoiding friendship. Although males and females thus differ slightly in their choices of some of the nonverbal indicants of liking, it is clear that both use high-immediacy nonverbal behaviors when they want to be liked.

In a similar study, Lefebvre (1975) instructed some subjects to get another person to like them and others to behave as they normally would. The people who were instructed to seek friendship smiled more and looked at the other more than did those who were not. The experimenters made videotapes of these interactions and showed them to another group of subjects who were asked to evaluate the people. These observers accurately perceived that subjects in the friendship-seeking condition were trying to ingratiate and wanted to be liked. Despite the accurate perception of these motives, though, those who were seeking friendship were still viewed as more charming, warm, and intimate than those who were not. Even when their motives are accurately diagnosed, people who use high-immediacy nonverbal behaviors come across as charming.

Predicting Reactions: Arousal and Liking

If all it took to get others to like us was to stand close to them, touch them, or look them in the eyes for hours on end, interpersonal relations would be much simpler than they are. Certainly, high-immediacy behaviors usually express liking and produce more positive reactions than low-immediacy behaviors. Yet we have all had the experience of having someone sit too close, touch too much, or gaze longingly while we conclude that we are not interested. The *context* of actions affects the reactions of the audience: is the actor violating social norms; is the situation one of cooperation or competition; is the actor handsome or ugly? The context of the action must be considered when predicting how the audience will react and hence the type of impression a particular behavior is likely to create.

Miles Patterson (1976) has proposed an *arousal model* of intimacy that allows us to generate predictions about how others will react to nonverbal behaviors. Patterson hypothesizes that any change in an existing level of intimacy in a relationship produces arousal. For example, suppose that two people are in the midst of a normal conversation. Soon, a particular level of intimacy becomes established. If one of them increases or decreases the intimacy level, by stepping slightly closer, say, or by engaging in more eye contact, the second person experiences an increase in arousal. The arousal is then cognitively labeled by the second person as either positive—liking, atttraction—or negative—disliking, repulsion, *depending on the context of the situation.* A woman who is saying goodnight to her date at the end of a pleasant evening is likely to interpret positively the arousal produced by an increase in his nonverbal immediacy behaviors; she might label it liking or love. On the other hand, if two people are negotiating a contract and one suddenly moves closer and starts staring, the arousal produced by the change is likely to be labeled "dislike" by the other.

It is hypothesized that if the arousal is labeled positive people react with *reciprocation*—that is, by increasing their own intimacy behaviors if the other person has increased his or by decreasing their intimacy behaviors if the other has decreased his. Through such reciprocation, relationships can grow or disintegrate depending on what the other person has done. If the arousal is labeled negative, however, people are hypothesized to react with *compensation*—that is, to engage in intimacy behaviors that reestablish the level that existed before the change. Compensation maintains equilibrium in the relationship (Argyle & Dean, 1965). Thus, if the other moves closer, and one doesn't like him, one might step backward or avert one's eyes.

To the degree that the model allows one accurately to predict, on the basis of one's own nonverbal initiatives, how people are going to react, it is relevant to impression management. First, if people already know the type of affect present in a relationship (positive or negative), they can predict whether any substantive change in their nonverbal immediacy behaviors is going to produce reciprocation or compensation. To employ a grossly simple example, one shouldn't move closer to a date if she is still quite angry (compensation will result), but one should move closer if she feels positive (reciprocation will result). Second, if people don't know the type of affect felt by the other toward them, they can perform a simple test to find out. Move closer to a date or increase eye contact and see if he reciprocates or compensates. One then has an idea of whether he feels positive or negative.

The model is not a complete explanation of all reactions to nonverbal immediacy behaviors—no single model can be—and it still has potential flaws. For example, it focuses exclusively on *reactions* to another's initiatives, yet people's behavior is rarely reaction alone. Others, too, have plans to accomplish goals and can use other people's initiatives in their own plans. This makes their "reaction" an action that is affected by their plans as modified by other people's initiatives. Thus, a female who steps back when her date steps closer may actually like him but be trying to act out the hard-to-get script to make him even more interested. Furthermore, this model seems most suited for interaction situations that don't involve the possibility of confrontation and aggression. In the midst of a heated argument in which physical blows are a possibility, the best way to provoke a fight is to take a step or two closer to an adversary while staring him straight in the eye. Although there is a possibility that he will back down (compensation), it is equally likely that he will reciprocate the action and perhaps swing the first blow. Clearly, the reciprocation in this case is generated by negative, not positive, affect, which is opposite to what the model would predict. Despite these potential flaws, however, the model does integrate a wide variety of data.

As the model would suggest, high levels of eye contact or extreme closeness can produce either positive or negative reactions in an audience. Eye contact seems to intensify whatever feelings are already present toward another (see Kleinke, 1975). For example, in one study, subjects were interviewed by a person who maintained a lot or very little eye contact, and the content of the interview was prearranged to be positive or negative (Ellsworth & Carlsmith, 1968). When the interview content was positive, subjects liked the interviewer who gazed at them more than the one who didn't; but, when the content of the interview was negative, subjects liked the one who avoided rather than sought eye contact.

Similarly, extreme closeness—interpersonal distances that violate people's cultural assumptions about the appropriate spacing in a given type of relationship—produces arousal and seems to intensify whatever feelings are already present in the relationship (Patterson, 1976; Schiffenbauer & Schiavo, 1976; Storms & Thomas, 1977). For example, people will turn away and pull in their elbows if a stranger comes up and sits close to them. If the stranger persists in the aberrant behavior, they will ultimately get up and leave (Sommer, 1969). When personal space is invaded by a stranger, people display more agonistic facial responses and less positive moods than they otherwise would (Efran & Cheyne, 1974). In contrast, people do appreciate closeness when the other is liked to begin with (see Kleinke, 1975).

Alternative Tactics: To Be Liked or Disliked

The most popular tactic for selling something, either a product or yourself, is to make the buyers like you (Carnegie, 1940). As we've seen, one of the most effective ways of doing that is for a person to make them believe that he is interested in and likes them. As Mehrabian (1971a, p. 122) notes, this is the "straightforward positive approach," and it can be implemented by using high-immediacy behaviors like smiles, eye contact, and forward lean. Door-to-door salespersons usually employ this technique. As people open the door they are greeted by a big smile, a lot of eye contact, rapid and well-rehearsed lines (to increase persuasiveness), questions about them and their family—every trick possible to show interest in and liking for the potential customer. If the tactic succeeds, they will become the owner of whatever commodity was being sold. During romantic encounters, people can display high-immediacy body language, such as touching the other, "accidently" sliding close to the other when the car rounds a turn, smiling and laughing, asking questions about the other's life and interests, and so on. Reciprocation and increased liking should follow.

Alternatively, Mehrabian notes that people sometimes attempt to increase liking by using the "aloof and unconcerned" approach—playing hard-to-get, so to speak. In business, the tactic is typified by the high-priced store whose sales personnel ignore the customers and seem quite uninterested in them. The message is conveyed that "we don't need you because this merchandise is good enough to sell itself." In some isolated cases, the tactic is pushed to the point of being disrespectful to customers, challenging them with the unspoken assertion that they are not good enough for the merchandise, if they can even afford it. Customers are then tempted to prove the sellers wrong. In romance, many people adopt the hard-to-get routine. They attempt to show that they are discriminating individuals: most people are not good enough for them; if you think you are you are welcome to try, but don't expect much encouragement. By communicating that you must prove yourself, rather than vice-versa, the discriminating individual both challenges people to the task and makes himself or herself appear to be rare and worthwhile. The aloofness tactic is a subcomponent of a strategy mentioned earlier—making oneself attractive by claiming images that significant others are believed to admire and like, in this case that of being discriminating.

The work of social scientists sometimes leaves the impression that people have only one major goal as far as liking is concerned—to increase the amount that others like them. This is hardly true. In many situations, people believe that their goals can best be achieved by being disliked by certain others. Examples are numerous. Some military officers believe that fear is the best motivator of men: "I want my men to fear me, not love me." High school bullies often believe that their threats are most credible when others fear and dislike them. In such cases, people engage in body language that communicates images of power and dislike.

NONVERBAL BEHAVIOR AND DECEPTION: THE CONCEALMENT AND DETECTION GAME

Sigmund Freud (1905/1959) said that "no mortal can keep a secret. If his lips are silent, he chatters with his fingertips; betrayal oozes out of him at every pore." Psychotherapist Fritz Perls (quoted in Fast, 1971, p. 166) remarked "I disregard most of the content of what the patient says and concentrate mostly on the nonverbal level, as this is the only one which is less subject to self-deception." Erving Goffman (1959) distinguished between expressions *given*, which are intentionally conveyed images that serve the goals of the actor, and expressions *given off*, which are images that don't seem to be governed by conscious monitoring and are conveyed primarily by nonverbal behavior. Goffman believes that audiences attend more closely to images that are given off than they do to those that are given, since the former are more likely to reflect the true state of the actor.

Is it true that the body doesn't know how to lie? Only in part. People can and do teach it to lie, and some people do a better job than others. When people are asked what behavior should be censored or controlled when attempting to deceive others, they mention facial expressions more than any other nonverbal cue (Ekman & Friesen, 1974). The face is what people attend to most during interactions, so it makes sense that this would be the first body area people think about when contemplating deception. Given this common knowledge, it should come as no surprise that liars are usually quite adept at controlling facial expressions that might suggest deceit. Facial expressions do not seem to serve as particularly accurate cues for detecting deception (Ekman & Friesen, 1969, 1974). After all, deceivers know the same truisms about lying that other people do: "Liars won't look you in the eye," "Liars have silly smiles on their faces," "Liars have guilty expressions," and so on. They can concentrate to insure that such cues don't give them away. In reviewing research on eye contact, smiling, and other facial expressions, LaFrance and Mayo (1978, p. 115) concluded that "facial cues don't seem to be too helpful in detecting deception."

Although people are successful at censoring facial expressions, cues to deceit leak through their guard in other areas. Nonverbal indicants of stress and anxiety seem to be the single most important class of cues related to deception. People who are lying as compared to those who are not have been found to engage in less frequent body movements, talk more slowly, exhibit more speech errors, and turn or lean away from their audience (Mehrabian, 1971c); engage in more self-touching, such as placing their hands to their face (Ekman & Friesen, 1974); be more hesitant in their speech (Harrison, Hwalek, Raney, & Fritz, 1978); have longer latencies when responding (Kraut, 1978); and use higher pitched voices (Streeter, Krauss, Geller, Olson, & Apple, 1977). All of these nonverbal behaviors are concomitants of stress.

It has also been suggested that "deceivers do too little or too much of what most people do when telling the truth" (LaFrance & Mayo, 1978, p. 115). Some studies find that liars talk more than nonliars (Harrison et al., 1978), others find they talk less (Kraut, 1978; Mehrabian, 1971c); and some find that liars smile more (Mehrabian, 1971c), while others find they smile less (McClintock & Hunt, 1975). In all likelihood, the skills of the actor and the context of the situation affect whether people who are lying will talk, smile, gesture, and so on more or less than people who aren't and whether their audience will even notice.

Unfortunately for the virtuous, deceit is not even as easy to detect as some of the above might suggest. First, audiences often have to attend quite closely to notice any difference between truth and falsity. For instance, although liars do speak in higher pitches than nonliars, listeners don't ordinarily seem to use such cues. They do so primarily when the semantic content of speech is artificially obliterated through laboratory machines and all they have left to listen to are the paralinguistic aspects (Streeter et al., 1977). Thus, audiences often miss cues that might signal deception. Second, the more an actor rehearses the part and concentrates on hiding deceit, the better the ensuing performance is likely to be—it may be virtually impossible to detect falsehoods without the aid of special equipment. For example, although an audience can recognize deceit through nonverbal cues when an actor is secretly videotaped while lying over an impersonal intercom, they are unable to do so when the actor is engaging in face-to-face interaction with another person from whom he is attempting to hide the deceptions (Krauss, Geller, & Olson, 1976). The whole point of professional acting is to take the role of another person and to do it in a way that convinces the audience that you *are* that person. The best actors are known for their versatility—they can convincingly claim a wide array of images. Just as professional actors can bring down the house with applause, so can amateurs in life's theater.

The idea of detecting lies through stress cues, of reading another person's mind, so to speak, when they are doing their best to hide their real feelings, has tremendous commercial appeal. So much the better if the person whose feelings are being probed is completely unaware of one's ability to get at the truth. Devices that purport to do just this are reaping dividends for their manufacturers. The "Hagoth" is a voice-stress analyzer that "purportedly measures changes in inaudible microtremors of the voice in order to detect when someone is lying" (Kleinfield, 1978). The device functions when attached to a telephone, and it is impossible for the person on the other end of the line to know that it is being used. It is about the size of a portable tape recorder, has eight green lights to indicate no stress and eight red lights to indicate stress, and sells for $1500. Questions can be raised about whether the instrument violates rights to privacy. Indeed, some states have laws that seem to make its use illegal. But it is used. For one thing, its use is virtually impossible to detect, so it is difficult to enforce such laws. For another, reasonable arguments can be raised to justify its use. Richard Bennett, the president and founder of the company that makes the device, believes that "This is no more an invasion of privacy than watching eye movements or analyzing handwriting. Everyone has the right to see if someone is smoking him or not."

Before worrying about whether the instrument is being used against you or boggling your mind with possible applications, it should be pointed out that the reliability and validity of the device are far from clear. If an identical voice tape is played through several times, different readings often result. Nonetheless, the company seems to have many satisfied customers (although most don't want their names to become public and have threatened to sue the company if their identities become known). One user remarked

> I use it to negotiate contracts. There have been instances where I would have settled for less money but the machine suggested I should press further and I wound up with a better deal. It's not a cure-all. You have to know how to interpret it. It's another club in the old golf bag.

Incidentally, some of the machines are bought by lawyers, psychologists, and movie stars, but most are purchased by people in big business, usually "heads of corporations with sales exceeding $10,000,000." The game of concealment and detection has endless variations.

SUMMARY

Nonverbal behaviors can be effectively employed to build and maintain images of oneself during social interaction. Their subtle impact on an audience often makes them a first choice among skilled impression managers when contemplating self-presentational devices. Body language, space-use behaviors, and paralanguage express feelings and images on the two major dimensions of social interaction—power and evaluation. These expressions can be controlled, consciously or through habit, to create particular impressions on an audience. Nonverbal behaviors that seem to express power-relevant images like status, dominance, and competence include maintaining relaxed but erect postures, exhibiting dynamic movements and gestures, using steady nonshifting gazes with less overall visual attentiveness, aggressively touching, maintaining larger personal spaces and territories, freely appropriating the territories of others, taking prominent seating positions, and employing powerful styles of speech. Nonverbal behaviors that are closely associated with expressions of liking include interpersonal closeness, forward body lean, direct head and body orientations, open body positions (for females), eye contact, smiling, affirmative head nods, and attentive paralanguage. These lists will undoubtedly be enlarged as research accumulates. The Association Principle allows us to deduce that people who are attempting to claim images that are relevant to interpersonal power or evaluation will engage in more of the associated nonverbal behaviors than people who are not.

N I N E

Judge not according to the Appearance.

John 7:24

It may be true that beauty is only skin deep, but the fact remains that the world judges you on appearance a great deal of the time.

Michael Korda

APPEARANCE, PROPS, AND SCENERY

People are judged by their appearance. We sometimes regret it and protest that such is not the way things should be; no one, however, argues that the assertion is incorrect. The human tendency to judge by appearance is sufficiently ingrained that one of the writers of the New Testament felt compelled to prescribe against it, perhaps in the hope that through conscious effort people could overcome it. Although people may attempt to guard against judgment by appearance, they cannot entirely eliminate it.

As soon as other people are encountered, we form some impressions of what they are like, how they are likely to behave, and how they should be treated. Everyone has stereotypes about others based on their hair color, eye color, complexion, race, sex, height, weight, clothes, jewelry, possessions, place of residence, home furnishings, and so on. Personal appearance, props, and scenery provide a major basis for identity.

As we will employ the term, *personal appearance* is composed of a person's physical features, makeup, and wardrobe. Physical features include the "natural" attractiveness of facial characteristics, body shape, and body proportions. Makeup consists of face and body enhancers (or, depending on your point of view, detractors) such as cosmetics and wigs. Wardrobe includes clothes and other body adornments that are physically secured to people, such as jewelry. *Props* are movable objects that affect a performance and might project relevant symbolic information. Props include a vast array of items such as briefcases, pipes, furniture, trophies, automobiles, friends, pets, wall hangings, books, records, sports equipment, and so on. *Scenery* consists of relatively permanent backdrops for performances, such as one's home, office, and places most frequented (bars, libraries, restaurants, churches, or whatever).

According to the Association Principle, people attempt to control their identities by claiming desirable images and disclaiming undesirable ones. It follows that personal appearance, props and scenery will be controlled and selected, within the limits of one's abilities and resources, to establish and support images. As writers of our own personal plays, the story lines we act out must be supported by what we believe are appropriate appearances, props, and scenic backgrounds. Inconsistencies between (a) verbal and nonverbal behavior and (b) personal appearance, props, and scenery are likely to cast doubt on the validity of the entire performance. No writer would place a naked clergyman in the bed of a prostitute unless he wanted to demonstrate to the audience the hypocrisy of the character. No writer would attire a supposedly devoted housewife and mother in a short and revealing dress, with heavy makeup usually reserved for ladies of the evening, and situate her in a singles bar, unless she wanted to make a point about her double life. True, people sometimes find themselves in such compromising situations. But people recognize that such inconsistencies refute the remainder of their projected identities, and they try to keep any such inconsistent information about themselves from coming to the attention of their usual audiences.

PERSONAL APPEARANCE

Personal appearance conveys an immediate impression of a person to an audience. Tom Landry, the highly successful coach of the Dallas Cowboys football team, always wears a suit, tie, and hat on the field during football games, which is in dramatic contrast to the way many coaches look. When asked why he takes such pains to establish an immaculate appearance, he responded "I've always felt the way you look is a perfect indication of what you represent. . . . Since we don't have the chance to meet our fans, they'll know what we are by the way we look." Landry clearly expresses the identity he wants to convey through his personal appearance, as do we all. Different people desire different identities, but, given the identity selected, personal appearance is controlled as much as possible to express it. Even though it is not wise to judge a book solely by its cover, advertisers know that books are made or broken by the appeal of their exteriors.

It is often said that looks can be deceiving, which is not surprising given the amount of time, energy, and money people expend attempting to create desirable impressions. The fashion and cosmetic industry is a multi-billion dollar enterprise around the world. Contemplate for a moment the lengths people go to in order to control their appearances: hair styling, wigs, makeup, tanning lotions and lamps, perfumes and deodorants, clothes, shoes, jewelry, contact lenses, false eyelashes and nails, body padding, girdles, and even cosmetic surgery. Ads for health spas, health foods, exercise programs, and exercise paraphernalia stress not only that users feel better but that they *look* better; the latter often takes precedence over the former in the design of the ad and the motivation of the patrons.

The modern Western world has no monopoly on fashion and the control of personal appearance. In ancient Egypt the hot climate permitted few clothes, so people from the upper classes concentrated on magnificent jewelry (some beyond today's craft standards) and face and body makeup as means of accentuating their social class and attractiveness (Durant, 1935). Every society around the world has some form of dress, makeup, or body features that they recognize as conveying attractiveness and status. These include various types of body painting, nose and ear rings, tattooing, and even more extreme alteration of natural features, as by inserting increasingly larger disks in the lips to produce a platter-shaped effect or by manipulating parts of the body to enlarge or otherwise modify them. In China, until well into the 20th century, young girls from the upper classes usually had their feet physically bound in infancy to constrain growth; tiny feet were considered fashionable. During the Victorian era in Western society, women forced themselves into painful corsets, which actually moved flesh around permanently and misplaced internal organs, in order to have the fashionable appearance of a small waist.

Personal appearance affects how people are regarded and treated both by themselves and others. People believe they can tell a great deal about a person on the basis of appearance alone. For example, people believe they can judge the personality, occupation, morality, hobbies, and educational level of someone from just their clothing (Gibbins, 1969). Similarly, people believe that physical attractiveness reveals much more about a person than merely looks (Berscheid & Walster, 1974; Kleinke, 1975). A what-is-beautiful-is-good attitude exists, particularly regarding females. Physically attractive people are assumed to possess a multitude of other attributes that are also socially desirable. Physically attractive people, compared to their less fortunate peers, are judged by audiences as more sexually warm, responsive, curious, complex, sensitive, perceptive, kind, interesting, confident, assertive, strong, poised, happy, amiable, sociable, modest, candid, serious, outgoing, pleasure-seeking, and flexible, and they are expected to procure better jobs, to marry better, and to live happier, more fulfilling lives. Attractive children are even evaluated by teachers as having higher intelligence than unattractive ones, a bias that might be self-fulfilling if it causes teachers to spend more of their time with the former. Although the enormous inferential leaps that people are willing to make about others on the basis of appearance alone should give one pause, they should hardly come as much of a surprise.

Personal appearance clearly affects the outcomes people receive from others. People whose appearances please rather than displease others are better liked, can exert greater influence over others' behaviors, have their actions interpreted and evaluated in a more positive manner, and therefore are more likely to receive a favorable reward/cost ratio. All else equal, people with pleasing personal appearances are better liked by others than those whose appearances are plain or unattractive (Berscheid & Walster, 1974). In dating relationships, for instance, physical appearance often takes precedence over personality and behavioral attributes. People usually profess to be looking for a wide variety of qualities in those they date, like friendliness, intelligence, maturity, and so on. However, one study found that when college couples are matched randomly for a "computer date," the single most important determinant of how much they liked their partner by the end of the evening was the partner's physical attractiveness—all other qualities that were measured were found to be totally unrelated to liking (Berscheid & Walster, 1974).

Physical attractiveness recedes in importance as relationships grow (Berscheid & Walster, 1974) and other qualities become more salient; no relationship can survive on appearance alone. Yet no matter what stage a relationship is in, appearances are never completely disregarded. Appearances still must be kept up or eventually the audience will discard the old constructs used to describe the actor and replace them with new and more accurate ones, which may generate less liking. Successful marriages are usually ones in which the partners care enough about one another that they don't abandon all concern for their personal appearances. They attempt to please one another with not only their behaviors but their looks. True, they will not always be on their best behavior or look the way they would for a night on the town. But a husband who never shaves or combs his hair on weekends, sits around in his underwear, allows beer to drip from his mouth to his post-nuptially acquired potbelly, and speaks to his wife only to request delivery of another sandwich will shatter any illusions she might have had about the man she married. Appearances can never be totally disregarded without dire consequences, even in supposedly long-term relationships.

People whose personal appearances are attractive have an advantage in being able to influence others; their attractiveness gives them greater social power. More attractive people find that audiences care more about their feelings, are more persuaded by their words, model their behaviors, follow their leads, and conform more to their presumed wishes (Lefkowitz, Blake, & Mouton, 1955; Mills & Aronson, 1965; Schlenker, 1975b; Sigall & Aronson, 1969; Sigall, Page, & Brown, 1971; Tedeschi et al., 1973). When people encounter situations in which they want to exert influence, they usually take extra precautions to insure that their personal appearance will be viewed as attractive by their audience. Examples include the concern for appearance that most people demonstrate before a date or job interview.

Identical actions are interpreted and evaluated differently depending on the personal appearance of the actor. In general, people whose personal appearances are more attractive discover that their actions are viewed in a more positive and socially desirable manner. For example, Landy and Sigall (1974) found that a writer's work was evaluated more favorably when the writer was more physically attractive, and this difference was greatest when the work was objectively poor. Children who misbehave are seen by both adults and peers as less naughty if they are attractive rather than unattractive (Berscheid & Walster, 1974). The effect of personal appearance extends even to serious crimes. One study (Sigall & Ostrove, 1975) found that defendants in a simulated criminal case received more lenient sentences from subject-jurors if their appearance was attractive rather than unattractive, but, interestingly, only if the crime was of a type in which their physical attractiveness was not useful in procuring their ill-gotten gains. If the defendant was charged with burglary (unrelated to attractiveness), a physically attractive perpetrator was given the more lenient sentence; but if the crime was a swindle (related to attractiveness), the physically attractive defendant received the more severe sentence. People will punish physically attractive people who use this asset to violate society's laws. Given the benefits that we grant attractive people, it is no wonder that audiences invoke stiff penalties against people who abuse those privileges.

Personal appearance also affects how people feel about themselves and how they are likely to behave. People who are satisfied with their physical appearance are also more satisfied with other aspects of their personalities and lives (Berscheid & Walster, 1974). Such correlational data do not prove that an attractive personal appearance produces greater personal satisfaction, but the hypothesis is reasonable. As the old saying goes: if you want to feel like a winner, look like a winner. It is sometimes remarkable to notice the change that comes over people when they wear a new suit of clothes or new piece of jewelry. People can't act the part they wish to play without looking the part; and when they look a part, they tend to act it. Clothes do make the man or woman.

The most successful Broadway producer during the first decades of the twentieth century was Florence Ziegfeld. His Ziegfeld Follies gained their reputation because of their success in being able to "glorify the American girl." Ziegfeld "repeatedly took some drab little creature that no one ever looked at twice and transformed her on the stage into a glamorous vision of mystery and seduction" (Carnegie, 1940, p. 37). He made actresses *feel* the parts they played by adorning them in gorgeous costumes and placing them in lavishly decorated stage scenes. To increase their feelings of importance, he sent opening night telegrams to his stars and inundated all of the performers with American Beauty roses and higher than normal salaries. When he finished, the aura induced around the actresses could not help but obtain the behavior he desired.

Personal appearance seems to be so important in affecting interpersonal relationships and feelings about oneself that psychotherapists are beginning to recommend the use of cosmetic surgery for patients who are troubled by their natural physical features (Berscheid & Walster, 1974). For example, an unattractive and rejected woman who worries about her inability to locate a husband may have her problems solved more easily by plastic surgery than by time-consuming, expensive, long-lasting psychotherapeutic sessions. Further, it has been found that ex-prisoners have lower recidivism rates, better job success, and improved self-concepts when unsightly physical characteristics (scars, disfigured noses) are corrected through surgery. Physical disfigurement has long been associated with social deviance (Berscheid & Walster, 1974). Changing the physical features can produce a corresponding transformation of behavior.

People's concerns about controlling appearance constantly show up in letters to advice columnists ("Should I wear a padded bra?"

"What attire is appropriate for a wedding?" "Should I have a face lift?")
and as chapters in popular how-to-do-it books. For example, Korda
(1977) devotes nearly a chapter to describing the types of clothes men
and women should wear if they want to be successful in the business
world. His basic hypothesis about dress is that "Your object is to set
yourself apart from other people in a quiet, dignified but unmistakable
manner, and to show that you are a winner" (p. 137). People then demonstrate sufficient conformity to group standards to be identified as a
part of the group while concomitantly demonstrating uniqueness that
displays the potential for leadership. Korda (1976, 1977) lists the brand
names that are currently "in," describes the ways clothes should be
tailored (the proper length for pants legs, the way a suit collar should fit
around a man's neck), and describes the kinds of shirts, ties, handker-
chiefs, belts, shoes, socks, and hats that should be worn. His attention to
detail is impressive. For women in the business world, he similarly lists
recommended apparel and notes that bright colors, tight pants suits,
short skirts, "fussy" clothes, and plunging necklines should be avoided
at all costs if one wants to overcome traditional feminine stereotypes.
He also strongly advises against long, lacquered fingernails, since they
generally make businesswomen "look as if they're incapable of performing any real work. . . . They represent a male-imposed symbol of sexual
possession—the proof that a woman is being kept and therefore doesn't
need to work" (1977, p. 147). He further notes "It's a small point, but the
kind of thing that gets noticed." Korda's remarks naturally represent
only his personal opinions, but they do illustrate the images that people
have of particular personal appearances and the degree of detail to
which people resort in order to create the "right" impression through
their appearance.

Virtually all images carry liabilities, at least in terms of the costs of
acquiring them and holding them. In attempting to build up an extensive and expensive wardrobe complete with mink coat and jewels, a
woman might drive herself into the poorhouse. Acquiring a pleasing
figure may take months of distressing dieting. Plastic surgery can be
both expensive and painful. People must weigh for themselves the costs
of acquiring an image against the perceived long-term benefits.

Eating is a topic that often isn't considered as within the purview
of impression management, perhaps because we all have to do it. Yet
there is a wide range of preference for particular types of food, amounts
to be eaten, and places to eat. Such selections can be judiciously
employed for impression-management purposes. Health food advocates
claim that, because of what they eat, they feel better, live longer, and
have more energy. They often claim to be more intelligent, more
dynamic, and in better condition than the average individual. Gourmets
delight in displaying their knowledge and talent by impressing others
with their choice of wines and their ability to name each of the spices

contained in their continental meals. Korda (1977) advises people in business to eat properly to keep up their energy and believes that "Successful people tend to eat sparingly during the day, not just to keep slim but to avoid that after-lunch slump that extends, in many cases, to quitting time" (p. 79). Stuffing oneself with an enormous meal with two double martinis is an almost certain way to debilitate oneself for several hours. Another example of eating in order to *avoid* certain types of impressions is the case of the British royal family, who eat low-bulk foods and drink little prior to important public appearances, thereby avoiding having to relieve themselves at inopportune times. Similarly, dieters bear the costs of their unappealing meals in order to avoid the appearance they know they would display if they ate what they wanted.

People who are dissatisfied with their appearance confront the dilemma of leaving "nature" alone versus attempting to claim more appealing images.The latter can be achieved either through the purchase of appearance modifiers like padded bras, wigs, elevator shoes, and girdles or by resorting to cosmetic surgery. The dilemma arises because many, perhaps most, people view such modifiers as phony attempts to try to be something one is not. When discovered, audiences often censure the actor's unsuccessful attempt through ridicule and lowered evaluations. According to letters to Dear Abby, many women who are dismayed by their small bust size would like to wear padded bras but fear that doing so would cause others to think less of them. Naturally, times change and so do people's beliefs about the appropriateness of particular appearance modifiers. Wigs go in and out of fashion; padded behinds (bustles), once the rage for women, now seem ridiculous. Further, beliefs about appropriateness are likely to differ for males and females. It is currently acceptable, for instance, for women to wear wigs, while male wig wearers are often kidded. Though perhaps overstating the case, Korda (1977, p. 135) warns men in business and politics "If there is the slightest chance that your wig will be noticed or even suspected, don't do it. Once you have been caught as a wig wearer, nobody is likely to trust you about anything else. It will be the only thing most people remember about you." As with all public claims to images, people must balance the expected worth of a successful claim against the expected negative sanctions of an unsuccessful one when deciding whether to proceed with appearance modification.

People can also control the impressions others form of them simply by associating publicly with people who are attractive and avoiding those who are unattractive. In Chapter 4 we discussed how people attempt to Bask in Reflected Glory by associating themselves with desirable people and events. The personal appearance of one's associates produces the same "rub off" effect. If an actor has a physically attractive spouse or date, for example, onlookers are likely to assume that he or she *must* have highly desirable attributes, even if these attributes are not evident on the surface. A rather average-looking man who has a beautiful woman dangling on his arm might be assumed by the audience to have an excellent personality or be rich, intelligent, or whatever. Why else would the attractive partner match up with him? Male and female professional escort services stay in business because they fill people's desires to be seen with, and hence associated with, attractive people.

Sigall and Landy (1973) demonstrated the association effect. In their first study, subjects were asked to evaluate an average looking male who had earlier been in the presence of a female who was either physically attractive ("tastefully dressed and made up to accentuate her natural good looks") or unattractive ("she wore an unbecoming wig, no makeup, and unflattering clothes"). It was made clear to the subjects either that the female was the girlfriend of the male or that she didn't know the male and was merely in the waiting room to meet someone else. It was found that subjects later expressed the most favorable overall impression of the male when he was described as the boyfriend of the attractive female; they expressed the least favorable impression of him when he was said to be the boyfriend of the unattractive female. A second study demonstrated that people do recognize that their choice of associates is going to affect how they are evaluated by others. Males believed they would be evaluated more favorably by observers if they were associated with an attractive female and less favorably if they were associated with an unattractive female. Indeed, male students even state that the main reason they do not like to be seen with an overweight female is fear of ridicule (Cahnman, 1968).

The association effect is sufficiently salient and dreaded by most people that anecdotes abound about how plain or unattractive partners are taken to dark deserted places where they won't be seen and how clandestine meetings in a motel room are set up after making it clear that each party must come from different directions and enter separately. (Of course, the unattractiveness of the partner may not be the only reason for employing such subterfuges.) Milder forms of such tactics are also observed. An individual might walk down the street next to a plain date while doing everything possible to avoid holding hands and making every effort to appear as if their close proximity was merely coincidental, such as by gazing in every direction but that of the partner or even walking a few steps in front or behind.

PROPS, SCENERY, AND SYMBOLS

Props and scenery communicate information about actors and can be judiciously used to add just the right touches to performances. A person who wants to display a "macho" identity might decorate his den with guns, gun racks, and mounted animal heads. A college professor might line the shelves of her office with hundreds of books, whether she reads them or not, thus allowing visitors to draw the conclusion that she must be sagacious. Doctors not only display medical books in their offices, but hang their diplomas, certificates, and awards (even if they are only for civic contributions) about in order to establish and substantiate claims to competence. Many people buy diplomas from fake diploma mills, where for anywhere from $25 to several hundred dollars they can acquire the "proof" of their expertise. The images people want to claim are usually readily apparent from just a quick look around their homes, dorm rooms, or offices.

Robert Ringer (1976) described how he created his own "Image Power" in the business world through the use of props. He was a land broker, a middleman who linked up buyers and sellers. He observed that after a deal was consummated he was no longer needed by the principals, so the seller would usually attempt to whittle down his fees or simply not pay him. Naturally, sellers would not pay him in advance because there was no guarantee that he would be able to sell their property, so he was caught in a bind. Believing that his skills and service more than justified the fees he asked, he concluded that he needed something more than just the ability to perform his job excellently. Contemplating what he knew about successful people, he found the answer.

> I realized that these people had something else going for them: image. I could no longer operate as "only a broker;" I had to have an image that would be awesome to the principals I worked with. They had to respect me so much that they would feel I—like wealthy people—had a "right" to earn big money [p. 125].[1]

He came to believe that "it's not what you say or do that counts, but what your posture is when you say or do it" (p. 124). He went to work on building a strong posture.

The first thing he did was to have a special calling card made up. It was an impressive brochure that cost about $5.00 per copy, measured 10″ by 10″, had a hard cover comparable to a book, and opened from the bottom to top instead of the more common right to left. In the middle of the glossy black cover was a "full-color photo of the earth as seen from an Apollo spaceship" (p. 144). He did not put his name on the front cover or even on the first page, the better to build suspense in the curious recipient. Upon opening the booklet, readers were greeted with these words:

[1]From *Winning through Intimidation*, by R. J. Ringer. Copyright © 1974 by Robert J. Ringer. (New York: Fawcett Books Group, a division of CBS Publications 1976.) This and all other quotations from this source are reprinted by permission.

Earth
To Life .... Support
To the Explorer .... A Base
To the Wise .... An Investment [p. 145]

The remainder of the booklet was equally elaborate and intimidating. When he first contacted prospective clients by telephone, he told them that he would send them some information about himself, and he forwarded the brochure. Recipients rarely threw it away, virtually never thereafter asked who he was or what his credentials were, and apparently concluded that he *must* be someone important. After carefully screening prospective clients to make sure that a deal was potentially profitable, he arranged a face-to-face meeting. He arrived in his private Lear jet accompanied by two or more secretaries. To heighten further the intimidating aura, he walked into a client's office with his *own* traveling office, with the secretaries transporting calculators, typewriters, mortgage rate books, extension cords, and a plethora of other equipment. He thus not only insured having everything he needed, but also tried to leave no doubt that here was a man to be taken seriously. Ringer attributes the use of these and other impression-management tactics to making the difference between his former modest income and a reported first-year gross after image building of $850,000.

People in business, the military, politics, social services, and even science usually resort to packaging their ideas in impressive demonstrations, replete with slides, graphs, models, and printed handouts. The strategy has its advantages. Shaw and Margulis (1974) point out that, "The mere fact that a communication is printed gives it an aura of significance, importance, and value that may have little to do with the quality of the communication" (p. 301). They had graduate students in psychology and college undergraduates read a scientific article that was packaged either in printed form, as it would appear in a journal, or in a mimeographed form that was merely typed by a secretary. When asked later for their evaluations of the article, those who read it in printed form rated it as more important than those who read it in mimeographed form. Whether the respondents were graduate students or undergraduates made no difference.

Titles are a type of symbolic prop that announces to audiences that the holder is someone important. History is replete with famous people who attempted to gain prestigious titles (Carnegie, 1940, p. 33): George Washington wanted to be referred to as "His Mightiness, the President of the United States;" Columbus asked for the title "Admiral of the Ocean and Viceroy of India;" Catherine the Great would not open any letter unless it was addressed to "Her Imperial Majesty." A title serves as public recognition that a person has a legitimate right to claim some highly attractive image. The holder no longer has to worry about proving himself to others. Many organizations capitalize on people's desires for recognition by using titles to reward members in lieu of tangibles such as money. Many businesses also use titles to impress clients. For example, a complaint department can be reorganized under a person who is given the title Chairman of the Executive Committee. When angry clients call in with complaints, they quickly become docile upon learning that *they* are thought enough of to be put in direct contact with such an important person (Townsend, 1971).

APPEARANCE AND POLITICS

Politics and public impression management have been linked throughout history. Machiavelli's 16th century advice to his prince is replete with recommendations about how princes should manage their public images to maximize their postures and power. One of the most detailed treatises on public impression management in a political context was Castiglione's *Il Cortegiano* (The Courtier), originally printed in 1514. Castiglione was an Italian contemporary of Machiavelli; his work shaped a profession and affected all the courts of Europe for centuries (Anglo, 1977). Castiglione gave definitive form to the image of the ideal courtier, who was an advisor and confidant of princes. To be successful, the courtier must appear to be praiseworthy, knowledgeable, articulate, cultivated, and skilled as a warrior. To assist enterprising courtiers in accomplishing their goals, Castiglione gave specific advice about how they should look, dress, speak, and occupy their time. He listed specific skills they should acquire, brave deeds they should perform, techniques they should use to flatter others, and occasions on which they should be braggartly or modest. For example, Castiglione believed that "Reputation is of paramount importance, and when the courtier is required to venture where he is unknown, he must help himself with wit and art so that 'there goes first a good opinion of him before he comes in person' " (Anglo, 1977, p. 42). When speaking, the courtier should recognize that "Particularly valuable in impressing people is the art of conversation; and it is suggested that when the courtier is required to speak on some topic he should, whenever possible, prepare himself in advance while pretending 'the whole to be done extempore' " (p. 42). When discussing topics about which he has meager knowledge, he should skirt and dart in such a fashion that his audience comes to the conclusion that he " 'hath a great deal more cunning therein than he uttereth.' Only when entirely ignorant is the courtier to confess it—and then only because he might be caught out and lose reputation" (p. 42). Ultimately, the goal of the courtier was to "ingratiate himself with his prince in order to influence him toward virtue;" coincidentally, the skilled courtier might also "ingratiate himself with his paramour in order to obtain her favours" (p. 43).

Castiglione met with abundant criticism from those who were repulsed by the affected style of life he described. When carried to such extremes, the courtier became nothing more than "a ceremonial puppet" (Anglo, 1977). Appearance, manners, and staging seemed to triumph over substance. It was a world of public impression management at its most conscious and tactical. In short, it was a life in which there were constant discrepancies between public and private claims, and the job of the courtier was to please the public while hiding the discrepancies.

Successful contemporary politicians still must be good at the art of public impression management. This is not to say that there are always discrepancies between their public and private beliefs; as with people in general, there are some politicians for whom there are frequent discrepancies and some for whom discrepancies occur only on occasion. It is to say, however, that, to be successful, politicians must advertise themselves and their ideas in ways that win support from a large segment of the public. Given the nature of the profession, politicians must be concerned about their public images.

Politicians are acutely aware of the power of public images, particularly since the advent of television. Prior to television, a political leader could focus on words, knowing that the print media reported *what* was said but often ignored the way it was said. Only the relatively few who saw the politician could react to the appearance and style of the orator. Television brought the style and appearance of the politician into people's homes, and they were then impressed (favorably or unfavorably) with that appearance, perhaps more than by substance. Ever since 1952—the first presidential election year following the widespread proliferation of television sets in America—presidential candidates have hired advertising firms to assist in building and sustaining their public images. The theatrical aspect of political campaigning reached a peak in Richard Nixon's 1968 presidential quest. In the book *The Selling of the President 1968* Joe McGinniss (1970) vividly chronicled the strategies. Nixon and his advisors, many from Madison Avenue advertising firms, believed that politics had "always been a con game" (p. 19) and sought to perfect the fine points. Going into the campaign, Nixon's reputation was not without flaws (such as the nickname "Tricky Dicky"), so one of their major goals was to seek improvement "not upon Nixon himself, but upon the image of him which was received by the voter" (p. 19). The backbone of the campaign was a reliance on television as a propaganda vehicle, based on the hypothesis that "On television it matters less that he [the politician] does not have ideas. His personality is what the viewers want to share. He need be neither statesman nor crusader. . . . Style becomes substance. The medium is the massage and the masseur gets the votes" (pp. 22–23). In massaging the public, Nixon and his advisors believed that they had to make use of personal images rather than concrete ideas. They felt that the public's reactions to candidates "tend to be more a gut reaction, unarticulated, non-analytical, a product of the particular chemistry between the voter and the *image* of the candidate. *We have to be very clear on this point: that the response is to the image, not to the man . . .*" (McGinniss, p. 31). The advertising men who ran Nixon's campaign saw it as pure art, the culmination of everything then known about the skills of public impression management. One assistant even showed copies of some of their television spots to representatives of the Museum of Modern Art in the hope that an exhibit could be built around them—the idea was rejected, coldly. Despite the rebuff, the Nixon camp still viewed their strategies as major innovations that would change the face of politics forever. Detractors termed his campaign deceptive, slick, trite, and theatrical.

One of the techniques used to great advantage was to create hour-long television encounters between Nixon and "the people," more accurately, between Nixon and about a half-dozen carefully selected individuals who queried him about his personal views in front of a studio audience. This "Man in the Arena" concept, as his advertising men called it, was designed to make him appear to be dynamic, vital, spontaneous, decisive, unafraid of hard questions, and able to think on his feet. Actually, the shows were carefully planned. Panels of questioners were selected with care, insuring that they would be of the type to ask easy questions and would contain a suitable proportion of women and minority group members. Nixon was prepared with pat answers to key questions that invariably popped up; he frequently recited his memorized responses even when questions were only remotely relevant. The scenery was set with precision. For instance, although a stage director had originally hung turquoise curtains in the background, the advertising men had them removed, remarking that Nixon "wouldn't look right unless he was carrying a pocketbook" (McGinniss, p. 60). They substituted plain wood panels to provide "clean, solid, masculine lines" in the background. Makeup was used to tone down Nixon's omnipresent "five o'clock shadow," and he carried a handkerchief soaked with witch hazel to wipe perspiration from his face. Audience applause was staged and cued, and the audience was instructed to swarm around Nixon at the end of the taping sessions, leaving the home viewer with the feeling that everyone loves Nixon to the point of euphoria. Reporters, who were expected to show antagonism toward the theatrics, were *not* permitted in the studio itself. They were seated in an adjacent studio and were only allowed to watch the proceedings on television monitors (providing them with the same product that was fed to the American public). The advertising men were worried that, otherwise, the only things the reporters would write about would be the applause cue cards and the instructions to mob Nixon at the conclusion.

After one of several "Man in the Arena" programs, a key Nixon advertising man wrote a strategy memorandum, replete with additional helpful impression-management hints for future programs. The memo contained four major headings: (1) The Look, (2) The Questions and Answers, (3) Staging, and (4) General. Its contents, which are noteworthy for their attention to detail, included the following (McGinniss, 1970):

> He looks good on his feet and shooting "in the round" gives dimension to him. . . . Standing adds to his "feel" of confidence and the viewers' "feel" of his confidence. . . . He still uses his arms a little too "predictably" and a little too often, but at this point it is better not to inhibit him. . . . He should, perhaps, be prepared with an optional cut in his closing remarks in case we get into time trouble getting off the air. I don't want to take a chance of missing the shots of the audience crowding around him at the end. . . . On one answer . . . he gave an unqualified "yes" and that was good. Whenever possible he should be that definitive. . . . There should be more women on the panel since over half the voters are women. Maybe combine a category, i.e., . . . negro woman. . . . The family [Nixon's] should be in the audience at every show [pp. 70–73].

The night before the election, Nixon's crew rented a studio in Burbank for a "live" program. Supposedly, anyone from any place in the country could call in and ask Nixon any question he or she wanted. According to announcements, operators would answer the calls and write down the question. Actually, edited versions of questions were sent to the announcer who read them to Nixon, who then read answers off a card. One of the key ad men commented

> It's sort of a semiforgery, isn't it? [A Nixon aide] has a bunch of questions he wants Nixon to answer. He's written them in advance to make sure they're worded properly. When someone calls with something similar, they'll use the prepared question and attribute it to the person who called [McGinniss, p. 154].

To try to counter the "contrived slickness" of the Nixon campaign, opponent Hubert Humphrey and his running mate Edmund Muskie designed their campaign around images of warmth, personalism, and the human touch. On the night before the election, Humphrey and Muskie also held a call-in telethon. Humphrey actually answered questions live and conversed with the callers. At home, viewers could see the whole stage, complete with cue cards, cameras, wires, folding chairs, and the producers and crew running around with their shirt-tails hanging out. This *carefully planned* scenario was designed to contrast sharply with Nixon's polished theatrics. Earlier in the campaign, a television spot was produced that showed Humphrey and Muskie, in their shirt sleeves, talking to people on the streets, in bowling alleys, and so on. In one scene, Humphrey was shown fishing in a stream, wearing a "stupid fisherman's hat" and getting his line snarled and fouled up. The spot "was the most effective single piece of advertising of the campaign" (McGinniss, p. 141). It "made a mockery of Richard Nixon's year-long quest for warmth. You can't create humanity, it said. You either have it or you don't. Hubert Humphrey has it. Guess who does not?" (p. 141). Humphrey's well-staged campaign almost worked, as it wiped out Nixon's huge early lead in the polls, but was not quite enough to gain him the election.

Gerald Ford, Nixon's successor, had the image of a plain, open, and, in some ways, common man. Yet while he was president, his public relations apparatus was larger and more sophisticated than that of his predecessors (Herbers, 1975). His staff tried to consolidate and capitalize on the images that they felt Ford could convey most successfully—those of a good, honest, down-to-earth human being. His writers infused his speeches with common touches; his staff members emphasized the virtues of his fundamental, nonflashy style. The result was a dramatized, more extreme version of Ford himself, an identity with which Ford ultimately became comfortable (Herbers, 1975).

Like all political campaigns, the 1976 race for the White House between Ford and Jimmy Carter was guided by consciously planned public impression-management strategies. Carter, the former governor of Georgia, built his campaign around information gathered from public opinion polls. A 1972 Carter poll indicated that voters were more concerned abut leadership than about specific issues, distrusted big government, and would be quite positive toward an outsider. He and his advisors therefore decided to run a campaign that emphasized his leadership ability, stressed the outsider aspect of his background, and promised to curtail drastically the Washington bureaucracy. He ran in all the primaries to get these points across and to obtain much-needed national exposure and free publicity. One member of the Atlanta advertising firm that helped organize the campaign pointed out that "Jimmy had an intangible something, a kind of charisma, that the other candidates lacked. And yet it was impossible to capture in print or in the conventional 30-second television spot, so we developed the five-minute commercial for him" (Weglowski, 1977). The commercials hammered home the themes mentioned above and generally avoided dealing with specifics. The commercials were aired immediately before the nightly news, so that viewers would associate them with news and not simply with advertising efforts.

During the campaign, Ford attempted to capitalize on the plain and open image he had built, but he may have carried it too far. Some of his commercials showed Joe Garagiola, a sports announcer who was an ex-athlete, chatting with Ford aboard Air Force One, trying to persuade viewers that Ford was a good guy. Many viewers thought it looked unpresidential. In contrast, Carter's commercials preached moral leadership, purpose, and vision. Carter's public relations men tried to capitalize on such contrasts whenever possible (Weglowski, 1977).

Ford and his advisors were cognizant of the dangers of appearing too unpresidential, so they tried to balance the plain and open image with other information designed to build up Ford's image of competence, consistency, and leadership. Ford stayed in the White House as much as possible during the campaign and played to the people via televised *Presidential* press conferences—portraying himself as *the* President, residing in *his* house, taking care of the nation's business. Early in the campaign, a series of dizzying "news" events were staged in which, during the course of one week, Ford and the White House became more visible to the public than they had been in the prior eight months (Naughton, 1976). Of course, the news correspondents who covered the events noted the transparency of it all and took offense at being used as political props. For example, at one news conference Ford's press secretary tried to prompt some of the reporters to ask a particular question that was relevant to the campaign. When none of the reporters responded to the prod, the question was answered anyway (Naughton, 1976).

Carter's campaign was not without its impression management mishaps, either. Shortly before the election a Carter campaign manual that was quite explicit in promoting the use of deception became public knowledge. The manual was prepared for Carter's advance men, who preceded him to campaign stops and did the brunt of the local planning and promotion. The manual described many "standard organizing techniques," but also advised the advance men to withhold information from the press, dribbling it out over time to obtain maximum publicity; withhold from campaign workers information that was over and above what they needed to know to do their jobs, since such restricted knowledge gave the advance men better control over events; make sure that the people who accompanied Carter on stage looked like they were middle American and were balanced by sex and race; and insure that television lights were judiciously placed to highlight Carter's hair, which was thought to be unusually good. Further, the manual advised staging displays of enthusiasm for Carter by scattering his most vocal supporters throughout the crowd and preinstructing groups to "spontaneously" cheer and chant when Carter arrived on the scene (Carter orders campaign . . . , Associated Press, October 11, 1976). After the manual reached the public's attention, a hurried announcement was made that Carter had never personally seen it and was going to have it rewritten immediately. People should never *appear* to be managing the impressions they convey.

SUMMARY

Personal appearance, props, and scenery communicate information to audiences about what people are like, how they are likely to behave, and how they should be treated. Across time and societies the symbolic meanings of appearance-related cues change. However, given an existing set of beliefs about what images are related to particular appearance cues, people can coordinate and control their personal appearance, props, and scenic background in order to construct specific identities before real or imagined audiences. People expend a tremendous amount of time, effort, and money in the judicious employment of appearance-related cues. Inconsistencies between the images conveyed by appearance-related cues, on the one hand, and verbal or nonverbal actions on the other, invalidate a performance. Consequently, these image-generating modes are coordinated by people in order to present coherent identities to others. As with verbal and nonverbal actions, people seem to manage their appearances so as to claim desirable images and disclaim undesirable ones.

Experimental social psychologists have devoted virtually no attention to how people go about constructing images through appearance and how they coordinate appearance with verbal and nonverbal actions. Although there is voluminous relevant material, it is stocked primarily with anecdotal descriptions. This lack of scientific attention is consistent with social psychologists' preoccupations with determining how people *react* when exposed to particular stimuli—how they are affected by the personal appearance of others, for example. Largely ignored is the question of how people *act* in order to establish particular images in front of others, such as by controlling their personal appearances, props, and scenic background. It is past time to redress this imbalance.

T E N

No society can tolerate the thought that those who choose to desert it may be acting in a rational manner. Society's deviants, like doctors' mistakes, have to be explained away, and the assumption that "the insane are not responsible for their actions" provides the proper and indeed the perfect explanation.[1]

Braginsky, Braginsky, & Ring

ABERRANT IMAGES

The emphasis in previous chapters has been on those impression-management tactics that construct the more popular and socially desirable types of identities. Most people want to be perceived as likable, competent, sociable, strong, influential, and dynamic. Even when reality pressures, norms, and stereotypes restrict the attractiveness of the images people claim, their self-demeaning presentations are still rational actions, perfectly understandable by observers. But what of the

[1]From *Methods of Madness: The Mental Hospital as a Last Resort*, by B. M. Braginsky, D. D. Braginsky, and K. Ring. Copyright 1969 by D. D. Braginsky. (New York: Holt, Rinehart and Winston, 1969.) This and all other quotations from this source are reprinted by permission.

individual who runs naked through the streets shouting profanities; the person who claims powerlessness, withdrawing from social relations, sitting almost paralyzed in a corner; or the person whose hallucinations include hearing the voices of people from the great beyond? Can there be any impression-management elements in such bizarre and deviant behaviors? Can such people possibly be claiming images? Can such obviously sick behavior be rational in any sense of the term?

There is increasingly convergent opinion among scientists that considerable rationality and purposefulness can be found in such statistically and socially aberrant behavior (Braginsky & Braginsky, 1971; Braginsky, Braginsky, & Ring, 1969; Carson, 1969; Goffman, 1961a, 1963b; Haley, 1962, 1963, 1971; Messinger et al., 1962; Scheff, 1966; Sullivan, 1953; Szasz, 1961). The concept of mental illness as a sickness comparable to physical illness may be as much a myth as possession by demons. Both serve the same function of explaining otherwise unintelligible behavior. It is important to note at the outset that it is not proposed that all forms of deviance are unrelated to physiological factors. Genetic defects can produce certain types of mental retardation, brain tumors and diseases can produce emotional and perceptual changes, and research suggests that there may be biochemical and genetic correlates of some of the "symptoms" of certain forms of "mental illness." But it is proposed that *most* people who are classified as mentally ill are acting in rational ways, given their personal resources, goals, and social environment. For numerous reasons, different people construct different sorts of identities. Impression management is used to establish and support aberrant identities just as it is used to maintain the ones we consider normal.

In this chapter we'll explore aberrant images—such as being mentally ill or violently anti-social—concentrating on impression-management aspects. To begin, we must consider the dimensions of interpersonal behavior.

DIMENSIONS OF INTERPERSONAL RELATIONS

There are a vast number of images that people claim through their actions—sexy, strong, sick, sociable, creative, weak, unique, stupid, and so on. Attempting to deal separately with each of the hundreds of possible images and millions of possible combinations would be a difficult task for the scientist interested in bringing conceptual order to the understanding of interpersonal relations. Consequently, attempts have been made to describe the basic dimensions of interpersonal behavior, to find some means of categorizing interpersonal behaviors into a workable scheme. Social scientists who have worked on this problem are in surprising accord that there are two basic dimensions of interpersonal relations that seem to apply universally: *power* and *evaluation* (Brown, 1965; Carson, 1969; Exline, 1971; Foa, 1961; Mehrabian, 1971a).

The power dimension is the superiority-to-inferiority continuum in relations, and its opposite poles are described with such terms as powerful/powerless, dominant/submissive, strong/weak, and high status/low status. Cutting across this continuum is the evaluative dimension, which reflects feelings from attraction to repulsion in a relationship. Its opposite poles are described with such terms as love/hate, approach/avoid, accept/reject, and like/dislike.

According to the rationale of this approach, any behavior or image can be classified as falling somewhere within the two-dimensional space formed by the intersection of the dimensions. In the upper right-hand quadrant are behaviors or images that express both power and liking, as in the case of a strong, respected, and considerate individual; the upper left-hand quadrant describes behaviors that express both power and disliking, as in the case of a strong, dictatorial, abhorrent despot. In the lower right-hand quadrant are behaviors expressing powerlessness and liking, as in the case of a weak but kind person; and in the lower left-hand quadrant are behaviors that express powerlessness and disliking, as in the case of a weak, spineless, rude, reprehensible individual. The more extreme or unusual the behavior is, the farther it is located from the point of intersection of the two dimensions. *All* interpersonal acts express something and can be located within these intersecting dimensions. Foa (1961) contends that by definition "an interpersonal act is an attempt to establish the emotional relationship of the actor toward himself and toward the other, as well as to establish the social relationship of the self and the other with respect to a larger reference group" (p. 350). Therefore, *every* interpersonal act "serves the purpose of giving or denying love and status to the self and to the other" (p. 351; see also Carson, 1969).

The most consistently admired set of images is located in the upper right hand quadrant—power and liking. Indeed, most of the experimental research social psychologists have conducted seems to illustrate that people try to appear to possess images from that quadrant. In most psychology laboratory experiments, most subjects are trying to be perceived as strong, competent, likable, and sociable, irrespective of what they privately believe about themselves.

Many perfectly normal identities rest on images that deviate somewhat from this most normatively attractive set of images. Some roles, for instance, dictate that the occupant usually display submissive behavior, such as the role of subordinate in an organization, the traditional role of woman, or in many cases the role of minority group members (recall the earlier discussion in Chapter 6 of stereotyping, particularly with regard to women and Blacks). Cries for Black Power and Women's Liberation further attest that people usually prefer to claim images that fall in the powerful rather than powerless side of that dimension or at least that they prefer to be allowed entry into that half. Further, a combination of reality constraints, roles, and situational pressures often make it profitable for people to be negatively rather than positively evaluated. For instance, in bargaining situations "tough" negotiators who present themselves as disliking their opponent and unwilling to compromise usually profit more if a settlement is ever reached (Tedeschi et al., 1973). Reality constraints, such as publicly known negative information about oneself, often make it nearly impossible for some people to claim anything but images of below-average competence, intelligence, power, popularity, and so on.

Some people present images of themselves that are far beyond these normal and understandable cases, generating statistical and social aberrance. The expression of images that are near any of the four poles of the two interpersonal dimensions qualify as abnormal. Extreme powerlessness is typified by some mental patients who express a complete loss of control in their lives, with catatonic schizophrenic symptoms of complete withdrawal epitomized by seemingly endless rigid positions. Extreme powerfulness is typified by the paranoid schizophrenic who seems to be under the delusion that he or she is either god or the devil. Extreme negativity is typified by the sociopathic individual, the extremely violent person who appears to have no regard for the feelings or physical well-being of others. Extreme positiveness is typified by the person who is so distressingly friendly, helpful, and optimistic that we wonder whether he or she is even remotely in touch with reality. These extremes, particularly the first three, usually seem inexplicable to observers. It is hard for most people to understand why anyone would habitually claim such images unless something was medically wrong with them. In centuries past, some such people may have been labeled demoniacs (possessed by demons). Today we label them mentally ill.

MENTAL ILLNESS

What is mental illness? Certainly it is nothing that can be transmitted and caught like the flu. In fact, the differences between mental illness and body illness seem to far outweigh the similarities (Szasz, 1960, 1961). The essence of the concept is usually found in terms of "problems in living" (Szasz, 1960), difficulties that people have in their *inter*personal relationships and communications. Mental illness is a label applied after someone has deviated sufficiently often, flagrantly, and publicly from social, cultural, and ethical prescriptions about how people should behave. Thomas Szasz believes that the traditional medical concept of mental illness is a myth and argues that mental illnesses "are for the most part communications expressing unacceptable ideas, often framed, moreover, in an unusual idiom" (1960, p. 16). Mental illness is a social reality, not a physical or medical one.

Not all social or ethical deviance is labeled mental illness. (There are always some people, of course, willing to call anyone "sick" who disagrees with them on matters of opinion.) To "legitimately" gain the label—that is, to have it applied by a psychiatrist who finds a problem sufficiently "serious" to send one to a mental institution—one must do something slightly more attention-getting. Based in part on the work of Scheff (1966), Robert Carson (1969) describes a disordered person as "someone who breaks residual rules in such a spectacular and/or persistent way that it is impossible for others to ignore the rule-breaking, or to discover 'normal' reasons for its occurrence" (p. 228).

Residual rules go beyond the simple rules of etiquette in a society that are easily written down. Residual rules are the *normally unchallenged assumptions people in a particular culture have about the very nature of reality, society, ethics, and human nature.* For example, residual rules. exist about how people should behave. Certain sexual acts are considered in particular societies to be perversions of human nature, even though the same acts might be considered normal in other cultures. There also are fundamentally accepted ways of dealing with people. A person who trembles when others approach, threatens others with no apparent reason, or constructs sentences that don't seem to make any sense appears to be abnormal. Further, residual rules exist about what people must believe if they are normal; in Western society a normal person doesn't believe in ghosts or think that inanimate objects can talk. Of course, such seemingly basic and unchallengeable assumptions about the world may not be accepted in another place or era. Thus, the belief that women should occupy a status equal to that of men, which was once viewed by almost everyone in Western society as an absurd contradiction of everything that was known about human nature, society, and religion, is now accepted. Similarly, people in another society who believe in ghosts and spirits that inhabit inanimate objects may scoff at Christian beliefs about the devil and hell. At a given time and place, though, residual rules are taken for granted by nearly everyone, since they seem to be so basic to the way the world is. "Deliberate violation of such norms is unthinkable for most of the society's members" (Carson, 1969, p. 227).

In actuality, most people seem to break such rules on occasion, but the behavior doesn't stabilize (Scheff, 1966). Children, for example, usually go through periods of having imaginary playmates and irrational fears of everything from the dark to goblins to inanimate objects. For children, of course, such behaviors are seen as normal, at least when exhibited in moderation. For adults, it is a different matter. Adults who believe in ghosts, conjure imaginary friends, or have strange beliefs about how society should be organized and who are incautious enough to discuss it publicly in a way that frightens or offends others are on their way to being labeled mentally ill.

Perhaps the most unthinkable aspect of this view of mental illness is that someone would deviate from residual rules *on purpose*. The purposive nature of such deviation is a theme explicitly stated or strongly implied in all of these social psychological analyses. Scheff (1966), for example, calls residual rule-breaking "a volitional act of innovation or rebellion." Such behavior can be as purposive as the behavior of any "normal" individual. The values and goals of people labeled mentally ill may partially differ from those of people labeled normal, but this is a far cry from the assumption that all those in the former group are mentally ill and must not be responsible for their actions. As with "normal" people, the values and goals of those labeled mentally ill can be quite varied.

Two of the most common sets of values and goals can be encompassed under the broad headings of (1) publicly displaying behaviors that claim images of powerlessness and incompetence and (2) publicly displaying behaviors that claim images that shock, offend, and frighten audiences. Seymour Krim (1968), a writer who was committed to mental institutions on two occasions, came to the conclusion that

> nine-tenths of the people I was quartered with were not "insane" by any of the standards a normally intelligent person would use: the majority had lost confidence in their own ability to survive in the world outside, or their families were *afraid* of them and had them palmed off on "experts" [pp. 116–117].[2]

In Krim's own case, the latter was true. He described himself as an intellectual who became tired of an unquestioned life of obedience to society's preoccupations and rules. He let his creative impulses run wild. He viewed himself as unique, impulsive, unorthodox, intellectual, Bohemian, and spontaneous, and he acted in ways that publicly demonstrated these self-images, much to the chagrin of others. He poignantly noted that upon hearing a psychiatrist

> literally equate sanity with current cliches of adjustment and describe Greenwich Village as a "psychotic community," I saw with sudden clarity that insanity and psychosis can no longer be respected as meaningful definitions—but are used by limited individuals in positions of social power to describe ways of behaving and thinking that are alien, threatening, and obscure to them [p. 118].

[2]From *Views of a Nearsighted Cannoneer*, by S. Krim. Copyright 1968 by E. P. Dutton & Company, Inc. This and all other quotations from this source are reprinted by permission of the publisher, E. P. Dutton.

Any claims to images that, by consensus of peers, are highly unattractive (like presentations of extreme power or extreme anti-socialness) are possible catalysts for being labeled mentally ill.

Many mental patients go in the opposite direction and claim images of powerlessness and incompetence, giving the impression that they can no longer function effectively in the world outside of the mental institution. It has been argued that feelings of powerlessness, incompetence, and low self-efficacy derive in part from consistent failures in certain situations (Bandura, 1969, 1977a). When people expect to fail publicly, they indeed are more self-demeaning in their presentations (Chapter 6). Further, it has been suggested that many mental patients come to value the rewards that can be achieved by creating the impression of powerlessness and incompetence (Braginsky et al., 1969; Carson, 1969; Sullivan, 1953). One can then escape from life's pressures, stresses, expectations, and responsibilities by no longer claiming to be capable of success. Responsibilities are abandoned and one can be provided for by others, allowing the others to take on the onerous aspects that freedom sometimes entails.

The escape from responsibility has an additional meaning. When people are caught in predicaments, they can attempt to escape by accounting for their behavior in a way that excuses them from responsibility (see Chapter 5). Many people who are labeled mentally ill do the same thing, but in more extreme fashion. For example, recall the case of David Berkowitz, the "Son of Sam," who accounted for his murder of six people by fabricating the story that it was commanded by demons via a talking dog (see Chapter 5). He was judged mentally ill and has not yet been tried for his crimes. His heinous actions deviate sharply from the rules of most societies and require an equally deviate explanation. His imagination provided it. Responsibility was removed from *him* and placed on coercive circumstances over which he supposedly had no control. Mental illness is a label that shifts responsibility from the individual as a purposive agent to something else—the coercive force that is presumed to accompany the label. Mental patients often contend that they can not be counted on, that they can not help what they do, that they should be excused for transgressions and embarrassing situations. In such cases, the label provides a suitable account for actions that other people have difficulty comprehending and excuses them from the typical sorts of negative sanctions.

There are, then, plausible reasons why people might claim aberrant images and break residual rules. Not every person who behaves strangely, though, is labeled mentally ill. According to Scheff (1966), the single most important factor in determining whether someone *is* mentally ill is the *societal reaction*. Audiences often try to ignore unusual behaviors, deny them, or even explain them away if they can find some understandable reason why the deviation might have occurred. For example, a person's antisocial behavior may be dismissed as due merely to short-lived drunkenness; extreme depression might be seen as manifesting only temporary stress brought on by being fired or divorced. However, if the audience is unduly frightened, shocked, offended or otherwise unable to ignore or explain the deviation, they are likely to apply the label "mentally ill." Actors may even come to doubt their own sanity if audience reactions continue to be those of shock or offense or if they can find no "acceptable" reasons for their own behavior.

Once it has been labeled, there is a strong possibility that reinforcement from others will stabilize the behavior (Carson, 1969; Scheff, 1966). If people are placed in mental institutions, the stabilization is likely to become even more rapid. Describing mental institutions, Goffman (1961a, pp. 151–152) notes that "the setting and the house rules press home to the patient that he is of little social weight, being hardly capable of acting like a full-fledged person at all." Gergen (1968, p. 301) points out the self-fulfilling nature of having been labeled: "the classification of 'mentally ill' may itself be encapsulating in that it serves to orient the behavior of others toward him. Perceiving the person as 'sick,' the attendant may effectively reinforce 'sick' behavior and fail to encourage conduct that is inconsistent with this perception." The individual is branded with the image, treated consistently with the image, and ultimately might come to the conclusion that it is more profitable to go along than resist.

David Rosenhan (1973) experienced first-hand the cycle that begins once the label has been applied. He and several of his colleagues feigned some of the symptoms of schizophrenia to gain admittance to a mental hospital. Immediately after admittance they acted as they normally did. They noted the tremendous feelings of powerlessness and depersonalization in the institution. They were rarely seen by hospital attendants, and, they reported, when they did speak with psychiatrists, on 71% of the occasions the psychiatrist did not even make eye contact. When they asked questions, such as whether they were eligible for special privileges, the psychiatrist would often ignore them and go about his business, such as saying "Good morning, how are you today?" and then turning to leave without waiting for a reply. Since the researchers were constantly taking notes to record their experiences, many of the other patients quickly sized up the situation, asking whether they were journalists or professors checking up on the hospital. On those occasions when their note-taking was commented on by the *staff*, however, it was seen as proof of compulsiveness, further justifying the original diagnosis of mental illness. Their audiences interpreted the behavior in terms of what they themselves expected to see. On the average, it took these pseudo-patients nineteen days to convince the staff that they were well enough to be discharged.

The staff of a mental institution has control over a staggering range of patient outcomes. As Goffman (1961a) has vividly detailed, patients usually confront a situation in which they are regarded and treated as nonpersons. Their ideas are not taken seriously, they must ask permission to do even the most trivial things, and control over nearly all aspects of their lives is taken by the staff of the institution. However, patients hardly give up hope for personal control over the outcomes they do care about (Goffman, 1961a; Braginsky et al., 1969). Braginsky, Braginsky, and Ring note that usually "the mental patient is not a passive and helpless victim who abjectly acquiesces to the enormous power" of such institutions (p. 50). Instead, they describe him "as a person who, within the limits of his situation, is concerned with living his life as he deems fit, just as any ordinary person of any other functioning community would be" (p. 50). The legitimate power of the staff, however, clearly limits the kinds of strategies patients can employ to gain a degree of counterpower and hence have a hand in affecting their own outcomes. Consequently, patients are virtually forced to rely on strategies that are "fundamentally subversive" in character (p. 5). They often attempt to undermine the legitimate authority of the staff by appearing to go along and acquiesce, but do so in a way that is privately recognized as mocking. This boosts their own morale and develops an in-group feeling of "us" versus "them." The book and movie *One Flew Over the Cuckoo's Nest* (Kesey, 1962) poignantly illustrates many of these subversive strategies.

Braginsky et al. (1969) challenge the traditional psychiatric assumptions that mental patients are incompetent, out of touch with reality, and incapable of highly purposive behavior. They have shown that patients are quite adept at using impression-management tactics in order to increase their counterpower in institutions. They argue that, "if anything, mental patients should be even more inclined" to use impression management and ingratiation than the average person, "because (1) their objective situation makes them more dependent on others for good outcomes, and (2) they are either in fact or normatively prevented from attaining their outcomes by more direct means (for example, by simply requesting permission to be allowed to go home for the weekend)" (pp. 51–52).

In their first study, they demonstrated mental patients' sensitivity to impression-management cues and their ability to control their own behavior for impression-management purposes. They had mental patients (most of whom were diagnosed as schizophrenics) fill out a questionnaire about their attitudes toward the hospital under conditions where their opinions were either completely anonymous or public information. Under the public conditions the patients should desire not to "rock the boat" or say anything that might get them in trouble with the staff, while under the anonymous conditions they would be freer to express their actual feelings and point out problems. Indeed, the patients were more negative toward the hospital staff, rules, and treatment of patients in the anonymous than public condition. Interestingly, the patients were not simply more negative about everything under the anonymous conditions, but only about things that the investigators believed represented legitimate and reasonable criticisms. Several items that were predetermined to be highly and unrealistically critical were included in the questionnaire; no differences between the conditions were found on these. Thus, just like anyone else, the mental patients refrained from criticizing those in power when their responses might get back to them but expressed legitimate grievances when assured of anonymity.

Many mental patients desire to remain in institutions, coming to like the freedom from responsibilities and doubting their own abilities to cope as well in the outside world. The research of Braginsky et al. supports the hypothesis that "the predominant motivations of the chronic patients . . . center around remaining in the hospital and being able to enjoy life as much as possible there" (p. 52). Seymour Krim (1968), the writer who was committed to institutions on two occasions, similarly observed that "The majority of people who stay in mental institutions for any length of time do not want to return to the uncertain conditions outside the wall" (p. 119). One of the sharpest differences in discharge rates of mental patients is simply between newcomers to the institution, who have not yet learned to value or take advantage of the rewards of institutional life, and oldtimers, who have; the former group has an 80% discharge rate and the latter, a 17% rate. Although the huge difference might be due to many factors, Braginsky et al. hypothesized that "to a very considerable extent this difference . . . may perhaps be attributable to nothing more esoteric than a patient's desire to stay or leave the hospital and his ability, through impression management, to achieve his particular goal" (1969, p. 59). To test that intriguing hypothesis, they gave some mental patients a standardized psychological test and told them that it was a test of *mental illness*—the more items they answered "true," the more likely the respondent would stay in the hospital for a long period of time. Other subjects were given the *identical* test but told it was a test of *self-insight*—the more items they answered "true," the more the patient would know about himself, the less the severity of the illness, and the greater the chances for release. If the hypothesis is correct, newcomers should want to manage the impression of mental health and hence should answer questions "false" on the mental illness test but "true" on the self-insight test. Old-timers, though, should want to manage the impression of mental illness in order to remain in the hospital and hence should answer "true" on the mental illness test but "false" on the self-insight test. This is precisely what was found. Although the newcomers and the old-timers were matched on the type and severity of their "psychopathology," they seemed to have different goals and hence desired to manage different impressions.

Some wards in mental hospitals are more desirable than others. Patients on open wards have freedoms and prerogatives that those on the closed back wards do not. Depending on the institution, the former can take advantage of a library, of shops and stores, bowling alleys and other recreational facilities. Old-timers on an open ward should prefer their location and therefore should walk a fine line between presenting themselves as so healthy that they are released and so sick that they are placed in the closed back wards. If they believe they look "too" healthy, they should compensate by displaying psychopathological symptoms that circumvent release; if they believe they look too sick, they should compensate by displaying healthy behaviors that circumvent placement in the back wards. In short, they should manage their impressions so that they can remain exactly where they are.

To ascertain whether mental patients will do so, and to determine whether their self-presentations have their intended effects on psychiatrists, Braginsky and Braginsky had a staff psychologist interview patients in open wards who were old-timers diagnosed as schizophrenic (reported in Braginsky, Braginsky, & Ring, 1969). Prior to the interview, they took each patient aside and told him "confidentially" that the interview was for a specific purpose. Some of the patients were told that the interview was to determine whether they should be allowed to remain on the open ward or should be placed on a closed ward; others were told that the interview was to determine if they were healthy enough to be released from the hospital; and still others were told that the interview was simply to see how they were feeling and what their mental status was. The first group, fearful of being viewed as too sick and hence being placed in the closed ward, should have presented themselves as relatively healthy; the second group, fearful of being released, should have done their best to demonstrate that they were still sick enough to stay in the hospital.

The results provided strong evidence of the patients' effectiveness at impression management. Tapes of the interviews were shown to three staff psychiatrists who were unaware of the purpose of the experiment and who were asked simply to give their independent opinions of the patients' mental states. Patients who believed they might be placed in the back wards were described as less mentally ill and less in need of treatment than subjects in either of the other conditions. Fearful of placement in the back wards, these subjects did not report *any* major or severe symptoms. People in the other two groups reported a high number of symptoms, such as hallucinations, and these were viewed by the psychiatrists as quite severe. The fact that patients in the "mental status" condition did not behave any differently from subjects who were concerned about the possibility of release suggests that old-time patients normally want to appear sufficiently ill to be allowed to remain in the hospital. As Braginsky, Braginsky, and Ring (1969) conclude, "when the self-interest of patients is at stake, they can present themselves *convincingly* as either 'sick' or 'healthy' depending on which mode of self-presentation is believed to increase the probability of desired outcomes" (p. 72).

Symptoms are communications that the mental patient can employ for impression-management purposes. Carson (1969), commenting on some of the observations of Artiss (1959), remarked that "the alleged hallucinations of schizophrenic persons might sometimes be merely lies, not qualitatively different from, 'I couldn't come to school yesterday because I was sick' " (p. 223). One of the traditional correlates and prime symptoms of schizophrenia is a much-slowed reaction time. Yet Fontana and Klein (1968) showed that schizophrenics can control their reaction time, making it either slower or exactly comparable to an average person's, depending on why they believe that symptom is being assessed. In a series of studies, Alan Fontana found that patients will manipulate their symptoms in order to remain in a hospital location they desire (Fontana & Gessner, 1969), resist all new treatment programs that might make them more responsible or accountable for their deviant actions or provide them with less of an excuse for deviance (Fontana & Corey, 1970), and attempt to manipulate staff in their everyday contacts (Fontana, 1971). Fontana concludes that mental illness involves a tremendous amount of self-presentation. He believes that "the creation of a sick incompetent impression on others is an intermediate goal which is instrumental to the attainment of other goals" (Fontana, Klein, Lewis, & Levine, 1968, p. 110). Further, there are numerous "rational" reasons why a person is motivated to present himself in this way:

> people are not likely to make demands on him or are not likely to persist in their demands. He cannot justifiably be held accountable for his actions, because no one can expect an irresponsible crazy person to know what he is doing. Passivity and gratification of dependency needs are legitimized, since society accepts the position that the sick cannot care for themselves and must be cared for. If the person is hospitalized, all these goals may be met by virtue of his status as a mental patient [Fontana et al., 1968, p. 111].

On the other hand, as Braginsky et al. have shown, there is a fine line between being perceived as sick enough to remain in the institution and so sick that one is confined to a back ward and denied freedoms. Although some people might actually want such complete withdrawal, most do not. Messinger et al. (1962) report the anecdotes of several mental patients who attempted to walk the line that separates freedom from responsibility and complete isolation. One patient remarked "Life is a pretense, I have to pretend every day I'm here. That I'm gay and happy in order to stay out of the isolation ward. So I laugh and pretend to be gay" (p. 101). Another patient took to playing Scrabble with her friends, which staff members interpreted as a sign of increasing mental health. After being insured of the confidentiality of her statements, the patient told an interviewer that "she and her friends had recently taken to playing Scrabble as a means of impressing the staff with their ability to think clearly and be sociable" (p. 99). Although many mental patients confidentially admit to using impression management, they frequently state that, if the interviewer ever mentions any such thing to the staff, they will deny it!

In further studies, Braginsky et al. (1969) found that mental patients, like everyone else, are quite selective in their familiarity with the types of facilities available for their use. Patients are highly familiar with the "recreational and hedonic aspects" of the hospital, such as bowling alleys, but are quite unfamiliar with the locations of "formal therapeutic services," such as where staff offices are located. They also found that "a more positive relationship exists between the patient's former weekend rather than weekday style of adaptation and his present everyday style of life in the hospital" (p. 134). In other words, the patients engaged in activities that they normally enjoyed only on their free time and did not do things that resembled their "work" in the outside world. This further suggests that the escape from onerous responsibilities drives many mental patients into institutions. They present the image of being too sick to be forced back into the patterns of life they detest but not too sick to be denied the activities they find rewarding. As additional evidence of the rationality of being labeled mentally ill, they note that admissions to mental institutions increase from neighborhoods surrounding those of a recently discharged person. This suggests that the former patients tell their friends about the "advantages" of institutionalization. "Virtually no one seeks admission during the warm summer months but . . . the demand starts to rise when the weather begins to grow less pleasant" (p. 161), suggesting that institutions serve the purpose of allowing people who are dissatisfied or disgusted with the conditions of their existence to seek asylum. They even label the mental institution as a "Last *Resort*," an obvious double entendre, suggesting that people who lack the means to afford a vacation in more conventional resorts seek relief from their miseries in mental hospitals.

In a subsequent book, *Hansels and Gretels* (1971), Braginsky and Braginsky demonstrated that children in institutions for the mentally retarded are quite adept at goal achievement. Once again, Braginsky and Braginsky view impression management as a form of counterpower, in this case "child counterpower." Despite the fact that the typical institutionalized child lacks formal education, has rejecting parents, and suffers from a "general impoverishment" that would virtually "ensure poor performance on intelligence tests," they found that the typical "Hansel and Gretel were resourceful, clever, manipulative children, capable of controlling the hostile environment into which they were cast" (p. 159).

This is not to suggest that patients in mental institutions do not have real problems. Virtually all seem to privately believe that something is "wrong" with them. They may have developed "ineffective" methods of coping with life's problems—ineffective as judged by the normal goals and standards of society, but perhaps not as judged by their own personal resources, goals, and situations. They may be failing to maximize the reward/cost ratios they *could* receive from life. However, they may be maximizing the outcomes they want or believe they can get from life. They may really feel incompetent or out of step with society or be so disillusioned with it that they no longer care to participate under the same rules and with the same responsibilities that most people unquestioningly accept. The problems they encounter in life may be more extreme than those encountered by the normal person, or at least they may seem more extreme. Consequently, more extreme solutions may be called for, allowing them to change their identities in more dramatic ways. Then, too, there is the possibility of physiological or genetic abnormality. An alternative interpretation of the problems, however, can be offered: "Of course, individuals who were (and still are) labeled as schizophrenic are individuals who have difficulties in living; so do we all" (Braginsky et al., 1969, p. 165). Or, as Krim (1968, p. 117) phrased it, "Who can not be conceived as [sick] in a world so complex ('The truth is there is a truth on every side' . . .) that each group has its own method for judging manners, behavior, ideas, and finally the worth of human values?"

MORE ABERRANT IMAGES

Impression management tactics are used to support a wide variety of aberrant images that best serve the goals and resources of particular types of people. Examples abound. Fortune tellers create an aura of mystery and occult power through the use of exotic dress and jewelry, props like crystal balls and tarot cards, and (sometimes) feigned foreign accents. Shamans, mystics, and others who claim to possess some extraordinary powers similarly employ impression-management tactics to convince audiences of their skills. Physically stigmatized people, such as those who are obviously physically handicapped or deformed, confront a variety of repugnant stereotypes about their conditions that are held by most normal audiences. Depending on their own goals and personal resources, the stigmatized can either go along with the stereotypes and play a role they might otherwise prefer not to or try to counteract the stereotypes by going out of their way to present convincing evidence that they are not what their audiences think they are. In either case, they are forced to monitor and control their actions carefully to convey only those images that will support the appropriate identity. Before leaving the area of aberrant images, let's briefly examine two additional examples—that of a witch in centuries past and that of an extremely anti-social character today.

Witchcraft

It has been estimated that approximately one-half million people in Europe were burned to death for witchcraft from the 15th to the 17th century (Harris, 1975). Many psychiatrists have contended that the witch craze was due in large part to the superstition and stupidity of the times concerning mental illness. The argument is put forth that most witches and demoniacs were actually hysterics whose mental illness produced hallucinations, delusions of occult power, and bizarre sexual fantasies. The victims believed they were witches, and the townspeople, failing to comprehend the poor wretches' plights, accepted their delusions at face value and persecuted them because of their own fear of the occult.

In point of fact, historical evidence appears to contradict these popular and fanciful psychiatric interpretations and leads to very different conclusions. Nicholas Spanos (1978) convincingly argues that witchcraft did not reflect mental disturbance on the part of the accused witches. Instead, the witch craze was due to complex sociopolitical and economic factors. (These factors are wide-ranging and include the Christian Church's decision to label political and religious dissidents and reformers—who were increasingly prevalent from the 11th century on—as heretics whose nefarious ideas were motivated by Satan. This action spared the Church the problem of dealing with people who might otherwise be viewed as rational individuals with potentially reasonable criticisms, and the money and property of witches was confiscated by the Inquisition on the continent of Europe—though not in England— and this revenue served as the means for the survival and prosperity of the Inquisitors.) Our major concern, though, is not with the causes of the fervor but with the reasons behind the behavior of the "witches." The vast majority of those accused of witchcraft did not freely admit to being witches. Only in a relatively few cases did people freely (not after torture) admit that they were witches and acted in highly "unusual" ways. In such cases, the individuals seemed to have rational reasons for behaving as they did, and they used impression management as a means to their ends.

Just as the concept of mental illness functions now, Spanos contends that in many instances in England "witchcraft accusations may have functioned as a means of defining the limits of acceptable behavior within a community" (p. 423). For example, in England in the 16th and 17th centuries, the typical accused witch was old, extremely poor, unmarried, female, and "described by her neighbors as foul-mouthed and unpleasant" (p. 423). She sustained herself almost exclusively by begging from neighbors who, though themselves poor, were better off than she. If your existence depended almost solely on handouts and your characteristics were comparable to those of the individual described above, how would you act, particularly if an initial request for aid was denied? As Spanos states, "She could become quite angry when her begging was met with refusal, and she sometimes cultivated the reputation of a witch in order to frighten people into generosity" (p. 423). The image of a witch with unusual powers would be one of the few types of identities that might allow her successfully to influence her neighbors and survive. When a refusal did occur, she was likely to heap invectives and curses on the misanthrope, perhaps hoping to change his mind. Of course, the tactic had its risks. Given the superstitions of the time, if an accident ultimately occurred to the cursed, his family, livestock, or property, the woman might be formally accused of witchcraft and executed. But the immediate alternative seemed to be starvation. This cycle of begging, refusal, curse, accident, and attribution of the accident to the "witch's" powers seemed to be repeated throughout England during the period. One 17th century description of the process (quoted in Spanos, p. 423) is that the accuser

> cryeth out of some poor innocent neighbor that he or she hath bewitched him. For, saith he, such an old man or woman came lately to my door and desired some relief, and I denied it, and, God forgive me, my heart did rise against her ... and presently my child, my wife, ... or somewhat, was thus and thus handled in such a strange manner, as I dare swear she is a witch, or else how should these things be? [p. 423]

My focus on England in the examples above was with good reason. On the continent of Europe, very different conditions prevailed, and the phenomenon was different in many respects. In England there were relatively few witch panics, largely limited to small-scale witch accusations, and few confessions of being a witch. On the continent, there were large scale panics, executions, and confessions of witchcraft that included elaborate bizarre accounts of witch sabbats, intercourse with demons, and traveling through the air. Was "mental illness" more prevalent on the continent? Actually, one of the major differences was that in England, the use of torture to extract confessions was prohibited by law. On the continent, unbelievably nefarious tortures were applied until the "witch" not only confessed but also named other witches.

Death was certain with or without a confession, but an elaborate and convincing confession would stop the torture and usually got the accused the quickest of the several possibilities for death, say, by strangulation before the flames were lit (Spanos, 1978). Since the accused was not allowed to die until others were named, the panics quickly spread as more and more innocent bystanders whose names might be known to the victims became implicated. The panics usually continued in an area until, "as the flames licked closer to the names of people who enjoyed high rank and power, the judges lost confidence in the confessions and the panics ceased" (Harris, 1975, p. 238). At the height of the craze, the bizarrre "hallucinations" of witches grew, with confessions extracted at the hands of professional witchhunters whose fees were generally based on the number of confessions they obtained. It seems that few, if any, accused people actually believed they were witches, at least on the continent (Spanos, 1978), since the liabilities of claiming that image there were extremely high.

Violent and Anti-Social Characters

Many people present themselves in ways that are negatively evaluated by others, such as seeming hostile, threateningly aggressive, unfriendly, and exploitive. Although these images seem to be statistically less frequent than their opposites, they still can serve impression-management functions. Relatively mild versions of these tactics are used by professional bargainers and negotiators (Tedeschi et al., 1973).

The more extreme case in contemporary society is that of the violent person who typically provokes confrontations that can result in physical fights, injuries, and death (Toch, 1969). The genesis of the violent individual is a complex mix of social learning, influence of group norms, lack of personal resources, and impression management (Bandura, 1973; Tedeschi & Lindskold, 1976; Toch, 1969; Yablonski, 1962). Violent people are usually reared in a subculture of violence in which coercion is the accepted means of resolving disputes. They establish an identity of being "macho," tough, and brutal and can influence others through their reputations alone. The violent person does not even have to win all of his fights. All that he has to do is to establish a reputation of being so tough that, even if others believe they can defeat him, they know it will come at great personal cost. The reluctance to risk the costs causes even some stronger opponents to back down and give in to their demands.

Not only do the norms of the subculture of violence encourage coercion, but the individual's personal resources often make alternative modes of influence unlikely. Violent men usually have low verbal skills and are from lower socioeconomic backgrounds (Toch, 1969). This makes it unlikely that they can settle disputes by logical argument, persuasion, verbal facility, or appeals to personal status in society at large. Instead, they are largely restricted to physical means of resolving interpersonal disharmonies—and reputations of such means. The images of masculinity, toughness, and violence that they cultivate and attempt to turn into reputations facilitate their goals.

Street gangs and juvenile toughs in contemporary society epitomize the strategy of "getting a rep." Many street gangs establish norms of aggression and make violence a prerequisite for membership and status. In one city gang, each physical assault upon a stranger was worth 10 points if observed by another club member, and 100 points were required for club membership (Bandura, 1973). As another example, a youth involved in a gang killing later told authorities "If I would of got the knife, I would have stabbed him. That would have gave me more of a buildup. People would say, 'There goes a cold killer' " (Yablonski, 1962, p. 8). Clearly, in some situations, a reputation for violence provides status and rewards.

Given such motivation, images of toughness are constructed through impression management. Appearance is tailored to suit the standards of the gang and might include particular dress styles (such as leather jackets), hair styles, and physical alterations (adding earrings, getting a tattoo). Potentially useful props (knife, gun) are carried. Verbal self-descriptions emphasize the actor's potential for violence and past anti-social deeds, and nonverbal behaviors include whatever mannerisms are prevalent in the group. All images have to be cultivated with the appropriate actions and supports, and the image of being anti-social is no different. Impression management permeates all styles of life.

SUMMARY

People differ in their goals, personal resources, and life situations. Not everyone either can be or wants to be rich, physically appealing, popular, sociable, wise, or successful in the traditional senses. For many reasons, different people construct different sorts of identities, sometimes willingly choosing a deviant identity and sometimes being forced into it by factors beyond their control such as physical deformity. Once identities are "selected," though, impression management is used to support and maintain them before real and imagined audiences.

Interpersonal acts and images can be categorized on two basic dimensions of interpersonal relations: power, the dimension of superiority/inferiority in relationships; and evaluation, the dimension of liking/disliking. Most people regard acts and images that connote power and liking more positively than other combinations, but there are often sound reasons why people present themselves in alternative ways. As a key example, *mental illness* is a term that describes "problems in living" and is typified by extreme self-presentations on any one of the four poles of the two dimensions (for example, appearing to be either completely powerless or omnipotent). People who are classified as mentally ill claim images that either (a) offend or frighten others or (b) give the appearance of being powerless, incompetent, and irresponsible. A cycle is created in which consistent public deviation from residual rules produces the labeling of the person as mentally ill, which generates even more impression-management behavior designed to maximize profits under adverse conditions, which produces more labeling, and, ultimately, institutionalization. Research suggests that mental patients are neither as out of touch with reality nor as completely incompetent as past medical analyses have led us to believe. Instead, they are quite adept at using impression management in order to maximize the outcomes they personally find desirable. Other instances where claims are made to extreme, unpopular, or statistically infrequent images also involve the use of impression management.

EPILOGUE

THE CURTAIN

When the curtain comes down on a performance and the audience files from their seats to return to their daily routines, the play's author invariably hopes that they carry away with them more than that with which they came. In the present, analogous case, the hope is multifold. It is hoped that readers, particularly those who had not had extensive prior exposure to social psychology, have acquired a new perspective on social behavior and interpersonal relations. Impression management is an integral part of interpersonal relations. Consciously or unconsciously, people attempt to control the images they project to real or imagined audiences. It doesn't matter whether a person is in the middle of a group and trying to achieve some goal, such as being liked or being elected leader; walking down the street and glancing surreptitiously at a store window, thinking about what an attractive image is cast there while nonchalantly straightening a few out-of-place hairs; or alone at home and judging one's own conduct with the help of an imagined audience of significant others—images determine how people see themselves and how they are viewed and treated by others. There is invariably some reason for people to control the images they project, since the reward/cost ratios people receive from social life are predicated in large part on these images.

Another hope, addressed particularly to those who once viewed impression management as a conscious, deceitful effort designed solely to procure illicit gains, is that the ethical overtones of this subject have been removed. There is nothing intrinsically unethical or ethical about impression management. In and of itself, it is ethically neutral. It can be used for unethical ends, of course, as people tell self-aggrandizing lies in order to procure illicit gains, such as jobs they don't really merit. It can be used for ethical ends, as when people are motivated to monitor and control the images they project in order to insure that others gain an honest picture of themselves. People who want to convey an accurate impression of themselves to others must monitor and control their actions in order to be sure they are faithfully conveying this impression, just as those who only want to con others monitor and control their actions to hide the deception. It is the motivation of the actor that determines whether impression management is "good" or "bad"; it is not the act itself.

Then, too, impression management is not always a conscious activity. Two states of self-awareness exist: objective self-awareness (the "Me" state), in which people focus their attentions on themselves and process information in terms of its self-relevance, and subjective self-awareness (the "I" state), in which people become focused on events and

304

lose a sense of personal awareness (see Chapter 3). At the times when people are subjectively self-aware, the habits of social life take over, and these habits frequently reflect impression-management tactics that have become well-ingrained over time. People encounter a social situation, and the "proper" ways of behaving become obvious immediately, because the appropriate cognitive script has been engaged. Cognitive scripts can be unconsciously engaged by cues in the situation, and the cognitive scripts that are relevant to most social situations are replete with many impression-management notions that have become incorporated into the etiquette of everyday life. People smile approvingly when an acquaintance tells a joke; they say "excuse me" when they bump into someone on the sidewalk; they unthinkingly congratulate those who achieve even a minor triumph; they nod acceptingly when others express (even dissimilar) opinions; they appear to pay attention to one who rambles through a boring description of last summer's vacation; and so on. Actions create impressions. The impressions that are created by actions are too potent for them not to affect behavior.

Impression management is sometimes viewed as "phony" even when it is not viewed as unethical: phony because people sometimes monitor and control their own actions instead of "acting naturally" or phony because people sometimes try to please others instead of pleasing themselves or being themselves. Some writers note that many people wear masks in public and that these masks hide people's "real selves" and cause them to act self-consciously. These writers prescribe that such people can never enter into truly healthy relationships; instead, people should "be themselves," shed their masks, and act without thinking about themselves and how their actions make them look. It is a fine thought, and it is probably good advice to individuals who overdo self-consciousness. Except for individuals at this extreme, however, it is an oversimplification and—like the adage "Judge not by the appearance"—it is utterly impossible to achieve in practice.

People *do* direct their attention inward and become objectively self-aware; this is a fact of human existence. People cannot avoid it. Moreover, it shouldn't be avoided, since it is responsible for meritorious as well as reprehensible conduct. The same self-reflection that causes people to monitor and control their actions in order to impress an audience can also cause them to contemplate acceptable, even lofty, standards for conduct. Conscience and the obedience to moral standards are predicated on people's abilities to reflect about themselves and their relationship to others. It is when people are objectively self-aware that they are most conscious of laudatory standards for conduct and can applaud or censure themselves for meeting or failing to meet these standards (Duval & Wicklund, 1972). The monitoring and control of actions thus takes different forms depending upon the actor's goals—it can be for the purpose of conning a real audience or satisfying an imagined audience in order to bring one's conduct up to the level of one's standards.

Further, there is nothing intrinsic to the concept of impression management that dictates that it must be directed toward only a real audience. Imagined audiences, which range from the generalized other (Chapter 3) to specific significant others (parents, teachers, siblings, spouse, admired heroes), can be conjured. These are often played to with more gusto than the immediate real audiences people encounter. What people usually mean when they say "be yourself" is to act in a way that would be approved by such significant imagined audiences rather than to act in a way that would only win the favor of (often less significant) immediate real audiences.

Thus, the concept of impression management does not simply imply that people are (a) behaving deceptively, (b) being unethical, (c) acting consciously and deliberately, (d) being "phony," (e) failing to live up to high standards, or (f) trying to please an immediate real audience. Future theorizing and research should focus more attention on the opposite sides of these ideas, exploring how impression management is employed to achieve personal consistency, the adherence to standards, and so on. It is unfortunate, although perhaps not too surprising, that most of the past work on impression management has focused on how it is used consciously to deceive unsuspecting audiences. People seem to be fascinated by how it is used in business, politics, and other fields to secure illicit gains. Such research should continue, but it is time to redress the imbalance.

Another hope, particularly relevant to those who already have solid backgrounds in social psychology, is that some "old" phenomena that were previously interpreted in terms of existing alternative approaches might now be interpreted from an impression-management perspective as well. The attribution of responsibility (Chapter 4), social comparison to maintain self-esteem (Chapters 4 and 5), attitude change in forced-compliance settings (Chapter 5), self-descriptions as a consequence of social feedback (Chapters 5 and 6), consistency in attitude statements (Chapter 7), the use of nonverbal actions and personal appearance (Chapters 8 and 9), some of the behaviors of mental patients (Chapter 10)—all can be viewed profitably from an impression-management perspective. The approach is a viable alternative or addition to many existing theoretical positions in social psychology.

In addition to reinterpretations of the "old," I hope I have specified enough "new" directions to occupy the attentions of researchers. Phenomena that might not be obvious targets for research from existing alternative theories emerge when an impression-management perspective is applied.

Another hope, addressed primarily to readers who espoused the view that human behavior is so spontaneous, complex, idiosyncratic, and rooted in unique historical circumstances to defy systematic examination, is that some of the general, predictable patterns of behavior have stood out. The idiosyncracy argument has been advanced in a number of overlapping ways. Some people focus on individual differences that exist in experiences, values, and beliefs, and they despair of finding commonalities. Others point out that the specific beliefs and values that people hold vary considerably over time and cultures, and they similarly despair. Still others point out that people are active agents, not passive puppets, implying that they have free will that allows them to avoid predictable reactions. All of these premises are true, at least in part. People are active agents who both affect and are affected by their environments (Chapter 2). People differ in their experiences, values and beliefs. And the specific beliefs and values people hold vary considerably over time and culture. Several writers have actually suggested that social science can never do more than simply record or catalog the beliefs, values, rules of etiquette, and behavior patterns that exist in a particular society at a given time. But it is incorrect to conclude that the study of impression management, or any other social psychological process, can't be done scientifically or that it amounts to nothing more than amassing the particular facts about behavior that exist at one particular intersection of an individual with time and place and is therefore not generalizable. Changes in beliefs and values can be studied in and of themselves to see how particular conditions affect them.

More importantly, though, *predictions* can be made about how one will behave, *given* a person's specific beliefs (for example, beliefs about which behaviors produce a particular image or which images produce particular consequences) and values (for example, how valued a particular image is). The Association Principle (Chapter 4) permits one to "plug in" the particular beliefs and values of an individual and emerge with predictions about the types of things that person is likely to do. Predictions can be made about the conditions under which a person is most likely to be motivated to convey a particular impression and the specific ways they might go about doing so. In Chapter 5, for instance, we examined the conditions under which people will be most motivated to act in predicaments and reviewed hypotheses about the factors that affect whether they attempt to excuse, justify, or apologize for undesirable events.

The general rule we've used to describe how people go about controlling images is expressed in shorthand in the Association Principle and its derivatives: people act to establish associations with desirable images and to disestablish associations with undesirable images. The principle integrates a wide array of findings in the domain of social psychology relevant to the self, cognitive social psychology, symbolic interactionism, and social influence. Through association (showing possession of, responsibility for, or connection to), we construct bridges between ourselves and images. We become linked to, and ultimately indistinguishable from, the images. Our selves are staked out in terms of images. The desirability of an image determines the worth of the bridge; a bridge that leads to an obnoxious or disliked destination is detonated if possible (that is, if reality permits), and one that leads to a rewarding destination is frequently traveled. Any action, object, attribute, or event can convey an image. People act to control (1) the ways in which actions, objects, attributes, and events are categorized (for example, whether the act of publicly agreeing with another person's opinion represents tactfulness, coincidence, or ingratiation); (2) the evaluation of the image (one could argue that ingratiation is good, not bad); and (3) the degree to which they are linked to the image (for example, their responsibility for an event or the degree to which they possess an attribute). Through these techniques of control governed by the Association Principle, people construct identities and maintain them against threatening events.

The Association Principle has been assumed to operate in private as well as in public; even when people are alone, they seem to think of themselves in ways that allow them to claim desirable images and disclaim undesirable ones. In this sense, impression management takes place before imagined audiences even when people are in the solitude of their rooms and ruminating about their attributes and conduct. Private beliefs and feelings, of course, are things the holder knows but others can only guess at. Because these are not accessible to direct observation by scientists, some researchers argue that such private phenomena are not really the proper subject of scientific investigation (there are fewer such researchers than several years ago, but there are still some). From a scientific point of view, there is no reason to insist on such direct observational purity. Social scientists cannot directly observe such private phenomena, but they can make often excellent inferences about them based on other objects or events that they can observe. In this pursuit, the social scientist's task is somewhat analogous to that of other scientists, who often make inferences about unseen phenomena on the basis of observable data (as when the physicist infers the existence and properties of an alpha particle from the trace it leaves in a cloud chamber or the astronomer infers the existence of unseen planets on the basis of perturbations in the orbits of planets that can be seen). The study of private impression management can draw on the same arsenal of methodological techniques now being used to investigate attitudes, beliefs, the self-concept, attributions, motives, and other private phenomena in the domain of cognitive social psychology. These include (a) placing subjects in situations that minimize or eliminate the pressures that arise from trying to impress the experimenter with their responses; (b) convincing subjects that it is in their best interests to report their private beliefs as accurately as possible—for example, by using the bogus pipeline, a technique designed to get subjects to tell the truth by convincing them that the experimenter has an accurate physiological measure of their private states (Jones & Sigall, 1971); (c) using measures that most subjects either can't consciously control (say, heart rate or galvanic skin response) or are less likely to control consciously (reaction time); (d) using unobtrusive measures in which subjects don't know that their responses are being assessed. Each of these techniques has advantages and disadvantages and can make research difficult. But this should not preclude the study of private impression management.

I also hope that the previous chapters assaulted the walls of demarcation between "psychological" social psychology and "sociological" social psychology. The former, composed largely of experimental social psychologists, and the latter, composed largely of symbolic interactionists, remain surprisingly aloof from one another, often ignoring one another's work and occasionally, when encountering work, demonstrating hostility. Yet they address similar issues and have much to share. We should strive for integration; impression management is an excellent area on which to focus that effort.

Symbolic interactionists are concerned with people's shared and symbolic experiences and how these affect the development and form of the self and of social interaction. Experimental social psychologists pursue a parallel course, emphasizing (among other things) cognitive social processes. The terminology of the groups differs, but the issues with which they deal are often identical. How people go about controlling the images that reflect their identities and self-concepts seems to be the ideal meeting point.

This list of hopes could go on and on, but I'll succumb to expressing only one more. I hope that, as the curtain is falling on our excursion into impression management and self-presentation, it is just rising on wider systematic study in this area.

REFERENCES

Abelson, R.P. Script processing in attitude formation and decision making. In J. S. Carroll & J. W. Payne (Eds.), *Cognition and social behavior*. Hillsdale, New Jersey: Erlbaum, 1976.

Abelson, R. P., Aronson, E., McGuire, W. J., Newcomb, T. M., Rosenberg, M. J., & Tannenbaum, P. H. (Eds.). *Theories of cognitive consistency: A sourcebook*. Chicago: Rand McNally, 1968.

Ackerman, B., & Schlenker, B. R. *Self-presentation: Attributes of the actor and audience*. Paper presented at the 83rd Annual Meeting of the American Psychological Association, Chicago, September 1975.

Adams, R. S. Location as a function of instructor interaction. *Merrill-Palmer Quarterly*, 1969, *15*, 309–321.

Addington, D. W. The relationship of selected vocal characteristics to personality perception. *Speech Monographs*, 1968, *35*, 492–503.

Ajzen, I., & Fishbein, M. A Bayesian analysis of attribution processes. *Psychological Bulletin*, 1975, *82*, 261–277.

Alexander, C. N., Jr., & Lauderdale, P. Situated identities and social influence. *Sociometry*, 1977, *40*, 225–233.

Allen, V. L. Role theory and consistency theory. In R. P. Abelson, E. Aronson, W. J. McGuire, T. M. Newcomb, M. J. Rosenberg, & P. H. Tannenbaum (Eds.), *Theories of cognitive consistency: A sourcebook*. Chicago: Rand McNally, 1968.

Allport, G. W. *Personality: A psychological interpretation*. New York: Holt, 1937.

Allport, G. W. The historical background of modern social psychology. In G. Lindzey & E. Aronson (Eds.), *The handbook of social psychology* (Vol. 1) (2nd ed.). Reading, Mass.: Addison-Wesley, 1968.

Anglo, S. The courtier: The Renaissance and changing ideals. In A. G. Dickens (Ed.), *The courts of Europe: Politics, patronage and royalty 1400–1800*. New York: McGraw-Hill, 1977.

Apsler, R. Effects of embarrassment on behavior toward others. *Journal of Personality and Social Psychology*, 1975, *32*, 145–153.

Archibald, W. P. Alternative explanations for self-fulfilling prophecies. Doctoral dissertation, University of Michigan, 1971.

Ardrey, R. *The territorial imperative*. New York: Dell, 1966.

Argyle, M. Non-verbal symbolic action: Gaze. In R. Harré (Ed.), *Life sentences: Aspects of the social role of language*. New York: Wiley, 1976.

Argyle, M., & Dean, J. Eye contact, distance and affiliation. *Sociometry*, 1965, *28*, 289–304.

Arkin, R. M., Gabrenya, W. K., Jr., Appelman, A. S., & Cochrane, S. T. Self-presentation, self-monitoring, and the self-serving bias in causal attribution. *Personality and Social Psychology Bulletin*, 1979, *5*, 73–76.

The Armed Forces Officer. Office of Armed Forces Information and Education, Department of Defense. Washington, D. C.: U. S. Government Printing Office, 1965.

Aronfreed, J. The nature, variety and social patterning of moral responses to transgression. *Journal of Abnormal and Social Psychology*, 1961, *63*, 223–240.

Aronson, E. Dissonance theory: Progress and problems. In R. P. Abelson, E. Aronson, W. J. McGuire, T. M. Newcomb, M. J. Rosenberg, & P. H. Tannenbaum (Eds.), *Theories of cognitive consistency: A sourcebook*. Chicago: Rand McNally, 1968.

Artiss, K. L. (Ed.), *The symptom as communication in schizophrenia*. New York: Grune & Stratton, 1959.

Austin, J. L. *Philosophical papers* (2nd ed.). New York: Oxford University Press, 1970. (Originally published, 1961.)

Austin, J. L. *How to do things with words.* Cambridge, Mass.: Harvard University Press, 1975. (Originally published, 1962.)

Austin, W., Walster, E., & Utne, M. K. Equity and the law: The effects of a harmdoer's "suffering in the act" on liking and punishment. In L. Berkowitz & E. Walster (Eds.), *Advances in experimental social psychology* (Vol. 9). New York: Academic Press, 1976.

Backman, C., Secord, P., & Peirce, J. Resistance to change in self-concept as a function of consensus among significant others. *Sociometry,* 1963, *26,* 102–111.

Bandura, A. *Principles of behavior modification.* New York: Holt, Rinehart & Winston, 1969.

Bandura, A. *Aggression: A social psychological analysis.* Englewood Cliffs, N. J.: Prentice-Hall, 1973.

Bandura, A. Behavior theory and the models of man. *American Psychologist,* 1974, *29,* 859–869.

Bandura, A. *Social learning theory.* Englewood Cliffs, N. J.: Prentice-Hall, 1977. (a)

Bandura, A. Self-efficacy: Toward a unifying theory of behavioral change. *Psychological Review,* 1977, *84,* 191–215. (b)

Bandura, A. The self system in reciprocal determinism. *American Psychologist,* 1978, *33,* 344–358.

Baron, P. H. Self-esteem, ingratiation, and evaluation of unknown others. *Journal of Personality and Social Psychology,* 1974, *30,* 104–109.

Bateson, G., Jackson, D. D., Haley, J., & Weakland, J. Toward a theory of schizophrenia. *Behavioral Science,* 1956, *1,* 251–264.

Baumeister, R. F., & Jones, E. E. When self-presentation is constrained by the target's knowledge: Consistency and compensation. *Journal of Personality and Social Psychology,* 1978, *36,* 608–618.

Becker, E. *The birth and death of meaning.* New York: Free Press, 1962.

Beckman, L. Effects of students' performance on teachers' and observers' attributions of causality. *Journal of Educational Psychology,* 1970, *61,* 76–82.

Bem, D. J. Self perception theory. In L. Berkowitz (Ed.), *Advances in experimental social psychology* (Vol. 6). New York: Academic Press, 1972.

Bem, D. J., & McConnell, H. K. Testing the self-perception explanation of dissonance phenomena: On the salience of premanipulation attitudes. *Journal of Personality and Social Psychology,* 1970, *14,* 23–31.

Berger, P. L., & Luckman, T. *The social construction of reality.* Garden City, N. Y.: Anchor Books, 1967.

Bergin, A. E. The effect of dissonant persuasive communications upon changes in self-referring attitudes. *Journal of Personality,* 1962, *30,* 423–438.

Berkowitz admits "inventing" demons. Associated Press. *Gainesville Sun,* February 23, 1979. p. 4B.

Berscheid, E., Graziano, W., Monson, T., & Dermer, M. Outcome dependency: Attention, attribution, and attraction. *Journal of Personality and Social Psychology,* 1976, *34,* 978–989.

Berscheid, E., & Walster, E. Attitude change. In J. Mills (Ed.), *Experimental social psychology.* New York: Macmillan, 1969.

Berscheid, E., & Walster, E. Physical attractiveness. In L. Berkowitz (Ed.), *Advances in experimental social psychology* (Vol. 7). New York: Academic Press, 1974.

Berscheid, E., & Walster, E. H. *Interpersonal attraction* (2nd ed.). Reading, Mass.: Addison-Wesley, 1978.

Biddle, B. J., & Thomas, E. J. (Eds.). *Role theory: Concepts and research.* New York: Wiley, 1966.

Birdwhistell, R. L. *Kinesics and context.* Philadelphia: University of Pennsylvania Press, 1970.

Blau, P. M. *Exchange and power in social life.* New York: Wiley, 1964.

Blumstein, P. W. Audience, Machiavellianism, and tactics of identity bargaining. *Sociometry,* 1973, *36,* 346–365.

Bogart, F., Geis, F., Levy, M., & Zimbardo, P. No dissonance for Machiavellians. In R. Christie & F. Geis, *Studies in Machiavellianism.* New York: Academic Press, 1970.

Bolles, R. C. Reinforcement, expectancy, and learning. *Psychological Review,* 1972, *79,* 394–409.

Braginsky, B. M., Braginsky, D. D., & Ring, K. *Methods of madness: The mental hospital as a last resort.* New York: Holt, Rinehart & Winston, 1969.

Braginsky, D. D. Machiavellianism and manipulative interpersonal behavior in children. *Journal of Experimental Social Psychology,* 1970, *6,* 77–99.

Braginsky, D. D., & Braginsky, B. M. *Hansels and Gretels: Studies of children in institutions for the mentally retarded.* New York: Holt, Rinehart & Winston, 1971.

Bramel, B., Taub, B., & Blum, B. An observer's reaction to the suffering of his enemy. *Journal of Personality and Social Psychology,* 1968, *8,* 384–392.

Bramel, D. A. A dissonance theory approach to defensive projection. *Journal of Abnormal and Social Psychology,* 1962, *64,* 121–129.

Bramel, D. A. Selection of a target for defensive projection. *Journal of Abnormal and Social Psychology,* 1963, *66,* 318–324.

Bramel, D. A. Interpersonal attraction, hostility, and perception. In J. Mills (Ed.), *Experimental social psychology.* New York: Macmillan, 1969.

Branden, N. *The psychology of self-esteem.* Los Angeles: Nash Publishing, 1969.

Braver, S. L., Linder, D. E., Corwin, T. T., & Cialdini, R. B. Some conditions that affect admissions of attitude change. *Journal of Experimental Social Psychology,* 1977, *13,* 565–576.

Brehm, J. W. *A theory of psychological reactance.* New York: Academic Press, 1966.

Brehm, J. W. *Responses to loss of freedom: A theory of psychological reactance.* Morristown, N. J.: General Learning Press, 1972.

Brewer, M. B. An information-processing approach to attribution of responsibility. *Journal of Experimental Social Psychology,* 1977, *13,* 58–69.

Brickman, P., & Seligman, C. Effects of public and private expectancies on attributions of competence and interpersonal attraction. *Journal of Personality,* 1974, *42,* 558–568.

Brittan, A. *Meanings and situations.* Boston: Routledge & Kegan Paul, 1973.

Brock, T. C., & Buss, A. H. Dissonance, aggression, and evaluation of pain. *Journal of Abnormal and Social Psychology,* 1962, *65,* 197–202.

Brock, T. C., & Buss, A. H. Effects of justification for aggression in communication with the victim on post-aggression dissonance. *Journal of Abnormal and Social Psychology,* 1964, *68,* 403–412.

Brown, B. R. The effects of need to maintain face on interpersonal bargaining. *Journal of Experimental Social Psychology,* 1968, *4,* 107–122.

Brown, B. R. Face-saving following experimentally-induced embarrassment. *Journal of Experimental Social Psychology,* 1970, *6,* 255–271.

Brown, B. R., & Garland, H. The effects of incompetency, audience acquaintanceship, and anticipated evaluative feedback on face-saving behavior. *Journal of Experimental Social Psychology,* 1971, *7,* 490–502.

Brown, R. *Social psychology*. New York: Free Press, 1965.

Burns, E. *Theatricality: A study of convention in the theatre and in social life*. New York: Harper & Row, 1973.

Byrne, D. *The attraction paradigm*. New York: Academic Press, 1971.

Cahnman, W. J. The stigma of obesity. *Sociological Quarterly*, 1968, *9*, 283–299.

Caine, B. T., & Schlenker, B. R. Role position and group performance as determinants of egotistical perceptions in cooperative groups. *Journal of Psychology*, 1979, *101*, 149–156.

Calder, B. J., Ross, M., & Insko, C. A. Attitude change and attitude attribution: Effects of incentive, choice, and consequences. *Journal of Personality and Social Psychology*, 1973, *25*, 84–99.

Carnegie, D. *How to win friends and influence people*. New York: Pocket Books, 1940.

Carroll, J. S., & Payne, J. W. (Eds.). *Cognition and social behavior*. Hillsdale, N. J.: Erlbaum, 1976.

Carson, R. C. *Interaction concepts of personality*. Chicago: Aldine, 1969.

Carter orders campaign manual rewrite. Associated Press. *Gainesville Sun*, Oct. 11, 1976.

Cartwright, D. (Ed.). *Studies in social power*. Ann Arbor: University of Michigan, Institute for Social Research, 1959.

Carver, C. S., & Scheier, M. F. Self-focusing effects of dispositional self-consciousness, mirror presence, and audience presence. *Journal of Personality and Social Psychology*, 1978, *36*, 324–332.

Chaikin, A. L., & Derlega, V. L. *Self-disclosure*. Morristown, N. J.: General Learning Press, 1974.

Child, I. L. Personality in culture. In E. F. Borgatta & W. W. Lambert (Eds.), *Handbook of personality theory and research*. Chicago: Rand McNally, 1968.

Christie, R., & Geis, F. Some consequences of taking Machiavelli seriously. In E. F. Borgatta & W. W. Lambert (Eds.), *Handbook of personality theory and research*. Chicago: Rand McNally, 1968.

Christie, R., & Geis, F. L. *Studies in Machiavellianism*. New York: Academic Press, 1970. (a)

Christie, R., & Geis, F. L. The ten dollar game. In R. Christie & F. Geis, *Studies in Machiavellianism*. New York: Academic Press, 1970. (b)

Cialdini, R. B. Attitudinal advocacy in the verbal conditioner. *Journal of Personality and Social Psychology*, 1971, *17*, 350–358.

Cialdini, R. B., Borden, R. J., Thorne, A., Walker, M. R., Freeman, S., & Sloan, L. R. Basking in reflected glory: Three (football) field studies. *Journal of Personality and Social Psychology*, 1976, *34*, 366–375.

Cialdini, R. B., Braver, S. L., & Lewis, S. K. Attributional bias and the easily persuaded other. *Journal of Personality and Social Psychology*, 1974, *30*, 631–637.

Cialdini, R. B., Cacioppo, J. T., Bassett, R., & Miller, J. A. Low-ball procedure for producing compliance: Commitment then cost. *Journal of Personality and Social Psychology*, 1978, *36*, 463–476.

Cialdini, R. B., Kenrick, D. T., & Hoerig, J. H. Victim derogation in the Lerner paradigm: Just world or just justification? *Journal of Personality and Social Psychology*, 1976, *33*, 719–724.

Cialdini, R. B., Levy, A., Herman, C. P., & Evenbeck, S. Attitudinal politics: The strategy of moderation. *Journal of Personality and Social Psychology*, 1973, *25*, 100–108.

Cialdini, R. B., Levy, A., Herman, C. P., Kozlowski, L. T., & Petty, R. E. Elastic shifts of opinion: Determinants of direction and durability. *Journal of Personality and Social Psychology*, 1976, *34*, 663–672.

Cialdini, R. B., & Mirels, H. L. Sense of personal control and attributions about yielding and resisting persuasive targets. *Journal of Personality and Social Psychology*, 1976, *33*, 395–402.

Cialdini, R. B., & Richardson, K. D. Two tactics of image management: Basking and blasting. *Journal of Personality and Social Psychology*, in press.

Cofer, C. N., & Appley, M. H. *Motivation: Theory and research*. New York: Wiley, 1964.

Collins, B. E., & Hoyt, M. F. Personal responsibility-for-consequences: An integration and extension of the "forced compliance" literature. *Journal of Experimental Social Psychology*, 1972, *8*, 558–593.

Cooley, C. H. *Human nature and the social order* (Rev. ed.). New York: Charles Scribner's Sons, 1922. (Originally published, 1902.)

Cooper, J., & Jones, E. E. Opinion divergence as a strategy to avoid being miscast. *Journal of Personality and Social Psychology*, 1969, *13*, 23–40.

Cooper, J., & Jones, R. A. Self-esteem and consistency as determinants of anticipatory opinion change. *Journal of Personality and Social Psychology*, 1970, *14*, 312–320.

Coopersmith, S. *The antecedents of self-esteem*. San Francisco: W. H. Freeman, 1967.

Costrich, N., Feinstein, J., Kidder, L., Maracek, J., & Pascale, L. When stereotypes hurt: Three studies of penalties for sex-role reversals. *Journal of Experimental Social Psychology*, 1975, *11*, 520–530.

Cozby, P. C. Self-disclosure: A literature review. *Psychological Bulletin*, 1973, *79*, 73–91.

Crowne, D. P., & Marlowe, D. *The approval motive*. New York: Wiley, 1964.

Dannenmaier, W. D., & Thumin, F. J. Authority status as a factor in perceptual distortion of size. *Journal of Social Psychology*, 1964, *63*, 361–365.

D'Arcy, E. *Human acts*. New York: Oxford University Press, 1963.

Davis, D., & Brock, T. C. Use of first person pronouns as a function of increased objective self-awareness and performance feedback. *Journal of Experimental Social Psychology*, 1975, *11*, 381–388.

Davis, K. E., & Florquist, C. C. Perceived threat and dependence as determinants of the tactical usage of opinion conformity. *Journal of Experimental Social Psychology*, 1965, *1*, 219–236.

Davis, K. E., & Jones, E. E. Changes in interpersonal perception as a means of reducing cognitive dissonance. *Journal of Abnormal and Social Psychology*, 1960, *61*, 402–410.

Davis, M. S., & Schmidt, C. J. The obnoxious and the nice. *Sociometry*, 1977, *40*, 201–213.

Deaux, K. K. Variations in warning, information preference, and anticipatory attitude change. *Journal of Personality and Social Psychology*, 1968, *9*, 157–161.

Deaux, K. K. Anticipatory attitude change: A direct test of the self-esteem hypothesis. *Journal of Experimental Social Psychology*, 1972, *8*, 143–155.

Dewey, J. *Human nature and conduct*. New York: Modern Library, 1922.

Dewey, J. A. Theory of valuation. In O. Neurath (Ed.), *International encyclopedia of unified science, II*. Chicago: University of Chicago Press, 1939.

Dickenberger, D., & Grabitz-Gniech, G. *Restrictive conditions for the occurrence of psychological reactance: Interpersonal attraction, need for social approval, and a delay factor*. Unpublished manuscript, University of Mannheim, West Germany, 1971.

Dickoff, H. Reactions to evaluations by another person as a function of self-evaluations and the interaction context. Doctoral dissertation, Duke University, 1961.

Diener, E., & Srull, T. K. Self-awareness, psychological perspective, and self-reinforcement in relation to personal and social standards. *Journal of Personality and Social Psychology*, 1979, *37*, 413–423.

Dillehay, R. C. On the irrelevance of the classical negative evidence concerning the effect of attitudes on behavior. *American Psychologist*, 1973, *28*, 887–891.

Dittes, J. E. Attractiveness of group as function of self-esteem and acceptance by group. *Journal of Abnormal and Social Psychology*, 1959, *59*, 77–82.

Dollard, J. Under what conditions do opinions predict behavior? *Public Opinion Quarterly*, 1949, *12*, 623–632.

Driedger, L. Ethnic self-identity: A comparison of ingroup evaluations. *Sociometry*, 1976, *39*, 131–141.

Durand, D. E. Power as a function of office space and physiognomy: Two studies of influence. *Psychological Reports*, 1977, *40*, 755–760.

Durant, W. *The story of civilization: Our oriental heritage.* New York: Simon & Schuster, 1935.

Dutton, D. G. Effect of feedback parameters on congruency versus positive effects in reactions to personal evaluations. *Journal of Personality and Social Psychology*, 1972, *24*, 366–371.

Duval, S. Conformity as a function of perceived level of personal uniqueness and being reminded of the object status of self. Doctoral dissertation, University of Texas at Austin, 1972.

Duval, S., & Wicklund, R. A. *A theory of objective self-awareness.* New York: Academic Press, 1972.

Eagly, A. H. Involvement as a determinant of responses to favorable and unfavorable information. *Journal of Personality and Social Psychology*, 1967, *7*, (3, Whole No. 643).

Earl of Chesterfield (Philip Darmer Stanhope). *Letters to his son* (Walter M. Dunne, Ed.). New York: Wiley, 1901. (Originally published, 1774.)

Edney, J. J. Territoriality and control: A field experiment. *Journal of Personality and Social Psychology*, 1975, *31*, 1108–1115.

Edney, J. J., & Jordan-Edney, N. L. Territorial spacing on a beach. *Sociometry*, 1974, *37*, 92–104.

Efran, M. G., & Cheyne, J. A. Affective concomitants of the invasion of shared space: Behavioral, physiological, and verbal indicators. *Journal of Personality and Social Psychology*, 1974, *29*, 219–226.

Ekman, P., & Friesen, W. V. Nonverbal leakage and clues to deception. *Psychiatry*, 1969, *32*, 88–106.

Ekman, P., & Friesen, W. V. Detecting deception from the body or face. *Journal of Personality and Social Psychology*, 1974, *29*, 288–298.

Ekman, P., & Friesen, W. V. *Unmasking the face.* Englewood Cliffs, N. J.: Prentice-Hall, 1975.

Ellsworth, P. C., & Carlsmith, J. Effects of eye contact and verbal content on affective response to a dyadic interaction. *Journal of Personality and Social Psychology*, 1968, *10*, 15–20.

Ellsworth, P. C., & Carlsmith, J. M. Eye contact and gaze aversion in an aggressive encounter. *Journal of Personality and Social Psychology*, 1973, *28*, 280–292.

Epstein, S. The self-concept revisited: Or a theory of a theory. *American Psychologist*, 1973, *28*, 404–416.

Erdelyi, M. H. A new look at the New Look: Perceptual defense and vigilance. *Psychological Review*, 1974, *81*, 1–25.

Erickson, B., Lind, E. A., Johnson, B. C., & O'Barr, W. M. Speech style and impression formation in a court setting: The effects of "Powerful" and

"Powerless" speech. *Journal of Experimental Social Psychology*, 1978, *14*, 266–279.

Essame, H. *Patton: A study in command.* New York: Scribner's, 1974.

Evreinoff, N. *The theatre in life.* New York: Benjamin Bloom, 1927.

Exline, R. V. Visual interaction: The glances of power and preference. In J. Cole (Ed.), *Nebraska symposium on motivation.* Lincoln: University of Nebraska Press, 1971.

Exline, R. V., Ellyson, S. L., & Long, B. Visual behavior as an aspect of power role relationships. In P. Pliner, L. Krames, & T. Alloway (Eds.), *Nonverbal communication of aggression.* New York: Plenum, 1975.

Exline, R. V., Thibaut, J., Hickey, C. B., & Gumbert, P. Visual interaction in relation to Machiavellianism and an unethical act. In R. Christie & F. Geis, *Studies in Machiavellianism.* New York: Academic Press, 1970.

Fast, J. *Body language.* New York: Pocket Books, 1971.

Fazio, R. H., Zanna, M. P., & Cooper, J. Dissonance and self-perception: An integrative view of each theory's proper domain of application. *Journal of Experimental Social Psychology*, 1977, *13*, 464–479.

Feather, N. T. Attribution of responsibility and valence of success and failure in relation to initial confidence and task performance. *Journal of Personality and Social Psychology*, 1969, *13*, 129–144.

Federoff, N. A., & Harvey, J. H. Focus of attention, self-esteem, and the attribution of causality. *Journal of Research in Personality*, 1976, *10*, 336–345.

Fenigstein, A. Self-consciousness, self-attention, and social interaction. *Journal of Personality and Social Psychology*, 1979, *37*, 75–86.

Festinger, L. *A theory of cognitive dissonance.* Evanston, Ill.: Row, Peterson, 1957.

Finck, H. T. *Romantic love and personal beauty: Their development, causal relations, historic and national peculiarities.* London: Macmillan, 1902.

Fischer, C. S. The effects of threats in an incomplete information game. *Sociometry*, 1969, *32*, 301–314.

Fishbein, M., & Ajzen, I. *Belief, attitude, intention and behavior: An introduction to theory and research.* Reading, Mass.: Addison-Wesley, 1975.

Fitch, G. Effects of self-esteem, perceived performance, and choice on causal attributions. *Journal of Personality and Social Psychology*, 1970, *16*, 311–315.

Fleming, D. Attitude: The history of a concept. *Perspectives in American History*, 1967, *1*, 287–365.

Foa, U. G. Convergences in the analysis of the structure of interpersonal behavior. *Psychological Review*, 1961, *68*, 341–353.

Folkes, V. S., & Sears, D. O. Does everybody like a liker? *Journal of Experimental Social Psychology*, 1977, *13*, 505–519.

Fontaine, G. Causal attribution in simulated versus real situations: When are people logical, when are they not? *Journal of Personality and Social Psychology*, 1975, *32*, 1021–1029.

Fontana, A. F. Machiavellianism and manipulation in the mental patient role. *Journal of Personality*, 1971, *39*, 252–263.

Fontana, A. F., & Corey, M. Culture conflict in the treatment of "mental illness" and the central role of patient leader. *Journal of Consulting and Clinical Psychology*, 1970, *34*, 244–249.

Fontana, A. F., & Gessner, T. Patients' goals and the manifestation of psychopathology. *Journal of Consulting and Clinical Psychology*, 1969, *33*, 247–253.

Fontana, A. F., & Klein, E. B. Self-presentation and the schizophrenic "deficit." *Journal of Consulting and Clinical Psychology*, 1968, *32*, 250–256.

Fontana, A. F., Klein, E. B., Lewis, E., & Levine, L. Presentation of self in mental illness. *Journal of Consulting and Clinical Psychology,* 1968, *32,* 110–119.

Foote, N. N. Identification as the basis for a theory of motivation. *American Sociological Review,* 1951, *16,* 14–21.

Forsyth, D. R., Riess, M., & Schlenker, B. R. Impression management concerns governing reactions to a faulty decision. *Representative Research in Social Psychology,* 1977, *8,* 12–22.

Forsyth, D. R., & Schlenker, B. R. Attributing the causes of group performance: Effects of performance quality, task importance, and future testing. *Journal of Personality,* 1977, *45,* 220–236. (a)

Forsyth, D. R., & Schlenker, B. R. Attributional egocentrism following performance of a competitive task. *Journal of Social Psychology,* 1977, *102,* 215–222. (b)

Freedman, J. L., & Fraser, S. Compliance without pressure: The foot-in-the-door technique. *Journal of Personality and Social Psychology,* 1966, *4,* 195–202.

French, J. R. P., Jr., & Raven, B. The bases of social power. In D. Cartwright (Ed.), *Studies in social power.* Ann Arbor: University of Michigan, Institute for Social Research, 1959.

Freud, S. Fragment of an analysis of a case of hysteria (1905). In *Collected papers* (Vol. 3). New York: Basic Books, 1959.

Frey, D. Reactions to success and failure in public and in private conditions. *Journal of Experimental Social Psychology,* 1978, *14,* 172–179.

Fromkin, H. L. Affective and valuational consequences of self-perceived uniqueness deprivation. Doctoral dissertation, Ohio State University, 1968.

Fromkin, H. L. Effects of experimentally aroused feelings of undistinctiveness upon valuation of scarce and novel experiences. *Journal of Personality and Social Psychology,* 1970, *16,* 521–529.

Fromm, E. *The sane society.* New York: Rinehart, 1955.

Gaes, G. G., Kalle, R. J., & Tedeschi, J. T. Impression management in the forced compliance situation. Two studies using the bogus pipeline. *Journal of Experimental Social Psychology,* 1978, *14,* 493–510.

Gaes, G. G., & Tedeschi, J. T. An evaluation of self-esteem and impression management theories of anticipatory belief change. *Journal of Experimental Social Psychology,* 1978, *14,* 579–587.

Gallup, G. G., Jr. Self-recognition in primates: A comparative approach to the bidirectional properties of consciousness. *American Psychologist,* 1977, *32,* 329–338.

Gallup, G. G., Jr., McClure, M. K., Hill, S. D., & Bundy, R. A. Capacity for self-recognition in differentially reared chimpanzees. *Psychological Record,* 1971, *21,* 69–74.

Garland, H., & Brown, B. R. Face-saving as affected by subjects' sex, audiences' sex, and audience expertise. *Sociometry,* 1972, *35,* 280–289.

Geis, F. The con game. In R. Christie & F. Geis, *Studies in Machiavellianism.* New York: Academic Press, 1970. (a)

Geis, F. Bargaining tactics in the con game. In R. Christie & F. Geis, *Studies in Machiavellianism.* New York: Academic Press, 1970. (b)

Geis, F., & Christie, R. Overview of experimental research. In R. Christie & F. Geis, *Studies in Machiavellianism.* New York: Academic Press, 1970.

Geis, F., Christie, R., & Nelson, C. In search of the Machiavel. In R. Christie & F. Geis, *Studies in Machiavellianism.* New York: Academic Press, 1970.

Geis, F., Weinheimer, S., & Berger, D. Playing legislature: Cool heads and hot issues. In R. Christie & F. Geis, *Studies in Machiavellianism.* New York: Academic Press, 1970.

Geller, V., & Shaver, P. Cognitive consequences of self-awareness. *Journal of Experimental Social Psychology*, 1976, *12*, 99–108.

Gemmill, G. R., & Heisler, W. J. Machiavellianism as a factor in managerial job strain, job satisfaction, and upward mobility. *Academy of Management Journal*, 1972, *15*, 51–62.

Gergen, K. J. Interaction goals and personalistic feedback as factors affecting the presentation of self. *Journal of Personality and Social Psychology*, 1965, *1*, 413–424.

Gergen, K. J. Personal consistency and the presentation of self. In C. Gordon & K. J. Gergen (Eds.), *The self in social interaction* (Vol. 1). New York: Wiley, 1968.

Gergen, K. J. *The concept of self.* New York: Holt, Rinehart & Winston, 1971.

Gergen, K. J., & Jones, E. E. Mental illness, predictability, and affective consequences as stimulus factors in person perception. *Journal of Abnormal and Social Psychology*, 1963, *67*, 95–104.

Gergen, K. J., & Taylor, M. G. Social expectancy and self-presentation in a status hierarchy. *Journal of Experimental Social Psychology*, 1969, *5*, 79–92.

Gergen, K. J., & Wishnov, B. Others' self-evaluation and interaction anticipation as determinants of self-presentation. *Journal of Personality and Social Psychology*, 1965, *2*, 348–358.

Gibbins, K. Communication aspects of women's clothes and their relation to fashionability. *British Journal of Social and Clinical Psychology*, 1969, *8*, 301–312.

Glass, D. C. Changes in liking as a means of reducing cognitive discrepancies between self-esteem and aggression. *Journal of Personality*, 1964, *32*, 520–549.

Goethals, G. R., & Reckman, R. F. The perception of consistency in attitudes. *Journal of Experimental Social Psychology*, 1973, *9*, 491–501.

Goffman, E. *The presentation of self in everyday life.* Garden City, N. Y.: Doubleday Anchor, 1959.

Goffman, E. *Asylums.* Garden City, N. Y.: Doubleday Anchor, 1961. (a)

Goffman, E. *Encounters.* Indianapolis: Bobbs-Merrill, 1961. (b)

Goffman, E. *Behavior in public places.* New York: Free Press, 1963. (a)

Goffman, E. *Stigma: Notes on the management of spoiled identity.* Englewood Cliffs, N. J.: Prentice-Hall, 1963. (b)

Goffman, E. *Interaction ritual.* Garden City, N. Y.: Doubleday Anchor, 1967.

Goffman, E. *Relations in public.* New York: Basic Books, 1971.

Goffman, E. *Frame analysis.* New York: Harper Colophon Books, 1974.

Goldman, H., & Schlenker, B. R. *Proattitudinal behavior, impression management, and attitude change.* Paper presented at the 85th Annual Meeting of the American Psychological Association, San Francisco, 1977.

Goldstein, I. L. The application blank: How honest are the responses? *Journal of Applied Psychology*, 1971, *55*, 491–492.

Gordon, C., & Gergen, K. J. (Eds.). *The self in social interaction* (Vol. 1). New York: Wiley, 1968.

Gouldner, A. The norm of reciprocity. *American Sociological Review*, 1960, *25*, 161–178.

Grabitz-Gniech, G. Some restrictive conditions for the occurrence of psychological reactance. *Journal of Personality and Social Psychology*, 1971, *19*, 188–196.

Greenwald, A. G., & Ronis, D. L. Twenty years of cognitive dissonance: Case study of the evolution of a theory. *Psychological Review*, 1978, *85*, 53–57.

Gross, E., & Stone, G. P. Embarrassment and the analysis of role requirements. *American Journal of Sociology*, 1964, *70*, 1–15.

Haas, H. T., & Maehr, M. L. Two experiments on the concept of self and the reaction of others. *Journal of Personality and Social Psychology,* 1965, *1,* 100–105.

Haley, J. The art of psychoanalysis. In S. I. Hayakawa (Ed.), *The use and misuse of language.* Greenwich, Conn.: Fawcett, 1962.

Haley, J. *Strategies of psychotherapy.* New York: Grune & Stratton, 1963.

Haley, J. (Ed.). *Changing families: A family therapy reader.* New York: Grune & Stratton, 1971.

Hall, E. T. *The silent language.* Garden City, N. Y.: Doubleday, 1959.

Hall, E. T. *The hidden dimension.* Garden City, N. Y.: Doubleday, 1966.

Hall, C. S., & Lindzey, G. *Theories of personality* (3rd ed.). New York: Wiley, 1978.

Hare, P. A., & Bales, B. F. Seating position and small group interaction. *Sociometry,* 1963, *26,* 480–486.

Harlow, H. F., & Harlow, M. K. Learning to love. *American Scientist,* 1966, *54,* 244–272.

Harlow, H. F., Harlow, M. K., & Suomi, S. J. From thought to therapy: Lessons from a primate laboratory. *American Scientist,* 1971, *59,* 538–549.

Harré, R. Blueprint for a new science. In N. Armistead (Ed.), *Reconstructing social psychology.* Baltimore: Penguin Books, 1974.

Harré, R. The ethogenic approach: Theory and practice. In L. Berkowitz (Ed.), *Advances in experimental social psychology* (Vol. 10). New York: Academic Press, 1977.

Harré, R., & Secord, P. F. *The explanation of social behavior.* Totowa, N. J.: Littlefield, Adams, 1973.

Harrell, W. A., & Hartnagel, T. The impact of Machiavellianism and the trust-fulness of the victim on laboratory theft. *Sociometry,* 1976, *39,* 157–165.

Harris, M. *Cows, pigs, wars, and witches: The riddles of culture.* New York: Vintage Books, 1975.

Harrison, A. A., Hwalek, M., Raney, D. F., & Fritz, J. G. Cues to deception in an interview situation. *Social Psychology,* 1978, *41,* 151–161.

Hart, H. L. A. *Punishment and responsibility: Essays on the philosophy of law.* New York: Oxford University Press, 1968.

Harvey, J. H., Ickes, W., & Kidd, R. F. (Eds.). *New directions in attribution research* (Vol. 1). Hillsdale, N. J.: Erlbaum, 1976.

Harvey, J. H., Ickes, W., & Kidd, R. F. (Eds.). *New directions in attribution research* (Vol. 2). Hillsdale, N. J.: Erlbaum, 1978.

Hass, R. G. Persuasion or moderation? Two experiments on anticipatory belief change. *Journal of Personality and Social Psychology,* 1975, *31,* 1155–1162.

Hass, R. G., & Mann, R. W. Anticipatory belief change: Persuasion or impression management? *Journal of Personality and Social Psychology,* 1976, *34,* 105–111.

Hastorf, A., & Cantril, H. They saw a game: A case study. *Journal of Abnormal and Social Psychology,* 1954, *49,* 129–134.

Heath, L. W., & Gurwitz, S. B. *Self-presentation and stereotypes: Is it smart to play dumb?* Paper presented at the 85th Annual Convention of the American Psychological Association, San Francisco, 1977.

Heider, F. *The psychology of interpersonal relations.* New York: Wiley, 1958.

Heider, F. A conversation with Fritz Heider. In J. H. Harvey, W. J. Ickes, & R. F. Kidd (Eds.), *New directions in attribution research* (Vol. 1). Hillsdale, N. J.: Erlbaum, 1976.

Heilbroner, R. L. *The worldly philosophers* (3rd ed.). New York: Simon & Schuster, 1967.

Hempel, C. G. *Philosophy of natural science.* Englewood Cliffs, N. J.: Prentice-Hall, 1966.

Hendricks, M., & Brickman, P. Effects of status and knowledgeability of audience on self-presentation. *Sociometry,* 1974, *37,* 440–449.

Henley, N. M. *Body politics: Power, sex, and nonverbal communication.* Englewood Cliffs, N. J.: Prentice-Hall, 1977.

Herbers, J. Ford now is a President in the recent tradition. New York Times Weekly Review. *Gainesville Sun,* May 19, 1975.

Hewitt, J., & Goldman, M. Self-esteem, need for approval, and reactions to personal evaluations. *Journal of Experimental Social Psychology,* 1974, *10,* 201–210.

Hilgard, E. R., & Bower, G. H. *Theories of learning* (4th ed.). Englewood Cliffs, N. J.: Prentice-Hall, 1975.

Hill, S. D., Bundy, R. A., Gallup, G. G., Jr., & McClure, M. K. Responsiveness of young nursery-reared chimpanzees to mirrors. *Proceedings of the Louisiana Academy of Sciences,* 1970, *33,* 77–82.

Hobbes, T. *Leviathan.* In R. M. Hutchins (Ed.), *Great books of the Western World.* Chicago: Encyclopaedia Britannica, 1952. (Originally published, 1651).

Hollingdale, R. J. Introduction to *Thus spoke Zarathustra,* by F. Nietzsche (R. J. Hollingdale, trans.). Baltimore: Penguin Books, 1961.

Holmes, D. S. Projection as a defense mechanism. *Psychological Bulletin,* 1978, *85,* 677–688.

Holstein, C. M., Goldstein, J. W., & Bem, D. J. The importance of expressive behavior, involvement, sex, and need-approval in inducing liking. *Journal of Experimental Social Psychology,* 1971, *7,* 534–544.

Homans, G. C. *Social behavior: Its elementary forms* (Rev. ed.). New York: Harcourt, Brace, Jovanovich, 1974.

Horney, K. *The neurotic personality of our time.* New York: Norton, 1937.

Howells, L. T., & Becker, S. W. Seating arrangement and leadership emergence. *Journal of Abnormal and Social Psychology,* 1962, *64,* 148–150.

Hoyt, M. F., Henley, M. D., & Collins, B. E. Studies in forced compliance: Confluence of choice and consequence on attitude change. *Journal of Personality and Social Psychology,* 1972, *23,* 205–210.

Hull, J. G., & Levy, A. S. The organizational functions of the self: An alternative to the Duval and Wicklund model of self awareness. *Journal of Personality and Social Psychology,* 1979, *37,* 756–768.

Hyman, H. H. The psychology of status. *Archives of Psychology,* 1942, *38: 269,* 1–94.

Jacobs, L., Berscheid, E., & Walster, E. Self-esteem and attraction. *Journal of Personality and Social Psychology,* 1971, *17,* 84–91.

James, W. *The principles of psychology.* In R. M. Hutchinson (Ed.), *Great books of the Western World.* Chicago: Encyclopaedia Britannica, 1952. (Originally published, 1890.)

Janis, I. L. *Victims of groupthink: A psychological study of foreign-policy decisions and fiascoes.* Boston: Houghton Mifflin, 1972.

Jellison, J. M., & Gentry, K. W. A self-presentation interpretation of the seeking of social approval. *Personality and Social Psychology Bulletin,* 1978, *4,* 227–230.

Jellison, J. M., & Ickes, W. J. The power of the glance: Desire to see and be seen in cooperative and competitive situations. *Journal of Experimental Social Psychology,* 1974, *10,* 444–450.

Jenkins, J. J. Remember that old theory of memory? Well, forget it! *American Psychologist,* 1974, *29,* 785–795.

Johnson, T. J., Feigenbaum, R., & Weiby, M. Some determinants and consequences of the teacher's perception of causation. *Journal of Educational Psychology*, 1964, *55*, 237–246.

Jones, E. E. *Ingratiation*. New York: Appleton-Century-Crofts, 1964.

Jones, E. E. Conformity as a tactic of ingratiation. *Science*, 1965, *149*, 144–150.

Jones, E. E. History of social psychology. In Kimble & Schlesinger (Eds.), *History of modern psychology*. New York: Wiley, in press.

Jones, E. E., & Archer, R. L. Are there personalistic effects of self-disclosure? *Journal of Experimental Social Psychology*, 1976, *12*, 180–193.

Jones, E. E., & Baumeister, R. F. The self-monitor looks at the ingratiator. *Journal of Personality*, 1976, *44*, 654–674.

Jones, E. E., & Berglas, S. Control of attributions about the self through self-handicapping strategies: The appeal of alcohol and the role of underachievement. *Personality and Social Psychology Bulletin*, 1978, *4*, 200–206.

Jones, E. E., & Davis, K. E. From acts to dispositions: The attribution process in person perception. In L. Berkowitz (Ed.), *Advances in experimental social psychology* (Vol. 2). New York: Academic Press, 1965.

Jones, E. E., Davis, K. E., & Gergen, K. J. Role-playing variations and their informational value for person perception. *Journal of Abnormal and Social Psychology*, 1961, *63*, 302–310.

Jones, E. E., & Gerard, H. B. *Foundations of social psychology*. New York: Wiley, 1967.

Jones, E. E., Gergen, K. J., & Davis, K. E. Some determinants of reactions to being approved or disapproved as a person. *Psychological Monographs*, 1962, *76*(2, Whole No. 521).

Jones, E. E., Gergen, K. J., Gumpert, P., & Thibaut, J. W. Some conditions affecting the use of ingratiation to influence performance evaluation. *Journal of Personality and Social Psychology*, 1965, *1*, 613–625.

Jones, E. E., Gergen, K. J., & Jones, R. G. Tactics of ingratiation among leaders and subordinates in a status hierarchy. *Psychological Monographs*, 1963, *77*(3, Whole No. 566).

Jones, E. E., Jones, R. G., & Gergen, K. J. Some conditions affecting the evaluation of a conformist. *Journal of Personality*, 1963, *31*, 270–288.

Jones, E. E., Kanouse, D. E., Kelley, H. H., Nisbett, R. E., Valins, S., & Weiner, B. (Eds.). *Attribution: Perceiving the causes of behavior*. Morristown, N. J.: General Learning Press, 1972.

Jones, E. E., & Sigall, H. The bogus pipeline: A new paradigm for measuring affect and attitude. *Psychological Bulletin*, 1971, *76*, 349–364.

Jones, E. E., Stires, L. K., Shaver, K. G., & Harris, V. A. Evaluation of an ingratiator by target persons and bystanders. *Journal of Personality*, 1968, *36*, 385.

Jones, E. E., & Wortman, C. *Ingratiation: An attributional approach*. Morristown, N. J.: General Learning Press, 1973.

Jones, R. G., & Jones, E. E. Optimum conformity as an ingratiation tactic. *Journal of Personality*, 1964, *32*, 436–458.

Jones, S. C. Self- and interpersonal evaluations: Esteem theories vs. consistency theories. *Psychological Bulletin*, 1973, *79*, 185–199.

Jones, S. C., & Schneider, D. J. Certainty of self-appraisal and reactions to evaluations from others. *Sociometry*, 1968, *31*, 395–403.

Jourard, S. M. *The transparent self: Self-disclosure and well-being*. Princeton, N. J.: Van Nostrand, 1964.

Jourard, S. M. *Disclosing man to himself*. Princeton, N. J.: Van Nostrand, 1968.

Jourard, S. M., & Remy, R. M. Perceived parental attitudes, the self, and security. *Journal of Consulting Psychology*, 1955, *19*, 364–366.

Kahn, A., & Young, D. L. Ingratiation in a free social situation. *Sociometry*, 1973, *36*, 579–587.

Kalven, J., Jr., & Zeisel, H. *The American Jury*. Boston: Little, Brown, 1966.

Katz, D. The functional approach to the study of attitudes. *Public Opinion Quarterly*, 1960, *24*, 163–204.

Katz, D., & Braley, K. W. Racial stereotypes of one hundred college students. *Journal of Abnormal and Social Psychology*, 1933, *28*, 282–290.

Keating, C. F., Mazur, A., & Segall, M. H. Facial gestures which influence the perception of status. *Sociometry*, 1977, *40*, 374–378.

Kelley, H. H. Attribution theory in social psychology. In D. Levine (Ed.), *Nebraska Symposium on Motivation*. Lincoln: University of Nebraska Press, 1967.

Kelley, H. H. *Attribution in social interaction*. New York: General Learning Press, 1971.

Kelly, G. A. *The psychology of personal constructs* (2 Vols.). New York: Norton, 1955.

Kelman, H. C., & Baron, R. M. Moral and hedonic dissonance: A functional analysis of the relationship between discrepant action and attitude change. In S. Himmelfarb & A. H. Eagly (Eds.), *Readings in attitude change*. New York: Wiley, 1974.

Kesey, K. *One flew over the cuckoo's nest*. New York: Signet Books, 1962.

Kiesler, C. A. *The psychology of commitment*. New York: Academic Press, 1971.

Kiesler, C. A., Collins, B. E., & Miller, N. *Attitude change*. New York: Wiley, 1969.

Kimble, G. A., & Perlmuter, L. C. The problem of volition. *Psychological Review*, 1970, *77*, 361–384.

Kinch, J. W. Experiments on factors related to self-concept change. *Journal of Social Psychology*, 1968, *74*, 251–258.

Kipnis, D. *The powerholders*. Chicago: University of Chicago Press, 1976.

Kipnis, D., & Vanderveer, R. Ingratiation and the use of power. *Journal of Personality and Social Psychology*, 1971, *17*, 280–286.

Kleinfield, H. R. Controversial new device detects telephone lying. New York Times News Service, *Gainesville Sun*, March 5, 1978.

Kleinke, C. L. *First impressions: The psychology of encountering others*. Englewood Cliffs, N. J.: Prentice-Hall, 1975.

Kleinke, C. L., Staneski, R. A., & Weaver, P. Evaluation of a person who uses another's name in ingratiating and noningratiating situations. *Journal of Experimental Social Psychology*, 1972, *8*, 457–466.

Knowing "lines" may reduce girls' pregnancies. N. Y. Times News Service. *Gainesville Sun*, April 3, 1977.

Koneya, M. Location and interaction in row-and-column seating arrangements. *Environment and Behavior*, 1976, *8*, 265–282.

Korda, M. *Power!* New York: Ballantine Books, 1976.

Korda, M. *Success!* New York: Random House, 1977.

Krauss, R. M., Geller, V., & Olson, C. *Modalities and cues in the detection of deception*. Paper presented at the 84th Annual Meeting of the American Psychological Association, Washington, D. C., 1976.

Kraut, R. E. Verbal and nonverbal cues in the perception of lying. *Journal of Personality and Social Psychology*, 1978, *36*, 380–391.

Kraut, R. E., & Price, J. D. Machiavellianism in parents and their children. *Journal of Personality and Social Psychology*, 1976, *33*, 782–786.

Krim, S. *Views of a nearsighted cannoneer*. New York: Dutton, 1968.

Kuhn, M. H. Self-attitudes by age, sex, and professional training. *Sociological Quarterly*, 1960, *1*, 39–55.

Lacey, R. *Majesty: Elizabeth II and the House of Windsor.* New York: Avon, 1977.

LaFrance, M., & Mayo, C. *Moving bodies: Nonverbal communication in social relationships.* Monterey, Calif.: Brooks/Cole, 1978.

Landy, D., & Sigall, H. Beauty is talent: Task evaluation as a function of the performer's physical attractiveness. *Journal of Personality and Social Psychology,* 1974, *29,* 299–304.

Langer, E. J. The illusion of control. *Journal of Personality and Social Psychology,* 1975, *32,* 311–328.

Langer, E. J. Rethinking the role of thought in social interaction. In J. H. Harvey, W. Ickes, & R. F. Kidd (Eds.), *New directions in attribution research* (Vol. 2). Hillsdale, N. J.: Erlbaum, 1978.

Lee, W. *Decision theory and human behavior.* New York: Wiley, 1971.

Lefebvre, L. Encoding and decoding of ingratiation in modes of smiling and gaze. *British Journal of Social and Clinical Psychology,* 1975, *14,* 33–42.

Lefkowitz, M., Blake, R., & Mouton, J. Status factors in pedestrian violation of traffic signals. *Journal of Abnormal and Social Psychology,* 1955, *51,* 704–706.

Lewittes, D. J., & Simmons, W. I. Impression management of sexually motivated behavior. *Journal of Social Psychology,* 1975, *96,* 39–44.

Longstreth, L. E. A cognitive interpretation of secondary reinforcement. In J. K. Cole (Ed.), *Nebraska Symposium on Motivation.* Lincoln: University of Nebraska Press, 1971.

Lott, D. F., & Sommer, R. Seating arrangements and status. *Journal of Personality and Social Psychology,* 1967, *7,* 90–94.

Lundgren, D. C. Public esteem, self-esteem, and interpersonal stress. *Social Psychology,* 1978, *41,* 68–73.

Lyman, S. M., & Scott, M. B. Territoriality: A neglected sociological dimension. *Social Problems,* 1967, *15,* 236–249.

Lyman, S. M., & Scott, M. B. *The drama of social reality.* New York: Oxford University Press, 1975.

Machiavelli, N. *The prince and selected discourses* (D. Donno, trans.). New York: Bantam Books, 1966. (Originally published, 1513.)

Maehr, M. L., Mensing, J., & Nafzger, S. Concept of self and the reaction of others. *Sociometry,* 1962, *25,* 353–357.

Maier, R. A., & Maier, B. M. *Comparative animal behavior.* Belmont, Calif.: Wadsworth, 1970.

Maracek, J., & Mettee, D. R. Avoidance of continued success as a function of self-esteem, level of esteem certainty, and responsibility for success. *Journal of Personality and Social Psychology,* 1972, *22,* 98–107.

Markus, H. Self-schemata and processing information about the self. *Journal of Personality and Social Psychology,* 1977, *35,* 63–78.

Martindale, D. Territorial dominance behavior in dyadic verbal interactions. *Proceedings of the 79th Annual Convention of the American Psychological Association,* Washington, D. C., 1971, 305–306.

Maslow, A. H. *Toward a psychology of being* (2nd ed.). New York: Van Nostrand, 1968.

McClintock, C. C., & Hunt, R. C. Nonverbal indicators of affect and deception in an interview setting. *Journal of Applied Social Psychology,* 1975, *5,* 54–67.

McCown, N. E. *The effects of self-monitoring, self-esteem, and partner positiveness on self-presentation.* Master's thesis, University of Florida, 1978.

McGinley, H., LeFevre, R., & McGinley, P. The influence of a communicator's body position on opinion change in others. *Journal of Personality and Social Psychology,* 1975, *31,* 686–690.

McGinniss, J. *The selling of the President 1968.* New York: Pocket Books, 1970.

McGuire, W. J., McGuire, C. V., Child, P., & Fujioka, T. Salience of ethnicity in the spontaneous self-concept as a function of one's ethnic distinctiveness in the social environment. *Journal of Personality and Social Psychology*, 1978, *36*, 511–520.

McGuire, W. J., & Millman, S. Anticipatory belief lowering following forewarning of a persuasive attack. *Journal of Personality and Social Psychology*, 1965, *2*, 471–479.

McGuire, W. J., & Padawer-Singer, A. Trait salience in the spontaneous self-concept. *Journal of Personality and Social Psychology*, 1976, *33*, 743–754.

McHugh, P. *Defining the situation*. Indianapolis: Bobbs-Merrill, 1968.

Mead, G. H. *Mind, self, and society*. Chicago: University of Chicago Press, 1934.

Meddin, J. Chimpanzees, symbols and the reflective self. *Social Psychology Quarterly*, 1979, *42*, 99–109.

Medow, H., & Zander, A. Aspirations of group chosen by central and peripheral members. *Journal of Personality and Social Psychology*, 1965, *1*, 224–228.

Mehrabian, A. Inference of attitude from the posture, orientation, and distance of a communicator. *Journal of Consulting and Clinical Psychology*, 1968, *32*, 296–308.

Mehrabian, A. *Silent messages*. Belmont, Calif.: Wadsworth, 1971. (a)

Mehrabian, A. Nonverbal communication. In J. K. Cole (Ed.), *Nebraska Symposium on Motivation*. Lincoln: University of Nebraska Press, 1971. (b)

Mehrabian, A. Nonverbal betrayal of feeling. *Journal of Experimental Research in Personality*, 1971, *5*, 64–73. (c)

Mehrabian, A. *Nonverbal communication*. Chicago: Aldine-Atherton, 1972.

Mehrabian, A., & Williams, M. Nonverbal concomitants of perceived and intended persuasiveness. *Journal of Personality and Social Psychology*, 1969, *13*, 37–58.

Meltzer, B. N. Mead's social psychology. In J. G. Manis & B. N. Meltzer (Eds.), *Symbolic interaction* (2nd ed.). Boston: Allyn & Bacon, 1972.

Meltzer, B. N., & Petras, J. W. The Chicago and Iowa schools of symbolic interactionism. In J. G. Manis & B. N. Meltzer (Eds.), *Symbolic interaction* (2nd ed.). Boston: Allyn & Bacon, 1972.

Merton, R. K. *Social theory and social structure* (Rev. ed.). Glencoe, Ill.: Free Press, 1957.

Messinger, S. E., Sampson, H., & Towne, R. D. Life as theatre: Some notes on the dramaturgic approach to social reality. *Sociometry*, 1962, *25*, 98–110.

Mettee, D. R., & Aronson, E. Affective reactions to appraisal from others. In T. L. Huston (Ed.), *Foundations of interpersonal attraction*. New York: Academic Press, 1974.

Miller, D. T. Ego involvement and attributions for success and failure. *Journal of Personality and Social Psychology*, 1976, *34*, 901–906.

Miller, D. T., & Norman, S. A. Actor-observer differences in perceptions of effective control. *Journal of Personality and Social Psychology*, 1975, *31*, 503–515.

Miller, D. T., & Ross, M. Self-serving biases in the attribution of causality: Fact or fiction? *Psychological Bulletin*, 1975, *82*, 213–225.

Miller, G. A., Galanter, E., & Pribram, K. H. *Plans and the structure of behavior*. New York: Holt, Rinehart & Winston, 1960.

Miller, G. R., & Hewgill, M. A. The effect of variations in noninfluency on audience ratings of source credibility. *Quarterly Journal of Speech*, 1964, *50*, 36–44.

Miller, N., Maruyama, G., Beaber, R. J., & Valone, K. Speed of speech and persuasion. *Journal of Personality and Social Psychology*, 1976, *34*, 615–624.

Miller, R. L., Brickman, P., & Bolen, D. Attribution versus persuasion as a means for modifying behavior. *Journal of Personality and Social Psychology*, 1975, *31*, 430–441.

Miller, R. S., & Schlenker, B. R. *Self-presentation as affected by a valid or invalid past performance.* Paper presented at the 86th Annual Meeting of the American Psychological Association, Toronto, August 1978.

Mills, C. W. Situated actions and vocabularies of motives. *American Sociological Review*, 1940, *5*, 904–913.

Mills, J., & Aronson, E. Opinion change as a function of the communicator's attractiveness and desire to influence. *Journal of Personality and Social Psychology*, 1965, *1*, 173–177.

Minsky, M. A framework for representing knowledge. In P. Winston (Ed.), *The psychology of computer vision.* New York: McGraw-Hill, 1975.

Mischel, W. Toward a cognitive social learning reconceptualization of personality. *Psychological Review*, 1973, *80*, 252–283.

Mischel, W., Ebbesen, E. B., & Zeiss, A. R. Selective attention to the self: Situational and dispositional determinants. *Journal of Personality and Social Psychology*, 1973, *27*, 129–142.

Mitchell, T. R., & Biglan, A. Instrumentality theories: Current uses in psychology. *Psychological Bulletin*, 1971, *76*, 432–454.

Miyamoto, S. F., & Dornbusch, S. M. A test of interactionist hypotheses of self-conception. *American Journal of Sociology*, 1956, *61*, 399–403.

Modigliani, A. Embarrassment and embarrassability. *Sociometry*, 1968, *31*, 313–326.

Modigliani, A. Embarrassment, facework, and eye contact: Testing a theory of embarrassment. *Journal of Personality and Social Psychology*, 1971, *17*, 15–24.

Moore, J. C. *A further test of interactionist hypotheses of self-conception* (Tech. Rep. 6). Stanford, Calif.: Stanford University, Laboratory for Social Research, 1964.

Morse, S., & Gergen, K. J. Social comparison, self-consistency, and the concept of self. *Journal of Personality and Social Psychology*, 1970, *16*, 148–156.

Mussen, P. H., Conger, J. J., & Kagan, J. *Child development and personality* (3rd ed.). New York: Harper & Row, 1969.

Mynatt, C., & Sherman, S. J. Responsibility attribution in groups and individuals: A direct test of the diffusion of responsibility hypothesis. *Journal of Personality and Social Psychology*, 1975, *32*, 1111–1118.

Nagel, E. *The structure of science: Problems in the logic of scientific explanation.* New York: Harcourt, 1961.

Naughton, J. M. Ford's strategy of wish-fulfillment: By acting "Presidential," he hopes to be elected President. *Gainesville Sun*, Sept. 13, 1976.

Neft, D. S., Johnson, R. T., & Cohen, R. M. *The sports encyclopedia: Baseball.* New York: Grosset & Dunlap, 1976.

Neisser, U. *Cognitive psychology.* New York: Appleton-Century-Crofts, 1967.

Neisser, U. *Cognition and reality.* San Francisco: W. H. Freeman, 1976.

Newcomb, T. M. An approach to the study of communicative acts. *Psychological Review*, 1953, *60*, 393–404.

Newtson, D., & Czerlinsky, T. Adjustment of attitude communications for contrasts by extreme audiences. *Journal of Personality and Social Psychology*, 1974, *30*, 829–837.

Novak, D. W., & Lerner, M. J. Rejection as a consequence of perceived similarity. *Journal of Personality and Social Psychology*, 1968, *9*, 147–152.

Patterson, M. L. An arousal model of interpersonal intimacy. *Psychological Review*, 1976, *83*, 235–245.

Peirce, C. S. The fixation of belief. In A. Rorty (Ed.), *Pragmatic philosophy.* Garden City, N. Y.: Doubleday Anchor, 1966. (a)

Peirce, C. S. How to make our ideas clear. In A. Rorty (Ed.), *Pragmatic philosophy.* Garden City, N. Y.: Doubleday Anchor, 1966. (b)

Pellegrini, R. J. Some effects of seating position on social perception. *Psychological Reports,* 1971, *28,* 887–893.

Pepitone, A. An experimental analysis of self-dynamics. In C. Gordon & K. J. Gergen (Eds.), *The self in social interaction* (Vol. 1). New York: Wiley, 1968.

Pollard, W. E., & Mitchell, T. R. A decision theory analysis of social power. *Psychological Bulletin,* 1972, *78,* 433–446.

Quarantelli, E. L., & Cooper, J. Self-conceptions and others: A further test of Meadian hypotheses. *Sociological Quarterly,* 1966, *7,* 281–297.

Quattrone, G. A., & Jones, E. E. Selective self-disclosure with and without correspondent performance. *Journal of Experimental Social Psychology,* 1978, *14,* 511–526.

Reece, M., & Whitman, R. Expressive movements, warmth, and verbal reinforcement. *Journal of Abnormal and Social Psychology,* 1962, *64,* 234–236.

Reeder, L. G., Donohue, G., & Biblarz, A. Conceptions of self and others. *American Journal of Sociology,* 1960, *66,* 153–159.

Regan, J. W. Liking for evaluators: Consistency and self-esteem theories. *Journal of Experimental Social Psychology,* 1976, *12,* 156–169.

Riess, M. *An impression management interpretation of aspects of spatial behavior.* Major area paper, University of Florida, 1977.

Riess, M., & Schlenker, B. R. Attitude change and responsibility avoidance as modes of dilemma resolution in forced compliance settings. *Journal of Personality and Social Psychology,* 1977, *35,* 21–30.

Ringer, R. J. *Winning through intimidation.* Greenwich, Conn.: Fawcett, 1976.

Ringer, R. J. *Looking out for number one.* New York: Harper & Row, 1977.

Rogers, C. R. *On becoming a person.* Boston: Houghton Mifflin, 1961.

Rogers, T. B., Kuiper, N. A., & Kirker, W. S. Self-reference and the encoding of personal information. *Journal of Personality and Social Psychology,* 1977, *35,* 677–688.

Rogers, T. B., Rogers, P. J., & Kuiper, N. A. Evidence for the self as a cognitive prototype: The "false alarms" effect. *Personality and Social Psychology Bulletin,* 1979, *5,* 53–56.

Rommetveit, R. *Social norms and roles: Explorations in the psychology of enduring social pressures.* Minneapolis: University of Minnesota Press, 1955.

Rosen, B., & Jerdee, T. H. Effects of employee's sex and threatening versus pleading appeals on managerial evaluations of grievances. *Journal of Applied Psychology,* 1975, *60,* 442–445.

Rosenberg, M. When dissonance fails: On eliminating evaluation apprehension from attitude measurement. *Journal of Personality and Social Psychology,* 1965, *1,* 28–42.

Rosenberg, M. Psychological selectivity in self-esteem formation. In C. Gordon & K. J. Gergen (Eds.), *The self in social interaction* (Vol. 1). New York: Wiley, 1968.

Rosenfeld, H. M. Effect of approval-seeking induction on interpersonal proximity. *Psychological Reports,* 1965, *17,* 120–122.

Rosenfeld, H. M. Approval-seeking and approval-avoiding functions of verbal and nonverbal responses in the dyad. *Journal of Personality and Social Psychology,* 1966, *4,* 597–605.

Rosenhan, D. L. On being sane in insane places. *Science,* 1973, *179,* 250–258.

Rosenthal, T. L., & Zimmerman, B. J. (Eds.). *Social learning and cognition.* New York: Academic Press, 1978.

Ross, L. D. Problems in the interpretation of "self-serving" asymmetries in causal attribution: Comments on the Stephan et al. paper. *Sociometry,* 1977, *40,* 112–114.

Ross, L., Bierbrauer, G., & Polly, S. Attribution of educational outcomes by professional and nonprofessional instructors. *Journal of Personality and Social Psychology,* 1974, *29,* 609–618.

Ross, M., & Sicoly, F. Egocentric biases in availability and attribution. *Journal of Personality and Social Psychology,* 1979, *37,* 322–336.

Rubin, Z. Measurement of romantic love. *Journal of Personality and Social Psychology,* 1970, *16,* 265–273.

Russell, B. *Power.* New York: Norton, 1938.

Russell, B. *A history of Western philosophy.* New York: Simon & Schuster, 1945.

Russo, N. F. Eye contact, interpersonal distance, and the equilibrium theory. *Journal of Personality and Social Psychology,* 1975, *31,* 497–502.

Sarbin, T. R., & Allen, V. L. Role theory. In G. Lindzey & E. Aronson (Eds.), *The handbook of social psychology* (Vol. 1). (2nd ed.). Reading, Mass.: Addison-Wesley, 1968.

Sattler, J. M. The relative meaning of embarrassment. *Psychological Reports,* 1963, *12,* 263–269.

Sattler, J. M. A theoretical, developmental, and clinical investigation of embarrassment. *Genetic Psychology Monographs,* 1965, *71,* 19–59.

Sattler, J. M. Embarrassment and blushing: A theoretical review. *Journal of Social Psychology,* 1966, *69,* 117–133.

Schank, R., & Abelson, R. *Scripts, plans, goals and understanding.* Hillsdale, N. J.: Erlbaum, 1977.

Scheff, T. J. *Being mentally ill.* Chicago: Aldine, 1966.

Scheff, T. J. Negotiating reality: Notes on power in the assessment of responsibility. *Social Problems,* 1968, *16,* 3–17.

Scherer, K. R., London, H., & Wolf, J. J. The voice of confidence: Paralinguistic cues and audience evaluation. *Journal of Research in Personality,* 1973, *7,* 31–44.

Schiffenbauer, A., & Schiavo, R. S. Physical distance and attraction: An intensification effect. *Journal of Experimental Social Psychology,* 1976, *12,* 274–282.

Schlenker, B. R. *Self-image maintenance and enhancement: Attitude change following counterattitudinal advocacy.* Paper presented at the 81st Annual Meeting of the American Psychological Association, Montreal, 1973.

Schlenker, B. R. Social psychology and science. *Journal of Personality and Social Psychology,* 1973, *29,* 1–15.

Schlenker, B. R. Self-presentation: Managing the impression of consistency when reality interferes with self-enhancement. *Journal of Personality and Social Psychology,* 1975, *32,* 1030–1037. (a)

Schlenker, B. R. Liking for a group following an initiation: Impression management or dissonance reduction? *Sociometry,* 1975, *38,* 99–118. (b)

Schlenker, B. R. Group members' attributions of responsibility for prior group performance. *Representative Research in Social Psychology,* 1975, *6,* 96–108. (c)

Schlenker, B. R. Social psychology and science: Another look. *Personality and Social Psychology Bulletin,* 1976, *2,* 384–390.

Schlenker, B. R. On the ethogenic approach: Etiquette and revolution. In L. Berkowitz (Ed.), *Advances in experimental social psychology* (Vol. 10). New York: Academic Press, 1977.

Schlenker, B. R. Attitudes as actions: Social identity theory and consumer research. *Advances in Consumer Research,* 1978, *5,* 352–359.

Schlenker, B. R., Bonoma, T. V., Hutchinson, D., & Burns, L. The bogus pipeline and stereotypes towards blacks. *The Journal of Psychology*, 1976, *93*, 319–329.

Schlenker, B. R., & Forsyth, D. R. On the ethics of psychological research. *Journal of Experimental Social Psychology*, 1977, *13*, 369–396.

Schlenker, B. R., Forsyth, D. R., Leary, M. R., & Miller, R. S. A self-presentational analysis of the effects of incentives on attitude change following counterattitudinal behavior. *Journal of Personality and Social Psychology*, in press.

Schlenker, B. R., & Miller, R. S. Egocentrism in groups: Self-serving biases or logical information processing? *Journal of Personality and Social Psychology*, 1977, *35*, 755–764. (a)

Schlenker, B. R., & Miller, R. S. Group cohesiveness as a determinant of egocentric perceptions in cooperative groups. *Human Relations*, 1977, *30*, 1039–1055. (b)

Schlenker, B. R., Miller, R. S., Leary, M. R., & McCown, N. E. Group performance and interpersonal evaluations as determinants of egotistical attributions in groups. *Journal of Personality*, 1979, *47*, 575–594.

Schlenker, B. R., & Riess, M. Self-presentations of attitudes following commitment to proattitudinal behavior. *Human Communication Research*, 1979, *5*, 325–334.

Schlenker, B. R., & Schlenker, P. A. Reactions following counterattitudinal behavior which produces positive consequences. *Journal of Personality and Social Psychology*, 1975, *31*, 962–971.

Schlenker, B. R., Soraci, S., Jr., & McCarthy, B. Self-esteem and group performance as determinants of egocentric perceptions in cooperative groups. *Human Relations*, 1976, *29*, 1163–1176.

Schneider, D. J. Tactical self-presentation after success and failure. *Journal of Personality and Social Psychology*, 1969, *13*, 262–268.

Schneider, D. J., & Eustis, A. C. Effects of ingratiation motivation, target positiveness, and revealingness on self-presentation. *Journal of Personality and Social Psychology*, 1972, *22*, 149–155.

Schneider, D. J., Eustis, A. C., Manzolati, J., Miller, R. S., & Gordon, J. Effects of visual contact on verbal self-presentation. *Proceedings of the American Psychological Association*, 1971, *6*, 303–304. (Summary)

Schneider, D. J., & Turkat, D. Self-presentation following success or failure: Defensive self-esteem models. *Journal of Personality*, 1975, *43*, 127–135.

Schopler, J. Social power. In L. Berkowitz (Ed.), *Advances in experimental social psychology* (Vol. 2). New York: Academic Press, 1965.

Scott, M. B., & Lyman, S. M. Accounts. *American Sociological Review*, 1968, *33*, 46–62.

Sereno, K. K., & Hawkins, G. J. The effect of variations in speakers' noninfluency upon audience ratings of attitude toward the speech topic and speakers' credibility. *Speech Monographs*, 1967, *34*, 58–64.

Shaffer, D. R., & Sadowski, C. This table is mine: Respect for marked barroom tables as a function of gender of spatial marker and desirability of locale. *Sociometry*, 1975, *38*, 408–419.

Shaver, K. G. *An introduction to attribution processes*. Cambridge, Mass.: Winthrop, 1975.

Shaw, M. E. New Science or nonscience? *Contemporary Psychology*, 1974, *19*, 96–97.

Shaw, M. E. *Group dynamics: The psychology of small group behavior* (2nd ed.). New York: McGraw-Hill, 1976.

Shaw, M. E., & Margulis, S. T. The power of the printed word: Its effect on the judgment of the quality of research. *Journal of Social Psychology*, 1974, *94*, 301–302.

Shaw, M. E., & Reitan, H. T. Attribution of responsibility as a basis for sanctioning behavior. *British Journal of Social and Clinical Psychology*, 1969, *8*, 217–226.

Shaw, M. E., & Sulzer, J. L. An empirical test of Heider's levels in attribution of responsibility. *Journal of Abnormal and Social Psychology*, 1964, *69*, 39–46.

Shaw, M. E., & Tremble, T. R. Effects of attribution of responsibility for a negative event to a group member upon group process as a function of the structure of the event. *Sociometry*, 1971, *34*, 504–514.

Shrauger, J. S. Responses to evaluation as a function of initial self-perceptions. *Psychological Bulletin*, 1975, *82*, 581–596.

Shrauger, J. S., & Schoeneman, T. J. Symbolic interactionist view of self-concept: Through the looking glass darkly. *Psychological Bulletin*, 1979, *86*, 549–573.

Sicoly, F., & Ross, M. Facilitation of ego-biased attributions by means of self-serving observer feedback. *Journal of Personality and Social Psychology*, 1977, *35*, 734–741.

Sigall, H., & Aronson, E. Liking for an evaluator as a function of her physical attractiveness and nature of the evaluations. *Journal of Experimental Social Psychology*, 1969, *5*, 93–100.

Sigall, H., & Landy, D. Radiating beauty: Effects of having a physically attractive partner on person perception. *Journal of Personality and Social Psychology*, 1973, *28*, 218–224.

Sigall, H., & Ostrove, N. Beautiful but dangerous: Effects of offender attractiveness and nature of the crime on juric judgment. *Journal of Personality and Social Psychology*, 1975, *31*, 410–414.

Sigall, H., Page, R., & Brown, A. C. Effort expenditure as a function of evaluation and evaluator attractiveness. *Representative Research in Social Psychology*, 1971, *2*, 19–25.

Simmel, G. The secret and the secret society. In K. Wolff (Ed.), *The sociology of George Simmel*. New York: Free Press, 1964.

Snyder, M. Self-monitoring of expressive behavior. *Journal of Personality and Social Psychology*, 1974, *30*, 526–537.

Snyder, M., & Monson, T. C. Persons, situations, and the control of social behavior. *Journal of Personality and Social Psychology*, 1975, *32*, 637–644.

Snyder, M., & Swann, W. B., Jr. When actions reflect attitudes: The politics of impression management. *Journal of Personality and Social Psychology*, 1976, *34*, 1034–1042.

Snyder, M., & Tanke, E. D. Behavior and attitudes: Some people are more consistent than others. *Journal of Personality*, 1976, *44*, 501–517.

Snyder, M. L., Stephan, W. G., & Rosenfield, D. Egotism and attribution. *Journal of Personality and Social Psychology*, 1976, *33*, 435–441.

Snyder, M. L., Stephan, W. G., & Rosenfield, D. Attributional egotism. In J. H. Harvey, W. Ickes, & R. F. Kidd (Eds.), *New directions in attribution research* (Vol. 2). Hillsdale, N. J.: Erlbaum, 1978.

Solar, D., & Bruehl, D. Machiavellianism and locus of control: Two conceptions of interpersonal power. *Psychological Reports*, 1971, *29*, 1079–1082.

Sommer, R. Small group ecology. *Psychological Bulletin*, 1967, *67*, 145–152. (a)

Sommer, R. Classroom ecology. *Journal of Applied Behavioral Science*, 1967, *3*, 489–503. (b)

Sommer, R. *Personal space*. Englewood Cliffs, N. J.: Prentice-Hall, 1969.

Sommer, R. *Design awareness*. San Francisco: Rinehart, 1972.

Sommer, R. *Tight spaces: Hard architecture and how to humanize it.* Englewood Cliffs, N. J.: Prentice-Hall, 1974.

"Son of Sam" suspect faces questioning on killings. Associated Press. *Gainesville Sun,* August 12, 1977.

Spanos, N. P. Witchcraft in histories of psychiatry: A critical analysis and an alternative conceptualization. *Psychological Bulletin,* 1978, *85,* 417–439.

Sperry, R. W. Bridging science and values: A unifying view of mind and brain. *American Psychologist,* 1977, *32,* 237–245.

Spiegel, J. P., & Machotka, P. *Messages of the body.* New York: Free Press, 1974.

Staneski, R. A., Kleinke, C. L., & Meeker, F. B. *Effects of ingratiation, touch, and use of name on evaluation of job applicants and interviewers.* Paper presented at the Meeting of the Western Psychological Association, Anaheim, Calif., 1973.

Stebbins, R. A. A theory of the definition of the situation. *Canadian Review of Sociology and Anthropology,* 1967, *4,* 148–164.

Steiner, I. D. Reactions to adverse and favorable evaluations of oneself. *Journal of Personality,* 1968, *36,* 553–564.

Stevens, L., & Jones, E. E. Defensive attribution and the Kelley cube. *Journal of Personality and Social Psychology,* 1976, *34,* 809–820.

Stires, L. K., & Jones, E. E. Modesty vs self-enhancement as alternative forms of ingratiation. *Journal of Experimental Social Psychology,* 1969, *5,* 172–188.

Stodgill, R. M. *Handbook of leadership.* New York: Free Press, 1974.

Stone, G. P. Appearance and the self. In A. M. Rose (Ed.), *Human behavior and social processes.* Boston: Houghton Mifflin, 1962.

Storms, M. D., & Thomas, G. C. Reactions to physical closeness. *Journal of Personality and Social Psychology,* 1977, *35,* 412–418.

Streeter, L. A., Krauss, R. M., Geller, V., Olson, C., & Apple, W. Pitch changes during attempted deception. *Journal of Personality and Social Psychology,* 1977, *35,* 345–350.

Streufert, S., & Streufert, S. C. Effects of conceptual structure, failure, and success on attribution of causality and interpersonal attitudes. *Journal of Personality and Social Psychology,* 1969, *11,* 138–148.

Strodtbeck, F. L., & Hook, L. H. The social dimensions of a twelve-man jury table. *Sociometry,* 1961, *24,* 297–315.

Sullivan, H. S. *Conceptions of modern psychiatry.* New York: Norton, 1953.

Szasz, T. S. The myth of mental illness. *American Psychologist,* 1960, *15,* 113–118.

Szasz, T. S. *The myth of mental illness.* New York: Delta, 1961.

Tankard, J. Effects of eye position on person perception. *Perceptual and Motor Skills,* 1970, *31,* 883–893.

Tedeschi, J. T. (Ed.). *The social influence processes.* Chicago: Aldine, 1972.

Tedeschi, J. T., & Lindskold, S. *Social psychology.* New York: Wiley, 1976.

Tedeschi, J. T., Schlenker, B. R., & Bonoma, T. V. Cognitive dissonance: Private ratiocination or public spectacle? *American Psychologist,* 1971, *26,* 685–695.

Tedeschi, J. T., Schlenker, B. R., & Bonoma, T. V. *Conflict, power and games: The experimental study of interpersonal relations.* Chicago: Aldine, 1973.

Tesser, A., & Rosen, S. The reluctance to transmit bad news. In L. Berkowitz (Ed.), *Advances in experimental social psychology* (Vol. 8). New York: Academic Press, 1975.

Thayer, S., & Schiff, W. Observer judgment of social interaction: Eye contact and relationship inferences. *Journal of Personality and Social Psychology,* 1974, *30,* 110–114.

Thibaut, J. W., & Kelley, H. H. *The social psychology of groups.* New York: Wiley, 1959.

Thomas, E. J. Role theory, personality, and the individual. In E. F. Borgatta and W. W. Lambert (Eds.), *Handbook of personality theory and research.* Chicago: Rand McNally, 1968.

Thomas, W. I. *The unadjusted girl.* Boston: Little, Brown, 1923.

Thorndike, E. L. The law of effect. *American Journal of Psychology,* 1927, *29,* 212–222.

Toch, H. H. *Violent men: An inquiry in to the psychology of violence.* Chicago: Aldine, 1969.

Toland, J. *Adolf Hitler.* New York: Ballantine Books, 1977.

Townsend, R. *Up the organization.* New York: Fawcett Crest, 1971.

Tulving, E. Episodic and semantic memory. In E. Tulving & W. Donaldson (Eds.), *Organization of memory.* New York: Academic Press, 1972.

Turner, R. G. Self consciousness and speed of processing self-relevant information. *Personality and Social Psychology Bulletin,* 1978, *4,* 456–460.

Turner, R. H. The self-conception in social interaction. In C. Gordon & K. J. Gergen (Eds.), *The self in social interaction.* New York: Wiley, 1968.

Upshaw, H. S., & Yates, L. A. Self-persuasion, social approval, and task success as determinants of self-esteem following impression management. *Journal of Experimental Social Psychology,* 1968, *4,* 143–152.

Videbeck, R. Self-conceptions and the reactions of others. *Sociometry,* 1960, *23,* 351–359.

Waller, W. *The sociology of teaching.* New York: Wiley, 1932.

Walster, E., Walster, G. W., & Berscheid, E. *Equity: Theory and research.* Boston: Allyn & Bacon, 1978.

Walster, E., Walster, G. W., Piliavin, J., & Schmidt, L. "Playing hard to get": Understanding an elusive phenomenon. *Journal of Personality and Social Psychology,* 1973, *26,* 113–121.

Weary, G., & Arkin, R. M. Attributional self-presentation and the regulation of self-evaluation. In J. H. Harvey, W. C. Ickes, & R. F. Kidd (Eds.), *New directions in attribution research* (Vol. 3). New York: Erlbaum, in press.

Weary Bradley, G. Self-serving biases in the attribution process: A reexamination of the fact or fiction question. *Journal of Personality and Social Psychology,* 1978, *36,* 56–71.

Webster, M., Jr. *Actions and actors: Principles of social psychology.* Cambridge, Mass.: Winthrop, 1975.

Webster's New World Dictionary of the American language (College edition). New York: World, 1960.

Weglowski, V. Speech reveals how advertising "sells" a president. *Independent Florida Alligator,* October 19, 1977.

Weinberg, M. S. Embarrassment: Its variable and invariable aspects. *Social Forces,* 1968, *46,* 382–388.

Weiner, B., Frieze, I., Kukla, A., Reed, L., Rest, S., & Rosenbaum, R. M. *Perceiving the causes of success and failure.* Morristown, N. J.: General Learning Press, 1971.

Weinstein, E. A., & Deutschberger, P. Some dimensions of altercasting. *Sociometry,* 1963, *26,* 454–466.

Weitz, S. (Ed.). *Nonverbal communication.* New York: Oxford University Press, 1974.

Wells, L. E., & Marwell, G. *Self-esteem: Its conceptualization and measurement.* Beverly Hills: Sage Publications, 1976.

White, R. Motivation reconsidered: The concept of competence. *Psychological Review,* 1959, *66,* 297–334.

Whyte, W. H., Jr. *The organization man.* New York: Simon & Schuster, 1956.

Wicklund, R. A. Objective self-awareness. In L. Berkowitz (Ed.), *Advances in experimental social psychology* (Vol. 8). New York: Academic Press, 1975.

Wilder, D. A. Perceiving persons as a group: Effects on attributions of causality and beliefs. *Social Psychology,* 1978, *41,* 13–23.

Wolosin, R. J., Sherman, S. J., & Till, A. Effects of cooperation and competition on responsibility attribution after success and failure. *Journal of Experimental Social Psychology,* 1973, *9,* 220–235.

Worchel, S., & Brehm, J. W. Effect of threats to attitudinal freedom as a function of agreement with the communicator. *Journal of Personality and Social Psychology,* 1970, *14,* 18–22.

Wortman, C. B. Causal attributions and personal control. In J. H. Harvey, W. G. Ickes, & R. F. Kidd (Eds.), *New directions in attribution research* (Vol. 1). Hillsdale, N. J.: Erlbaum, 1976.

Wortman, C. B., Costanzo, P. R., & Witt, T. R. Effects of anticipated performance on the attributions of causality to self and others. *Journal of Personality and Social Psychology,* 1973, *27,* 372–381.

Wyer, R. S., Jr. *Cognitive organization and change: An information processing approach.* Hillsdale, N. J.: Erlbaum, 1974.

Wylie, R. C. *The self-concept: A critical survey of pertinent research literature.* Lincoln: University of Nebraska Press, 1961.

Wylie, R. C. The present status of self theory. In E. F. Borgatta & W. W. Lambert (Eds.), *Handbook of personality theory and research.* Chicago: Rand McNally, 1968.

Wylie, R. C. *The self-concept: A review of methodological considerations and measuring instruments* (Vol. 1). (Rev. ed.). Lincoln: University of Nebraska Press, 1974.

Wylie, R. C. *The self-concept: Theory and research on selected topics* (Vol. 2). (Rev. ed.). Lincoln: University of Nebraska Press, 1979.

Yablonsky, L. *The violent gang.* New York: Macmillan, 1962.

Zaidel, S., & Mehrabian, A. The ability to communicate and infer positive and negative attitudes facially and vocally. *Journal of Experimental Research in Personality,* 1969, *3,* 233–241.

Zanna, M. P., & Pack, S. J. On the self-fulfilling nature of apparent sex differences in behavior. *Journal of Experimental Social Psychology,* 1975, *11,* 583–591.

Zweigenhaft, R. Signature size: Key to status awareness. *Journal of Social Psychology,* 1970, *81,* 49–54.

NAME INDEX

SUBJECT INDEX